Passing the Georgia High School Graduation Test in Social Studies

Kindred Howard

Katie Herman

Edited by
Devin Pintozzi
Rob Hunter
Jason Kirk

American Book Company
PO Box 2638
Woodstock, GA 30188-1383
Toll Free: 1 (888) 264-5877 Phone: (770) 928-2834
Toll Free Fax: 1 (866) 827-3240
Web site: www.americanbookcompany.com

ACKNOWLEDGEMENTS

The authors would like to gratefully acknowledge the editing and technical contributions of Marsha Torrens and Yvonne Benson.

We also want to thank Charisse Johnson and Eric Field for their expertise in developing the graphics for this book.

PO Box 2638
Woodstock, GA 30188-1318

Printed in the United States of America

01/08 02/09

Table of Contents

PREFACE

Passing the Georgia High School Graduation Test in Social Studies (3rd Edition) will help students who are learning or reviewing material for the HSGT Test. The materials in this book are based on the GPS based testing standards as published by the Georgia Department of Education.

This book contains several sections. These sections are as follows: 1) General information about the book; 2) A Diagnostic Test; 3) An Evaluation Chart; 4) Chapters that teach the concepts and skills that improve graduation readiness; 5) Two Practice Tests. Answers to the tests and exercises are in a separate manual. The answer manual also contains a Chart of Standards for teachers to make a more precise diagnosis of student needs and assignments.

We welcome comments and suggestions about the book. Please contact us at

American Book Company
PO Box 2638
Woodstock, GA 30188-1383

Toll Free: 1 (888) 264-5877
Phone: (770) 928-2834
Fax: (770) 928-7483
Web site: www.americanbookcompany.com

ABOUT THE AUTHORS

Kindred Howard is a 1991 alumnus of the University of North Carolina at Chapel Hill, where he graduated with a B.S. in Criminal Justice and national honors in Political Science. In addition to two years as a probation & parole officer in North Carolina, he has served for over twelve years as a teacher and writer in the fields of religion and social studies. His experience includes teaching students at both the college and high school level, as well as speaking at numerous seminars and authoring several books on US history, American government, and economics. Mr. Howard is currently completing both a M.A. in history from Georgia State University and a M.A. in biblical studies from Asbury Theological Seminary. In addition to serving as Social Studies Coordinator for American Book Company, Mr. Howard is the president/CEO of KB Howard Writing, Consulting, and Administrative Services and lives in Kennesaw, Georgia, with his wife and three children.

Katie Herman is a senior at Kennesaw State University and will graduate in May 2008 with a Bachelor's degree in English. Her experience includes working as a writing tutor and editor at the collegiate level, as well as authoring several academic essays. After graduation, she plans to pursue a M.A. in professional writing. Ms. Herman currently lives in Woodstock, Georgia.

TEST-TAKING TIPS

1. Complete the chapters and practice tests in this book. This text will help you review the skills for the Georgia High School Graduation Test in Social Studies. The book also contains materials for reviewing skills under the Research standards.

2. Be prepared. Get a good night's sleep the day before your exam. Eat a well-balanced meal, one that contains plenty of proteins and carbohydrates, prior to your exam.

3. Arrive early. Allow yourself at least 15–20 minutes to find your room and get settled. Then you can relax before the exam, so you won't feel rushed.

4. Think success. Keep your thoughts positive. Turn negative thoughts into positive ones. Tell yourself you will do well on the exam.

5. Practice relaxation techniques. Some students become overly worried about exams. Before or during the test, they may perspire heavily, experience an upset stomach, or have shortness of breath. If you feel any of these symptoms, talk to a close friend or see a counselor. They will suggest ways to deal with test anxiety. Here are some quick ways to relieve test anxiety:
   - Imagine yourself in your most favorite place. Let yourself sit there and relax.
   - Do a body scan. Tense and relax each part of your body starting with your toes and ending with your forehead.
   - Use the 3-12-6 method of relaxation when you feel stress. Inhale slowly for 3 seconds. Hold your breath for 12 seconds, and then exhale slowly for 6 seconds.

6. Read directions carefully. If you don't understand them, ask the proctor for further explanation before the exam starts.

7. Use your best approach for answering the questions. Some test-takers like to skim the questions and answers before reading the problem or passage. Others prefer to work the problem or read the passage before looking at the answers. Decide which approach works best for you.

8. Answer each question on the exam. Unless you are instructed not to, make sure you answer every question. If you are not sure of an answer, take an educated guess. Eliminate choices that are definitely wrong, and then choose from the remaining answers.

9. Use your answer sheet correctly. Make sure the number on your question matches the number on your answer sheet. In this way, you will record your answers correctly. If you need to change your answer, erase it completely. Smudges or stray marks may affect the grading of your exams, particularly if they are scored by a computer. If your answers are on a computerized grading sheet, make sure the answers are dark. The computerized scanner may skip over answers that are too light.

10. Check your answers. Review your exam to make sure you have chosen the best responses. Change answers only if you are sure they are wrong.

Georgia HSGT
Diagnostic Test

The purpose of this diagnostic test is to measure your knowledge in social studies. This test is based on the GPS-based Georgia HSGT in Social Studies and adheres to the sample question format provided by the Georgia Department of Education.

General Directions:

1. Read all directions carefully.

2. Read each question or sample. Then choose the best answer.

3. Choose only one answer for each question. If you change an answer, be sure to erase your original answer completely.

4. After taking the test, you or your instructor should score it using the evaluation chart following the test. Circle any questions you did not get correct and review those chapters.

Use the following table to answer the question below.

Position	Role
president	chief executive
vice president	presides over the Senate
Electoral College	elects president and vice president
president pro tempore	X

1 **Which of the following should appear in place of the X in the table above?** SSCG10

A leader of the House of Representatives

B makes sure that party members vote the way the party leadership wants them to

C commander in chief

D presides over the Senate when the vice president is absent

2 **Which of the following is TRUE regarding African slaves in the thirteen colonies?** SSUSH2

A African slaves came from common cultures in Africa and shared the exact same beliefs.

B African slaves originally spoke different languages, had different religious beliefs, and were familiar with different traditions.

C African slaves lacked any cultural background and immediately tended to fully accept the Christian beliefs and English language of their masters.

D African slaves refused to accept any new traditions of the British, including the languages or religions of America

3. **The US failed to join the League of Nations for which of the following reasons?** SSUSH15

A President Woodrow Wilson greatly opposed it.

B Germany would not be allowed to join and, in protest, the US refused to join as well because they felt such an exclusion would encourage future wars.

C European powers were not willing to grant US demands to leave a small number of troops in Europe to help prevent future aggression by Germany.

D Isolationism had again become popular in the US following the horrifying death and destruction of the war in Europe, and too many people feared that involvement would eventually drag the US into another war.

Use the timeline below to answer the following question.

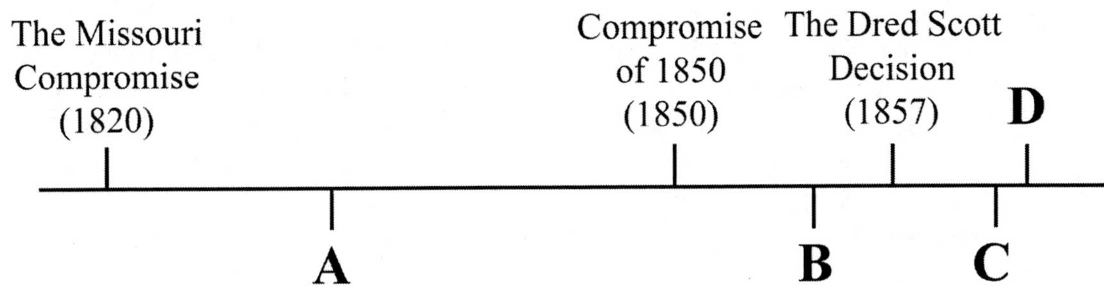

4 Where on the timeline above would you place the Kansas-Nebraska Act, The battle of Antietam, and the battle of Vicksburg, in that order? SSUSH9

A B, C, D **B** A, B, C **C** C, B, D **D** A, D, C

5 Landforms, climate, natural vegetation, and animal life are all SSWG1

A human characteristics of geography.

B aspects of culture.

C physical characteristics of geography.

D physical characteristics of culture.

6 The belief that citizens surrender some of their freedom in order to allow governments to maintain order is consistent with SSCG2

A the Declaration of Independence.

B the Social Contract Theory.

C natural rights.

D the letters of enlightenment.

7 Simon Bolivar and Jose de San Martin were both SSWH14

A leaders of Latin American nationalist movements during the 1960s.

B Spanish generals who fought Napoleon at Waterloo.

C leaders of successful Latin American revolutions that led to independence.

D leaders of anti-US nationalist movements in Central America during the 1970s and '80s.

8 Who is not elected by the people but appointed by the president for life? SSCG4

A vice president

B Speaker of the House

C judges in the judicial branch

D cabinet members

Go On

Read the quote below and answer the following question.

> **"The position of the United States is quite clear. If any foreign power attempts to claim territory in the Americas, this nation will view such action as an act of aggression. No longer is this hemisphere a land to be conquered by European tyrants."**
>
> **US Public official, 1820**

9 The above quote is MOST LIKELY referring to SSUSH6

A The Declaration of Independence.

B The Missouri Compromise.

C The Monroe Doctrine.

D Manifest Destiny.

10 How were the classical works of Rome and Greece viewed during the Renaissance? SSWH9

A with skepticism because modern ideas were seen as superior

B with little interest because people were so familiar with them that they wanted new ideas and literature

C with praise because many felt there was a need to reconnect with such works and ideas

D with interest because no one knew where they came from

11 Which of the following dates affected US citizens in much the same way as September 11, 2001? SSUSH9

A July 4, 1776

B December 7, 1941

C December 12, 2000

D August 8, 1974

12 Certain African tribal weddings are called 'jumping the broom'. These weddings are said to have originated from the Deep South during the American Civil War when slave weddings were not permitted and so an alternative commitment ceremony had to be found. In this ceremony, the broom is placed on the floor and the couple jumps over it. The gesture is said to symbolize jump from single-hood into matrimony or sweeping away the old and welcoming the new. This ritual is an example of a SSWG2

A human characteristic.

B custom or tradition.

C population pattern.

D physical characteristic.

13 This law was passed in 1935 and created a board to monitor unfair management practices such as firing workers who joined unions. It demonstrated a strong shift by the federal government towards supporting the interests of workers and made Roosevelt extremely popular among laborers and union leaders. Which law was it? SSUSH18

A Revenue Act

B Wagner Act

C Social Security Act

D Agricultural Adjustment Act

Use the following map to answer question 14.

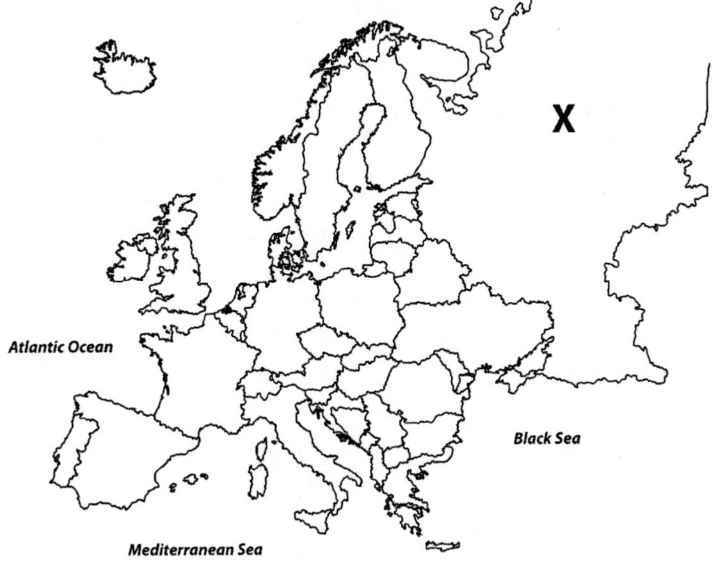

14 What landform lies along the X on the map? SSWG6

A the Pyranees

B the Alps

C the Ural Mountains

D the Rhine River

15 Which of the following is TRUE regarding World War I? SSWH16

A It originally began as a conflict between American powers, but it eventually involved Europe and many other nations as well.

B Because of the size of the conflict, as well as the incredible amount of death and destruction it produced, it came to be called "The Great War."

C Great Britain, France, and The United States formed an alliance called the Triple Entente.

D Germany and Russia created an alliance called the Central Powers.

16 What impact did the Puritan faith have on New England? SSUSH1

A It was one of several major religions to develop during colonial New England.

B It led to the establishment of New Amsterdam.

C It defined religion and government in the region.

D It led to King Philip's War as an attempt to end religious dissent.

Read the quote below and answer the following question.

> "Society is produced by our wants, and government by wickedness; the former promotes our happiness positively by uniting our affections, the latter negatively by restraining our vices. The one encourages intercourse, the other creates distinctions. The first is a patron, the last a punisher. Society in every state is a blessing, but government in its best state is but a necessary evil."

17 What is this quote from? SSUSH3

A *Common Sense*

B Treaty of Paris in 1763

C Hamilton's Economic Plan

D Doctrine of Nullification

18 Why must citizens pay taxes? SSCG7

A to ensure they are not making too much money

B to allow the government to remain adequately funded and fulfill its role for society

C to give the government money to increase their annual salaries

D to maintain that the wages of the people are balanced in regards to how much they make each year

19 Which nation is most affected by deforestation? SSWG7

A Israel

B Australia

C Brazil

D Canada

20 The Truman Doctrine stated that SSUSH20

A the US would not hesitate to intervene to help foreign nations resist communism.

B the US would not allow Communism in the US.

C the US would support Mao's Chinese revolution.

D the US would not cross the 38th parallel during the Korean War.

21 Why do few people live in the Himalayas? SSWG5

A because of the many wild animals that inhabit the mountains

B because of the lack of natural resources

C because of the rough terrain, high altitude, and harsh conditions

D because of the many bodies of water that take up livable land

22 What was a major idea introduced by the Renaissance? SSWH10

A Human beings are limitless in what they can accomplish.

B Humans should focus on the one thing they are gifted in.

C specialization

D Modernization is superior to ancient ideas.

Look at the map below and answer the following question.

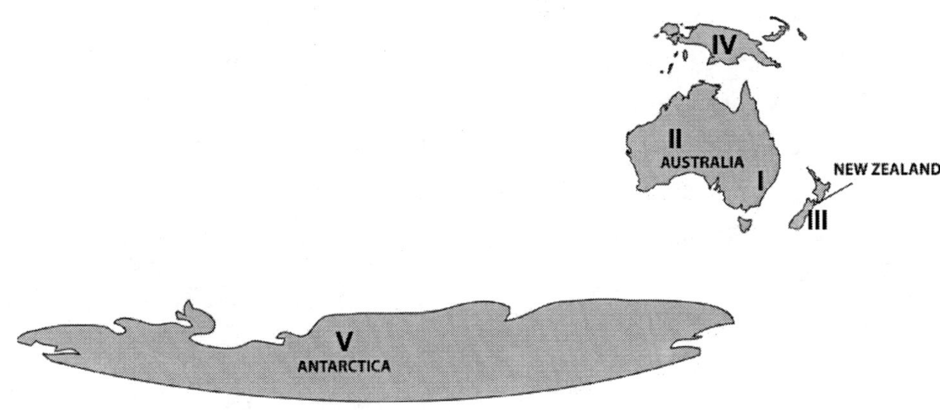

23 Where would one most likely find the largest urban population? SSWG9

A I B II C III D V

24 Although Vice President Al Gore won more votes in 2000 than Governor George W. Bush, Bush still won the presidential election because of his narrow victory in Florida. Many critics point to this election as evidence that SSCG8

A Bush's election was unconstitutional.

B Florida's vote should not have counted.

C too many people are voting in elections to keep an accurate count.

D the Electoral College is outdated and should no longer be used.

25 Many Native Americans contracted smallpox and died as a side-effect of the SSWH10

A Protestant Reformation.

B Great War.

C Glorious Revolution.

D Columbian Exchange.

26 Which of the following correctly list the world's continents in order of size, from largest to smallest? SSWG1

A Asia, Africa, Antarctica, South America, Australia, North America, Europe

B Asia, Africa, North America, South America, Antarctica, Europe, Australia

C Asia, Africa, South America, Australia, North America, Antarctica, Europe

D Europe, Africa, Asia, North America, South America, Antarctica, Australia

> ". . .No state shall make or enforce any law which shall abridge the privileges or immunities of citizens of the United States; nor shall any state deprive any person of life, liberty, or property, without due process of law . . ."
>
> – the Fourteenth Amendment

27 The Fourteenth Amendment has which of the following effects? SSCG6

A gives all people living in the US the right to vote

B strengthens segregation

C increases the power of state governments

D extends the Bill of Rights to the states

28 According to the supremacy clause, SSCG5

A the Constitution is superior to the Declaration of Independence.

B state laws are protected from federal interference.

C federal laws override state laws.

D the president is above Congress.

29 Bill is one of two people representing Georgia in the house of Congress in which he serves. He is elected to a six year term and, just last week, voted to affirm the president's appointment of a federal judge. Bill is a SSCG9

A US representative.

B US senator.

C presidential cabinet member.

D member of the judiciary.

30 The Ottoman Empire finally collapsed in large part because SSWH16

A Hitler invaded its territory and the European powers refused to oppose him.

B it allied itself with the Soviet Union during the Cold War.

C it fought with Germany during WWI and lost.

D it was conquered by Napoleon.

31 What impact did the bombing of Pearl Harbor eventually have on many Japanese Americans? SSUSH19

A It caused many to burst with pride and a desire to help their "homeland" win the war against the United States.

B It had little effect because most of these Japanese Americans had lived in the US so long that no one identified them with Japan any longer.

C The federal government and citizens of the United States viewed many of them with suspicion. As a precaution, they were rounded up and forced to relocate to internment camps where the government could monitor them.

D It inspired many Japanese Americans to leave the US and return to Japan.

32 What has contributed MOST to the growth and development of cities in Africa? SSWG4

A Lack of natural resources in Africa's rainforests

B overpopulation of coastal regions

C more advanced technology and better job opportunities due to modernization

D nomadic lifestyles

33 Which of the following was an example of decolonization? SSWH19

A establishment of the mandate system

B the French Revolution

C establishment of Indian independence and Pakistan

D Zionism

34 Which of the following is an example of how the US Constitution recognizes individual rights? SSUSH5

A The minimum wage amendment guarantees the right to a living wage.

B Article II grants the president the right to veto proposed laws.

C Article III grants judges life-long terms, as long as they maintain good behavior.

D The 4th Amendment prevents searches and seizures without a warrant.

35 Which of the following effects did the US Supreme Court's decision in *Plessy v. Ferguson* have on US society? SSUSH13

A It affirmed segregation laws as constitutional.

B It granted women the right to vote.

C It ended segregation in public places.

D It made abortion legal throughout the US.

Look at the map below and answer the following question.

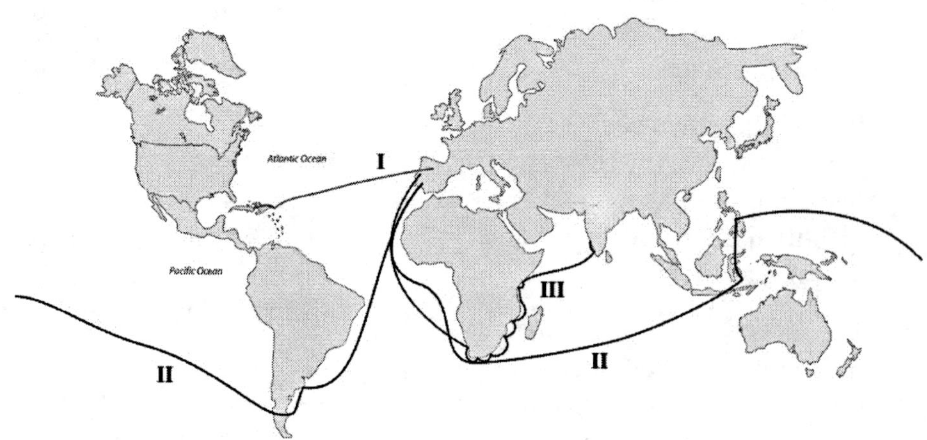

36 Route III depicts the voyage of SSWH10

A Christopher Columbus.

B Magellan.

C Vasco da Gama.

D Amerigo Vespucci.

37 Which of the following is NOT a power and responsibility of Congress? SSUSCG4

A impeaching public officials

B setting foreign policy

C proposing taxes and ways to raise revenue

D declaring war

38 Someone who believes in the Qur'an, and reveres Muhammad as God's greatest prophet is a member of what religion? SSWG3

A Judaism

B Christianity

C Islam

D Hinduism

39 A man who is a gifted architect, inventor, mathematician, and poet could be described as a SSWH9

A Machiavellian.

B Totalitarian.

C Renaissance man.

D Humanist.

40 Henry Ford contributed to the United States' growth as an industrial nation by introducing such innovations as SSUSH16

A the electric light and buying stock on the margin.

B new methods of mass production and a more efficient assembly line.

C the cotton gin and interchangeable parts.

D the phonograph and the moving picture camera.

41 Which of the following bodies of government has the "sole power of impeachment." (Article 1, US Constitution) SSCG14

A the cabinet

B Supreme Court

C US Senate

D US House of Representatives

42 Who was appointed by the Continental Congress to command the Continental Army? SSCG14

A Thomas Paine

B General Horatio Gates

C George Washington

D Lord Cornwallis

43 What was most significant about Yorktown? SSUSH4

A It ended the Revolution.

B It gave Cornwallis more power in the war.

C Washington was forced to surrender to Cornwallis.

D It allowed Marquis de Lafayette to command his own army for the first time.

Read the quote below and answer the following question

> "This is our hope. This is the faith with which I return to the South. With this faith we will be able to hew out of the mountain of despair a stone of hope. With this faith we will be able to transform the jangling discords of our nation into a beautiful symphony of brotherhood. With this faith we will be able to work together, to pray together, to struggle together, to go to jail together, to stand up for freedom together, knowing that we will be free one day."

44 Who was this quote MOST LIKELY spoken by? SSUSH22

A President Truman

B Martin Luther King

C Rachael Carson

D General Eisenhower

SESSION II

Look at the picture below and answer the following question.

45 The picture most likely depicts SSWH14

A the Reign of Terror.

B the Holocaust.

C the Russian Revolution.

D the Counter Reformation.

46 Where did Roosevelt, Churchill, and Stalin meet and agree to launch an invasion of Europe? SSWH18

A Potsdam

B Tehran

C Yalta

D Paris

47 The idea that it was the United State's sovereign duty to conquer the West under God's will was called SSWH18

A sectionalism.

B Supreme Law of the Land.

C Temperance.

D Manifest Destiny.

48 Which of the following is true about the Mississippi River? SSWG8

A It connects Canada to the United States.

B It stretches from Georgia to Maine.

C It is part of the largest river system in North America.

D It is only navigable five months a year.

49 The national government is responsible for foreign policy and trade. State, governments, however, set guidelines regarding public education. Such division of power is known as SSCG3

A separation of powers.

B popular sovereignty.

C checks and balances.

D federalism.

50 What impact did the nation's railroads have on steel and other industries following the Civil War? SSUSH11

A Very little because it was almost 1900 before the first railroads were available for use in the United States.

B They competed with steel and forced manufacturers to become more creative.

C Industries thrived because railroads made it easier to ship products and materials.

D They hurt the steel industry by allowing builders to get iron more easily.

51 Multinational corporations, the United Nations, and the World Trade Organization are all examples of SSWH21

A international treaties.

B diplomacy.

C the need for decolonization.

D the impact of globalization.

Read the list below and answer the following question.

1. political participation
2. running for political office
3. paying taxes and obeying laws
4. participation in jury duty
5. taking private land for public use

52 Which are examples of civic responsibilities? SSCG7

A 1,3,4

B 2,4

C 1,2,4

D 1,5

53 What agreement admitted California to the Union as a free state? SSUSH8

A The Compromise of 1850

B Kansas-Nebraska Act

C Dred Scott Case

D Wilmot Proviso

Look at the cartoon below and answer the following question.

54 The artist who drew this carton would MOST LIKELY agree with which one of the following statements? SSCCG4

A Congress and the president usually cooperate.

B Congress' powers are rarely checked.

C The Supreme Court usually has no say in what becomes a law.

D The Supreme Court has a great deal of power over what laws actually stay in place.

55 Which of the following individuals would have been MOST LIKELY to visit Ellis Island in 1900? SSUSH12

A a Native American

B a wealthy industrialist

C a Chinese laborer

D a European immigrant

56 The continent with the greatest population is SSWG5

A Africa.

B Europe.

C Asia.

D North America.

Read the quote below and answer the following question.

> **"Mr. Vice President, Mr. Speaker, members of the Senate and the House of Representatives: yesterday, December 7, 1941 — a day which will live in infamy — the United States of America was suddenly and deliberately attacked by naval and air forces of the Empire of Japan... I ask that the Congress declare that since the unprovoked and dastardly attack by Japan on Sunday, December 7, 1941, a state of war has existed between the United States and the Japanese Empire."**
>
> **President Franklin D. Roosevelt**
> **speech before Congress, December 8, 1941**

57 The speech quoted above was made in response to SSUSH19

A Japan's invasion of the Philippines.

B the attack on Pearl Harbor.

C the battle of Midway.

D Japan's decision to take Germany's side in WWII.

58 What is significant about Russia? SSWH17

A It became the first communist state.

B It was led by Adolf Hitler.

C It became the first democracy in Europe.

D It was the birthplace of Fascism.

59 The President of the United States would have the authority to do which of the following? SSCG12

A declare war on a foreign country

B order US military forces into action

C make a treaty signed by the US official

D declare a law passed by Congress unconstitutional

60 What effect did the end of Reconstruction have on African Americans? SSUSH10

A It presented them with more opportunities because it meant the end of racist policies.

B It resulted in greater opportunities for education, the chance to hold political office, and the revival of the African American church.

C It led to oppression because southern states had more sovereignty and used it to implement things like Jim Crow laws, literacy tests, and poll taxes.

D It meant the loss of political influence because it made the Republicans more powerful and most African Americans were Democrats.

61 Petrarch, Dante, and Erasmus are all remembered for their contributions to SSWH9

A the Reformation.

B the Counter Reformation.

C the Enlightenment.

D Humanism.

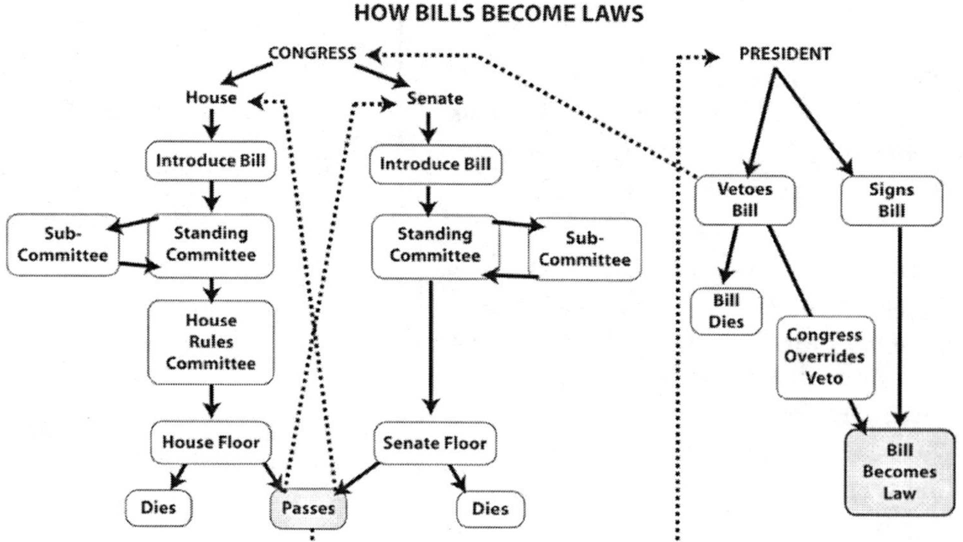

62 The chart above depicts SSCG10

A the nomination process.

B the election process.

C the judicial process.

D the legislative process.

63 The Columbian Exchange contributed to SSWH10

A World War I.

B the Renaissance.

C the French Revolution.

D the spread of disease.

64 Which of the following inspired African Americans to fight for the Union during the Civil War? SSUSH9

A the Declaration of Independence

B the Articles of Confederation

C the Emancipation Proclamation

D the Thirteenth Amendment

65 Candice opposes big government. She believes that the government should simply provide law and order, structure for society, national defense, and economic policies that allow the market to function as freely as possible. Candice can BEST be described as what? SSCG8

A a liberal

B a conservative

C a moderate

D an independent

Read the list below and answer the following question.

- Secretary of State
- Attorney General
- Secretary of Defense
- Secretary of the Treasury
- Secretary of the Interior

66 The best title for the above list is SSCG15

A members of the legislative branch.

B officials appointed for life.

C members of the president's cabinet.

D elected members of the executive branch.

67 Englishman Isaac Newton is considered one of the greatest geniuses of all time for his ability to SSWH13

A design the astrolabe.

B develop the first telescope.

C create an accurate globe of the earth.

D explain gravity's role in the universe.

68 Which of the following is NOT a characteristic of Jacksonian democracy? SSUSH7

A Laissez-faire economics

B strict interpretation of the Constitution

C Spoils System

D the doctrine of nullification

Read the quote below and answer the following question

> **"A long habit of thinking a thing wrong, gives it a superficial appearance of being right, and raises at first a formidable outcry in defense of custom... Everything that is right or natural pleads for separation. The blood of the slain, the weeping voice of nature cries, *'tis time to part'...***
>
> **Thomas Paine**
> ***Common Sense*, 1776**

69 According to the quote above, Paine believed that SSUSH3

A tradition is more valuable than what is superficial.

B Americans should embrace independence as their natural right.

C Just because colonists might long for independence, that doesn't make it right.

D Colonists should revolt against the king, even though they may have no natural right to do so.

70 Who used non-violent protest and pled for unity among Indians of different faiths as he led his nation's independence movement? SSWH19

A Toussaint L'Ouverture

B Mohandas Gandhi

C Martin Luther King, Jr.

D Lenin

Go On

Look at the map below and answer the following question.

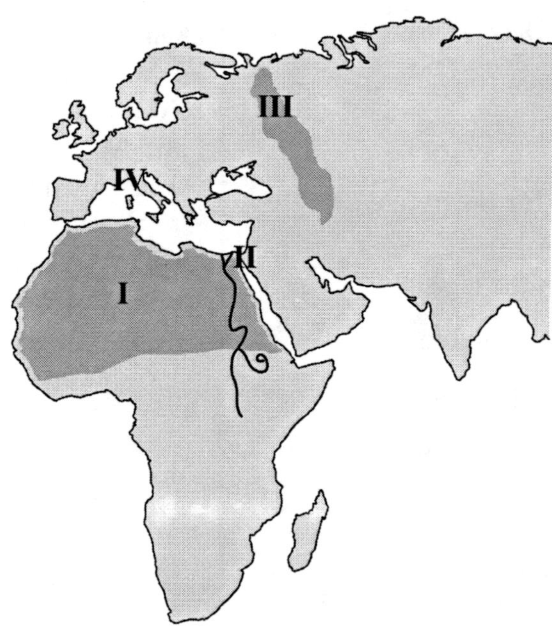

71 In which areas would one expect to find the greatest concentration of population? SSWG1

A I and III

B I

C II and IV

D III

72 The authority of the Supreme Court to declare acts of Congress unconstitutional was established in which court case? SSCG16

A *Marbury v. Madison* (1803)

B *McCullough v. Maryland* (1819)

C *Korematsu v. United States* (1944)

D *Brown v. Board of Education* (1954)

73 Labor unions formed primarily for the purpose of SSUSH12

A helping business owners better conduct their operations.

B assisting the government to draft new laws.

C increasing economic production and profits.

D organizing workers to bring about better pay and working conditions.

Look at the lists below and answer the following question.

1	2
raise revenue	open a national bank
provide a national defense	buy territory
regulate trade	authorize a draft
declare war	establish federal departments

74 Which of the following statements is accurate regarding the above lists? SSCG5

A Column 1 lists implied powers, while column 2 lists enumerated powers.

B Column 1 lists federal powers, while column 2 lists powers reserved for the states.

C Column 1 lists enumerated powers, while column 2 lists implied powers.

D Column 1 lists the powers of government, while column 2 lists rights protected by the first ten amendments to the Constitution.

75 After WWII, the United States implemented the Marshall Plan. The purpose of this plan was to SSUSH20

A supply West Berlin with much needed supplies despite the Soviets' decision to block access to the city.

B provide European nations with the money they needed to rebuild after WWII in order to prevent the spread of communism.

C prevent communists from taking over countries in Southeast Asia.

D provide returning US soldiers with jobs, homes, and educational opportunities as they returned from the war.

76 The president of the United States meets with the leaders of Canada, Great Britain, Russia, France, Germany, and a number of other western nations. Collectively, they decide to restrict trade with North Korea and limit financial aid to that country. They hope that by taking such action they will force North Korea to give up its attempts to develop nuclear weapons. They are attempting to change North Korea's behavior through SSCG20

A diplomacy.

B negotiations.

C sanctions.

D military action.

Go On

Look at the map below and answer the following question.

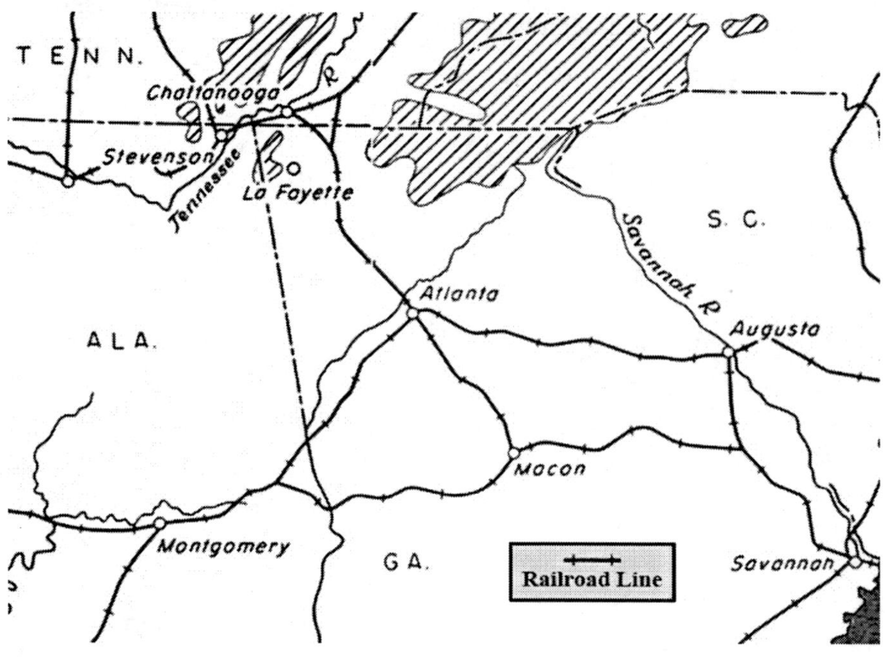

77 Based on the map above, what reason might a Union general have for wanting to capture Atlanta? SSUSH9

A It was the capital of the Confederacy.

B It was an important center in terms of transporting confederate supplies and troops.

C It was the only major city between Grant's and Lee's armies.

D It was an important confederate port.

78 The First Amendment to the United States Constitution guarantees SSCG6

A freedom of speech.

B due process.

C trial by jury.

D the right to bear arms.

79 A strong Federalist would have MOST LIKELY supported which of the following? SUSH5

A the Jeffersonian-Republicans

B the Articles of Confederation

C the Bill of Rights

D the Constitution prior to any amendments

Read the song lyrics below and answer the following question.

> **"...Once I built a railroad, made it run, made it race against time.**
>
> **Once I built a railroad; now it's done. Brother, can you spare a dime?**
>
> **Once I built a tower, up to the sun, brick, and rivet, and lime;**
>
> **Once I built a tower, now it's done. Brother can you spare a dime."**

80 The above song was most likely written during SSUSH17

A World War II.

B the Civil War.

C the civil rights movement.

D the Great Depression.

81. The term "Cold War" referred to which of the following? SSUSH20

A the war between Germany and the USSR

B the war between the US and Germany

C the tension and potential for war that existed between the US and USSR after WWII.

D the dividing line between the democracies of Western Europe and the communist nations of Eastern Europe

82 Which of the following best defines culture? SSWG2

A a system of shared beliefs, values, customs, and behaviors that shape how members of society live and view their world

B traditions passed down from one generation of a group to the next

C the natural land formations that make up the surface of an area

D the study of how human characteristics define a region

83 Nicholas Davis is extremely disappointed. Although the president of the United States nominated him to serve on the Supreme Court, the US Senate voted down his nomination. This scenario is an example of which principle at work? SSCG3

A separation of powers

B popular sovereignty

C the legislative branch

D checks and balances

84 Increased US industrialization in the years following the Civil War led to SSUSH11

A rapid population growth in urban areas.

B increased reliance on agriculture as the foundation of the US economy.

C fewer immigrants arriving in the US.

D less call for reforms from progressives.

85 Which of the following acts as a natural barrier affecting the climate of the Mediterranean coast? SSWG6

A the Alps

B the European Great Plain

C the Rhine

D the Urals

86 For what purpose did the United States want to build the Panama Canal? SSUSH14

A It would make it easier for manufacturers in New York to reach western markets.

B It would allow eastern US cities to trade more easily with Europe.

C It would allow US ships to travel between the Atlantic and Pacific more easily.

D It would make it easier for US troops to reach Cuba to fight the Spanish.

87 Why did Sputnik concern leaders of the United States? SSUSH21

A They feared it would jeopardize their relationship with the USSR.

B They feared it would cause a communist revolution in North America.

C It revealed the superiority of Soviet technology in comparison to the US.

D It launched the Bolshevik revolution.

Read the description below and answer the following questions.

This region is one of the coldest on Earth. In the winter, the weather can reach -50 degrees farenheit. There is very little evaporation. The permafrost lies six inches below the ground. Trees and plants have a hard time growing in these conditions.

88 What region in Europe does this describe? SSWG6

A tundra

B mediterranean

C arctic

D subtropical

89 Why do few people live in the region described in question 88? SSWG6

A They do not want to interfere with the short growing season for trees and plants.

B The harsh conditions make it difficult to live in.

C The many wolves and polar bears that inhabit the region frighten the people.

D The lack of open territory for settling reduces population growth.

90 NOW was founded as a result of SSUSH24

A the civil rights movement.

B the temperance movement.

C the women's movement.

D the environmental movement.

Go On

EVALUATION CHART FOR GEORGIA HSGT IN SOCIAL STUDIES DIAGNOSTIC TEST

Directions: On the following chart, circle the question numbers that you answered incorrectly, and evaluate the results. These questions are based on the *standards and benchmarks published by the Georgia Department of Education.* Then turn to the appropriate chapters, read the explanations, and complete the exercises. Review other chapters as needed. Finally, complete the Practice test(s) to assess your progress and further prepare you for the **Georgia High School Graduation Test in Social Studies**.

Note: Some question numbers may appear under multiple chapters because those questions require demonstration of multiple skills.

Chapter	Diagnostic Test Question(s)
Chapter 1: United States Government	1, 6, 8, 28, 29, 37, 41, 42, 49, 54, 59, 62, 66, 72, 74, 76, 83
Chapter 2: Civil Rights and Civic Responsibility	18, 24, 27, 52, 65, 78
Chapter 3: European Settlement Through the War of 1812	2, 9, 16, 17, 34, 43, 69, 79
Chapter 4: United States History: Industrial Revolution Through the Civil War	4, 11, 47, 53, 64, 68, 77
Chapter 5: United States HIstory: Reconstruction Through World War I.	3, 35, 50, 55, 60, 73, 84, 86
Chapter 6: United States History: Roaring 20s to the Modern Age	13, 20, 31, 40, 44, 57, 75, 80, 87, 90
Chapter 7: World Geography: Africa and Asia	5, 12, 21, 26, 32, 38, 56, 71, 82, 85
Chapter 8: World Geography: Europe, the Americas, and Oceania	14, 19, 23, 48, 88, 89
Chapter 9: World History: From the Renaissance Through Napoleon	7, 10, 22, 25, 36, 39, 45, 61, 63, 67
Chapter 10: World History: World War I to Modern Day	15, 30, 33, 46, 51, 70, 58, 81

Chapter 1
United States Government

GPS	SSCG2: The student will analyze the natural rights philosophy and the nature of government expressed in the Declaration of Independence. (QCC standards US6, US9)
	SSCG3: The student will demonstrate knowledge of the United States Constitution. (QCC standards CC3, CC8)
	SSCG4: The student will demonstrate knowledge of the organization and powers of the national government. (QCC standards CC3, CC4, CC6, CC7, CC8)
	SSCG5: The student will demonstrate knowledge of the federal system of government described in the United States Constitution. (QCC standards CC3, CC4, CC8, US9)
	SSCG9: The student will explain the differences between the House of Representatives and the Senate, with emphasis on terms of office, powers, organization, leadership, and representation of each house. (QCC standard CC4)
	SSCG10: The student will describe the legislative process including the roles played by committees and leadership. (QCC standard CC4)
	SSCG20: The student will describe the tools used to carry out United States foreign policy (diplomacy; economic, military, and humanitarian aid; treaties; sanctions; and military intervention). (QCC standards CC4, CC6)

1.1 Natural Rights, Social Contract, and the Declaration of Independence

Natural Rights and Social Contract Theory

Beginning in the late 1600s, Europe experienced the *Enlightenment.* The Enlightenment was a time of revolutionary ideas in philosophy and political thought that later helped form American ideas about government. England's John Locke was one of the most influential figures of this period. John Locke challenged the old view that monarchs possess a God-given right to rule, with citizens obligated to obey. Locke believed that people were born with certain **natural rights** that no government could morally take away. These rights include life, liberty, and property. He also advocated ***social contract theory***. According to this philosophy, there is an implied contract between government and citizens. For the good of society, people agree to give up certain freedoms and empower governments to maintain order. If, however, a government failed to serve the public good, Locke believed, citizens could rightfully replace it.

John Locke

The Declaration of Independence

Thomas Jefferson

In June 1776, the delegates to the Second Continental Congress decided to declare independence from Great Britain. They appointed a committee to prepare a statement outlining the reasons for this separation. One of the committee's members, a young delegate named Thomas Jefferson, drafted the statement. Strongly influenced by the ideas of the Enlightenment, Jefferson asserted the principle of *egalitarianism* (the idea that all men are created equal) and proclaimed that men are born with certain **inalienable rights** (natural rights that government cannot take away). Among these rights are "life, liberty, and the pursuit of happiness." The document became known as the **Declaration of Independence**. The Continental Congress formally adopted this declaration on July 4, 1776.

Signing of the Declaration of Independence

The Declaration of Independence begins by echoing the theories of John Locke and asserting the "natural rights" to which all men are entitled. It proclaims that governments obtain their power to rule from the free consent of the people. If the government fails to serve its citizens, those citizens have the right to resist and/or replace it with a new system. The document then lists the many ways in which England had failed to rule properly and states why, therefore, the colonies should rule themselves. It concludes with a formal declaration of independence and the signatures of those serving as delegates to the Second Continental Congress.

Sadly, the rights trumpeted by the Declaration of Independence were not applied to everyone. African Americans were not recognized as citizens and remained slaves in most states. Women were not afforded the same rights as men. Native Americans were not recognized as having the same human rights, despite having lived in North America much longer than any Europeans. Still, the Declaration was a revolutionary document for its emphasis on egalitarianism and natural rights. Once adopted it also fueled debate that, in time, led to the end of slavery, equal rights for women, and recognition of the rights of minorities.

Jamil Round

Practice 1.1: Natural Rights, Social Contract, and the Declaration of Independence

1. What document formally proclaimed the American colonies' independence from Great Britain?

   A. the social contract

   B. the letters of Enlightenment

   C. the Declaration of Independence

   D. the writings of John Locke.

2. Rights which human beings are born with and which no government has a right to take away are called

   A. declaratory rights.
   C. social rights.

   B. natural rights.
   D. alienable rights.

3. Together with four or five classmates, read a copy of the Declaration of Independence and evaluate its arguments. Does it make a persuasive case for natural rights and the duties of government? What are its strengths and weaknesses? Do you agree with the idea of "natural rights" and "social contract"? Why or why not?

1.2 The United States Constitution

Need and Purpose

Daniel Shays' Rebellion

Following the adoption of the Declaration of Independence, the newly independent states were cautious about giving too much authority to a central government. For this reason, Congress drafted the **Articles of Confederation**. Finally ratified in 1781, this document failed because it did not give enough power to the federal (national) government. In order for any law passed by Congress to be final, at least nine of the thirteen states had to agree. Since the states often had different interests, such agreement was rare. Also, the Articles did not grant Congress the power to impose taxes. The federal government had to *ask* the states for money. As you might imagine, this was not very effective and made it practically impossible to administer the government or provide for a national defense. Change finally came as a result of **Daniel Shays' Rebellion** in 1786. After the war, the United States experienced an economic crisis. The value of US currency was very low and falling farm prices left many farmers unable to repay outstanding loans. At the same time, in order to pay war debts, the state of Massachusetts raised taxes (the national government could not impose taxes, but state governments could). Outraged, a Massachusetts farmer and Revolutionary War veteran named Daniel Shays led a number of farmers in rebellion. With Congress helpless to do anything, Massachusetts had to raise its own army to put down the uprising. This rebellion supported the argument that a stronger central government was needed.

THE CONSTITUTIONAL CONVENTION AND COMPROMISE

Constitutional Convention

James Madison

In 1787, a delegation met in Philadelphia to revise the Articles of Confederation. Soon after the convention began, however, the delegates decided to do away with the document altogether and write a new set of laws. The result was the **United States Constitution**.

All the delegates in attendance (only Rhode Island did not send representatives) agreed that change was necessary. However, how the national government should be reorganized was a matter of much debate. As a result, a number of compromises emerged. Edmund Randolph and James Madison of Virginia introduced the *Virginia Plan*. They proposed a federal government made up of three branches: a legislative branch to make laws, an executive branch to enforce laws, and a judicial branch to make sure laws were administered fairly. For the legislative branch, the Virginia Plan called for two houses with representatives from each state. In each house, the number of representatives per state would be determined by population. The greater a state's population, the more representatives it would have. Larger states loved the idea, but smaller states hated it because they would have less representation. As a result, one of New Jersey's delegates proposed the *New Jersey Plan*. Like the Virginia Plan, it also called for three branches of government, but it wanted the legislative branch to consist of only one house with each state getting a single vote. In the end, the delegates decided on a compromise. It became known as the **Great Compromise**, or the *Connecticut Plan*, because it was proposed by Roger Sherman of Connecticut. It established a legislative branch with two houses. One house, called the House of Representatives, would be elected directly by the people, with each state granted a certain number of seats based on population. The other house, called the Senate, would be elected by state legislatures, with each state having two senators, regardless of population. Together, the two houses would comprise Congress.

Slavery also proved to be a point of contention. Northern states had fewer slaves and argued that, since slaves were not voting citizens, they should not be counted as part of the population. Southern states, however, had far more slaves and wanted to count them. The answer to this question was important because it affected how many representatives each state would have in

Congress. Again, a compromise was reached. It was known as the **Three-fifths Compromise** because it stated that each slave would count as "three-fifths of a person." In other words, for every five slaves, a state would be credited for having three people. Meanwhile, debate about the slave trade resulted in a **slave trade compromise**. Under this agreement, Northerners and delegates from the Upper South (Maryland and Virginia) who opposed the slave trade agreed to allow it to continue unregulated for twenty years, though Congress could impose regulations. This was important to delegates from the Deep South who insisted that their economy could not survive without the slave trade. Though US involvement in the Atlantic slave trade finally ended in 1808, slavery continued until 1865.

Fundamental Principles of the Constitution

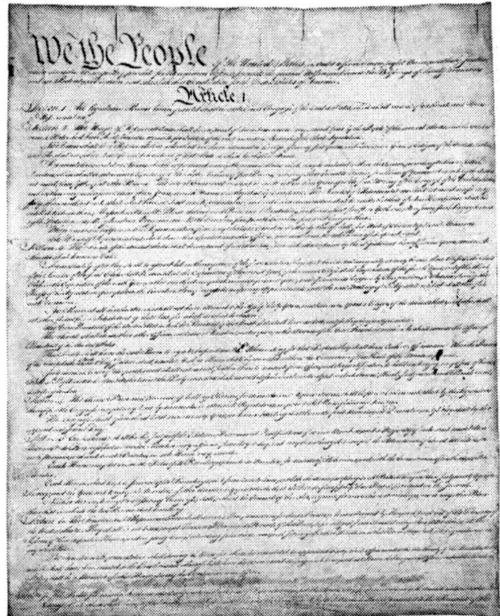

Constitution

The Constitution establishes a government based on *limited government, separation of powers, checks and balances, federalism,* and *the rule of law.* The **rule of law** simply means that the United States is a society governed by set laws, not the independent will of a monarch or small body of rulers. Every citizen, leader, and body of government must obey the nation's laws. In the United States, the US Constitution is the highest authority and defines what laws govern the country.

Limited government is the principle that even governments must obey a set of laws and respect the rights of citizens. They are "limited" in what powers they have and what they can do. The Founding Fathers intended the Constitution to provide such limitations. They wanted a government that respects and upholds the natural rights of citizens.

Separation of powers divides authority to govern between different branches of government. Under the Constitution, the federal government divides its power between three branches: legislative, executive, and judicial. The legislative branch (Congress) is responsible for making the laws of the country. The executive branch, led by the president, is responsible for enforcing the laws. Finally, the judicial branch (the federal court system, with the US Supreme Court serving as the highest court in the land) makes sure the laws are applied fairly and appropriately.

Checks and balances in the Constitution allow each branch to check the powers of the other two. By dividing power between different branches and allowing each to check the others, the Founding Fathers designed a model of government that keeps any one branch from becoming too authoritative.

Finally, **federalism** means that power is divided between different levels of government. In the United States, the national and state governments share power. The **Tenth Amendment** to the Constitution states that those powers not restricted by the Constitution or delegated to the national government are reserved for the states. In other words, states have the authority to make many of their own laws.

Separation of Powers

Judicial

Legislative

Executive

Government Branches

Another important political principal is ***popular sovereignty***. Popular sovereignty is the belief that the government is empowered by, and is subject to, the will of its people (John Locke's social contract theory). In the early years of the US, many leaders interpreted this to mean that the will of the people was best expressed through a republic in which an "elite" class of educated individuals would elect leaders and be selected to rule on the people's behalf. Later, particularly during the early 1800s, more and more citizens believed that popular sovereignty demanded that all citizens (or, at least, all white male citizens) be given the right to vote in elections and have a voice in government.

RATIFICATION

Although the new document was an amazing improvement from the Articles of Confederation, it was not without controversy. A number of states refused to ratify it, claiming it did not do enough to guarantee the rights of citizens. Finally, in late 1788, the last of the nine states needed for ratification (acceptance) approved the Constitution, once Congress agreed to consider a number of amendments protecting civil liberties (Georgia was the fourth state to ratify the Constitution). Only North Carolina and Rhode Island waited until after these amendments had actually been submitted to Congress. When Congress met in 1789, one of its first orders of business was to pass the **Bill of Rights**. Consisting of the first ten amendments (additions) to the Constitution, its purpose is to protect citizens' rights and maintain limited government. (See chapter 2, section 2.1)

FEDERALISTS VS. ANTI-FEDERALISTS

Alexander Hamilton

Controversy also surrounded the new Constitution concerning what role and powers the national government should have. Many favored the Constitution because they believed that the United States needed a strong federal government with a powerful president at its head. Others opposed the Constitution because they feared that a powerful federal government would trample on their rights. Because of the debate, political leaders split into opposing factions. A **faction** is a group of people who are bound by a common cause, usually against another group bound by an opposing cause.

The **Federalists** favored a strong central government and supported the Constitution. Among their leaders were **Alexander Hamilton** and **James Madison**. Madison played a key role in drafting the Constitution and devising its model of government. He is often referred to as the "Father of the Constitution." Long before leaders decided to call a convention to revise the Articles of Confederation, Madison believed that a new framework for government would eventually be needed. He spent years prior to 1787 developing a more effective system for governing. Since many of the ideas that framed the Constitution were introduced by Madison, such as dividing power among three branches of government, it is not surprising that he was originally a Federalist who supported ratification. Federalists also tended to have a "loose interpretation" of the Constitution. They believed that the Constitution allowed the federal government to take actions not specifically stated, so long as they were deemed necessary for carrying out the government's constitutional responsibilities.

Thomas Jefferson

Anti-federalists had a different view. Author of the Declaration of Independence, Thomas Jefferson, was an Anti-federalist. However, he was not present at the Constitutional Convention because he was serving as the US ambassador to France. Anti-federalists, like Jefferson, were more suspicious of the Constitution and feared that it gave too much power to the central government. Anti-federalists held to a "strict interpretation" and believed the federal government could only do what the Constitution specifically said. Anti-federalists did not want a small faction of leaders becoming too powerful and using the national government to trample on the rights of citizens.

To make their case for the Constitution, Hamilton and Madison helped author a series of essays known as the ***Federalist Papers***. The essays were written to persuade New York's legislature to ratify the Constitution by easing fears that the document left the government susceptible to any one faction seizing too much power. Eventually, with the support of men like George Washington, Alexander Hamilton, and John Adams, the Federalist view won. Anti-federalists did succeed, however, in securing the Bill of Rights.

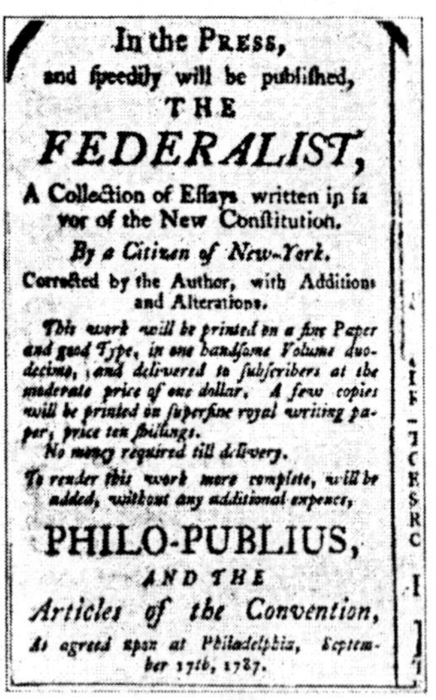

In the PRESS,
and speedily will be published,
THE
FEDERALIST,
A Collection of Essays written in favor of the New Constitution.
By a Citizen of New-York.
Corrected by the Author, with Additions and Alterations.
This work will be printed on a fine Paper and good Type, in one handsome Volume duodecimo, and delivered to subscribers at the moderate price of one dollar. A few copies will be printed on superfine royal writing paper, price ten shillings.
No money required till delivery.
To render this work more complete, will be added, without any additional expence,
PHILO-PUBLIUS,
AND THE
Articles of the Convention,
As agreed upon at Philadelphia, September 17th, 1787.

Federalist Papers

Practice 1.2: The United States Constitution

1. The idea of a legislative branch making the laws, an executive branch enforcing the laws, and a judicial branch overseeing application of the law is consistent with
   A. separation of powers.
   B. checks and balances.
   C. federalism.
   D. popular sovereignty.

2. Which of the following states that governments are empowered by and exist for the people they govern?
   A. federalism
   B. popular sovereignty
   C. anti-federalism
   D. checks and balances

3. Explain the difference between *Federalists* and *Anti-federalists*. How did they view the role of the central government and interpret the Constitution differently?

1.3 The Federal Government

The Legislative Branch

The first sentence of the US Constitution is known as the *Preamble*. It serves to explain the purpose and intent of the document. It reads as follows:

> *"We the people of the United States, in order to form a more perfect union, establish justice, insure domestic tranquillity, provide for the common defense, promote the general welfare, and secure the blessings of liberty to ourselves and our posterity, do ordain and establish this Constitution for the United States of America."*

US Capitol Building

The Preamble is followed by three articles that establish the three branches of US government. *Article I* establishes the **legislative branch**, known as Congress. It is the role of the legislative branch to make the laws. Congress consists of two houses. Population determines how many representatives each state has in the **House of Representatives**. The greater a state's population, the more representatives that state has. Voters elect representatives to the House every two years. Once in office, these representatives then elect a **speaker of the House** (usually from the majority party) to preside over the House of Representatives.

The second house is the **Senate**, which is comprised of two senators from each state. Originally, state legislatures, rather than the people, elected senators. However, in 1913, the Seventeenth Amendment changed this. Now, citizens directly elect US senators, who serve six year terms. Under Article I / Section 3, one-third of the sitting senators are elected every two years. States usually stagger senatorial elections (make sure that their two senators are elected in different election years) so as to always have at least one experienced senator in Congress at all times. The senator who has represented a particular state in Congress the longest is referred to as that state's "senior senator," while the senator who has served less time is referred to as the "junior senator." The Senate is presided over by the vice president; however, there is also a **president pro tempore**. This person is usually the most senior member of the majority party and is the highest ranking member of the Senate. He/she presides over the Senate in the vice president's absence.

U.S. Congress		
	House of Representatives	U.S. Senate
Representation	by population	2 per state
length of terms	2 years	6 years
leadership	led by the Speaker of the House	led by vice president and president pro tempore

Powers and Limitations of Congress

The Constitution grants each house of Congress certain powers and responsibilities. Some powers are shared by both houses. Others belong to one house, but not the other. For instance, both houses must approve a bill (a proposed law) before it can become a law (a rule which society is legally bound to uphold and abide by). On the other hand, only the House of Representatives may introduce tax bills or impeach public officials. In the same way, only the Senate has the power to block or confirm presidential appointments (people the president nominates to fill cabinet positions, seats on the federal courts, or other public offices) and ratify treaties. Below are some of the powers given to one or both houses of Congress and limitations specifically stated in the Constitution.

POWERS:

1. *Impeach* (charge with wrongdoing while in office) public officials.
2. Try impeachment cases and decide the guilt or innocence of impeached public officials.
3. Confirm (accept) or reject presidential appointments.
4. Ratify or reject treaties with foreign nations.
5. Propose taxes and means of raising revenue.
6. Introduce bills and pass new laws.
7. Raise revenue in the form of taxes, etc. for the purpose of maintaining a national defense and the general welfare of the US.
8. Borrow money and regulate foreign and interstate trade.
9. Coin money, establish rules by which foreign immigrants become citizens, establish bankruptcy laws, post offices, and provide copyrights and patents.
10. Declare war and maintain a national military force.

LIMITATIONS:

1. Congress cannot suspend *Writ of Habeas Corpus*. This is the right of an arrested person to go before a judge within a reasonable amount of time to determine if their incarceration is justified. Congress may not suspend this right except in cases of rebellion, invasion, or to ensure public safety.

2. Congress may not pass "bills of attainder" which are legislative acts convicting people of a crime without a trial.

3. Congress may not establish *ex post facto* laws (laws that make some past activity illegal, even though it was not illegal at the time). For instance, if the government established a law making profanity on television illegal, it could not prosecute people for using profanity on TV prior to the law being passed.

4. Congress may not grant "titles of nobility." Sorry, but no matter what you do, Congress cannot name you the *Duke* or *Duchess of Georgia.*

5. Congress is limited in what kinds of taxes and duties it may establish and how it may govern trade.

Congressional Leadership

As mentioned before, the top post in the House of Representatives is the **Speaker of the House**. He/she is elected by the members of the House and is, therefore, usually a member of the majority party. The **vice president** presides over the Senate. However, the vice president only votes if his/her vote is needed to break a tie. When the vice president is not present, the **president pro tempore**, takes his/her place. However, these are not the only positions of leadership in Congress. The two major parties (Republican and Democrat) within the Senate and House of Representatives also have leaders. The **majority leader** is the elected leader of the majority party. Conversely, the **minority leader** leads the minority party. There is also a **majority and minority whip**. The whip makes sure that members of the party vote the way the party leadership wants them to. There are also **committee chairpersons** within each house who are over the various committees considering bills and other legislative actions. We will discuss committees more when we look at the legislative process.

Speaker of the House Nancy Pelosi

President Pro Tempore Robert Byrd

ARTICLE II (THE EXECUTIVE BRANCH)

George Washington

Abraham Lincoln

Franklin Roosevelt

Ronald Reagan

Barack Obama

Article II establishes the **executive branch** of government to enforce the laws. The **president of the United States** serves as the chief executive of this branch and the nation's head of state. Under Article II / Section 2, the president is elected to office by the **Electoral College**. This is a body of delegates that meets every four years solely to elect the president and the **vice president**. The vice president becomes president should the president die or become incapable of finishing his/her term. Originally, the vice president was simply whoever had the second highest number of votes in the Electoral College. However, in 1804, the Twelfth Amendment changed this by stating that the delegates to the Electoral College are to cast separate votes for the two offices. Each state's delegation in the Electoral College equals its number of representatives and senators in Congress. Today, this body serves as more of a formality since delegates' votes are predetermined in a general election (see chapter 2, section 2.3).

Once elected, the president and vice president are then inaugurated (swear an oath to uphold the duties of their respective office and the Constitution) and serve four year terms. Although the Constitution did not originally place limits on how many terms a president may serve, none served more than two terms until 1940. That year, Franklin Delano Roosevelt broke tradition and became the only president in history elected to a third term (he was eventually elected four times). Later, in 1951, the Twenty-second Amendment limited presidents to no more than two terms.

Responsibilities of the President and Vice President

The Constitution lists the qualifications for president in Article II / Section 5 and defines his/her powers and responsibilities in Article II / Sections 3 – 4.

POWERS AND RESPONSIBILITIES OF THE PRESIDENT:

1. The president is the country's **chief executive**. He/she is the nation's recognized leader and head of the executive branch of government and is ultimately responsible for enforcing the nation's laws.
2. The president is to serve as **commander in chief** of the nation's military. He/she is the top military commander.
3. The president is responsible for **foreign policy**. The president plays the major role in deciding how the United States will deal with foreign countries and international situations. He/she is responsible for negotiating treaties and agreements with other nations (treaties must be ratified by the Senate before they are official). The president is the nation's chief of state and its foremost representative.

President Clinton Meeting with Foreign Leader

4. He/She appoints public officials (i.e., heads of federal departments and federal judges) which must be approved by the Senate.

The president also acts as the head of his/her **political party**. Political parties are organizations that seek to impact public policy by sponsoring and supporting candidates for political office.

As in the case of Congress, the Constitution also takes steps to make sure that the president is bound by the rule of law. Article II / Section 4 states that the president may be **impeached** (charged with wrongdoing while in office) by the House of Representatives if he/she is suspected of treason, bribery, or "other high crimes and misdemeanors." If this occurs, the president then stands trial in the Senate. If two-thirds of the Senate finds him/her guilty, then he/she is removed from office. Only two presidents have ever been impeached: Andrew Johnson and Bill Clinton. Neither was found guilty.

Clinton During Impeachment

The vice president is also part of the executive branch and he/she presides over the Senate. He/she has no vote, however, unless there is a tie; then the vice president casts the tie-breaking vote. Article II / Section 1 says that if the president cannot fulfill his/her term in office, then the vice president shall assume the duties of the presidency. This wording was originally confusing because it was not clear whether this meant that the vice president became president, or if it merely meant that he/she remained vice president but assumed the responsibilities of the president. In 1967, the Twenty-fifth Amendment settled this issue by plainly stating that, if the president could not fulfill his/her term, then the vice president would become the president.

THE PRESIDENT'S CABINET

Secretary of State Hillary Clinton

One part of the executive branch that became an important part of US government, but is not officially established by the Constitution, is the **president's cabinet**. The cabinet evolved over time and consists of the heads of various federal departments. It serves as the president's official panel of advisors and representatives regarding certain issues. For instance, the secretary of state advises the president on foreign affairs and often acts as the president's representative in dealing with leaders of foreign governments. The secretary of defense presides over the defense department and, as a civilian, has authority over the nation's military commanders. The attorney general is the nation's top law enforcement official and, as head of the justice department, presides over agencies like the FBI. These are just a few examples of officials who serve on the president's cabinet. They are appointed by the president and must be approved by the Senate before they can take office. Usually, they serve until the president who appointed them leaves office, although it is not uncommon for some to resign sooner. The **federal departments** which they oversee are part of the executive branch of government. Together, they form what is known as the **federal bureaucracy** (government structure put in place to regulate certain areas). A few of these agencies are:

- Department of Energy
- Department of Education
- Defense Department
- Justice Department
- State Department
- Department of Homeland Security
- Department of Labor
- Department of Health and Human Services

Former President George W. Bush's Cabinet

ARTICLE III (THE JUDICIAL BRANCH)

John Marshall

Article III created the **judicial branch**. This branch consists of the federal court system, with the Supreme Court acting as the highest court in the land. The role of the judicial branch is to make sure that laws are applied appropriately. Since Article III is somewhat vague about how this branch should be organized and what powers the Supreme Court shall hold, Congress passed the Judiciary Act of 1789 to establish both the federal court system and the authority of the Supreme Court.

One of the most important powers of the judicial branch is not specifically granted by the Constitution, but rather was established by precedence in 1803. *Precedence* means a court uses past legal decisions to make rulings because the law is open to interpretation or there is no written statute. In 1801, Thomas Jefferson (an Anti-federalist and leader of a political party known as the "Jeffersonian Republicans") became president. However, just before leaving office, his predecessor, John Adams (a member of an opposing political party known as the Federalists), appointed a number of federal judges. Although the Senate had confirmed these judges and Adams had signed their appointments, the documents making their appointments official had not yet been delivered when Jefferson took office. Fearing that Federalist judges might interfere with his plans, Jefferson refused to deliver the documents, preventing some of the judges from ever taking office. When several of the appointees challenged this move, the Supreme Court intervened to hear the case. In ***Marbury v. Madison (1803)***, Chief Justice John Marshall stated that the appointees were entitled to their commissions, *but* that the US Supreme Court did not have authority under the Constitution to force the president to issue them. In so doing, Marshall led the court in striking down part of the Judiciary Act of 1789 which gave such authority to the Court, thereby establishing the Court's authority of **judicial review**. Judicial review is the judicial branch's power to declare acts of Congress and/or state legislatures "unconstitutional." This means that even if Congress passes a law and the president signs it, the federal courts can still nullify the law by ruling that it violates the Constitution.

US Supreme Court

Chief Justice

Associate Justices

Unlike the president, vice president, and members of the legislative branch, judges who serve in the judicial branch are not elected. Rather, they are **appointed** (given their position) for life by the president. The reason they are appointed rather than elected is so they will be free to make their decisions based strictly on the law without having to worry about popular opinion or political pressures. The Supreme Court consists of nine judges, called *justices*. One justice serves as the *chief justice* (lead justice) while the other eight serve as *associate justices*. These justices serve as the highest court in the land and have appellate jurisdiction (the authority to review the decisions of lower courts) over all federal and state court cases. Under Article III / Section 2, the Supreme Court also has original jurisdiction (authority to hear a case first) over, "cases affecting ambassadors, other public ministers and consuls and those in which a state shall be a party." Underneath the Supreme Court are the US Court of Appeals, US District Courts, and US Special Courts. In each case, judges who preside on these courts must be appointed by the president and confirmed by the US Senate before they take the bench.

U.S. Court System

Some cases are heard ONLY by federal courts rather than state courts. They include:

- cases over which the Supreme Court has original jurisdiction.
- cases that involve violations of a federal rather than a state law.
- cases concerning bankruptcies, patents and/or copyrights.
- civil suits brought against the US government.

The chart below depicts the various levels of the federal court system and the jurisdictions which they cover:

UNITED STATES SUPREME COURT

Highest court in the nation which has appellate jurisdiction over all lower courts and original jurisdiction over cases affecting ambassadors, other public ministers and consuls, and those in which a state shall be a party. It may also hear cases appealed from state supreme courts.

UNITED STATES COURT OF APPEALS

Federal mid-level appellate court. Appellate jurisdiction over decisions rendered by the US District Courts and US Special Courts.

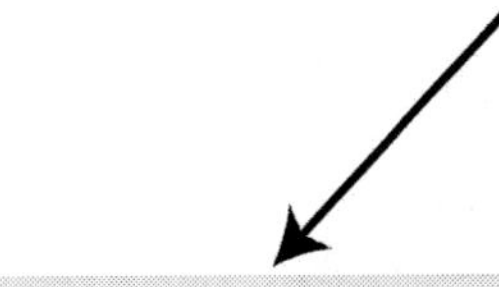

US DISTRICT COURTS

Act as the federal court system's trial courts for both criminal and civil cases that involve the federal government or alleged violations of federal laws.

US SPECIAL COURTS

Have original jurisdiction over special kinds of cases (i.e., international trade).

Cases Before the Supreme Court

Although the Supreme Court does have original jurisdiction over certain types of cases, most of the cases it hears involve appeals from lower courts. An appeal is when a party that loses a case in one court "appeals" to a higher court with more authority and asks it to review the case. The Supreme Court hears appeals from lower federal courts and from state supreme courts. Citizens and businesses may appeal both civil and criminal cases. A **civil case** consists of one

Chief Justice Roberts

party (person, business, etc.) claiming that another party (person, business, etc.) has wronged them is some way. A **criminal case** involves the state or federal government accusing someone of committing a crime. The diagram below depicts how cases may reach the Supreme Court:

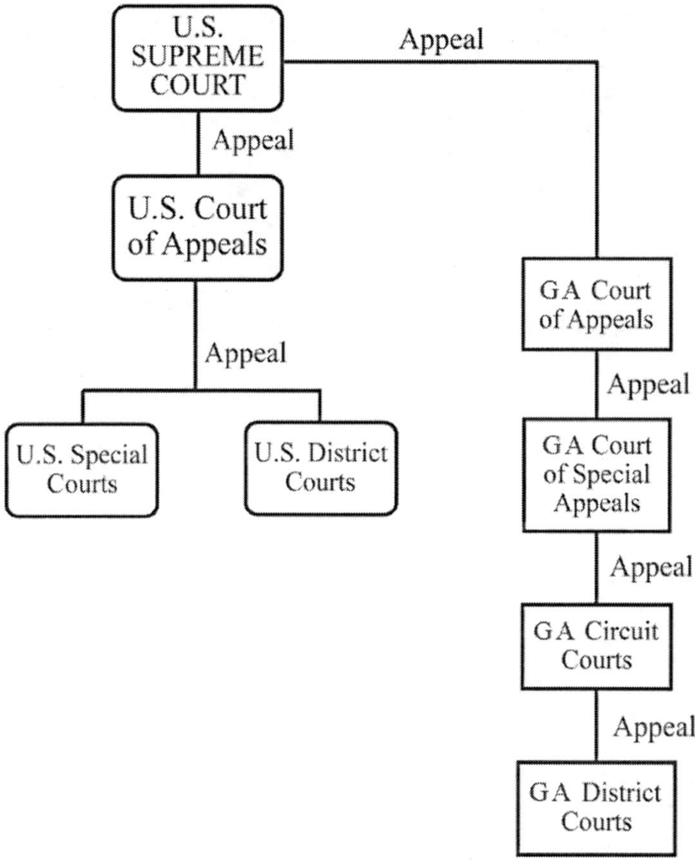

Georgia Supreme Court

As you notice from the diagram, both state and federal cases may be appealed to the Supreme Court. Although hundreds of cases may be appealed every year, the Court is not obligated to hear them all. The Supreme Court chooses which cases it will hear and which ones it will not. If the Court refuses to hear a case, then the decision of the lower court stands. However, if the Supreme Court accepts a case, then lawyers for both sides will present **written briefs** (legal arguments) before arguing the case before the justices. During the *oral arguments,* the justices ask questions of the lawyers as they argue their case. Ultimately, the justices are suppose to apply the Constitution in making their decision. After hearing all the arguments, the justices will then meet and vote on which way they will rule. Since there are nine justices, five form a majority. Whichever side wins five of the justice's votes wins the case. If the court upholds (agrees with) a lower court's decision, then the case is over, and the lower court's decision stands. However, if the court overturns (reverses) a lower court's decision, it can mean several things. In criminal cases, it often means that the defendant (person convicted of a crime in a lower court) is entitled to a new trial. In many cases, it means that a law passed by Congress or a state legislature is ruled "unconstitutional" because the Court finds that it violates the Constitution.

Practice 1.3: The Federal Government

1. List the three branches of the federal government.

2. What are the duties and responsibilities of the president of the United States?

3. *Judicial Review* refers to
   A. the president's authority to appoint judges.
   B. the cabinet's responsibility for overseeing federal departments.
   C. the Supreme Court's authority to strike down laws as unconstitutional.
   D. the Senate's power to refuse presidential appointments.

1.4 The Legislative Process

Bills and Legislative Debate

In order for a proposal (idea for a new law) to become a national law, it must first be introduced as a **bill** in either the House of Representatives or the US Senate. The president of the United States may submit bills to Congress for consideration, but they must be formally introduced by members of either the House or Senate. Under the Constitution, a bill must pass both houses of Congress by a majority vote and be signed by the president in order to become a law. If either house rejects the bill, or if the president refuses to sign it (called a **veto**), then the bill "dies" and does not become a law.

President Bush signing a Bill

Committees

In addition to the guidelines of the Constitution, a legislative process has evolved by which bills become laws. Before a bill goes before the entire House or Senate for a vote, **committees** within each house take time to consider it. Each committee consists of members of the particular house and will examine, debate, and perhaps even question outside individuals concerning bills under consideration. Then, it will decide whether to recommend the bill for approval to the entire house. Committee chairpersons are chosen, and committee seats allotted, according

Committee in Session

to a *seniority system*. Traditionally, the longer one has served and faithfully represented the interest of their political party, the more consideration one receives. Certain committees tend to exercise greater power and receive more public attention than others. Senators and representatives desire positions on these committees because they give them greater influence in Congress and greater publicity. Such publicity can help them gain even more political support when they eventually run for re-election or attempt to gain a higher office (i.e., when a senator runs for president). Since committee chairpersons and members are appointed by House and Senate leadership, committee chairs and many of the best positions tend to go to members of the majority party.

DEBATE

Bills that make it out of committee to the House or Senate floor are then debated and voted on by the entire house. Senators who are opposed to a bill have the option of using a *filibuster*. According to Senate rules, debate on a bill cannot end so long as a senator is still speaking. A filibuster is a tactic in which a senator delays a vote on a bill he/she fears will pass by continuing to talk. Senators have been known to read books out loud and tell jokes just to avoid shutting up. Usually, while this is happening, other senators are attempting to sway as many votes as they can. To prevent a handful of senators from using a filibuster to halt the passage of an otherwise popular bill, the Senate adopted *cloture*. Under this procedure, if at least three fifths of the present senators (60 if all 100 are present) are in favor of ending a debate, then the filibuster is ended and a vote can occur.

PRESIDENTIAL VETOES

Often, the president will *veto* a bill. A **veto** is when both houses of Congress pass a bill, but the president refuses to sign it. If this happens, the bill does not become law *unless* two-thirds of both the Senate and the House vote to override the president's veto. Occasionally, the president may exercise a *pocket veto*. Under the Constitution, the president has ten days (not counting Sundays) to either sign or veto legislation. If he/she does nothing, then the bill becomes law. The one exception is if Congress adjourns (ends its session) prior to the ten days expiring. If this happens and the president takes no action, then the legislation effectively dies. A pocket veto is when the president intentionally takes no action on a bill because he/she knows Congress is not in session and the bill will die. The president is said to "put the bill in his/her pocket."

Signing a Bill into Law

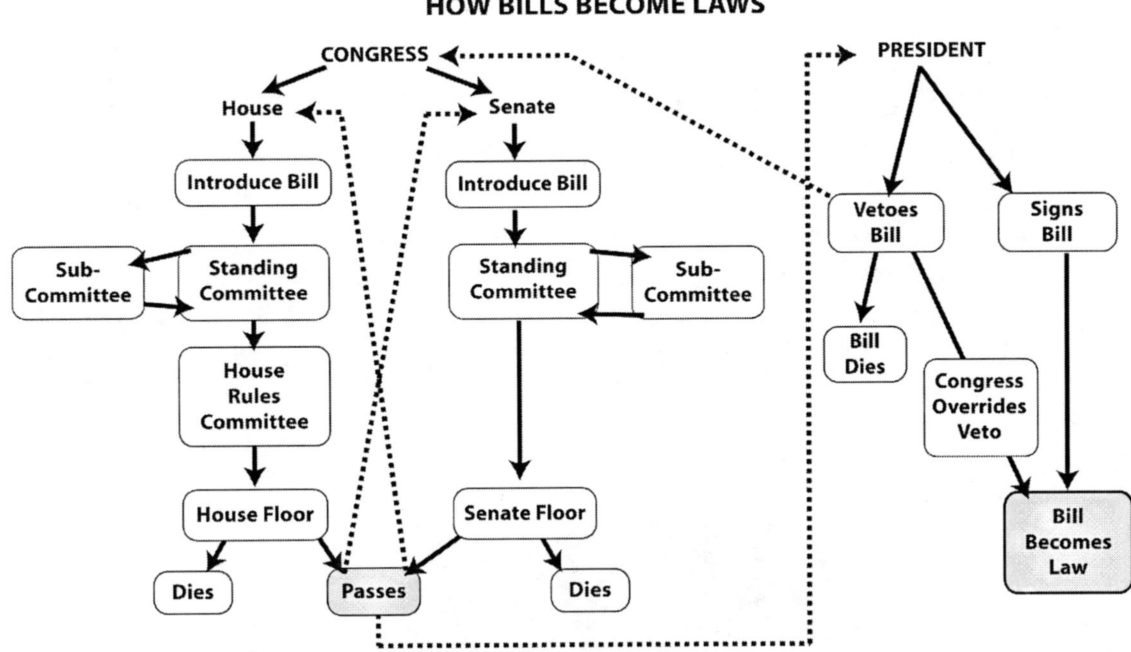

Practice 1.4: The Federal Legislative Process

1. A proposal that has been introduced by a member of Congress to be considered as a potential law is called what?

   A. a resolution
   B. an act of Congress
   C. a bill
   D. a veto

2. Of the following, which one is NOT a power enjoyed by the president during the legislative process?

   A. veto
   B. overriding judicial reviews
   C. pocket veto
   D. signing bills into law

3. Describe the role of congressional committees in the legislative process. Why do members of Congress desire certain committee positions?

1.5 The National Government and Federal System at Work

Separation of Powers

Earlier in this chapter, we discussed the importance of ***separation of powers*** and ***checks and balances*** as principles on which the Constitution is based. Each branch has different powers under the Constitution. Congress passes laws. The president sets foreign policy, domestic policy, and makes sure that existing laws are enforced. The courts make sure that the Constitution is applied fairly and appropriately. By dividing power between the branches, no one branch is able to exercise all the power. This prevents any one party from seizing too much power and protects the rights of citizens.

Checks and Balances

Congress in Session

Even though each branch has certain powers, the other two branches are able to "check" and make sure that no branch is abusing its authority. We actually saw the principle of checks and balances in action when we looked at the legislative process. Although Congress has the power to make laws, the president may use his/her veto power to *check* Congress. Congress, however, may return the favor by overriding the veto and making the bill a law anyway. The Founding Fathers granted such powers to both branches in order to make sure that no bills violating the rights of citizens became law. However, there is another check in the legislative process we did not mention earlier. Even if Congress passes a bill and the president signs it into law, the judicial branch can rule that the law is unconstitutional, in which case it ceases to be an enforceable law. Congress, however, can make sure that the Court cannot strike down a law by moving to amend the Constitution. Since the Court's duty is to uphold the Constitution, it cannot strike down any law that is explicitly expressed in the document.

FDR Prepares Speech Declaring War

The legislative process is just one example of checks and balances at work. Other examples include federal appointments. The president appoints judges and officials, but the Senate must confirm them. The president may order certain military actions, but Congress must approve such decisions and controls military funding. The list goes on and on. The good thing about checks and balances and separation of powers is that these principles help prevent abuses of power. The bad thing is that they often make it harder for the government to reach important decisions in a timely fashion. Issues often go unresolved and problems drag out because members of the federal government become bogged down in political debate and disagreements.

Amendments to the Constitution

The representatives to the Constitutional Convention wanted to ensure that the Constitution would last a long time and remain relevant to changing circumstances. Therefore, they provided a process by which it could be *amended.* An **amendment** is simply a change to the Constitution that is added later. In the case of the US Constitution, all amendments are added at the end of the document. The first amendments were ratified in 1791. The most recent was added in 1992. Remarkably, the US Constitution has only been amended 27 times in its more than 200 year history.

There are two ways that amendments may be added to the Constitution. First, if two-thirds of both houses of Congress vote in favor of a change, it is then presented to the states. If three-fourths of the states approve the proposed amendment, then it is added to the Constitution. The second way that an amendment can be added is when two-thirds of the states call for a *constitutional convention.* Any amendments adopted by the convention must then be ratified by three-fourths of the states in order to become part of the Constitution. Because it tends to emphasize principles and leaves room for interpretation and debate, the Constitution has proved to be flexible and able to adjust to changing times. For this reason, it has often been referred to as a "living document."

Enumerated and Implied Powers

Enumerated powers are powers explicitly granted by the Constitution. For instance, the Constitution specifically grants Congress the power to coin money, levy taxes, and oversee interstate commerce. It also officially gives the president the power to negotiate treaties and agreements with foreign nations. By contrast, **implied powers** are powers *not* specifically mentioned in the Constitution. They are, however, *implied* based on enumerated powers. For instance, during the early years of the nation, Congress established a national bank. Many opposed this move because the Constitution does not grant such power. The Supreme Court upheld the law, however, stating that Congress' enumerated power to coin money implied it could take reasonable measures it deemed necessary to fulfill its responsibility. In the same way, President Thomas Jefferson signed an agreement with France purchasing the Louisiana Territory in 1803. Even though the Constitution does not authorize the president to acquire additional territory, Jefferson justified the move, and Congress approved it, based on the president's authority to negotiate with foreign nations. Today, establishing federal departments not mentioned in the Constitution but deemed necessary to carry out constitutional responsibilities is another good example of implied powers at work. Because there is room for disagreement over what is implied by the Constitution and what is not, government powers are often a source of intense debate in US politics.

The Relationship Between State and National Government

Under our federal system of government, power is divided between states and the national government. (Review section 1.2 regarding *federalism*.) According to the Tenth Amendment, any powers not specifically granted to the national government are reserved for the states. However, any powers expressly denied the national government (i.e., enforcing *ex post facto laws* or violating rights guaranteed to citizens) are also denied to the states. No state government may pass a law that violates the US Constitution. Article VI of the Constitution contains what is known as the **Supremacy Clause**. It states that the US Constitution shall be, "...the supreme law of the land...." and take precedence over any state or local laws.

Georgia Governor Sonny Perdue and President Bush

Practice 1.5: National Government and Federal System at Work

1. The president appoints judges to serve on the federal courts. However, the Senate must first approve these appointments. Eventually, after they are on the bench, these judges will have the power to strike down laws passed by Congress and signed by the president as unconstitutional. This illustrates

   A. federalism.

   B. separation of powers.

   C. checks and balances.

   D. judicial review

2. Explain the difference between enumerated and implied powers.

3. What is made explicitly clear by the Supremacy Clause?

1.6 United States Foreign Policy

Another important aspect of US government is **foreign policy**. Foreign policy refers to the United States' relations with other nations and how it handles international situations. As mentioned earlier, the president is the one predominantly responsible for determining the US' foreign policy. However, even in matters of foreign policy, there are checks and balances.

President Bush with Foreign Leader

Foreign Aid

Humanitarian Aid

There are a number of ways the United States government engages in foreign policy. One is through **economic, humanitarian, and military aid**. In other words, the United States often offers aid to countries that are either less developed or hurting as the result of a natural disaster, etc. Economic aid may be in the form of money or economic investment to help develop or rebuild a particular region. Humanitarian aid may consist of money, supplies, and even manpower to help relieve those hurting in foreign nations from poverty or the devastation of war or some catastrophic event. Finally, military aid might involve the US military coming to the rescue of an oppressed people, or using US soldiers to assist getting supplies to those in need. Often times, in dangerous and unstable regions, the US military may be sent to help restore stability and prevent the outbreak of chaos, violence, and suffering.

Treaties

Treaties are formal international agreements between nations. Some treaties deal with trade. Others are promises between countries to protect each other in the event one nation is attacked. Sometimes treaties are between nations that have traditionally been hostile to one another and now agree to stop fighting. Treaties usually come after periods of negotiation and compromise between leaders. Any treaty signed by the president of the United States must be ratified by the US Senate before it becomes official.

Diplomacy, Sanctions, and Military Intervention

Inevitably, conflicts arise between the United States and other nations. Hopefully, most of these conflicts can be settled peacefully through **diplomacy**. Diplomacy is the process of nations coming together to find peaceful solutions. In order for diplomacy to work, both sides have to be willing to compromise to a certain point, and both have to feel that they are reaching a conclusion that is ultimately better for their country than escalated conflict.

North Korean Leader Kim Jong-il

When diplomacy doesn't work, the next step is often **sanctions**. Many times, these sanctions are economic. For instance, in recent years, North Korea has pursued the development of nuclear weapons. The US has responded by calling on a number of nations to impose sanctions that would limit trade with North Korea and produce economic pressure for it to change its behavior. Sanctions are most effective when a number of nations unite in imposing them against nations they view as violating international agreements. Ideally, they bring nations back to diplomacy and, ultimately, peaceful solutions.

The most drastic measure for dealing with international conflicts is **military intervention**. At times, the US government decides that the only solution is military force against another nation.

US Soldiers in Iraq

Because it inevitably involves death and destruction, military intervention is generally the very last resort and is almost never engaged in without some degree of controversy. The current US involvement in Iraq is an example of military intervention. When diplomacy broke down between Iraq and the United Nations, and Iraqi leader, Saddam Hussein, refused to abide by UN sanctions, the United States and a number of allies elected to send in their militaries rather than risk the possibility that Saddam might have weapons of mass destruction. The Iraq war is a good example of when the US might elect to use military intervention and the controversy such actions ignite. Today, military interventions in Iraq along with Afghanistan remain crucial fronts in the global war on terror.

Practice 1.6: United States Foreign Policy

1. How the US chooses to interact with other nations and handle international situations is known as

   A. diplomacy.
   B. foreign policy.
   C. military intervention.
   D. international sanctions.

2. What are treaties, why might the United States engage in them, and what must occur for the US to officially become bound to one?

Chapter 1 Review

Key terms, people, and concepts

natural rights
social contract theory
inalienable rights
Declaration of Independence
Articles of Confederation
Daniel Shays' Rebellion
United States Constitution
Great Compromise
Three-fifths Compromise
slave-trade compromise
rule of law
limited government
separation of powers
checks and balances
federalism
popular sovereignty
Bill of Rights
faction
Federalists
Alexander Hamilton and James Madison
Anti-federalists
Federalist Papers
legislative branch
House of Representatives
Speaker of the House
Senate
president pro tempore
powers of Congress
limitations on Congress
House/Senate majority leader
House/Senate minority leader
House/Senate majority and minority whip
executive branch
president of the United States
vice president of the United States
Electoral College
powers and responsibilities of the president
impeachment
president's cabinet
federal departments
federal bureaucracy
judicial branch
US Supreme Court
Marbury v. Madison
judicial review
appointment of judges
cases that come before the US Supreme Court
bill
veto
committees
constitutional amendment
implied powers
enumerated powers
Supremacy Clause

Multiple Choice Questions

1. The Constitution delegates some powers to the federal government while reserving other powers for the states, this is evidence that the US government is based on:
   A. republicanism.
   B. democracy.
   C. separation of powers.
   D. federalism.

2. Congress passes a new federal law making it illegal to call public officials "boneheads." The president gladly signs it. However, the Supreme Court nullifies the law by ruling that it violates citizens' First Amendment right to free speech. What power has the Court exercised?

   A. the power to impeach
   B. judicial appointment
   C. judicial review
   D. constitutional amendment

3. Which of the following BEST describes how the president of the United States is elected?

   A. Whichever candidate wins the most individual votes becomes president.
   B. Whichever candidate is elected by both houses of Congress becomes president.
   C. Whichever candidate wins the most states becomes president.
   D. Whichever candidate wins the most votes in the Electoral College becomes president.

4. A proposal that has been introduced by a member of Congress to be considered as a potential law is called what?

   A. a resolution
   B. an act of Congress
   C. a bill
   D. a veto

5. The Great Compromise settled what issue at the Constitutional Convention?

   A. representation in Congress
   B. the legality of slavery
   C. the slave trade
   D. how many branches of government there would be

6. What point do you believe the political cartoon below is trying to make?

A. Congress and the president usually get along.

B. It is the duty of the courts to remind Congress and the president to do their jobs.

C. The judicial branch is more important than the other two branches of government.

D. Laws passed by Congress and signed by the president can be struck down by the Court.

7. Congress is composed of

A. the federal judiciary.

B. the House of Representatives and the US Senate.

C. the executive branch.

D. the cabinet and the federal bureaucracy.

8. Because it is empowered specifically by the Constitution to levy taxes, Congress passed a law establishing the Internal Revenue Service. Which of the following statements is true?

A. Both raising taxes and establishing the IRS are enumerated powers.

B. Both raising taxes and establishing the IRS are implied powers.

C. Raising taxes is an enumerated power while establishing the IRS is an implied power.

D. Raising taxes is an implied power while establishing the IRS is an enumerated power.

9. Filibusters, committees, debate, vetoes, and overrides are all part of

A. amending the Constitution.

B. the legislative process.

C. federalism.

D. the Supremacy Clause.

10. Because the president is the commander-in-chief, he/she has the authority to
    A. order the US military into action.
    B. sign a treaty with a foreign country.
    C. represent the US at international conferences.
    D. appoint the heads of federal departments.

11. The US and Russia are experiencing some conflict over fishing rights in the North Atlantic. However, the secretary of state and Russian foreign minister are able to sit down and come up with a formal, international agreement that settles the issue. Which of the following statements is true?
    A. Neither country would ever engage in military action to protect international interests.
    B. The actions of these officials represent diplomacy.
    C. The US has offered Russia humanitarian aid.
    D. The US and Russia have agreed on North Atlantic sanctions.

12. When nations sit down to discuss their differences in search of peaceful resolutions, it is called
    A. humanitarian aid.
    B. political intervention.
    C. sanction.
    D. diplomacy.

Chapter 2
Civil Rights and Civic Responsibility

GPS	SSCG6: The student will demonstrate knowledge of civil liberties and civil rights. (QCC standards CC3, CC7, CC14, US11, US21)
	SSCG7: The student will describe how thoughtful and effective participation in civic life is characterized by obeying the law, paying taxes, serving on a jury, participating in the political process, performing public service, registering for military duty, being informed about current issues, and respecting differing opinions. (QCC standard CC14)
	SSCG8: The student will demonstrate knowledge of local, state, and national elections. (QCC standards CC15, US21, US29, US30)

2.1 The Bill of Rights

The **Bill of Rights** consists of the first ten amendments (additions) to the United States Constitution. It was added in 1789 for the purpose of protecting civil rights and providing **equal protection** under the law. "Equal protection" means that the document is intended to guarantee the rights of *all citizens*, not simply a privileged few. Originally, the government did not extend the rights guaranteed by the Constitution equally to women and minorities. Today; however, the Constitution has been amended so that, at least in theory, every US citizen is given equal protection under the law regardless of skin color, gender, age, wealth, etc.

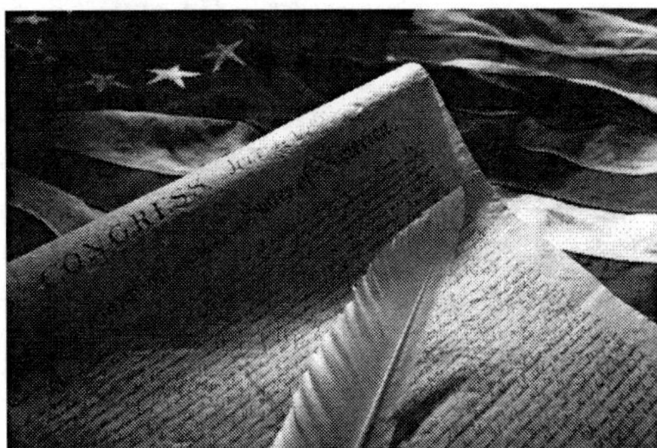

Bill of Rights

The First Ten Amendments

The **First Amendment** guarantees citizens' *freedom of speech, freedom of the press, freedom to petition the government* and *freedom to assemble*. It also protects *freedom of religion* and establishes the principle of separation of church and state. The *free exercise clause* forbids Congress from making any law prohibiting the free exercise of one's religious beliefs. Meanwhile, the *establishment clause* forbids Congress from establishing a religion.

The **Second Amendment** guarantees the *right to bear arms*. There is much debate today about the extent to which firearms should be available to private citizens. In the early days of the nation, however, firearms were considered crucial for maintaining local militias. In fact, the first shots of the American Revolution were fired because the British attempted to take arms stored by private citizens at Concord, Massachusetts.

The **Third Amendment** restricts *quartering* (housing) of federal troops in the homes of US citizens. Prior to the revolution, the British angered colonists by forcing them to house British soldiers.

The **Fourth Amendment** protects citizens against *unreasonable searches and seizures*. Supporters of the Bill of Rights insisted on this amendment because Great Britain had used search warrants known as *writs of assistance* to board and search American ships prior to the colonies declaring independence.

The **Fifth Amendment** clearly defines criminal proceedings by which a person may be arrested and charged with a crime. It ensures that no person shall be imprisoned or deprived of his or her property without ***due process***. In other words, the government must obey the laws governing criminal and civil proceedings before it can put someone in jail or strip them of their property. Due process prevents government abuse and ensures that citizens who are charged with a crime are not denied their rights during judicial proceedings. In addition, this amendment also protects citizens from *double jeopardy* (being charged with the same crime again after being found "not guilty"), *self-incrimination* (having to testify against oneself in court, or being forced to confess to a crime) and places limits on *eminent domain*. Eminent domain is the government's power to take private property for public use. Under the Constitution, the government cannot take a citizen's property without paying "just compensation" (i.e., if the government takes someone's house, then they must pay that person what the house is worth).

The **Sixth Amendment** protects the rights of the accused. This includes the right to a *public and speedy trial by jury*. A trial by jury means that a group of an accused person's peers decides his or her guilt or innocence, rather than a single government official. This amendment also guarantees a defendant's right to be informed of the nature of the charges against them, the right to call and confront witnesses, and the right to be represented by *legal counsel* (a lawyer). The **Seventh Amendment** extends the right to a trial by jury to civil cases (i.e., when one person sues another for money).

The **Eighth Amendment** protects those arrested or found guilty of a crime. It prohibits the government from imposing *excessive bail* and/or *fines*. Bail is money an arrested person must pay to get out of jail until the date of their trial. Fines, on the other hand, are amounts of money imposed as punishment for a crime one has been found guilty of. The Eighth Amendment also forbids *"cruel and unusual punishment"* of those convicted of a crime. Of course, what constitutes "cruel and unusual" punishment is often an issue of debate.

The **Ninth Amendment** simply says that the rights specifically mentioned in the Bill of Rights are not necessarily the only ones guaranteed to the people. Meanwhile, the **Tenth Amendment** says that those powers not restricted by the Constitution, nor delegated to the US government, are *"reserved for the states."* In other words, the Constitution grants the states the authority to decide certain matters of law.

First Amendment Freedoms

Statue of Liberty

Perhaps no part of the Constitution has caused as much debate and controversy as the **First Amendment**. While most citizens agree that freedom of speech, freedom to assemble, freedom of the press, etc. are good things, many disagree on how they are defined. Does freedom of speech mean a person can say anything they want, regardless of where they are and what the circumstances may be? Does restricting the use of profanity, to safeguard what children hear, violate free speech? Does censoring what is printed in a school paper constitute a violation of freedom of the press? Does having a prayer at school or displaying a nativity scene on public property during Christmas go against separation of church and state? Because citizens often interpret such concepts differently, the First Amendment has been the source of heated disagreements and numerous court cases. As a result, the courts have played an important role in helping to establish what is, and is not, protected by the First Amendment.

DUE PROCESS

Due process refers to the principle that a citizen who is accused of a crime is entitled to certain rights, and that the government must obey certain laws when carrying out its investigation, prosecution, and sentencing of a defendant. The Fifth Amendment guarantees due process. Following the Civil War and the end of slavery, Congress ratified the **Fourteenth Amendment**. The Fourteenth Amendment is special because it defines US citizenship to include all races and proclaims that any citizen of the US is automatically a citizen of the state in which he/she resides. The amendment also makes it illegal for any state government to pass laws denying liberties guaranteed under the Bill of Rights. For example, since the Fifth Amendment guarantees due process, no state may do anything to deny due process in a state case. In short, the Fourteenth Amendment guarantees the same rights under state governments that are guaranteed under the Bill of Rights.

INDIVIDUAL LIBERTIES VERSUS PUBLIC INTEREST

Sometimes conflict can arise between the need to protect individual liberties and the need to protect public interest. **Individual liberties** are the personal freedoms every citizen enjoys under the Constitution. **Public interest** refers to those things in which citizens have a common interest: public safety, national security, a healthy environment, protection from dangerous products in the market place, etc. At times, protecting public interest can infringe on individual liberties. For instance, following the terrorist attacks of September 11, 2001, the US government passed the PATRIOT Act. This law grants government officials greater freedom to monitor phone calls, emails, and other forms of communication between citizens that might alert the US to potential terrorist plots. Many appreciate such a law because it protects the public. Others, however, say that such laws go too far because they invade citizens' privacy and violate individual liberties. How far should law enforcement be allowed to go to investigate crimes and arrest those suspected of offenses? How thoroughly should people be searched before boarding aircraft? What speech or print can the government censor in order to maintain public safety? Such questions demonstrate the tension between personal rights and public welfare.

Practice 2.1: The Bill of Rights

1. The purpose of the Bill of Rights is to
   A. ensure the civil rights of citizens.
   B. postpone equal protection.
   C. ensure the government's right to enforce laws.
   D. protect the government from rebellious citizens.

2. The Fifth and Fourteenth Amendments are both meant to provide
   A. freedom of speech.
   B. protection against future terrorist plots.
   C. due process.
   D. separation of church and state.

3. Explain how public interest and individual rights can sometimes be in conflict. Give examples.

2.2 Participation in Civic Life

Civic Responsibilities

Along with the many civil rights we enjoy, US citizens must fulfill a number of **civic responsibilities** in order for US society to function. These are responsibilities that every citizen should live up to as part of their *civic duty*.

Obeying Laws

Police Station

Obeying and upholding the laws passed by local councils, state legislatures, and the United States Congress is an important part of fulfilling one's civic duty. If citizens fail to obey laws, then society suffers and it becomes harder for the government to maintain law and order without infringing on individual rights. Obeying the laws that are in place is one of the best ways citizens show an appreciation for the many freedoms the Constitution gives them.

Paying Taxes

Citizens must pay taxes. Taxes allow the government to remain funded and fulfill its role. Through taxes, local governments pay for local services like police and fire protection, sanitation, parks and recreational services, etc. State governments use tax revenue to provide schools, highways, and disaster relief. Finally, the national government uses tax dollars to provide for a national defense, social programs, social security for retired citizens, national disaster relief, and a number of other services. When citizens fail to pay the taxes that they owe, it hinders the government and often results in citizens having to pay even more taxes in the future.

Jury Duty

Jury

The Sixth and Seventh Amendments guarantee the right to a jury in criminal and civil cases. The right to a jury is an important civil right because it keeps decisions about guilt, innocence, and punishment in the hands of average citizens rather than government officials. However, such a system depends on citizens being willing to serve on juries. Citizens usually learn that they have been selected for **jury duty** by receiving a notice in the mail. In most cases, jury duty is mandatory unless one is released from duty by the court. Citizens can be released from jury duty either by showing that they are not qualified to serve, proving that they have a just cause for being dismissed from service, or as part of the *voir dire*. The *voir dire* is a process that occurs prior to the actual trial, in which attorneys for both sides ask potential jurors questions. If one of the attorneys feel that a certain citizen might be biased against his/her side, then that attorney may dismiss that potential juror from service. Juries usually consist of 12 members.

Citizens must be willing to pay the **costs of serving on a jury**. For instance, jury duty takes *time*. In some cases, a juror might only sacrifice a day. However, sometimes, jurors might have to spend days or even months serving. In more serious cases, such as a murder trial or a civil case worth millions of dollars, a jury might have to be "sequestered." In other words, the jury may have to be isolated in order to assure that its decision will not be influenced by factors outside of the courtroom (i.e., media coverage, public opinions about a high-profile case, etc.). As a result, jurors often have to spend long periods of time away from family, work, and other pursuits. For jurors whose jobs pay an hourly wage, jury duty often means *financial sacrifice*. While the government usually pays a set amount of money for each day a juror serves, it is normally less than an average salary. Even for those whose pay is not affected, the inconvenience and problems created by missing days of work often leads to additional stress and tension. There is also the *emotional cost* of jury duty. For some, deciding whether or not another human being goes to prison creates great anxiety. In some cases, such as extremely violent crimes, jurors may have to hear testimony and view evidence that is emotionally disturbing as well. Time, money, and emotional strain can all be costs of participating in the judicial process.

Performing Public Service

Responsible citizens perform invaluable public services everyday. Volunteering to help with community projects and charitable organizations, deal with the effects of a natural disaster, improve schools, facilitate elections, etc. are all important ways citizens perform public service. Citizens may serve as part of a volunteer fire department or police force. Some even run for and serve in political office. While such service is important, it also has costs. People must be willing to sacrifice time, money, and, in the case of political office, their own privacy in order to fulfill such civic roles.

Military Duty

Another way citizens serve the public is by **registering for military duty**. Once male citizens and legal aliens turn eighteen years of age, they must register with a selective service (branch of the military). Registering makes it easier for the government to find them should the need ever arise for a military draft. (A draft is when the government selects and requires certain individuals to serve in the military rather than waiting for them to volunteer.) Of course, some citizens do enlist in the military. They volunteer to serve in the military either full-time or as part of the Reserves or National Guard. Those who serve in the Reserves or National Guard serve on a part-time basis. They usually serve one weekend a month and two weeks during the summer. However, they can be called up by the governor or even the president for extended duty if the need arises. Recently some reservists and guardsmen have served a year, or longer, in Iraq and Afghanistan as part of the United States' "war on terror."

Political Participation

Political Protests

US citizens have a right to know what is going on in their government, judicial system, and the world in general. Freedom of the press helps ensure that they remain informed. Citizens have the privilege of deciding who their leaders will be and participating in the **political process**. Citizens take part in the political process in a number of ways. By *voting*, they are able to influence who serves in a particular public office. Through *volunteering*, citizens can take a more active part in the campaigns of candidates they support. Some volunteers pass out pamphlets. Some canvass neighborhoods trying to inform residents about their candidate. Still others answer phones at campaign headquarters. Volunteers play a key role in effective campaigns. Some citizens join *PACS* or *interest groups* in an effort to influence elections and political policies. A "PAC," or political action committee, is a group organized to ensure that the candidates who will back issues most important to the PAC get elected and remain in office. PACs primarily contribute money to the campaigns of candidates they support. By comparison, interest groups are groups advocating a certain cause. They use the political process (supporting candidates, campaigning for their position, lobbying politicians, etc.) in an attempt to either encourage or prevent change to existing policies. Because of the controversies that arise regarding the Constitution, such groups have come to be an important force in US politics. In most important debates, there are interest groups fighting for both sides. Some citizens participate in *political protests*. Protests usually consists of a group of people gathering to make known their disapproval of some aspect of the government. Finally, some citizens actually run for and serve in public office.

Yet, for all the great benefit, there are also **costs of political participation**. Voting, volunteering, and serving all take time. Time that could be spent with family, earning money, or engaging in some leisure activity is sacrificed for the sake of participating in the political process. In many cases, citizens donate money to campaigns and PACs that could have been saved or spent on something else. In the case of those who choose to run for political office, there is the loss of privacy and the likelihood of political attacks. News media often makes public nearly every aspect of a candidate's past, and political opponents are likely to publicly attack a candidate's motives, character, and/or past record of service. In addition, campaigns require lots of time and energy. In some cases, candidates may have to make appearances all over the state, or even the country, within a few hours. As a result, many qualified people choose not to seek office due to the high cost it requires of both themselves and their families.

Staying Informed and Respecting Opinions

Part of being a good citizen is staying **well-informed**. Citizens need to remain aware of what is happening locally, nationally, and around the world. Televised newscasts, radio, newspapers, magazines, and an ever-growing number of on-line resources are some of the major ways citizens stay educated regarding the important events of the day. Responsible citizens learn about such issues as taxes, the environment, government spending, military actions, natural disasters, the economy, the state of education, etc. Inevitably, they form opinions as well. These opinions ultimately affect how citizens

Staying Informed

vote, what role they want their government to play, and what economic, social, and political philosophies they hold to. While it is good for citizens to increase their knowledge and form strong opinions, it is also important to remember that others have the right to come to different opinions about the same issues. The key is to figure out how to champion one's views in a constructive manner. Good citizens show **respect for other citizens' right to their own opinions**, without compromising their own convictions.

Practice 2.2: Participation in Civic Life

1. Which of the following is a civic responsibility?
   - A. being an active member of your church
   - B. taking good care of the car your dad let you borrow
   - C. showing up for work on time
   - D. volunteering your weekends to build houses for low-income families

2. Citizens must be willing to serve on juries because juries are
   - A. an important part of the political process.
   - B. an important part of protecting our civil liberties.
   - C. guaranteed by the Fifth Amendment.
   - D. important interest groups.

3. Describe some of the ways citizens participate in the political process.

2.3 Elections and Political Parties

Political Parties

The United States Constitution says nothing about political parties. In fact, President George Washington warned the nation that forming such parties would have harmful effects on US government. Despite Washington's pleas, political parties have become an important part of US politics.

Party Systems

Political parties are organizations that promote political beliefs and sponsor candidates (people running for political office). Many of the world's democracies operate on what is called a *multi-party system*. In such a system, there are numerous political parties that hold government seats. The Netherlands, Israel, and Denmark are just a few examples of countries operating on this kind of system. In a multi-party system, parties receive representation in government proportional to the number of votes they receive in an election. For example, say that there are 10 seats available in Parliament. Party A receives 40% of the vote, party B receives 30%, and parties C, D, and E each receive 10%. Proportional representation means that party A gets 4 seats, party B 3 seats, and parties C, D, and E each get 1 seat. All five parties will be represented in Parliament, with party A having most of the influence. Under a multi-party system, parties only need to receive a *plurality vote*, rather than a *majority vote*, to remain in power. A majority vote involves a party gaining more than 50% of votes cast in order to win the election. In a plurality vote, a party does not need to win a majority of votes; it simply needs to win more than the other parties. Think about the example we just gave featuring parties A, B, C, D, and E. Party A did not receive a majority of votes (it received only 40%), but it did win the plurality (more than any of the other parties).

By contrast, the United States operates on a *two-party system.* This is a system in which only two primary parties dominate a nation's politics. In the United States, these two parties are the **Democrats** and **Republicans**. Both operate at the federal, state, and local levels of government. Why does the US feature a two-party system while many other nations have multi-party systems? The answer is largely due to the way the US conducts elections. Take, for example, congressional elections. In a multi-party system based on proportional representation, each party receives a number of seats based on the number of votes it gets. But in the United States, things are done differently. If a state is entitled to 15 representatives, then that state is divided into 15 individual voting districts. Each district elects one representative. This means that if the Democratic candidate wins 51% of the vote, the Republican 42%, the Libertarian 6%, and the Reform Party 1%, then there is still just one winner — the Democrat. Only the Democratic candidate will go to Congress; the other three are flat out of luck. As a result, it is more beneficial in the United States to align oneself with one of the two major parties that actually have a chance of winning. Sometimes, however, **third parties** (parties other than the Republicans and Democrats) and **independents** (those not affiliated with a party) do play an important role in US politics. Third parties usually arise and gain momentum when citizens don't feel that either of the two major parties adequately represents their views. In the late 1800s, the Peoples Party (also known as the Populists) initiated a number of key reforms. In 1912, Theodore Roosevelt actually won more votes for president as the Progressive Party candidate than did the incumbent Republican. In 1992, Bill Clinton (a Democrat) won the election with only 43% of the popular vote, in large part due to Ross Perot's independent campaign that pulled support away from Republican President George HW Bush. Historically, while third party candidates and independents have won some government offices and influenced policies, they generally do not win the White House or a large number of seats in Congress. This is largely because they face challenges that the major parties do not. They have less funds and fewer members than the Republican and Democratic parties. Also, many citizens feel traditionally tied to one of the major parties and are unwilling to vote for third party candidates they doubt can win. Also, because third parties usually rally around a single issue or regional concern, they often have trouble appealing to a widespread audience.

Some countries use a *one-party system,* in which only one party is allowed to operate. As a result, citizens' ability to have a say in their government is greatly limited under such a system. China's Communist Party is an example of a one-party system.

U.S. Party Structure and Function

Political parties serve several functions. They nominate candidates for office, structure the voting choice (limit the list of candidates to those who have a real chance of winning — usually the Republican and Democratic candidates), coordinate the actions of government officials (i.e., facilitate the different branches of government working together) and establish party *platforms*. The *platform* is the party's statement of programs and policies it will pursue once its candidates are in office. It is made up of several *planks*. The term "plank" refers to an individual policy within the platform. For example, if the Republican platform states that the party opposes abortion, favors increased military spending, and supports a constitutional amendment against flag burning, then each one of these issues represents one plank of the platform. Parties normally adopt their platform every four years at their national convention. The **national convention** consists of delegates (representatives) from each state and US territory that meet to nominate (choose) candidates for president and vice president in the upcoming general election.

1976 Republican National Convention

Party Constituencies

Each party has its general *constituency.* The **constituency** is the people who make up and are represented by the party. Although each party consists of all kinds of people with various backgrounds and beliefs, there are general trends regarding who makes up each party. In general, Democrats are identified as more **liberal**. Liberals tend to favor a more active government. They advocate government programs to provide welfare, health care, job assistance, etc. Liberals view government as having a broad role. They believe government should help provide for the physical needs, education, and monetary security of its citizens. Republicans, however, are generally more **conservative**. Conservatives believe that less government is better. They believe the role of government is simply to provide law and order, protection of its citizens' rights, and a national defense against foreign threats. Conservatives believe that it is government's job to provide citizens with the opportunity for success, not guarantee it. Of course, in reality, some Democrats are conservative and some Republicans are liberal. Both parties also have *moderates*. **Moderates** are those whose beliefs fall somewhere in the middle, between liberal and conservative.

Traditionally, minorities, union members, many lower-income individuals, people favoring a woman's right to have an abortion, and those with more progressive views regarding religion, morality, gender roles, etc. tend to lean towards the Democratic Party. Meanwhile, middle to upper class whites, business owners, people opposed to abortion, and those holding more traditional views regarding morality, etc., tend to identify with the Republican Party. Often, it is not uncommon for people to start out as members of one party, then switch or become an independent later in life due to changing circumstances and/or views.

Party Coalitions

Coalition

Since third parties rarely win elections in the US, most interest groups choose to align themselves with one of the two major parties, rather than branching out on their own. This leads to interesting coalitions. **Coalitions** are the banding together of different groups for the purpose of achieving political success. For instance, auto workers in Michigan and civil rights activists in the South may, on the surface, not seem to have much in common. However, they may band together to support candidates that will back both their interests. Some groups within a party might be seen as *radical* because they hold extreme opinions. For instance, those advocating massive government reforms and/or government control over certain institutions are often tagged as "radicals" (i.e., those favoring government control of businesses or health care). Other groups are seen as *reactionary* because they "*react*" to what they view as radical changes or movements. Reactionary groups tend to value the status quo or want to see a return to more traditional ways. Since both groups tend to be seen as "too extreme" by many citizens, they find it advantageous to be part of a larger coalition within one of the major parties.

Elections

Election Process

Local, state, and federal officials are voted into office by means of a **general election**. These elections are held in November of an election year (usually even-numbered). This is when voters choose between the Republican, Democratic, and any third party/independent candidates for public office. However, before the general election is held, each party must first decide which candidate will represent them. After all, there may be ten Democrats who want to be the party's nominee for president, or six Republicans who want to run for governor. To decide on a single nominee, each major party holds primary elections a few months prior to the general election. In **primary elections**, voters choose between candidates within the same party. The candidate who wins the most votes receives the party's nomination. However, as is the case in general elections, if there are several candidates running and no one wins a clear majority, then there will be a **run-off election** between the top vote getters (usually the top two). When this happens, the top vote getter in the run-off election wins. It is important to note, however, that run-off elections do not occur in presidential elections. If a presidential candidate fails to win a majority of electoral votes, then the winner is decided by the House of Representatives. Some states (i.e., Iowa) choose their party's nominee for president by means of a **caucus** rather than a primary. In the caucus system, party members hold local meetings to choose delegates to vote in favor of nominating a certain candidate at the national convention.

There are also "special elections." A **recall election** is an election that is called to determine if voters want to remove a sitting official from office before his/her elected term is up. This occurred in California in 2003, when Governor Gray Davis was recalled and defeated by Arnold Schwarzenegger. An **initiative** is when citizens force a vote on a particular issue by getting enough citizens to sign a petition. Citizens may also vote on **propositions**, such as whether or not they support a certain policy or changes in the law.

THE ELECTORAL COLLEGE

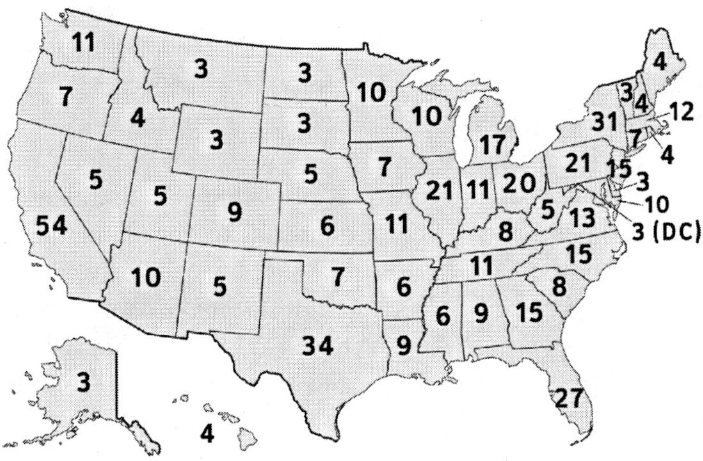

Electoral College Map

In presidential elections, the winner is not directly chosen by the people, but by the **Electoral College**. Each state possesses a certain number of electoral votes (1 for each of its senators and representatives in Congress). In a general election, whichever presidential candidate wins the most votes in a particular state is awarded *all* of that state's votes in the Electoral College (called *electoral votes*). For example, based on the 2000 US Census (official US population count that is conducted every ten years) the state of Georgia has 15 electoral votes for the elections of 2004 and 2008. Let's say Randolph and Helen are facing one another in a presidential election. After months of heavy campaigning in Georgia, Randolph barely wins with 51% of the state's vote. Helen wins the other 49%. Close election, right? However, because he won the most votes, Randolph gets all 15 of Georgia's electoral votes even though almost half the state voted for Helen. Under the Constitution, it is the presidential candidate who wins the majority of electoral votes, rather than individual votes (called the *popular vote*) who is elected president. If, however, no candidate wins a majority of electoral votes, then the election is decided by the House of Representatives. This has happened twice: 1800 and 1824. Usually, the winner in the Electoral College is also the winner of the popular vote. However, a few times in history this has not been the case. Most recently, this occurred in 2000. Democrat Al Gore actually won the popular vote, but Republican George W. Bush won the electoral vote. Under the Constitution, it was Bush, not Gore, who was elected.

CAMPAIGNS

In order to win an election, a candidate must have an effective **campaign** (strategy for winning). If the candidate is their party's nominee, then they can count on the support of the party. In addition, campaigns are often supported by political action committees (PACS). Most funding for campaigns come from private resources, such as PACs or private donors. However, since 1976, presidential candidates also have access to *public funding*. Candidates must demonstrate that they have broad support and raise a certain amount of money privately first. Once these conditions are met, candidates in both the primary and general elections may accept public funds, but they must agree to limit their campaign spending.

Jimmy Carter Campaigning

Campaign Volunteer

Money is just one aspect of a successful campaign. They also require wise strategy and lots of hard work. To get their supporters to the polls, parties often rely on "grassroots" efforts. Like the roots that lie unseen below the surface, yet are necessary for grass to grow, grassroots campaign efforts are those efforts made by volunteer and local party members who actively educate, campaign, and encourage citizens to get out and vote for the party's candidates. Although their labor is "unseen," it is crucial for effective campaigns. Volunteers *canvass* neighborhoods by going door-to-door or stationing themselves in public places to encourage citizens to vote for their candidate. *Political endorsements* (statements of support) from influential leaders and/or organizations are also valued, because they often lead to large numbers of votes. For instance, when a conservative group formally endorses a Republican candidate or a union endorses a Democrat, people who respect or are affiliated with these organizations are more likely to vote for the candidate.

To win votes, campaigns also produce a great deal of propaganda. *Propaganda* is information meant to influence voters to support a specific candidate over another. The information may, or may not, be true, but it is always biased (meant to favor one candidate). **Positive campaigning** often tries to appeal to mainstream voters by portraying the candidate as "just plain folk." This is because the candidate wants to be seen as relatable to voters. By contrast, **negative campaigning** often takes the form of name calling, in which candidates accuse one another of terrible offenses, incompetence, and/or past betrayals of public trust. In order to avoid alienating voters, candidates often speak in "glittering generalities" during election campaigns. In other words, they say things that appeal to emotions or are consistent with popularly held values without getting so specific as to offend voters. For example, a candidate may say something like, "We must protect Social Security at all costs," but he/she will not say that they intend to raise taxes to do so. This is because they realize that most citizens support Social Security but hate paying taxes.

The Voting Process

On Election Day, voters report to **polling places** to cast their votes. Schools, churches, community centers, and public facilities are all commonly used as polling places. Which polling place a voter reports to is determined by the **voting district** and **precinct** in which they live. A voting district determines which candidates a person may vote for. A citizen may vote only for candidates that are running to represent his/her district. By comparison, a precinct is that area to which one has been assigned to vote. There are normally several voting precincts within a given district. In order to vote, one must make sure that they are properly registered. The purpose of **voter registration** is to make sure that only qualified citizens vote, and that they only vote once. In most states, voters must register prior to election day. In a few, however, voters may register at their polling place. Voters cast their votes on a **ballot**, which is simply a list of the candidates to choose from.

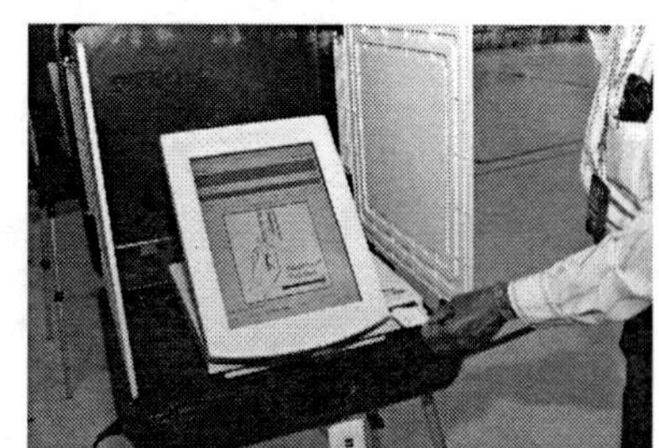
The Voting Process

One thing that can impact voting is **exit polls**. These are unofficial polls taken when people who have voted reveal who they chose, prior to any votes being counted. Candidates' campaign organizations and the media both tend to conduct exit polls. The media uses them to try and predict who has won a particular election. Sometimes, however, exit polls can be wrong. In 2004, presidential candidate John Kerry thought he had won the election when early exit polls taken by his campaign suggested he had the votes needed to win. As the day wore on, however, it became evident that his polls were wrong, and the election went to President Bush. Even more infamous were the erroneous exit polls of 2000. Early in the evening, exit polls suggested that Vice President Al Gore had won in Florida. Later, however, as more votes poured in, it became apparent that the vote was too close to call. Then, late that night, the press reported that George W. Bush had won Florida and, with it, the election. Gore called Bush to congratulate him, then got into a limo and headed for a gathering of supporters to make his concession speech (speech made by the losing candidate in an election, in which he/she congratulates the winner and publicly admits defeat). On the way, however, he learned that fewer than 1,000 votes separated him and Bush. He withdrew his concession and it wasn't until a month later that the election was finally settled in Bush's favor. To this day, people debate whether or not inaccurate exit polls kept some citizens from voting and possibly changing the outcome of the 2000 election. (If citizens who haven't voted yet believe exit polls are accurate they might decide not to go to the polls because they think their vote won't make a difference.)

Constitutional Amendments Affecting Voting

Originally, only white, male, property owners could vote. Later, this was amended to include all white males, then African American males, women, and other minorities. Below are constitutional amendments that greatly impacted voting in the United States.

Fifteenth Amendment (ratified 1870): Extended the right to vote to blacks following the abolition of slavery. Officially, it guarantees that no citizen shall be denied his right to vote due to race, color, or previous condition of servitude (slavery).

Nineteenth Amendment (ratified 1920): Granted women the right to vote in nationwide elections (some states already allowed women to vote in local elections).

Twenty-fourth Amendment (ratified 1964): Protected the rights of minorities to vote by outlawing poll taxes (taxes one must pay before they can vote; they were often used as a means to keep blacks and other minorities from voting).

Practice 2.3: Elections and Political Parties

1. Organizations that promote political beliefs and sponsor candidates for public office under the organization's name are called
   A. PACs.
   B. political parties.
   C. political platforms.
   D. interest groups.

2. A party's nominee for president will be officially nominated at the
   A. primary election.
   B. party platform.
   C. national convention.
   D. presidential caucus.

3. An election in which the Republican, Democratic, and any third party/independent candidates face one another for a particular office is called a/an
   A. primary election.
   B. caucus.
   C. recall election.
   D. general election.

4. Describe the role of the Electoral College in presidential elections.

5. How did the Fifteenth and Nineteenth amendments impact voting in the United States?

CHAPTER 2 REVIEW

Key terms, people, and concepts

Bill of Rights
equal protection
First Amendment
due process
Fifth Amendment
Fourteenth Amendment
conflict between individual liberties and public interest
civic responsibilities
jury duty
costs of serving on a jury
registering for military duty
costs of political participation
being a well-informed citizen
respecting the rights of others to their own opinions
political parties
Democrats
Republicans
third parties
independents
national convention
party constituency
liberals
conservatives
moderates
coalitions
general election
primary election
run-off election
caucus
recall election
propositions
Electoral College
campaign
positive versus negative campaigning
polling places
voting district
voting precinct
voter registration
ballot
exit polls
Fifteenth Amendment
Nineteenth Amendment
Twenty-fourth Amendment

Multiple Choice Questions

1. The Democratic and Republican candidates for lieutenant governor have just squared off in a tough election. After all the votes were counted, the Democratic candidate pulled out a narrow victory. He will be the state's next lieutenant governor. This describes what?

   A. the results of a general election
   B. the results of a primary election
   C. the results of the state caucus
   D. the results of the Electoral College

2. Miriam's congressional campaign has just launched a series of ads. Half of the ads feature her past accomplishments and talk about her patriotism. The other half criticize her opponent and point out that he was investigated by the IRS. ALL of Miriam's ads are examples of what?

   A. negative campaigning
   B. positive campaigning
   C. canvassing
   D. propaganda

3. Party leaders gather at the national convention to nominate their candidates for president and vice president. While there, they draft a list of policies and programs the party will support. What is this list of policies and programs called?
   A. the party plank
   B. the party platform
   C. the party machine
   D. the party system

4. In the United States, only the Republican and Democratic parties truly dominate the political scene. This demonstrates that the US operates on which kind of political system?
   A. multi-party
   B. a republic
   C. two-party
   D. coalition

5. The results of an election are very close. Candidate A wins 49% of the vote, candidate B wins 48% of the vote, and candidate C wins the remaining 3% of the vote. There is a good chance that candidates A and B will have to meet again in what kind of election?
   A. a primary election
   B. a recall election
   C. a general election
   D. a run-off election

6. David is a liberal politician. He believes that the government should provide health care, welfare, and job training for unemployed citizens. He also believes that those who make more than $100,000/year should have their taxes raised in order to help pay for government programs. Although David could be a member of any political party, he is most likely a member of which major US party?
   A. Democrat
   B. Republican
   C. Libertarian
   D. Independent

7. Phil has spent nearly three weeks serving on the jury of a criminal trial. Because he works from home as an independent contractor, the 8 hours/day he has had to be at the courthouse has meant that he has been unable to pursue new clients. It has also prevented him from spending as much time with his wife and kids. Phil is experiencing which of the following?
   A. the benefits of jury duty
   B. the cost of political activism
   C. the cost of fulfilling his civic responsibility
   D. the inconvenience of civil lawsuits

8. The Bill of Rights specifically ensures
   A. the right to vote.
   B. the right to run for political office
   C. the right to due process.
   D. the rights of minorities.

9. Austin is opposed to US policies in the Middle East. In protest, he stands on the steps of the courthouse, burns a US flag, and calls for the recall of all his state's representatives in Congress and the impeachment of the president. Austin's actions are protected by
   A. the First Amendment.
   B. the Fifth Amendment.
   C. the Fifteenth Amendment.
   D. the Nineteenth Amendment.

10. Madeline is disturbed to learn that the US government has been monitoring personal phone calls made from her office over the last three months. However, she is also relieved when she learns that, as a result of the government's actions, the FBI was able to stop a terrorist plot involving one of her co-workers that would have involved the death of a number of innocent civilians. Madeline is experiencing firsthand

    A. the benefits of the First Amendment.
    B. the impact of the Fifteenth Amendment.
    C. the costs of active citizenship.
    D. the tension between individual liberties and public interest.

Chapter 3
United States History: European Settlement through the War of 1812

GPS	**SSUSH1:** The student will describe European settlement in North America during the 17th century. (QCC standards US1, US2, US3)
	SSUSH2: The student will trace the ways that the economy and society of British North America developed. (QCC standards US3, US5)
	SSUSH3: The student will explain the primary causes of the American Revolution. (QCC standards US5, US6)
	SSUSH4: The student will identify the ideological, military, and diplomatic aspects of the American Revolution. (QCC standards US6, US7)
	SSUSH5: The student will explain specific events and key ideas that brought about the adoption and implementation of the United States constitution. (QCC standa4rds US8, US9, US11, US12)
	SSUSH6: The student will analyze the nature of territorial and population growth and the impact of this growth in the early decades of the new nation. (QCC standards US8, US13)

3.1 The Colonial Period

Virginia

Jamestown, Virginia

It wasn't until the fifteenth and sixteenth centuries that the first Europeans arrived in North America and began establishing colonies (territories established by a government in a foreign land). The Spanish were the first to establish strong settlements. They dominated much of South America, modern-day Mexico, and what eventually became the US Southwest, Florida, and parts of Georgia. Next came the French, who took advantage of rivers and inland waterways to control parts of the interior. Because of the abundant forests and vast wilderness that covered much of these regions, France made great amounts of money from their fur trade. They obtained fur either by trapping animals or trading with Native Americans, then sold their products for great profit in Europe.

Jamestown

Jamestown, Virginia became the first successful English colony in 1607. A joint-stock company (a company owned by a group of investors) called the Virginia Company sponsored the colony and hoped to make money off of its products and raw materials. Many new settlers came to the colony hoping to get rich and obtain land. The first few years, however, were hard. The new Virginians were often not used to doing the kind of hard, manual labor it took to build a colony. Many of them wanted to search for gold in hopes of getting rich quick, rather than raising crops the colony needed to survive. In addition, colonists established Jamestown in a swampy area, making them vulnerable to disease-carrying mosquitoes. As a result, freezing winters, infectious diseases, and starvation killed many of the settlers. Ultimately, a man named John Rolfe saved the colony when he discovered a new crop: **tobacco**! Because tobacco was often associated with corrupt behavior, many in England were not thrilled to see it become the colony's chief source of income. However, the crop proved very profitable for growers, produced large revenues for the British government in taxes, and created a class of wealthy, large land owners in Virginia. In part to attract more settlers to the colony to help cultivate as much tobacco as possible, Virginia instituted the *headright system*. This system promised 50 acres of land to those who settled in the colony. As a result, the colony's population grew.

VIRGINIANS AND NATIVE AMERICANS

Settlers and Natives

When British colonists arrived in Virginia, they found that Native Americans already lived in the land. Most of these Native Americans lived under a tribal confederation (loose alliance) led by **Chief Powhatan**. Initially, hostility broke out when roughly 200 Native Americans attacked the Jamestown settlement. After using their cannons to turn back the attackers, the Virginia settlers negotiated an uneasy peace. Powhatan, however, kept a close eye on the newcomers. He probably hoped to establish a profitable trade with the colony, but he was always cautious about the British settlers' true intentions.

At times, Native American and British relations were good. In fact, it is likely that the colony would not have survived its first winter had Native Americans not given them food. At other times, however, relations were tense. British settlers often looked down on the Native Americans as lazy and effeminate because they valued leisure time and were not interested in working for the colonists. From time to time, violence even broke out. In March 1622, Powhatan's brother and successor, Opechancanough, led a surprise attack on Jamestown that killed about 300 colonists. Residents of Jamestown struck back within days, killing at least as many Native Americans. Finally, in 1644, when he was almost 100 years old, Opechancanough attacked again. Once more, his plan failed and Virginians shot and killed him in the streets of Jamestown. From then on, it was clear that the European settlers had control of the colony. However, conflicts with Native Americans in the western regions of Virginia continued for several more decades.

Virginia's Social Structure and Bacon's Rebellion

Nathaniel Bacon

In Virginia, society eventually became divided between large landowners, poor farmers, indentured servants, and slaves. **Indentured servants** were people who could not afford to come to North America on their own. They agreed to work for a landowner for up to seven years in exchange for the landowner paying for their trip. Once their seven years were up, these servants then became small landowners. Eventually, this caused strains on Virginia's social order. As more indentured servants became free landowners, land became less available in the colony. As a result, settlement pushed further and further west. Ultimately, poor farmers in western Virginia experienced increased conflicts with Native Americans along the frontier. They also grew impatient with the governor in Jamestown. Westerners viewed the governor as favoring the rich in eastern Virginia. They believed he was not doing enough to help western Virginians acquire and protect land. In 1676, this tension led to an armed conflict known as **Bacon's Rebellion**. Nathaniel Bacon, a Virginia planter and wealthy aristocrat, rallied forces to fight Native Americans on the Virginia frontier. When the colony's governor condemned his actions, Bacon turned his army of small landowners, discontented servants, and even a few African slaves on Jamestown. The governor was forced to flee and Bacon's men burned Jamestown to the ground! Bacon's sudden death led to the end of the rebellion, but his uprising showed that colonists expected a government that served more than just the wealthy few. They wanted a government where even "ordinary" citizens have a voice. Bacon's Rebellion also alerted the wealthy, ruling class of Virginia to the discontent that existed among the lower classes and the need to deal with shortages of land. As a result, Virginia began relying less on indentured servants who would eventually be entitled to land and, instead, turned to another source of labor: slavery.

Slavery Arises in Virginia

Slaves

Slavery is a system in which people are "owned" like property. Although it existed in Virginia prior to Bacon's Rebellion, it became more essential to the colony's economy as indentured servitude decreased. Eventually, English colonists, like other Europeans, viewed Africa as their most efficient source for slaves. The first Africans in the English colonies arrived in 1619 at Jamestown. Originally, most did not come as slaves but as indentured servants. As such, they attained their freedom after a set number of years, owned land, and some even became masters of indentured servants and/or slaves themselves. In time, however, economic concerns, racism, and rationalizations on the part of white European settlers led to the institution of African slavery. Although they served in a variety of roles, most Virginia slaves worked to harvest crops like tobacco. As a result, the institution of slavery helped to firmly establish the **plantation system** in

Virginia and throughout the southern colonies. Plantations were huge farms owned by wealthy landowners who raised cash crops (crops grown for trade and profit). Because these plantations required lots of manual labor, slavery became an important part of the southern economy. By the late1600s, slavery was firmly rooted throughout the colonies.

Virginia's Government

House of Burgesses

Due to the colonies' great distance from England, the British adopted a policy known as *salutary neglect.* In other words, except for limited efforts by the crown to assert its control in the mid 1600s, the English government basically let the colonists govern themselves. While colonial governors appointed by the crown were technically in charge, colonial legislatures consisting of local residents came to possess most of the power. These legislatures typically consisted of two houses (much like the British Parliament). One was an advisory council appointed by the governor, while the other was a body elected by eligible voters. Conflict sometimes arose between governors concerned with serving the king and legislatures concerned with serving the colony. Eventually, in 1619, Virginians established the colonies' first elected legislative body: the **House of Burgesses.** The Burgesses were selected directly by the people and, along with the governor and his appointed council, comprised Virginia's government. In general, only white, male property owners could vote and those who they elected usually came from the wealthy upper classes of society. Still, the House of Burgesses helped lay a foundation for the ideas about representative government that would develop in the colonies.

New England

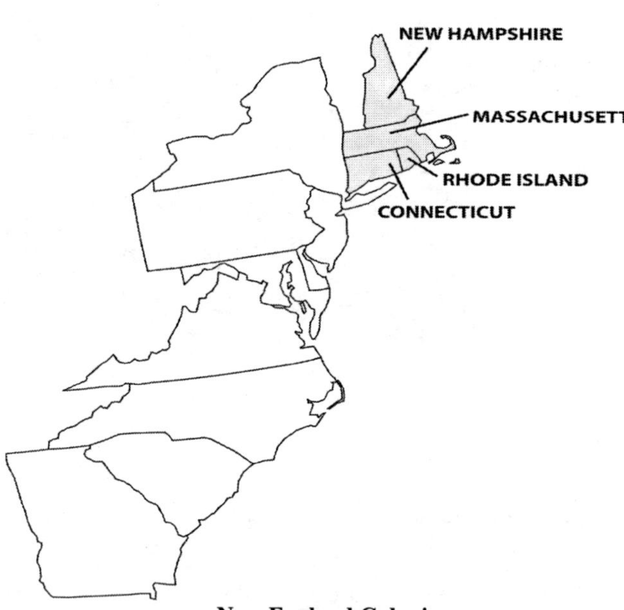

New England Colonies

Historians (people who study history for a living) traditionally divide the British colonies into three geographic regions. The **New England colonies** included Massachusetts, New Hampshire, Rhode Island, and Connecticut. The **middle colonies** consisted of New York, New Jersey, Pennsylvania, and Delaware. The **southern colonies** were made up of Maryland, Virginia, North Carolina, South Carolina, and Georgia. Some colonies were established as *royal colonies*, governed directly by the king through an appointed royal governor. Other colonies were *proprietary* or *charter colonies*. Proprietary colonies were colonies the king granted to a group of private owners for development, while charter colonies were colonies to which the crown granted a charter for the purpose of establishing a government. Georgia was the last colony Britain established in North America in 1733. It began as a charter colony and became a royal colony in 1752.

In addition to wealth, there were other reasons people came to North America. **Religious dissent** (disagreement with the Anglican Church) was one of the most common. Since Europeans strongly identified religion with nationality, English leaders viewed any protest or refusal to follow Anglican church teachings as a betrayal. As a result, those with different religious views saw North America as a place to escape persecution. One such group was the **Puritans**. In 1620, a group of Puritans established a colony at Plymouth, Massachusetts. These Puritans became known as the "Pilgrims" and celebrated the first Thanksgiving in 1621. Later, another group of Puritans settled further north and established the Massachusetts Bay Colony.

New England Government

In New England, the first efforts at self-government were defined in the *Mayflower Compact*. The Puritan settlers at Plymouth drafted this document while still on board the Mayflower (the ship that transported them to North America). It established an elected legislature and asserted that the government derived its power from the people of the colony. It also implied the colonists' desire to be ruled by a local government, rather than England. This belief in representative government often took the form of **town meetings**, in which local, tax-paying citizens (usually property owners) met to discuss and vote on issues. Once again, it gave citizens a say in their government and helped to establish a belief in democratic ideals. However, despite advocating representative government in principle, the Puritans still believed that government should seek to enforce the will of God rather than satisfy the will of the people. For this reason, power tended to rest in the hands of church leaders who were often very authoritative, dictating to colonists what the rules of society would be.

Town Meeting

Religion and Dissent

Puritans

The Puritan church was a central part of life in New England. In Massachusetts, every settler had to attend and support the Puritan church. Dissenters (those who disagreed with church leaders) were often banished from the colony. Eventually, Roger Williams and Anne Hutchinson both left Massachusetts because they disagreed with teachings of the Puritan church in the colony. Each played key roles in the founding of **Rhode Island** as a new colony. In addition, Thomas Hooker also disagreed with the church and left Massachusetts in 1636 to found **Connecticut**. He and his followers wrote a new body of laws for their settlement known as the *Fundamental Orders of Connecticut.* It stated that the government's power came only from the "free consent of the people" and set limits on what the government could do. Such principles eventually provided a foundation for the government of the United States following the American Revolution.

Eventually, unrest in Massachusetts took its toll. The colony **lost its charter** in 1684. In 1691, despite the Puritans' best attempts to resist the Crown, Massachusetts became a royal colony under the leadership of the king's appointed governor. The Crown also established a new, representative legislature and abolished the requirement that every member must be a member of the church.

The Half-way Covenant and the Salem Witch Trials

Salem Witch Trials

Puritanism affected society in other ways as well. Original settlers to New England shared deep religious convictions that led them to travel across the Atlantic to establish a new homeland. As many of these settlers died and a new generation took their place, many Puritans feared that their offspring would not share the same "conversion experiences" (experience of coming to faith in Christ). Since a valid "conversion experience" was necessary to obtain Puritan church membership, this threatened the very core of New England society. To fix the problem, the church adopted the **Half-way Covenant**. It established partial membership in the church for the children and grandchildren of full members regardless of any conversion experience. So long as the partial member was baptized, they were considered a church member, but without certain privileges, such as voting on church matters. Church leaders hoped that, despite growing attraction to the non-religious world around them, many younger Puritans would come to see the value in full church membership and would eventually embrace Puritan teachings. Some Puritans, however, opposed the Half-way Covenant and saw it as a sinful compromise.

In 1692, commitment to protect the Puritan faith resulted in one of the darkest episodes in American history—the **Salem Witch Trials**. Claiming that certain citizens had been possessed by the devil, several young girls in Salem, Massachusetts accused various townspeople of being witches. Before it was over, colonial authorities actually brought the accused to trial and condemned at least 25 people to death.

New Englanders and Native Americans

At first, relations between colonial settlers and Native Americans in New England were peaceful. Native Americans actually taught the Pilgrims of Plymouth how to raise corn that helped them survive the harsh winters. Eventually, however, a series of wars broke out as settlers continued to move west, pushing Native Americans off lands that they had occupied for generations. Finally, in 1675, a Native American leader known as "King Philip" (his Native American name was Metacom) united Native Americans in New England in an unsuccessful attempt to drive out English settlers. Despite killing nearly 2,000 colonists, Metacom's forces eventually had to retreat when the settlers struck back. Colonial soldiers finally cornered Metacom in a Rhode Island cave and shot him through the heart, putting an end to the conflict. The confrontation became known as **King Philip's War** and resulted in English colonists gaining firmer control over New England.

King Philip's War

The Middle Colonies

Sandwiched between the New England and southern colonies were the middle colonies. Because of their geographic location and the degree of religious tolerance, and because other nationalities (i.e., the Swedes and Dutch) had successfully colonized parts of the region before England, the middle colonies were the most culturally diverse.

NEW YORK
PENNSYLVANIA
NEW JERSEY
DELAWARE

Middle Colonies

Diversity in the Middle Colonies

Under the leadership of William Penn, Pennsylvania became a homeland for **Quakers**. This religious group did not recognize class differences, promoted equality of the sexes, practiced pacifism (non-violence), and sought to deal fairly with Native Americans. They also made **Pennsylvania** a place of religious tolerance, thereby attracting not only the English Quakers, but German Lutherans, Scotch-Irish Presbyterians, and Swiss Mennonites as well. Because New York was originally a Dutch colony, its residents spoke languages other than English and exhibited a great deal of cultural diversity and religious differences. Jews, as well as Christians, made New York their home, making the city the site of the colonies' first synagogue (Jewish place of worship). Because of the diversity and tolerance that the middle colonies tended to offer, the region featured a frontier that was continually pushing west as more and more settlers made their way from other colonies and overseas. Meanwhile, as urban areas continued to grow and develop (Philadelphia eventually became the colonies' largest city), a social order also emerged. Merchants who dealt in foreign trade formed the upper class "aristocracy" of the region, while sailors, unskilled workers, and artisans comprised the lower classes. The middle class consisted of craftsmen, retailers, and businessmen.

From "New Amsterdam" to "New York"

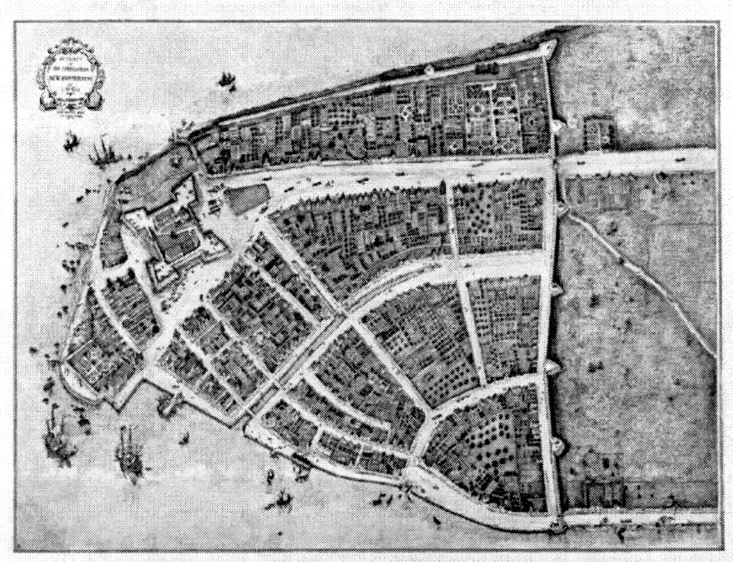

New Amsterdam

The area we know as New York was originally settled by the Dutch (Europeans from the Netherlands). They named their new colony "New Netherland" and, in 1625, established its key trading post at the mouth of the Hudson River: **New Amsterdam**. The Dutch colonists quickly built a very successful trading industry with Europe and other colonies. They traded furs, local goods, and agricultural products like wheat and rye. Because of its location, New Amsterdam also became a key port that featured inhabitants from various countries. As a result, much of the diversity mentioned earlier arose during the days of Dutch colonization.

England did not fail to notice New Netherland's prosperity. In 1664, King Charles II decided he wanted the region and declared the entire area under the rule of his brother, the Duke of York. Unable to resist the British, New Amsterdam surrendered and was immediately renamed **New York**. With its most prized city lost, the rest of New Netherland soon surrendered as well.

Practice 3.1: The Colonial Period

1. Which of the following best describes Jamestown?

   A. It was the first English colony in North America.
   B. The colony thrived most before tobacco was discovered.
   C. Colonists constantly lived in peace with Native Americans.
   D. Slavery became less important after Bacon's Rebellion.

2. What were plantations and how did they help make slavery an important part of colonial culture?

3. The House of Burgesses was the

   A. first legislative body in New England.
   B. court responsible for conducting the Salem Witch Trials.
   C. first representative body of government in the colonies.
   D. governmental body formed by the Half-way Covenant.

4. Describe New Amsterdam. Why did the English decide to take it over and what did they rename it?

3.2 Colonial Culture and the American Revolution

Slavery and African Americans

The Atlantic Slave Trade

Slave Trade Route

Beginning in the fifteenth century, Portugal established what would become the **Atlantic slave trade.** It involved Europeans shipping slaves from Africa to the Americas. Although relatively small at first, this trade grew drastically from the fifteenth to the nineteenth centuries, finally ending in the 1800s. When the Portuguese first arrived in Africa in the 1400s, they discovered an abundant slave trade already in existence. When African kingdoms fought one another, they often sold prisoners of war into slavery. Sometimes the conquerors sold their slaves to other Africans. At other times, they sold them to foreign traders (often from the Mediterranean). The Portuguese tapped into this system and quickly adopted it to ship slaves all the way to the Americas. Soon, the Dutch, British, Spanish, and French participated in the slave trade as well. Thanks to American colonization and the demand for plantation labor it produced, the Atlantic slave trade became extremely profitable for both European and African slave traders. As a result, slave ships carried millions of African slaves to the Americas. By the 1700s, black slaves actually outnumbered white settlers in Latin American colonies and in the British colony of South Carolina. These slaves normally arrived by way of the **Middle Passage** (the route taken by ships carrying slaves from Africa to North America). The trip was called the "Middle Passage" because it was the middle leg of the "triangular trade route" (trade between 3 points: Europe, Africa, and the Americas). Africans were forced to live in cramped quarters aboard slave ships and often suffered inhumane treatment during their voyage. Due mostly to disease and poor sanitation, many of them died before ever reaching the Americas.

Colonial African American Culture

Colonial Slavery

Today, we often think of the African slaves who came to America as coming from a common culture and being very similar to one another. In reality, however, they came from many different cultures within Africa. As a result, the slave population on any particular plantation or within a community usually consisted of Africans from a variety of backgrounds. They often spoke different languages, had different religious beliefs, and were familiar with different traditions. Still, because of the burden of slavery that they shared, African slaves developed tight-knit communities over time. Slaves quickly began to adopt the English language in British North America because it was the common language of their masters and, therefore, the one language that they were all exposed to regardless of their backgrounds. Slaves also adopted aspects of the Christian religion. However, they often mixed it with their own African religious traditions.

In the South, where plantations dominated, most slaves tended to work on farms harvesting crops and processing agricultural products. In the North and in urban areas, it was not uncommon to find slaves living in cities, sometimes independent of their masters, and working as artisans. Sometimes, they even earned their own money and bought their freedom. Slaves with special skills, such as blacksmiths, barrel makers, or carpenters tended to be more valued on large plantations and in cities, whereas healthy young slaves who could work hard were in high demand for field work. Over time, as racial divisions increased and laws became more restrictive, slaves in the British colonies became less and less mobile and their treatment more harsh. Southern slaves especially suffered as the South's entire economy came to rely on the institution of slavery.

It is worth noting that, while the majority of blacks in the British colonies were slaves, some were free as well. A few managed to buy their freedom or have it "awarded" to them by "benevolent" masters. Others were born free because their parents had been freed from slavery. Still others fled slavery and began *maroon settlements* (communities formed in frontier areas by escaped slaves). Interestingly, some free blacks became slaveowners themselves. In general, however, even free blacks saw the few rights they had decline over time in colonial North America.

Maroon Settlers

MERCANTILISM AND TRADE

Why did nations like England establish colonies in the first place? One of the main reasons was Europeans' acceptance of **mercantilism**. Under this theory, countries grow wealthier and maintained their national security by consistently exporting (selling goods to other nations) more than they import (buy goods from other nations). As a result, countries tried to maintain a "favorable balance of trade" (export more than they import). To maintain such a balance, nations needed colonies for additional resources and markets. Thus, American colonists began a profitable **trans-Atlantic trade** in which they shipped many of the colonies' products and raw materials to England and places like the West Indies. In 1660, England began passing a series of laws known as the Navigation Acts. These laws were largely based on mercantilism, and required the British colonies to sell certain goods only to England. England would then use them or trade them to foreign nations. The few products the colonies could sell to other countries were charged a British duty (tax). Colonists did not like such policies because they could make more money selling goods directly to other nations or colonies. Therefore, colonists often traded illegally with other nations besides just Britain. Strict enforcement of the Navigation Acts ultimately contributed to the call for revolution.

THE ROAD TO REVOLUTION

THE FRENCH AND INDIAN WAR

As British colonists moved west, they found themselves fighting French settlers and Native Americans. In 1754, this tension between French and British colonials resulted in the **French and Indian War**. It was so named because Britain fought the war against France and its Native American allies (some Native Americans helped the British). After nine years of fighting, France, Great Britain, and Spain (a French ally) signed the **Treaty of Paris in 1763**. France gave up its claims in Canada and all lands east of the Mississippi River. In addition, Spain ceded Florida to the British. Great Britain now stood alone as the one colonial power in eastern North America. In addition, the French and Indian War soon became part of a much larger conflict. Two years after fighting broke out in North America, war engulfed Europe. It involved all the major European powers and extended to colonies around the globe.

French-Indian War

TENSIONS RISE BETWEEN GREAT BRITAIN AND THE COLONIES

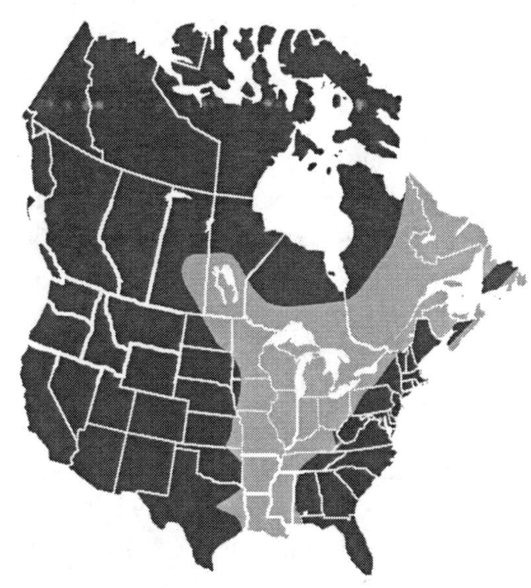

1763 Proclamation

Soon after the French and Indian War, relations between England and its colonies deteriorated. After fighting beside the British against the French, many colonists lost respect for Britain's military. They viewed it as ill-prepared and unsuited for fighting on the American terrain. Meanwhile, Great Britain was heavily in debt after fighting to defend its colonies and felt that the Americans should help pay for the expense. It also possessed vast new territories and felt that it needed to find a way to control them. As a result, it took a number of steps the colonists found offensive. The first was the king's **Proclamation of 1763**. It forbade colonists from settling west of the Appalachian Mountains and put the territory under British military control. While the proclamation was intended to manage Britain's new territories and ensure peace with Native Americans, colonists resented the king's restrictions and many ignored the proclamation.

Acts By Parliament and Colonial Reaction

Stamp Act

Beginning in the mid 1760s, Parliament passed a series of laws and taxes that infuriated the Americans. One of the most offensive was the **Stamp Act**. Under this law, the British government taxed nearly all printed material by requiring that it bear a government stamp. In protest, the colonies imposed a boycott of British goods. A boycott means that they refused to buy them, thereby withholding money that would otherwise go to English businesses. Groups known as the **Sons of Liberty** and **Daughters of Liberty** sprang up throughout the colonies to support and enforce the boycotts. The Sons of Liberty often used violence to intimidate any merchant or royal official who might otherwise use the stamps. Meanwhile, the Daughters of Liberty used their skills to weave fabric and other products that were usually bought from Britain. Of all the colonies, only Georgia ever issued any of the stamps, prompting angry South Carolinians to threaten an invasion of Savannah. The boycotts, along with violent responses to the Stamp Act, eventually led England to repeal (cancel) the law.

Many colonies also formed groups dedicated to organizing resistance against British laws. They were known as **committees of correspondence**, and they made sure that colonists remained discontent with British rule. One such group took bold action in December 1773. Recent British laws enabled British traders to gain an unfair advantage in the trade of tea (a popular colonial drink). In protest, Massachusetts' committee of correspondence led a group of radicals who dressed as Mohawk Indians and marched to Boston Harbor. There, in what became known as the "Boston Tea Party," the group raided ships hauling British tea and threw the crates overboard. In response, Parliament passed the Coercive Acts (because of their harshness, the colonists labeled them the **Intolerable Acts**). These acts closed Boston Harbor and placed a military governor over Massachusetts. In addition, England expanded the Canadian border, thereby taking land away from certain colonies.

A Revolution Begins

Thomas Paine

To deal with the crisis, representatives from nearly every colony (only Georgia did not attend) gathered for the First Continental Congress in September 1774. In a statement to the king, the Congress wrote that the colonists had a right to be represented in their government. Since the colonies were not represented in Parliament, they were entitled to govern themselves. Then, in April 1775, all hope of a peaceful resolution was lost when fighting broke out at Lexington and Concord. As British troops were on their way to seize arms and ammunition stored by colonists at Concord, Massachusetts, they were met at Lexington by colonial militia (voluntary, local military units consisting of private citizens rather than full-time soldiers). It was there that someone (to this day no one is sure who) fired the "shot heard 'round the world" that started the American Revolution. Less than a month later, colonial delegates met for the Second Continental Congress to discuss how to deal with the situation. The following January, in 1776, **Thomas Paine** published his famous pamphlet, ***Common Sense***. In it, he made a compelling case for independence that won many to the cause. Due to the influence of Paine and others, the Second Continental Congress eventually stopped seeking resolution with England and chose, instead, to declare independence.

THE AMERICAN REVOLUTION

THE FIRST YEAR OF WAR

General Washington

Washington Crossing Delaware

In July 1776, the Second Continental Congress formally signed the Declaration of Independence (review chapter 1, section 1.1). In actuality, the American Revolution began long before the document was ever written. By the summer of 1776, colonists and British forces had been fighting for over a year. Following Lexington and Concord, nearly 20,000 Patriots (colonists who supported the fight for independence) surrounded Boston where British soldiers were stationed. In June 1775, British troops launched a series of attacks against two hills occupied by American forces. The British eventually won the battle but suffered far greater casualties than the Americans. A month later, General **George Washington** arrived, after being appointed by the Continental Congress to command the American army. In March, 1776, the British left Boston and eventually made their way to New York. There, despite his best efforts, the British forced Washington to abandon the city and start a long and humiliating retreat. Plagued by a lack of supplies, undisciplined soldiers, and the desertion of many of his troops (either illegally or because their enlistments had expired), Washington and his army seemed on the brink of defeat. Then, in December 1776, Washington made a daring move. He surprised his enemy by **crossing the Delaware River** on Christmas night and attacking the Hessians (Germans hired to fight for the British) encamped at Trenton, New Jersey. Having finally tasted victory, Washington's troops did not let up. Leaving their campfires burning so as to make the enemy think they were still there, Washington's army slipped away in the middle of the night to launch another surprise attack at Princeton. Washington's victories in New Jersey greatly lifted American morale and gave people hope that, perhaps, the revolution could actually succeed.

General George Washington

George Washington was a Virginian and former surveyor who eventually became a soldier, wealthy landowner, and respected delegate to the Continental Congress. As a young military officer, he served with the British during the French and Indian War. Because of his military experience, the Continental Congress chose him to command its new army after declaring independence from Great Britain.

Washington faced many **challenges to building an army**. Not only was he fighting one of the most powerful military forces in history, but he also had to form an army out of a band of undisciplined farmers, frontiersmen, and volunteers. Many of his men enlisted for only short periods and planned on returning home after only a few weeks of service. Washington was constantly short of men and begging soldiers to remain longer than they were obligated. In addition, he normally found himself short of supplies and money. As a result, his men usually had to camp in cold and wet conditions with very few clothes and often no pay. Many times, his soldiers did not have shoes, even in the dead of winter. Still, Washington turned out to be an amazing leader. His willingness to ride into the heat of battle, risking his own life to lead his men, greatly inspired and won the loyalty of his soldiers. Although leaders in Congress often criticized him for not winning more of his early battles, Washington's ability to hold his army together and frustrate the British allowed the Continental Army the time it needed to grow its ranks and become better trained. His ability to lead the American forces to victory in light of the obstacles he faced and the enemy that opposed him makes George Washington one of the greatest military leaders of all time.

The Northern War

In September 1777, General Horatio Gates won praise for another key US victory at Saratoga, New York. (In reality, however, it was one of Gates' subordinate generals, Benedict Arnold, who really won the battle.) This victory was especially important because it convinced the French that the US could possibly win the war. As a result, France and the United States forged an alliance that proved crucial in defeating Great Britain.

Following the victory at Saratoga, the Continental Army (official name given the US forces) endured a harsh winter at **Valley Forge**, Pennsylvania. Poorly supplied and lacking warm clothes, many of Washington's men proved too sick to serve. A number of them even died. Fortunately, thanks to the efforts of Washington and a Prussian named Baron Friedrich Von Steuben, the army effectively used its time at Valley Forge to become better trained. Once the warm weather returned, Washington's army returned to battle more determined and better prepared to meet the British.

Valley Forge

The Southern War

Lord Cornwallis

In late 1778, the British began focusing more effort on the South. Many Southerners were *Tories* (colonists who remained loyal to England; for this reason the British called them "Loyalists"). Britain believed these Tories would support their cause and help them crush the revolution. By the summer of 1780, the British had seized both Savannah and Charleston and were ready to try to bring all of the Carolinas under their control. British forces under the command of General **Lord Cornwallis** sought to invade North Carolina following their victory at Camden, but were defeated and turned back by Patriot victories at Kings Mountain and Cowpens.

The French Alliance

As mentioned earlier, the US relied heavily on an alliance with the French to defeat the British. Although the colonists had a great amount of desire for independence and the willingness to fight, they had no navy, barely an army, and very little money for supplies and weapons. France, however, could supply all these things. Shortly after signing the Declaration of Independence, the Continental Congress sent **Benjamin Franklin** to Paris to try to convince the French to form an open alliance with the US. After the American victory at Saratoga, the French finally agreed. France promised money, troops, and the support of the French navy. Following the US-French treaty, Great Britain and France were soon at war with each other in Europe as well, forcing the British to fight on two continents.

Benjamin Franklin

Marquis de Lafayette

Even before the official treaty, a Frenchman known as the **Marquis de Lafayette** made his way to America to fight for the revolution. Although only 19 years old, he proved to be a talented and valiant soldier who quickly won the confidence of General Washington. Congress eventually gave Lafayette his own command. He finally asked to return to France in 1778 in order to fight for his homeland against the British following France's treaty with the US.

Victory at Yorktown

Surrender at Yorktown

Eventually, Cornwallis regrouped and invaded North Carolina. He pursued the southern US forces, now under the command of Nathanael Greene, hoping to force them into a decisive battle. After leading the British on a long chase that extended into Virginia and forced Cornwallis to exhaust many of his supplies, Greene eventually engaged the British forces at the Battle of Guilford Courthouse at what is today Greensboro, NC. Cornwallis won, but at a heavy cost. To win the battle, he had to fire his cannons into the midst of the battle, killing many of his own men. In need of supplies, he marched his forces north to the coastal town of Yorktown, Virginia, where he hoped to receive what he needed from British ships.

Realizing that Cornwallis was now trapped on the Virginia peninsula, Washington marched south to pin him between the Continental Army and the Atlantic Ocean. Meanwhile, the French navy provided a blockade that prevented British ships from coming to Cornwallis' rescue. On October 19, 1781, Cornwallis surrendered to Washington at **Yorktown**. So humiliated was the British general that he could not even deliver his sword in person. (In those days, the losing general gave his sword to the victorious general as part of a formal ceremony of surrender.) Although negotiations went on for two more years, Yorktown effectively ended the revolution. The Americans and British finally signed the **Treaty of Paris in 1783**, in which Great Britain officially recognized the independence of the United States.

Practice 3.2: Colonial Culture and the American Revolution

1. Who was the Virginian chosen to command the American Continental Army during the Revolutionary War?

   A. George Washington
   B. Lord Cornwallis
   C. Benjamin Franklin
   D. Marquis de Lafayette

2. Describe George Washington as a military leader and discuss some of the challenges he faced when building the Continental Army.

3. In what ways did the French contribute to the revolution's success?

4. The colonial business in which Europeans transported African slaves to America and sold them to white slave owners was called what?

   A. mercantilism
   B. triangular trade route
   C. individualism
   D. the Atlantic slave trade

5. Which of the following is true regarding African Americans in the American colonies?
   A. Most of them were slaves who gained their freedom after seven years of service.
   B. They came to America from a variety of different cultural backgrounds.
   C. They were all slaves because the law prevented blacks from ever being free.
   D. Most worked in northern colonies.

6. What was significant about the French and Indian War?
   A. It was the first major war between French settlers and Native Americans.
   B. It settled the issue of which European nation would dominate eastern North America.
   C. It left the colonies deeply in debt and begging Great Britain to pass new taxes.
   D. It was the first war the British ever lost, thereby giving the colonists hope that they could also defeat the king's army.

7. Who was Thomas Paine and what was *Common Sense*?

3.3 The Early Nation

The First Presidents

Following the victory of the revolution, the new nation's leaders watched in frustration as the country's first national body of laws, the Articles of Confederation, failed. In 1787, the Constitutional Convention met and drafted the United States Constitution, which established a new national government with three branches of government. It was ratified in 1788 and granted power to both the national and state governments (review chapter 1, section 1.2).

President George Washington

President George Washington

Delegates to the Electoral College unanimously elected **George Washington** the first president of the United States in 1789, and again in 1792. He was initially inaugurated in New York City, which served as the nation's capital for Washington's first year in office. The government then moved to Philadelphia. Congress eventually approved plans for a new capital city to be built along the Potomac River between Virginia and Maryland. President Washington himself chose the site, but ironically was the only president never to live there. The new capital was eventually named Washington, DC.

Alexander Hamilton

Washington's new presidency faced several challenges. When the new US government took power in 1789, the nation was deep in debt and the value of the new currency was low. Alexander Hamilton, Washington's secretary of the treasury, developed a plan to help. **Hamilton's economic plan** proposed that the federal government take on state debts that were largely due to the war. To raise revenue, Hamilton wanted a tax on whiskey. He reasoned that such a tax would not only raise money, but would also serve to demonstrate the power of the federal government. He also supported tariffs (taxes on imports). Not only did he believe that these tariffs would raise much needed money, he also saw them as necessary to strengthen and protect US business interests from foreign competition. Hamilton believed this was necessary to give US manufacturers a chance to succeed. Finally, Hamilton proposed establishing a national bank. Hamilton had a loose interpretation of the Constitution and believed that its *necessary and proper clause* gave the government the right to charter a bank if it was necessary to exercise its constitutional duties (in this case, coining money).

Hamilton's plan gained the support of President Washington, but it was not without controversy. Many opposed Hamilton's views. One such opponent was Washington's secretary of state and author of the Declaration of Independence, Thomas Jefferson. Jefferson had a strict interpretation of the Constitution and argued that the federal government must restrict itself to those powers specifically stated in the document. Since the Constitution did not give the federal government the authority to open a national bank, Jefferson argued that it could not. Many southerners also opposed Hamilton's plan because they were against tariffs that would lessen competition from foreign countries and raise prices on finished goods. They also feared that such measures would encourage other countries to respond with tariffs of their own, thereby raising prices on southern exports and hurting the South's economy. Many saw Hamilton's plan as evidence that the federal government intended to support the business interests of a wealthy few over the needs of farmers who made up the bulk of the nation's population.

Finally, the whiskey tax was very unpopular among farmers in the western regions of Pennsylvania, Maryland, Virginia, and North Carolina. Many of these farmers made their living converting grain into whiskey. Their protest eventually resulted in the **Whiskey Rebellion**. Pennsylvania farmers refused to pay the tax and resorted to violence. The uprising ended when President Washington organized a military force that marched into Pennsylvania and halted the resistance. While the event showed that the new government had the power to enforce its laws, it also led many farmers and frontiersmen to see Hamilton's form of government as tyrannical. More of them flocked to Thomas Jefferson as a defender of states' rights and a champion of their cause.

Whiskey Rebellion

Washington and Neutrality

While the new US government tried to establish itself, European powers Great Britain and France were once again at war with one another. President Washington, recognizing that the country could not afford a fight with either side, made a **Proclamation of Neutrality**. He stated that the US would not take sides. The conflict still had consequences for the United States, however. The British began intercepting US ships they believed bound for France and impressing seamen (taking US sailors captive and forcing them to serve the British). These actions were intended to injure the French, but they also hurt the United States' ability to trade and operate on the high seas. In response, Chief Justice John Jay went to London to broker an agreement with the British. To the disappointment of many in the US, Jay returned with a treaty that primarily benefited Great Britain and did little to further the interests of the United States.

The Rise of Political Parties

Formation of Political Parties

Shortly before leaving office, President George Washington gave a farewell address in 1796 in which he emphasized three key points. First, Washington believed the United States should stay neutral and avoid permanent alliances with other nations. Second, he believed that good government is based on religion and morality. Third, he spoke about the dangers of forming political parties. He warned that political parties would cause people to work for their special interests rather than for the public good. Despite Washington's warnings, opposing political parties did indeed form. The **Federalist** party was created even prior to the ratification of the Constitution. Alexander Hamilton, James Madison and John Adams were among its leaders. The Federalists supported ratification of the US Constitution because they supported a strong national government. They also supported large landowners, merchants, and the interests of business over agriculture. Therefore, they supported tariffs and other measures meant to help US businesses. Most New Englanders were Federalists. Meanwhile, the **Republicans** arose in opposition to the Federalists. Their leader was Thomas Jefferson. For this reason, they are sometimes referred to as "Jeffersonian Republicans" to distinguish them from today's Republican Party. The Jeffersonian Republicans favored stronger state governments and a weaker national government. For this reason, many of them originally opposed the Constitution because they feared it made the national government too strong. In addition, the Republicans tended to favor the interests of small farmers and debtors, rather than those of business. Therefore, they opposed many Federalist policies and saw them as an attempt by the wealthy upper class to limit economic opportunities for small landowners. Most Southerners were Jeffersonian Republicans.

President John Adams

John Adams

Following his second term as president, George Washington retired from public life. **John Adams**, the same man who had nominated Washington to serve as commanding general of the Continental Army and who had served him as vice president, now succeeded him as the nation's second president. He was a Federalist and, therefore, often found himself at odds with Thomas Jefferson. He also had to deal early on with a French government that was very angry over Jay's treaty with the British. Although many in the US saw the treaty as a weak document, it angered the French because they saw it as an alliance with Great Britain. In an attempt to improve US-French relations, the United States sent three diplomats (Charles Pinckney, Elbridge Gerry, and John Marshall) to France. The three were not officially received, but after several days they were informed by an unofficial delegation that, with a bribe and the promise of a US loan to France, they might be given access to French leaders. This infuriated the US representatives, who rejected the suggestion and returned home. It also angered citizens in the United States when they learned of what happened. The event was known as the *XYZ Affair*, because the unofficial French delegation consisted of three men known only as "X, Y, and Z." As a result, the US broke off its relations with France. Fearing it could not remain both neutral and safe, the United States began building up its military force. Fortunately, with the *Convention of 1800*, France and the United States were able to negotiate some of their differences, reopen trade, and re-establish diplomatic relations. The convention also formally ended the US-French alliance that had existed since the revolution, making the US officially neutral. The US could now engage in trade without appearing to violate a treaty with France or aid a war against Great Britain.

Federalist and Republican Hostilities

The Federalists in Congress passed several laws during John Adams' administration that alarmed Jeffersonian Republicans. The Naturalization Act required foreign immigrants to live in the United States for fourteen years before they could be US citizens. The **Alien Act** allowed the government to arrest, detain, or remove foreigners deemed untrustworthy. Of even greater concern was the **Sedition Act** that severely limited free speech and expression. Federalists often used the Alien and Sedition Acts to silence critics (usually Republicans). These acts tended to help the Federalists because immigrants who had been in the country for only a short time were usually poorer and often drawn to the Republicans who represented the "common man." Under these laws, such people could not vote in elections.

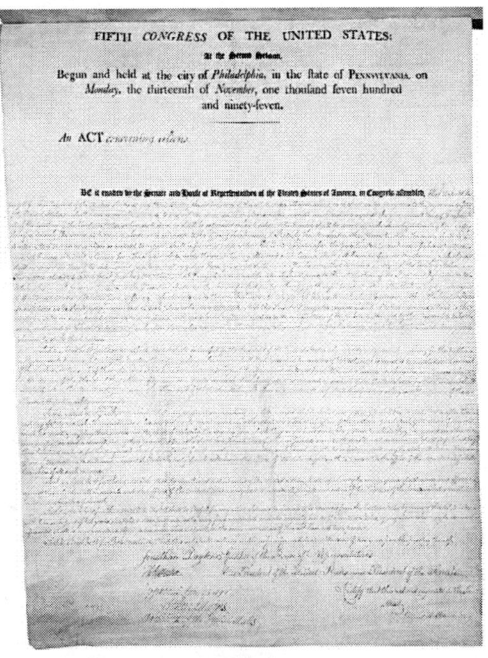

FIFTH *CONGRESS* OF THE UNITED STATES:

Begun and held at the city of *Philadelphia*, in the ſtate of PENNSYLVANIA, on *Monday*, the thirteenth of *November*, one thouſand ſeven hundred and ninety-ſeven.

An ACT

Alien Act

Jefferson and others saw these acts as abuses of power. He and James Madison (a former Federalist) produced a response to the Alien and Sedition Acts in the form of the Virginia and Kentucky Resolutions. These resolutions stated that if a state believed a federal law to be unconstitutional, then it did not have to obey or enforce it. The resolution was so named because the state legislatures of Virginia and Kentucky adopted it. The idea that individual states have such a right came to be known as the **doctrine of nullification**, because it claims that states can nullify a national law that they believe violates the Constitution. The debate surrounding states' rights versus federal authority ultimately played a major role in events leading up to the Civil War.

The Election of 1800

The battle between the Federalists and Republicans culminated in the election of 1800. It was a nasty election that pitted the Federalist president against Thomas Jefferson. Republicans accused Adams of wanting to be a king, a huge insult so soon after the revolution, while Federalists proclaimed Jefferson to be an anarchist (someone who is against any structure of government). When the electoral college finally voted, two Republican candidates, Thomas Jefferson and Aaron Burr, ended up tied with 73 votes each. As a result, the House of Representatives had to decide the winner. In an ironic twist, Alexander Hamilton played a major factor in deciding who won. Although Hamilton did not agree with Jefferson's politics, he hated Aaron Burr as a person. Hamilton supported Thomas Jefferson, making him the third president of the United States. Burr never forgave Hamilton for his decision and the two remained at odds. They ultimately met in a duel, with Burr shooting and killing the former secretary of the treasury.

Thomas Jefferson and the Louisiana Purchase

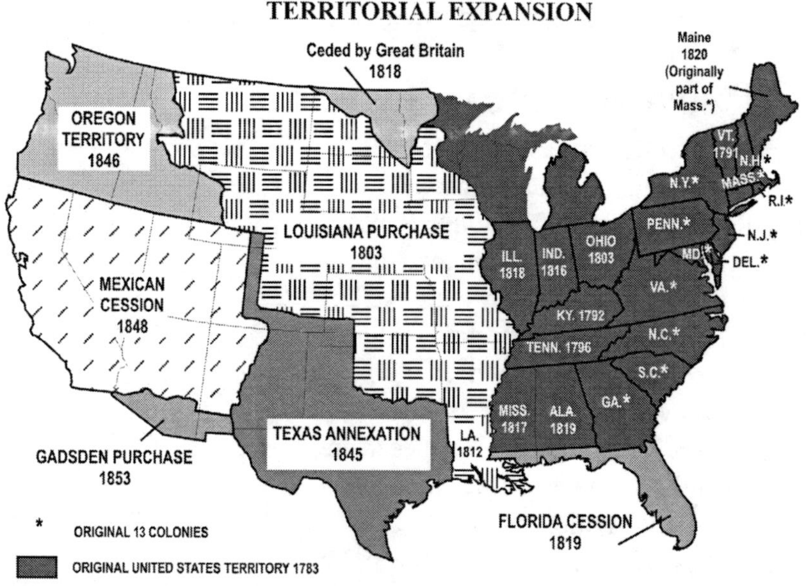

Map of Louisiana Purchase

Once in office, President Thomas Jefferson wanted to secure United States trading on the Mississippi River. For this reason, he sent representatives to France to negotiate the purchase of New Orleans. Initially, Napoleon was not interested in selling New Orleans because he hoped to revitalize the French colonial empire in the Western Hemisphere. However, when slaves in the French colony of Saint-Domingue (later known as Haiti) revolted and Britain resumed its war with

France, the French emperor surprised Jefferson by offering to sell not only New Orleans, but the entire Louisiana region. Because he believed it was important for citizens in a republic to have access to land, and due to the resources the new territory offered, Jefferson accepted the offer. The **Louisiana Purchase** of 1803 was the United States' largest land purchase, roughly doubling the country's size. It marked a turning point for the new nation economically, as it began to pursue prosperity within its own borders rather than from foreign nations.

THE LEWIS AND CLARK EXPEDITION

Even before the Louisiana Purchase in 1803, President Jefferson appointed his personal secretary, Meriwether Lewis, to find a water route to the Pacific Ocean. Lewis chose William Clark to help him lead the expedition that departed from St. Louis in May of 1804. Finally, in November of 1805, the **Lewis and Clark Expedition** reached the Pacific Northwest coast. Many people thought the explorers had died along the way, but the group returned to St. Louis in September of 1806 with valuable information about the Oregon and Louisiana territories. This exploration led to the rapid migration of settlers to the Pacific Northwest. The pathway these settlers followed from Missouri became known as the *Oregon Trail.*

Lewis and Clark

THE WAR OF 1812

War of 1812

As US settlers attempted to move west, they encountered Native American resistance. Many settlers blamed the British for encouraging such resistance in order to protect their own interests. They also felt threatened by the British presence in Canada. This, combined with the British navy's policy of impressing US sailors, led many in the United States to demand war. Finally, on June 18, 1812, Congress declared war on Great Britain. The **War of 1812** began with many in the US hoping to win land from the British in Canada and the Spanish in Florida (Spain had ties to the British). At times, it appeared that the US was in trouble, especially when the British invaded and burned Washington, DC. The US persevered, however, winning an inspiring victory at the battle of Fort McHenry. The bravery of the US soldiers who held the fort despite intense British fire inspired Francis Scott Key to write his initial draft of the *Star Spangled Banner* (today's US national anthem). Eventually, with Andrew Jackson's victories at the battles of Horseshoe Bend and New Orleans, the US secured the signing and ratification of a treaty ending the war (the battle of New Orleans actually occurred after the treaty, but the US victory ensured that the British would honor its terms). The Treaty of Ghent did not grant any official land gains to the US, but it did keep the Mississippi River and the frontier open, thereby encouraging further western migration. It also showed that the United States could defend itself and assert its interests in North America against foreign powers. Meanwhile, due to its opposition to the war, the Federalist party lost its credibility and faded from importance in national politics.

A National Identity

Star Spangled Banner

Perhaps most importantly, the War of 1812 helped produce a stronger sense of **national identity** among US citizens. People felt a great deal of pride after standing up to the mighty British — again! In addition, before the war, US manufacturing had lagged far behind the Europeans. However, once the war started, US ships could not safely carry products overseas, nor could other nations' products reach the US. Instead, US citizens had to supply themselves with the products they needed. As a result, US manufacturing and agriculture improved and grew prosperous. Northern manufacturers sold more and more of their products to other regions of the country, while the South's plantation economy exploded as the nation's only major supplier of cotton. By the time the war ended, US citizens had a new sense of national pride and both US manufacturers and planters had established themselves as respectable players in domestic and international trade.

The Monroe Doctrine

James Monroe

With the end of the War of 1812 and the Federalist party, the United States entered a period of national pride and political unity known as the *Era of Good Feelings*. It was during this period that President James Monroe issued the **Monroe Doctrine** in 1823. The United States would not tolerate European intervention in the affairs of any independent nation in the Americas, nor were the American continents open to European colonization any longer. The US would view any future attempts to colonize them as acts of aggression. Finally, the president promised that the United States would not interfere in the internal affairs of other American countries, nor in those of European nations.

Practice 3.3: The Early Nation

1. Who were the first and second presidents of the United States?

   A. George Washington and Thomas Jefferson
   B. George Washington and Alexander Hamilton
   C. George Washington and John Adams
   D. John Adams and Thomas Jefferson

2. Which of the following best describes a Federalist?

   A. someone who favors farmers over businessmen
   B. someone who believes in a strong government that helps US businesses
   C. someone who opposes tariffs that might hurt small landowners
   D. someone who supports Thomas Jefferson over John Adams

3. What challenges did George Washington face when he became president?

4. Explain the importance of the Louisiana Purchase and give Jefferson's reasons for supporting it.

5. The War of 1812 served to

   A. divide the country between manufacturers who supported the war and farmers who opposed it.
   B. hurt US manufacturing and farming.
   C. improve US manufacturing and farming.
   D. discourage the US from wanting to expand west.

6. What did the Monroe Doctrine state?

CHAPTER 3 REVIEW

Key terms, people, and concepts

Jamestown
Chief Powhatan
indentured servants
Bacon's Rebellion
slavery
plantation system
House of Burgesses
New England colonies
middle colonies
southern colonies
religious dissent
Puritans
town meetings
Rhode Island
Connecticut
Massachusetts losing its charter
Half-way Covenant
King Philip's War
Quakers
Pennsylvania
New Amsterdam
New York
Atlantic slave trade
Middle Passage
mercantilism
trans-atlantic trade
French and Indian War
Treaty of Paris (1763)
Proclamation of 1763
Stamp Act
Sons and Daughters of Liberty
committees of correspondence
Intolerable Acts
Thomas Paine
Common Sense
George Washington
crossing the Delaware River
challenges faced by Washington when building an army
Valley Forge
Lord Cornwallis
Benjamin Franklin
Marquis de Lafayette
Yorktown
Treaty of Paris (1783)
Hamilton's economic plan
Whiskey Rebellion
Proclamation of Neutrality
Federalists and Republicans
John Adams
Alien and Sedition acts
doctrine of nullification
Louisiana Purchase
Lewis and Clark Expedition
War of 1812
national identity
Monroe Doctrine

Multiple Choice Questions

1. What was the land purchase that roughly doubled the size of the US in 1803?
   A. the Northwest Ordinance
   B. the Land Ordinance
   C. the Northwest Territory
   D. the Louisiana Purchase

2. "The president has firmly established that any further attempts to colonize this hemisphere shall be viewed by the United States as an act of aggression. I commend his resolve and hope that this nation is willing to take all steps necessary to uphold this position."

   The above quote is expressing support for which of the following?

   A. the Declaration of Independence
   B. the Erie Canal
   C. the Louisiana Purchase
   D. the Monroe Doctrine

3. As a result of the War of 1812, US manufacturing

   A. suffered and declined.
   B. grew and eventually prospered.
   C. ceased to exist until after the war.
   D. survived but no longer dominated world trade.

4. The following quote is most likely from whom?

   "The institution of slavery is vital to our economy. Why, I bet we have as many African slaves as we do free Europeans...perhaps even more. Without them, we could not begin to produce the tobacco for which there is a market in England and elsewhere."

   A. a Puritan leader in New England
   B. a Quaker in Pennsylvania
   C. a rich landowner in Massachusetts
   D. a plantation owner in Georgia

5. A politician goes before Parliament and passionately proclaims that the American colonies are crucial to the British economy. He tells his colleagues that it is important that England export more products to other countries than it imports. Otherwise, England's wealth and security will be in jeopardy. He believes the colonies are important because they provide both resources for production and markets for English goods. This politician is advocating which of the following?

   A. salutary neglect
   B. protection of the triangular trade route
   C. mercantilism
   D. repeal of the Navigation Acts

6. Which of the following is the correct chronological order in which the people listed arrived in North America?

   A. Spanish explorers, Native Americans, African Americans, English colonists
   B. Native Americans, colonists in Jamestown, colonists in Massachusetts, the first African Americans in the English colonies
   C. French trappers, Iroquois, Spanish missionaries, Jamestown colonists
   D. Spanish explorers, Jamestown colonists, first African Americans in the English colonies, the Pilgrims

7. Who was Powhatan?
   A. a Native American chief who made peace with the Pilgrims and helped them through their first winter.
   B. a Native American chief who ruled over much of the Virginia territory when English settlers arrived
   C. a Native American chief who was shot and killed by New Englanders in Rhode Island
   D. the first African slave to arrive in Virginia by way of the Middle Passage.

8. Which of the following best describes the Atlantic slave trade?
   A. It was an illegal trade because no country would formally support it.
   B. The Atlantic slave trade began when Virginians started demanding slaves.
   C. It included a cruel ocean voyage known as the "Middle Passage."
   D. Only Europeans bought and sold slaves as part of the trade.

9. Which of the following groups founded Massachusetts?
   A. Puritans
   B. Quakers
   C. Anglican ministers
   D. tobacco farmers

10. Committees of correspondence would have been most devoted to which of the following?
    A. raising tobacco
    B. enforcing the Stamp Act
    C. protecting the king's reputation
    D. encouraging discontent among the colonists

11. Someone inspired by the writings of Thomas Paine in 1776 would most likely support which of the following statements?
    A. "Long live King George!"
    B. "The colonies must proclaim their independence!"
    C. "Laws passed by Parliament must be respected."
    D. "Slavery is a moral outrage and must be abolished."

12. The US victory at Saratoga was especially important for which of the following reasons?
    A. It was the first US victory of the American Revolution.
    B. It was the result of a daring move by General Washington on Christmas night 1776.
    C. It convinced France that the US could win the war, thereby giving the US a crucial ally.
    D. It resulted in Britain's immediate surrender and served as the final decisive battle of the war.

13. Which of the following is the best description of George Washington as a military leader?
    - A. He was a weak leader who had trouble winning the respect of his men.
    - B. He was a gifted leader who never lost a single battle during the revolution.
    - C. Although Congress did not want him to serve as general, he was elected to that post by the army and surprised everyone with his skill as a commander.
    - D. He was an exceptional leader who somehow overcame defeats and hardships to lead the US to victory.

14. The early political party that favored strong state governments, looked to Thomas Jefferson as its leader, opposed Hamilton's plan, and favored the interests of farmers over big business was which of the following?
    - A. the Federalists
    - B. the Tories
    - C. the Republicans
    - D. the Patriots

15. Which of the following was a major area of concern for George Washington during his presidency?
    - A. slavery
    - B. fires in Washington, DC
    - C. relations with Great Britain and France
    - D. problems with the Articles of Confederation

Chapter 4
United States History: Industrial Revolution Through the Civil War

GPS	SSUSH7: Students will explain the process of economic growth, its regional and national impact in the first half of the 19th century, and the different responses to it. (QCC standards US14, US15, US16, US17)
	SSUSH8: The student will explain the relationship between growing north-south divisions and westward expansion. (QCC standards US14, US15, US16, US18)
	SSUSH9: The student will identify key events, issues, and individuals relating to the causes, course, and consequences of the Civil War. (QCC standards US18, US20)

4.1 Industrial Revolution and Manifest Destiny

The Growth of Industry

During the late eighteenth and early nineteenth centuries, the western world experienced the **Industrial Revolution**. It was a time when advances in technology led to massive economic changes. Before the Industrial Revolution, national economies tended to rely on artisans, merchants, and farmers. As a result, manufacturing was slow, as products had to be crafted individually by hand. With industrialization, however, factories that relied on mechanization (use of machines) began to transform manufacturing and replace manual labor with industry. The "revolution" began in Great Britain, but it soon spread throughout the western world, impacting trade and economies around the globe.

Watt Steam Engine

Eli Whitney

One of the United States' most important figures during the industrial revolution was **Eli Whitney**. In 1793,he invented his famous **cotton gin**. The machine allowed people to process harvested cotton much faster and made the South a "cotton kingdom" (nickname given to the South as cotton became its most profitable crop and the basis of the South's economy during the 1800s). Because the cotton gin led to a boom in cotton plantations, it also made the South very dependent on slave labor.

While Whitney's cotton gin impacted the South, it was another of his innovations that transformed the economy of the North. After the cotton gin, Whitney began to manufacture muskets. In this industry, he introduced the idea of **interchangeable parts**. For the first time, each part of the musket was produced with such precision that it could fit with parts from any other musket. Whitney's concept of interchangeable parts spread to other industries and became a key principle behind industrial development.

Eli Whitney

Sectionalism

The Industrial Revolution also had another, unforeseen circumstance: **sectionalism**. Sectionalism refers to the economic, social, cultural, and political differences that exist between different parts of the country. As Whitney's cotton gin helped transform the South into a plantation system dependent on slaves and cotton, the North became a region growing more dependent on factories and immigrant labor. Such economic differences caused strains on the nation that led to bitter disputes. Meanwhile, the West became a growing frontier as technology like the steel plow, barbed wire, and railroads allowed small landowners and aspiring plantation masters to move west.

Manifest Destiny

As the United States approached the middle of the nineteenth century, many leaders and citizens believed it was God's sovereign will for the US to expand and possess territory all the way to the Pacific Ocean. They considered it the nation's sacred duty to conquer the West, and labeled their ideology **Manifest Destiny**.

Texas and Oregon

James K Polk

In 1821, Mexico gained independence from Spain. Along with its independence, Mexico also gained control of **Texas**, a region which included a large number of US settlers. Fifteen years later, in 1836, Texans fought for and won their independence from Mexico. Wanting to become part of the United States, Texas asked to be annexed (made part of the US). President Andrew Jackson favored annexing Texas, but he could not overcome northern opposition. Northerners knew that Texas would be admitted as a slave state. They also feared that, because of its large size, the area might be divided into *several* slave states, thereby giving slave states an advantage in Congress. Texas remained an independent nation and became a key issue during the election of 1844. James K. Polk took a strong stand as the Democratic candidate, calling for the annexation of both Texas and Oregon (the northwest territory explored years before by Lewis and Clark). Polk ultimately defeated the Whig candidate, Henry Clay, and won the presidency. (The Whigs and Democrats were the two dominant political parties at the time.) Inspired by Polk's victory, his predecessor, President John Tyler, called for a joint resolution of Congress prior to leaving office. At his urging, Congress passed a resolution admitting Texas to the Union as a slave state in 1845.

With the question of Texas settled, Polk turned his attention to acquiring **Oregon**. In 1827, the US and Great Britain reaffirmed their agreement to occupy the Oregon territory jointly. Beginning in 1843, thousands of US settlers moved to Oregon seeking a better life. President Polk approached Britain, arguing that the US had rightful claim to the territory up to 54°40'N latitude. Thus arose the slogan, "54-40, or fight!" Polk's aggressive tone irritated the British, but they were ready to give up Oregon because the territory was no longer profitable. Furthermore, the United States had become an important consumer of British goods, leading Britain to desire friendly terms with the US. The United States accepted a treaty declaring the 49th parallel as the official boundary and, in 1846, Oregon became a US territory.

War With Mexico and the Gadsden Purchase

In 1846, disputes over the US-Mexican border led to **war with Mexico**. The war was a series of US victories leading up to September 14, 1847, when General Winfield Scott finally marched his troops into Mexico City and forced Mexico to surrender. After months of negotiations, the US and Mexico finally ended the war with the Treaty of Guadalupe-Hidalgo on February 2, 1848. The treaty required Mexico to surrender the New Mexico and California territories to the United States in exchange for financial compensation. However, in 1853, boundary disputes with Mexico still remained. President Franklin Pierce sent James Gadsden to settle the problem and to purchase land for a southern transcontinental railroad. The **Gadsden Purchase** gave the

United States parts of present-day New Mexico and Arizona in exchange for $10 million. The acquisition of these territories all but completed the continental expansion envisioned by those who believed in Manifest Destiny.

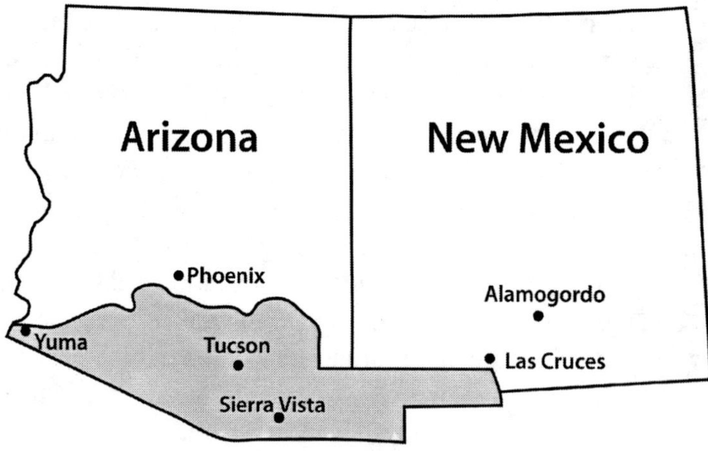

Gadsden Purchase Map

CALIFORNIA

In 1848, settlers discovered gold just north of Sacramento, California. The following year, gold seekers came from all over the world as part of the California **Gold Rush of 1849**. These new arrivals came to be known as "49ers," and they rapidly increased California's population. This growth produced a need for stable government, almost overnight. When the debate over slavery prevented Congress from organizing the territory, Californians took matters into their own hands by drafting and approving their own constitution. Finally, thanks to the Compromise of 1850, Congress admitted California as a free state on September 9, 1850. (see section 4.2.)

California Gold Rush Sign

Sutters Mill

Practice 4.1 Industrial Revolution and Manifest Destiny

1. What effect did the US war with Mexico have?

   A. The US invaded and annexed Texas.
   B. The US marched into Sacramento and forced Mexico to surrender California.
   C. The US agreed to give back Texas in exchange for California.
   D. The US acquired territory that eventually became Arizona and New Mexico.

2. Define "Manifest Destiny."

3. Who invented the cotton gin and interchangeable parts?
   A. Eli Whitney
   B. Samuel Slater
   C. Robert Fulton
   D. Cyrus McCormick

4. In what ways did the Industrial Revolution impact both the northern and southern United States? How did it impact western territories?

4.2 Social and Political Reform

Jacksonian Democracy

Andrew Jackson

One great supporter of Manifest Destiny was **Andrew Jackson**. He was a war hero who had defeated the British at New Orleans in 1814 and forced concessions from the Spanish that led to Florida becoming a US territory in 1819 (it became a state in 1845). In addition, Jackson was a "common man." Unlike previous US political leaders, he was not born into the privileged upper class. Instead, he achieved his success despite growing up relatively poor and uneducated. As a result, he was very popular with western frontier settlers and "common folk." In 1824, he decided to take advantage of his popularity and ran for president. He lost. However, Jackson returned victoriously in 1828 to become the nation's first "common man" president.

Universal (White Male) Suffrage

Jackson's brand of politics and the changes he inspired came to be called **Jacksonian Democracy**. Jackson believed strongly in western expansion and the rights of white frontier settlers. He, like many westerners, resented "eastern elites" and political leaders who seemed to favor the upper class and passed laws favoring the wealthy. As a result, Jackson backed **universal suffrage**. In other words, he believed that all white men should be free to vote, not just those who owned property. With the support of men like Jackson, all but a few states dropped property requirements for voting. Expanding suffrage made the nation more democratic and enabled "simpler men" like Jackson to win public office, rather than simply those from the upper class. (It is important to remember, however, that even Jacksonian Democracy did not attempt to extend the right to vote to women, blacks, or Native Americans.)

The "Spoils System," Strict Interpretation, and Laissez-Faire Economics

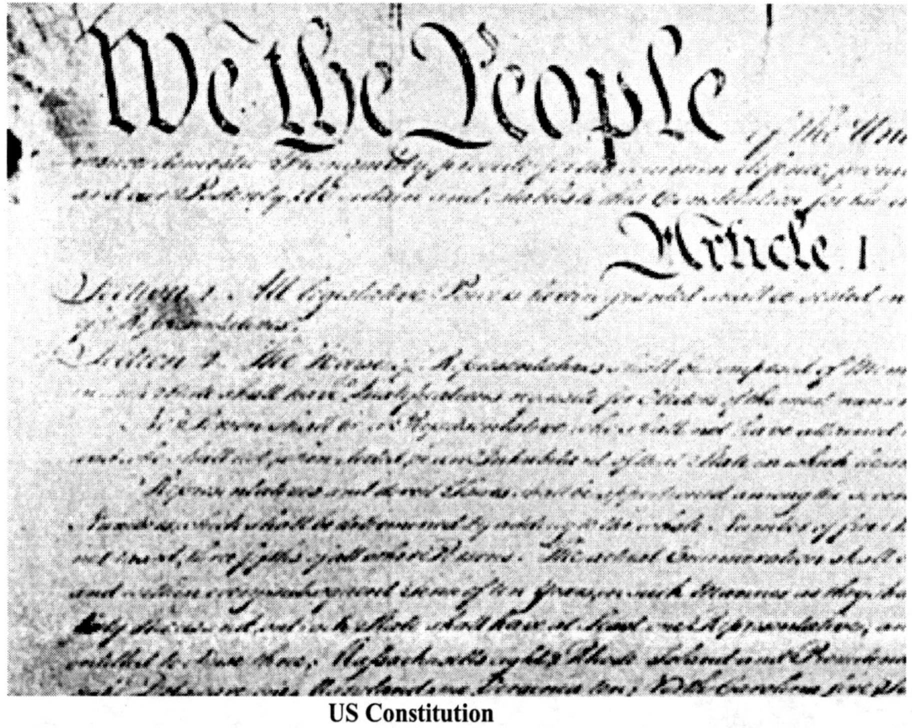

US Constitution

Once in office, Jackson instituted a policy of rewarding his political supporters with government positions. This policy became known as the *spoils system*, and set a precedent for rewarding faithful supporters with government jobs. Jackson believed it was a great way to encourage common people to become politically involved and ensure that wealthy politicians would not continually dominate the government. However, it ultimately led to corruption and a call for reform.

Jackson and his followers also favored *laissez-faire economics*. In other words, they did not think that the government should either regulate business or pass policies to help US businessmen. They believed that such measures tended to favor wealthy easterners while hurting southern farmers and western landowners. Jackson did not want to hurt large US businesses and landowners, but he did want to make sure that smaller merchants and small landowners had as much chance to succeed as rich manufacturers. Therefore, he sometimes supported tariffs he did not see as a threat to small farmers.

Jackson also had a *strict interpretation of the Constitution*. Although he often pushed the bounds of presidential power and was even accused by his enemies of acting more like a king than a president, Andrew Jackson believed that the federal government should be restricted to only those powers the Constitution specifically gave it.

INDIAN REMOVAL

Trail of Tears

As mentioned earlier, Jackson believed in Manifest Destiny and westward expansion. He saw the Native Americans that occupied territories to the west as an obstacle to be removed. As a result, he supported **Indian Removal**. Under this policy, the US government forced Native Americans off lands it wanted for white settlement. Perhaps the most famous example of Jackson's support for this policy was his refusal to help the Cherokee in north Georgia and the western Carolinas. Despite the fact that the Cherokee had helped Jackson defeat his enemies at the battle of Horseshoe Bend during the War of 1812, Jackson supported Georgia's efforts to remove the tribe from their lands during the 1830s. Jackson's policies ultimately led to the forced removal of the Cherokee in 1838. Their march west to Oklahoma became known as the **Trail of Tears** because of the many Cherokee who suffered and died along the way.

RETURN OF THE TWO-PARTY SYSTEM

Eventually, sharp differences between Jackson and men like Henry Clay, Daniel Webster, and John C. Calhoun led to a break in the Jeffersonian Republican Party. Jackson's wing took the name "Democrats" while his opponents adopted the name "National Republicans." Eventually, many of the National Republicans formed a new party, the "Whigs." They chose this name because it was the name of the British party that opposed King George III during the Revolutionary War. Since they accused Jackson of acting like "King Andrew," they adopted the name "Whig" as well. After an "era of good feelings," the **two-party system** returned to national politics with a vengeance. Jackson left office after his second term, and Vice President Martin Van Buren succeeded him in office.

SOCIAL REFORMS

Horace Mann

A number of **social reform movements** began during the 1800s. These movements aimed to transform society in beneficial ways. Horace Mann was an influential American educator who advocated **education reform**. He wanted both men and women to have access to public education and believed that education was essential to the success of democracy. He helped to create the state Board of Education in Massachusetts, the first of its kind in the United States. Such efforts in Massachusetts inspired other states to make reforms in education as well. During the early nineteenth century, the **temperance movement** began gaining popularity. Members of this movement wanted to moderate the use of alcohol. Later, they advocated total abstinence from alcohol and succeeded in convincing several states to pass laws prohibiting its sale. The temperance movement owed much of its success to the efforts of women and church leaders in the US. In the 1830s, the **abolitionist movement** gained momentum despite being seen by most as a movement of fanatics. As always, slavery remained a hot topic in the nation. The South found itself dependent on the practice for economic support. Meanwhile, in the North, a movement to abolish slavery was growing. White members of this movement were mostly middle class, educated church people from New England (many of whom were Quakers). Black abolitionists were mostly former slaves. Eventually, the movement gained enough support and respectability that it helped give birth to a new political party and changed the course of the nation. (see section 4.3)

Women's Rights Movement

Women had participated in the abolitionist and temperance movements, only to face discrimination from the men with whom they'd served. The offense these women suffered led to the birth of the **Women's Rights Movement**. Women such as **Elizabeth Cady Stanton** helped organize the first women's rights convention, known as the **Seneca Falls Conference**, in 1848. Stanton used the occasion to call for **women's suffrage** (women having the right to vote). Such boldness shocked many of her fellow activists. Although some felt Stanton went too far by demanding suffrage, the conference went a long way in drawing attention to the issue of women's rights.

Practice 4.2 Social and Political Reform

1. Who would have most likely supported Andrew Jackson?

   A. a wealthy, eastern businessman
   B. a National Republican
   C. a western farmer
   D. a Whig

2. What was Andrew Jackson's view concerning suffrage?

   A. he believed everyone living in the US should be allowed to vote.
   B. he believed any white man should be allowed to vote.
   C. he favored restricting suffrage to landowners.
   D. he thought that whites and Native Americans should be allowed to vote, but not blacks.

3. Describe Jackson's views regarding the government's role in economic matters and interpretations of the Constitution.

4. Elizabeth Cady Stanton is most identified with

   A. Jacksonian democracy.
   B. education reform.
   C. abolition.
   D. women's suffrage.

5. What was significant about the Seneca Falls conference?

4.3 Slavery, Secession, and the Civil War

Slavery and States' Rights

Slaves Working

Tensions over **slavery** continued to rise during the mid nineteenth century. Planters in the South depended on slaves to provide labor for their huge cotton plantations. Because the South's economy depended heavily on agriculture and large plantations, southern politicians fought to uphold slavery and see that it was expanded into new territories. Meanwhile, the North's economy did not depend on slave labor because it was more industrialized. As a result, many northern states had already emancipated (freed) their slaves and outlawed slavery by the mid 1800s. Therefore, northern politicians wanted to see the expansion of slavery halted, if not the entire institution brought to an end. Some leaders took this stand on moral grounds, seeing slavery as an abomination. Others opposed it for economic and/or political reasons. The struggle between the two regions led to constant battles for power in the national government. Each side knew that whoever controlled Congress could ultimately pass laws either strengthening or dismantling slavery.

Southerners responded to the political struggle over slavery by advocating **states' rights**. Supporters of state's rights believed that the federal government should restrict itself to powers specifically stated in the Constitution and that all else should be left to the states. This was in large part because they did not trust northern politicians whom they believed were out to end slavery.

South Carolina Nullification Crisis

John C Calhoun

The conflict between state's rights and federal authority reached a boiling point in the early 1830s. President Jackson experienced a serious test when South Carolina began protesting high tariffs on British goods (tariffs are taxes on imports). Southerners often opposed such measures because they believed the national government used tariffs to help rich, northern businessmen at the expense of small landowners and southern planters. One of South Carolina's senators (and, for a time, Jackson's vice president), **John C. Calhoun**, took center stage when he wrote a pamphlet entitled *Exposition and Protest.* Calhoun argued for states' rights and asserted that any state could refuse to enforce a law it saw as unconstitutional. In 1832, South Carolina threatened to invoke this right and **secede** (leave the Union) if the offensive tariffs were not repealed. Although President Jackson did not like tariffs either, he recognized Congress' authority to pass them and he expected states to comply. Enraged, he threatened to hang Calhoun personally and prepared to call up federal troops to force South Carolina's compliance. Fortunately, Senator Henry Clay of Kentucky proposed a compromise that both sides could accept. Clay's compromise ended the **South Carolina Nullification Crisis**, but the issues of states' rights and secession remained alive until the end of the Civil War. The crisis also served to harden the sectionalism between the North and South. Northerners began to call more and more on the national government to limit slavery. Meanwhile, the South rallied around the banner of state's rights, making men like John C. Calhoun regional heroes.

THE ABOLITIONIST MOVEMENT

While some sought merely to limit slavery's expansion into new territories, others were determined to end the institution completely. They advocated the abolition of slavery and became known as **abolitionists**. Among key white figures in this movement was **William Lloyd Garrison**. Garrison founded an influential, anti-slavery newspaper called *The Liberator* in 1831 and helped establish the *American Anti-Slavery Society*. Meanwhile, important African American abolitionists included men like **Frederick Douglass**. After escaping slavery in Maryland, Douglass educated himself and became the most prominent African American speaker for the abolition of slavery. In addition to Douglass, many other African American men and women played key roles in the abolitionist movement.

Frederick Douglass

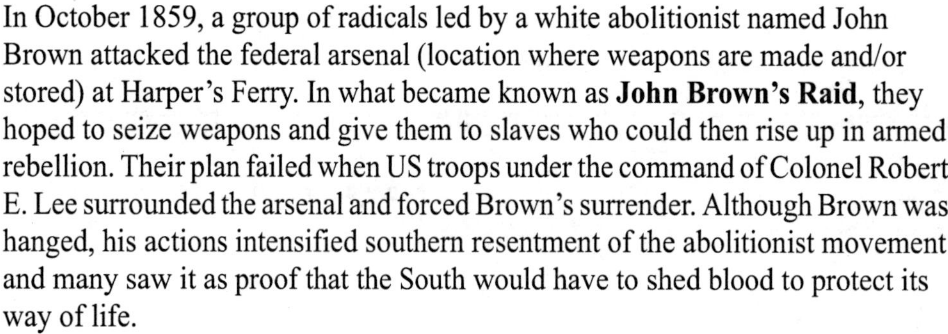

In October 1859, a group of radicals led by a white abolitionist named John Brown attacked the federal arsenal (location where weapons are made and/or stored) at Harper's Ferry. In what became known as **John Brown's Raid**, they hoped to seize weapons and give them to slaves who could then rise up in armed rebellion. Their plan failed when US troops under the command of Colonel Robert E. Lee surrounded the arsenal and forced Brown's surrender. Although Brown was hanged, his actions intensified southern resentment of the abolitionist movement and many saw it as proof that the South would have to shed blood to protect its way of life.

John Brown

SLAVERY AND NEW TERRITORIES

As the US acquired new territories in the West, the debate over slavery grew more intense. New territories would eventually become states. States would send representatives and senators to Congress. Therefore, whether or not these territories should allow slavery was the object of much heated debate among political leaders.

THE MISSOURI COMPROMISE

Free northern states opposed the addition of new slave states. Conversely, southern states feared that the addition of free states would leave them at a political disadvantage. In 1819, a debate raged in Congress over Missouri's application for statehood. Slave states and free states were equally represented in the Senate, and Missouri's admission would disrupt the balance of power. Missouri was also the first territory applying for statehood west of the Mississippi River. How Missouri entered the union would set the stage for future US expansion. Senator Jesse B. Thomas of Illinois proposed a bill calling for the admission of Missouri as a slave state and Maine as a free state. In addition, the southern boundary of Missouri, 36°30' N, would become a dividing line for any new states admitted to the Union. All new states north of that line would be free states, while those to the south would be slave states. Congress passed the bill and President Monroe signed it into law in 1820. It became known as the **Missouri Compromise**, and it was designed to maintain the balance of power in Washington, DC.

The Wilmot Proviso

As discussed earlier, the United States went to war with Mexico in 1846. Even before the war was over, it became evident that the issue of slavery would once again be a major problem. Victory over Mexico would mean new territories and the question of whether or not they should allow slavery. During the conflict, a Pennsylvania congressman named David Wilmot put forth what would come to be known as the **Wilmot Proviso**. This *proviso,* or condition, proposed banning slavery from any land purchased from Mexico. Northerners embraced the idea, but southerners denounced it. Congress eventually voted down the Wilmot Proviso. Still, it stirred debate exposing the serious divisions over slavery that existed in the country.

The Compromise of 1850

Compromise of 1850

Another key piece of legislation was the **Compromise of 1850**. The compromise admitted California to the Union as a free state and declared the unorganized western territories free as well. The Utah and New Mexico territories, however, were allowed to decide the issue by **popular sovereignty** (the will of the majority). The people living in these territories would vote on whether or not to allow slavery. Attached to the compromise was the *Fugitive Slave Law.* This law required that northern states forcibly return escaped slaves to their owners in the South. Because the law was unpopular in the North, however, many northern citizens refused to obey it.

The Kansas-Nebraska Act

In 1854, Congress passed the **Kansas-Nebraska Act**. This act allowed the previously free and unorganized territories of Kansas and Nebraska to choose whether or not to permit slavery by popular sovereignty. Its guidelines effectively repealed the Missouri Compromise and reignited the slavery issue. Both supporters of slavery and abolitionists rushed into Kansas, eventually setting up rival governments. The territory became known as "Bleeding Kansas" as armed clashes between the two sides became common. Meanwhile, in Washington, the act inspired emotional reaction. Charles Sumner, a fiery senator from Massachusetts who opposed slavery, strongly denounced the act and the act's writers in a speech that spanned two days. A couple of days after the speech, a South Carolina congressman, Preston Brooks, approached Sumner on the Senate floor. He was insulted by Sumner's words both because he was from the South and because he was related to one of the act's authors. Brooks beat Sumner with a heavy cane, almost killing him. The attack caused Sumner to be absent from the Senate for three years while he recovered from his injuries. The Sumner-Brooks incident was a brutal example of how inflamed passions had become over slavery.

The Dred Scott Decision

The 1857 **Dred Scott case** threw the nation further into turmoil. Dred Scott, a slave in Missouri, went with his owner into free territory where he lived for four years. The owner later returned to Missouri, where he died. After his death, Dred Scott sued for his freedom. The Supreme Court ruled that Scott had no right to sue because, as a slave, he was not a citizen. It also declared that a slave owner could not be deprived of his "property" without due process of law. The decision struck down the Missouri Compromise because it declared that it was a violation of the Fifth Amendment to declare slaves free of their owners without due process of law — even if that slave had entered a free state. The decision outraged both abolitionists and those who favored popular sovereignty because it suggested that slaveholders could keep their slaves in any state.

Dred Scott

The Civil War

Lincoln and the Election of 1860

Jefferson Davis

Abraham Lincoln

In 1854, a coalition of northern Democrats who opposed slavery, Whigs, and Free Soilers (a party opposing slavery in new territories) came together and formed the *Republican Party.* While the Republicans did not call for the immediate abolition of slavery, they did adopt the Free Soilers' position of opposing the extension of slavery into new US territories. In 1860, Abraham Lincoln ran for president as the Republican candidate. The South felt threatened by Lincoln's candidacy because he considered slavery a moral evil. The southern states feared that Lincoln would seek not only to prevent slavery in the new territories, but to dismantle it in the South as well. When Lincoln won the election, South Carolina responded by **seceding** (withdrawing) from the Union on December 20, 1860. Within two months, six other states had seceded as well: Mississippi, Alabama, Georgia, Florida, Louisiana, and Texas. In February 1861, southern delegates from the seceded states met in Montgomery, Alabama to draft their own constitution and elected **Jefferson**

Davis to serve as president of the new *Confederate States of America.* (They chose a Georgian, Alexander Stephens, to be their Vice President.) The Civil War began a few months later when Confederate forces fired on Union troops at Fort Sumter, South Carolina.

Key Figures of the Civil War

Abraham Lincoln: President of the United States of America during the Civil War and the first Republican president in history.

Ulysses S. Grant: Initially an effective general in the Union's western battles, he eventually assumed command of the entire Union army in 1864. He defeated the South and accepted Robert E. Lee's surrender at Appomatox Courthouse. He went on to become the 18th president of the United States.

William T. Sherman: Union general who took command of the western forces after Grant decided to remain with troops in the East. His capture of Atlanta in 1864 signaled to both the North and the South that the war was all but won for the Union and helped Lincoln win re-election in 1864. He is most remembered for his "march to the sea," in which he burned and destroyed southern cities and railways in an effort to disrupt the Confederate war effort and trap Lee between himself and General Grant.

Jefferson Davis: First and only president of the Confederate States of America.

Robert E. Lee: Assumed command of the Confederacy's Army of Northern Virginia after General Joseph Johnston was injured. Despite winning several impressive victories during the course of the war, he did not have nearly enough men to sustain the war effort past early 1865. He eventually surrendered to General Grant.

Thomas "Stonewall" Jackson: Confederate general and right-hand man to Robert E. Lee. Noted for his ability to use geography to his advantage, he swiftly navigated the Shenandoah Valley which stretched from the Allegheny Mountains in northern Virginia north towards Washington, D.C. One of his most brilliant moves came at the battle of Chancellorsville, when he successfully marched his troops over 12 miles undetected and attacked the unsuspecting Union forces. Jackson was such an effective leader that many believe the South would have won the war had he lived to fight at Gettysburg.

Ulysses S Grant

Robert E Lee

Thomas "Stonewall" Jackson

Antietam and The Emancipation Proclamation

On land, the war was fought on two primary fronts, or *theaters*: eastern and western. In 1862, Robert E. Lee assumed command of the Army of Northern Virginia after General Joseph Johnston was wounded. After defeating the Union army at the Second Battle of Bull Run, he devised a plan to invade the North. Lee and his generals tried to maintain secrecy as they made preparations for their invasion. Meanwhile, General McClellan (the Union's commanding general), remained unaware of the Confederate army's whereabouts until a copy of Lee's orders was found wrapped around some cigars at an abandoned Confederate camp. Now aware of Lee's plans, McClellan saw to it that Lee met a prepared Union force at Antietam Creek, Maryland. The battle of **Antietam** proved to be the bloodiest single day of the war, halting the Confederate advance. McClellan hesitated, however, and Lee's army slipped away to fight another day.

On January 1, 1863, following the much needed Union victory at Antietam, Maryland, President Lincoln issued the **Emancipation Proclamation**. This proclamation freed the slaves in the Confederate States, while maintaining slavery in the few slave states that had remained loyal to the Union. Lincoln still needed the support of these states and could not yet risk alienating them by forcing them to give up slavery. With this executive order, Lincoln hoped to give the war a moral focus beyond just saving the Union. He also hoped to undermine the South's reliance on slave labor and ensure the support of England and France — both of which had already abolished slavery. The Emancipation Proclamation also encouraged free African Americans to serve in the Union army. Although originally not allowed to enlist, early Union defeats led Congress to authorize accepting African Americans into the army in 1862. On warships, whites and blacks served side by side. In the army, however, African Americans served only in all black regiments under the command of white officers. Seeing their battle as one to free their own people from the bonds of slavery, African Americans served notably during the war.

Emancipation Proclamation

Chancellorsville and Gettysburg

Gettysburg

The battle of Chancellorsville is known by many as "Lee's perfect battle" because of the great planning and good fortune that aided the Confederates. Thanks to the efforts of his most gifted general, **Thomas "Stonewall" Jackson**, Lee's army defeated more than 70,000 Union troops with only 40,000 Confederate soldiers. Unfortunately for the Confederacy, however, Jackson was accidently shot by his own troops while scouting the enemy's position at night. His left arm had to be amputated, leading to Lee's famous quote, "Jackson has lost his left arm, but I have lost my right." Although his injuries did not initially seem life threatening, Jackson died after contracting pneumonia during his recovery. As a result, Robert E. Lee was without his most talented and reliable commander at Gettysburg.

Fought just outside Gettysburg, Pennsylvania, the battle of **Gettysburg** was a key turning point in the war. Without Jackson to assist him, Lee's forces proved less aggressive than usual and failed to win valuable high ground early in the battle. Union forces under the command of General George Meade defeated Lee's army and ended any hope the South had of successfully invading the North. With more than 51,000 soldiers killed, wounded, or missing, Gettysburg was the bloodiest battle of the entire Civil War.

Vicksburg

In the late spring of 1863, the town of **Vicksburg**, Mississippi was the last Confederate obstacle to total Union control of the Mississippi River. Ignoring advice to withdraw, General Ulysses S. Grant laid siege to Vicksburg for almost two months. A siege is when an army surrounds a city, cuts off its supplies, and starves it into surrendering. By the time the town finally surrendered on July 4, residents had been reduced to eating horses, mules, dogs, and even rats.

Sherman's Atlanta Campaign

William T Sherman

In 1864, Lincoln appointed Grant to be overall commander of the entire Union army. Grant decided to take command of the eastern forces and put his most trusted general, **William T. Sherman**, in charge of his western forces. In May 1864, Sherman began an invasion of Georgia. He wanted to reach Atlanta because of its importance as a railway hub. If Sherman took Atlanta, he could seriously hurt the South by disrupting its major rail lines. As Sherman advanced south, General Johnston's Confederate forces tried to delay his march with several small attacks. Johnston did not want to meet Sherman in a full-scale battle because Sherman had more men and Johnston feared that a defeat would mean the end of his army. Finally, after a series of bloody fights, Johnston's forces prepared to make their stand just north of Atlanta at Kennesaw Mountain. When a direct assault on Kennesaw Mountain failed, Sherman decided to flank (move around) Johnston's army to reach Atlanta. The move worked and, on July 8, the first Union forces crossed the Chattahoochee River to reach the outskirts of Atlanta.

Jefferson Davis was furious with Johnston for not engaging Sherman in a full-scale battle and replaced him with General John Bell Hood. By then, however, it was too late. Hood evacuated the city on September 1, 1864, and Sherman's army moved into Atlanta the very next day. Sherman's successful **Atlanta campaign** not only placed the city under Union control, it also reignited support for President Lincoln in the North. Before Atlanta, many northerners wanted to negotiate with the South and end the war. After Sherman's success, however, people in the Union believed victory was in sight and re-elected Lincoln to a second term.

Sherman's March to the Sea

After taking Atlanta, Sherman ordered much of the city burned. He then began a march from Atlanta to Savannah that became known as his **march to the sea**. On its way to the coast, Sherman's army burned buildings, destroyed rail lines, set fire to factories, and demolished bridges. Sherman hoped to cripple the South's ability to make and ship supplies, so that it could not keep fighting. People in Savannah were so terrified by news of the destruction that, when Sherman finally reached the city, they surrendered without a fight. Sherman then turned north into the Carolinas. All the while, General Joseph Johnston continued trying to resist Sherman as best he could.

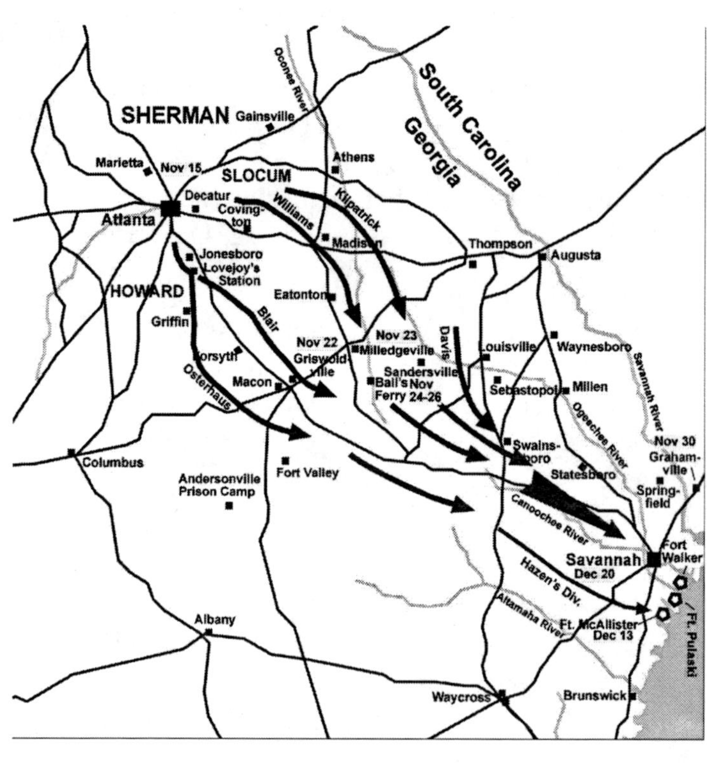

Sherman's March

Union Victory

In March of 1864, President Lincoln put Ulysses S. Grant in command of the Union army. Grant, knowing he had far more men than Lee, began a campaign designed to crush the Confederate army in a series of head-to-head confrontations. Pushing south, Grant engaged Lee in a number of bloody battles. In less than two months, Grant's army suffered some 65,000 casualties. Still, the Union's overwhelming numbers meant that the Confederates were the ones on the retreat. Finally, when Lee's army found itself surrounded in Virginia, the Confederate general elected to surrender rather than see more lives lost. On April 9, 1865, Robert E. Lee surrendered to Ulysses S. Grant at **Appomattox Courthouse**. Although some fighting continued afterwards, this effectively ended the war. Two weeks later, the largest and last major surrender of the war took place when General Joseph Johnston surrendered his Confederate army to General William T. Sherman at a farm house in Durham, North Carolina, known as the Bennett Place.

Looking back, it is not hard to understand why the Union ultimately won the war. The North had a much larger **population**. As a result, the Union army had more men and the Union had more labor to produce war supplies and keep the economy running during the conflict. The North also possessed more **railroads,** allowing the Union to move supplies more efficiently. Finally, the northern economy had much more **industry**. Its factories allowed the Union to produce weapons, ammunition, clothes, blankets, and other supplies much easier and in greater numbers than the South. Although southerners possessed a fiery determination to defend their homeland and way of life, in the end, they could not overcome the North's advantages long enough to win.

Northern Industry

Practice 4.3 Slavery, Secession, and the Civil War

1. It was a major turning point in the war that ended the South's hopes of successfully invading the North. In addition, many believe that had General "Stonewall" Jackson been alive the South would have won this battle and, quite possibly, the war. Which battle was it?

   A. Gettysburg
   B. Antietam
   C. Vicksburg
   D. Chancellorsville

2. How did Sherman's taking of Atlanta greatly impact the election of 1864?

   A. It allowed Lincoln to suspend the *writ of habeas corpus* in Georgia, thereby assuring that only Lincoln's supporters went to the polls.
   B. It inspired faith in military generals, thereby leading to General McClellan being nominated for president.
   C. It assured people in the North that victory was in sight, thereby increasing the popularity of President Lincoln and allowing him to win re-election.
   D. It led to Lincoln's defeat because he lost the support of Southerners whom Sherman had abused.

3. What was the Emancipation Proclamation, what impact did it have on the role of African Americans in the Civil War, and why did it have this impact?

4. Describe some of the advantages the Union had during the war and explain how they contributed to the Confederacy's defeat.

Chapter 4 Review

Key terms, people, and concepts

industrial revolution
Eli Whitney
cotton gin
interchangeable parts
sectionalism
Manifest Destiny
Texas
Oregon
war with Mexico
Gadsden Purchase
Gold Rush of 1849
Andrew Jackson
Jacksonian Democracy
universal suffrage
Indian Removal
Trail of Tears
two-party system
social reform movements
education reform
temperance movement
abolitionist movement
women's rights movement
Elizabeth Cady Stanton
Seneca Falls Conference
women's suffrage

slavery

states' rights
John C. Calhoun
South Carolina Nullification Crisis
William Lloyd Garrison
Frederick Douglass
John Brown's Raid
Missouri Compromise
the Wilmot Proviso
the Compromise of 1850
Kansas-Nebraska Act
Dred Scott Case
Abraham Lincoln
secession
Jefferson Davis
Ulysses S. Grant
William T. Sherman
Robert E. Lee
Thomas "Stonewall" Jackson
Emancipation Proclamation
Gettysburg
Vicksburg
the Atlanta campaign
march to the sea
Appomatox Courthouse
northern advantages (population, industry, railroads)

Multiple Choice Questions

1. A time that featured new technology and economic change and led to the rise of men like Eli Whitney was known as
   - A. the Civil War.
   - B. Jacksonian Democracy.
   - C. era of good feelings.
   - D. the industrial revolution.

2. The South's heavy reliance on slaves and cotton, along with the North's increased dependency on immigrant labor and industry, contributed to
   - A. Manifest Destiny.
   - B. Jacksonian Democracy.
   - C. sectionalism.
   - D. war with Mexico.

3. Which of the following were passed by Congress to deal with the issue of slavery in newly acquired territories?
   - A. the Wilmot Proviso and the Nullification Compromise
   - B. the Missouri Compromise and the Compromise of 1850
   - C. the Doctrine of Nullification and the Emancipation Proclamation
   - D. the Doctrine of Nullification and the Missouri Compromise

4. A southern politician in the 1800s would have MOST LIKELY supported which of the following?
   - A. the Republicans
   - B. abolition
   - C. tariffs
   - D. states' rights

5. Why was the issue of slavery in new US territories so politically heated in the 1800s?
   - A. Most politicians knew that they could not win enough votes to stay in office if they did not openly oppose slavery.
   - B. Settlers in new territories opposed slavery and did not like Congress requiring them to allow the practice.
   - C. Southern pro-slavery leaders and northern anti-slavery leaders both wanted to maintain their power in Washington and spread their ideology to new territories that would eventually become states.
   - D. Nearly every new state allowed slavery while almost all politicians in Washington, DC had decided that the practice should be outlawed.

6. "It was a horrible scene. For well over a month, the enemy sat encamped around the city. They let no one out, and no supplies in. We held out as best we could, but by the end, we were eating mules, rats... anything we could get our hands on. Finally, we had no choice but to surrender."

The above quote was MOST LIKELY made by whom?

   - A. a slave forced to fight at Gettysburg
   - B. a citizen of Vicksburg
   - C. a citizen of Atlanta
   - D. a Confederate making a stand at Appomatox

7. Sherman wanted to capture Atlanta because
   A. it was a major railroad hub and its capture would disrupt southern industry.
   B. it was the southern capital and its capture would end the war.
   C. it was the only city that interfered with Union trade on the Mississippi River.
   D. it was home to Robert E. Lee's Army of Northern Virginia.

8. In the end, the South could not defeat the Union because
   A. the South never won any battles.
   B. the South had too many railroads and factories to keep manned with labor.
   C. the North had too much manpower and industry.
   D. the North did not have to worry about protecting railroads.

9. "Slavery is an evil straight from hell. They may have hanged him as a criminal, but rest assured, he will sing in glory next to the holy angels, while them that hanged him for trying to free his fellow man will burn in the devil's fire for all eternity."

Who most likely made the above statement and who were they most likely talking about?

   A. an advocate of states' rights talking about John Brown
   B. an abolitionist talking about Dred Scott
   C. a supporter of popular sovereignty talking about Dred Scott
   D. an abolitionist talking about John Brown

10. What effect did Manifest Destiny have?
   A. It improved relations between the US and Mexico.
   B. It made Texas a free republic.
   C. It extended US territory all the way to the Pacific.
   D. It resulted in universal suffrage.

11. Someone who believed women should have the right to vote in the 1800s would have most likely supported
   A. Andrew Jackson.
   B. Elizabeth Cady Stanton.
   C. Eli Whitney.
   D. Horace Mann.

12. Andrew Jackson would have been most supportive of
   A. a slave's right to freedom.
   B. woman's suffrage.
   C. the Whig Party.
   D. white frontiersmen having a voice in politics.

Chapter 5
United States History: Reconstruction Through World War I.

GPS	SSUSH10: The student will identify legal, political, and social dimensions of Reconstruction. (QCC standard US21)
	SSUSH11: The student will describe the growth of big business and technological innovations after Reconstruction. (QCC standards US22, US23, US24)
	SSUSH12: The student will analyze important consequences of American industrial growth. (QCC standards US22, US23, US24)
	SSUSH13: The student will identify major efforts to reform American society and politics in the Progressive Era. (QCC standards US22, US24, US25, US27, US29, US30)
	SSUSH14: The student will explain America's evolving relationship with the world at the turn of the twentieth century. (QCC standards US24, US26, US28)
	SSUSH15: The student will analyze the origins and impact of U.S. involvement in World War I. (QCC standards US29, US30)

5.1 Southern Reconstruction

Andrew Johnson and the Radical Republicans

Presidential Reconstruction

With the Union preserved, Lincoln introduced a plan for rebuilding, rather than punishing, the South. Sadly, however, Lincoln would not live to see the nation healed. On April 14, 1865, just five days after the surrender at Appomattox Courthouse, a Confederate sympathizer named John Wilkes Booth assassinated the president as he attended a play at Ford's Theatre. With Lincoln's death, the presidency fell to Andrew Johnson. Johnson proved sympathetic to the South and pursued his own plan of **Presidential Reconstruction**. Under Presidential Reconstruction:

Lincoln Assassination

1. Southerners who swore allegiance to the Union were pardoned (forgiven of any crimes against the US).

2. Former Confederate states could hold constitutional conventions to set up state governments.

3. States had to void (cancel) secession and ratify the **Thirteenth Amendment** to the Constitution, which ended slavery throughout the nation.

4. Once the Thirteenth Amendment was ratified, states could then hold elections and be part of the Union.

Andrew Johnson

Johnson initially enacted his brand of reconstruction while Congress was not in session. Under its provisions, many of the same southerners who led the Confederacy held on to their positions of influence in the southern states. Southern states also enacted ***black codes*** (laws that limited the rights of freed blacks so much that they were basically still living like slaves). For instance, blacks had curfews which made it illegal for them to gather after sunset, could be whipped or sold into forced labor (slavery) if they were convicted of vagrancy (not working), had to agree to work for at least a year for whites, and were often restricted to renting land only in rural areas. Such restrictions allowed whites to continue to control and profit from the labor of African Americans even though slavery did not officially exist.

Radical Reconstruction

Radical Republican Leaders

Conflict quickly arose between Johnson and the **Radical Republicans**. The Radical Republicans were members of the Republican party who favored a much tougher stance with the former Confederate states. They believed that Johnson's approach did not do enough because it failed to offer African Americans full citizenship rights. They also believed that Congress, not the president, should oversee Reconstruction, and that the majority of each state's voting population should have to pledge allegiance to the United States before a state could be readmitted to the Union. The Radical Republicans ultimately pushed the Reconstruction Act through Congress in 1867. The law established much stricter guidelines on the South that came to be known as **Radical Reconstruction**. Under Radical Reconstruction:

1. The southern states were put under military rule.

2. Southern states had to hold new constitutional conventions.

3. African Americans were allowed to vote.

4. Southerners who had supported the Confederacy were temporarily not allowed to vote.

5. Southern states had to guarantee equal rights to African Americans.

6. Southern states had to ratify the **Fourteenth Amendment** which made African Americans citizens of their respective states as well as the nation.

FEDERAL LEGISLATION

Thaddeus Stevens

Prior to Lincoln's death, Congress passed the **Thirteenth Amendment** to the Constitution. The Thirteenth Amendment ended slavery throughout the United States. The **Fourteenth Amendment** guaranteed that no person, regardless of race, would be deprived of life, liberty, or property without due process of law. It granted national and state citizenship to African Americans. Finally, the last major piece of Reconstruction legislation was the **Fifteenth Amendment**. Ratified during the presidency of Ulysses S. Grant, it guaranteed African Americans the right to vote in elections.

JOHNSON'S IMPEACHMENT

The battle between Congress and President Johnson came to a head in 1868. Johnson tried to fire Secretary of War Edwin Stanton because he was closely tied to the Radical Republicans. However, such a move violated the Tenure in Office Act, which limited the president's power to hire and fire government officials. Led by a fiery Radical Republican congressman named Thaddeus Stevens, Congress voted to **impeach** (charge with wrongdoing in order to remove from office) the president of the United States. On May 16, 1868, the Senate voted to spare Johnson's presidency by just one vote.

AFRICAN AMERICANS AND RECONSTRUCTION

FARMING AND THE FREEDMEN'S BUREAU

The Thirteenth Amendment freed the slaves. Next, African Americans in the South had to adjust to life after slavery. In order to survive, many turned to **sharecropping**. Under this practice, a family farmed a portion of a white landowner's land in return for housing and a share of the crop. Many sharecroppers, unfortunately, fell victim to dishonest landowners who subjected them to what amounted to slavery. Sharecroppers who were fortunate enough to have an honest landowner and good crops sometimes advanced to **tenant farming**. Tenant farmers paid rent to farm the land and owned the crops they grew. Although tenant farmers were less at the mercy of white landowners than sharecroppers, both lived under systems designed to keep African Americans working white-owned land.

Sharecropper

In an effort to help freed slaves, Congress created the **Freedmen's Bureau** in 1865. As the first federal relief agency in US history, the Freedmen's Bureau provided clothes, medical attention, food, education, and even land to African Americans coming out of slavery. Lacking support, it eventually ended in 1869. However, during its brief time, it helped many slaves transition to freedom throughout the South.

White Resistance

Freedmans Bureau

After the Radical Republicans passed the Reconstruction Act, the black codes passed under Presidential Reconstruction lost much of their power. Many southern whites, however, continued to resist giving African Americans equal rights. Some even advocated violence against freed blacks. Perhaps the most notorious group to use such tactics was the **Ku Klux Klan**. A secretive organization whose members often dressed in hooded white robes, the Klan used violence, murder, and threats to intimidate blacks and those who favored giving African Americans equal rights. The Klan practiced lynchings (mob initiated murders in which the victim is kidnapped and murdered) and other acts of violence against blacks until the mid twentieth century.

The End of Reconstruction

Ku Klux Klan

Reconstruction finally ended in 1877. After a controversial presidential election in 1876, Democrats finally agreed to give the presidency to the Republican candidate, Rutherford B. Hayes, in exchange for Washington loosening its grip on the southern states. With the end of Reconstruction and the rise of groups like the Ku Klux Klan, African Americans soon lost whatever political position they gained in the years following emancipation. Southern states passed **Jim Crow laws** that required blacks and whites to use separate public facilities. Many states also tried to avoid upholding the Fifteenth Amendment by requiring citizens to pass **literacy tests** or pay **poll taxes** in order to vote. Literacy tests required that a citizen prove he could read/write, while poll taxes required voters to pay a set amount of money in order to vote. Since most African Americans in the South tended to be poor and uneducated, the new laws prevented many of them from voting. In order to keep these laws from hindering poor and illiterate whites, some states instituted **grandfather clauses**. These clauses exempted citizens from restrictions on voting if they, or their ancestors, had voted in previous elections or served in the Confederate military. Since whites had enjoyed the right to vote for years and because it was mostly whites who had fought for the Confederacy, grandfather clauses allowed poor and illiterate whites to vote, while excluding African Americans.

Practice 5.1 Southern Reconstruction

1. Describe the differences between Presidential Reconstruction and Radical Reconstruction. Who backed each view and which one eventually won?

2. The purpose of the Fourteenth Amendment was to
   A. end slavery.
   B. ensure African Americans had the right to vote.
   C. make sure that African Americans were recognized as citizens.
   D. place military rule over southern states during Reconstruction.

3. The Amendment to the Constitution that was intended to give African Americans the right to vote was the
   A. Thirteenth Amendment
   B. Fourteenth Amendment
   C. Fifteenth Amendment
   D. Reconstruction Act of 1867

5.2 Industrial Growth and Western Expansion

Railroads and Giants of Big Business

Railroads and the West

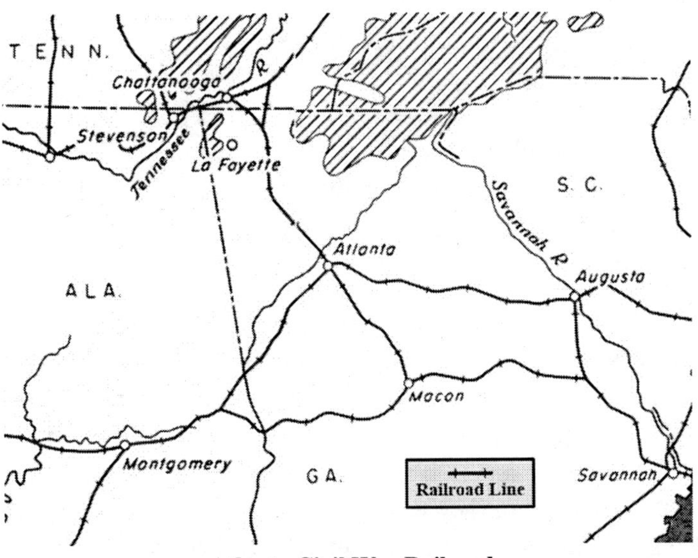

Atlanta Civil War Railroad

Following the Civil War, the US continued to expand and become more and more industrialized. **Railroads** played a major role in this industrial growth and expansion. Railroads made life in the West possible by allowing farmers, ranchers, and other settlers access to eastern markets and resources. They also made it easier for people to move west and populate territories at a rapid rate. In 1862, Congress coordinated an effort among the railroad companies to build a *transcontinental railroad.* Union Pacific (an eastern rail company) and Central Pacific (a rail company from Sacramento, California) joined their tracks at Promontory, Utah, in 1869. The completion of the transcontinental railroad would not have been possible without the contribution of thousands of **Irish and Chinese immigrants**. These immigrants often worked under very dangerous conditions. Laying railroad track could cause injury or even death. Attacks from hostile Native Americans were always a possibility. Railroad workers labored in the blistering heat of summer months and freezing snowstorms during winter. All the while, their employers paid them very little money. In addition, Chinese workers were often the victims of racism and abuse because of their Asian features and cultural differences. Many who worked on the railroads lost their lives or suffered serious injury in the process of opening the West for further expansion.

Chinese Immigrants

Railroads and Big Business

Railroads also contributed to the rise of the **steel industry and big business**. In the 1850s, a man named Henry Bessemer developed a new method for making steel known as the *Bessemer process*. Using this process, manufacturers could make steel much cheaper. As a result, steel became more affordable, leading to faster expansion of railroads and more construction. Thanks to steel, buildings could be constructed taller than ever before. By building taller buildings, cities like New York could hold more people and industry even though land was limited. Thus, steel became very important to the nation's economy.

Before railroads, most goods had to be transported by water. People couldn't load something like steel beams on wagons and transport it over land very easily. Even if they tried, they would not be able to haul very much. Therefore, water was the only way. Unfortunately, shipping products by water meant that boats had to follow the route of the river and greatly limited what areas had access to goods. Railroads, however, changed this. Since railroads were much larger and faster than wagons, they became a practical and economical way to ship sizeable products over land. As a result, resources necessary for manufacturing things like steel could be transported to the factories where they were produced, while finished goods could reach the people and places that demanded them more easily. Because of their ability to carry goods and resources long distances in a timely fashion, railroads contributed greatly to the growth of big business.

JOHN D. ROCKEFELLER

John D Rockefeller

As industry grew, a few men became incredibly rich. Cornelius Vanderbilt rose to prominence in the railroad industry. Andrew Carnegie dominated the steel industry. Perhaps none was more important than **John D. Rockefeller**. Rockefeller made it big in the oil business and his company, **Standard Oil**, was the nation's first **trust**. A trust is a business arrangement under which a number of companies unite into one system. In effect, trusts serve to destroy competition and create **monopolies** (a market in which there is only one supplier of a product and no market competition). Through the trust, Rockefeller was able to dictate prices, eliminate competition, and control the US oil industry.

URBAN IMPACT OF INDUSTRIALIZATION

New York City in the late 1800s

From the end of the Civil War until the beginning of the 20th century, the size of US cities increased rapidly. When cities increase in size, it is called **urban growth**. In the West, new towns grew out of nothing as railroads and western settlements took hold. Many of these towns grew into bustling cities. Meanwhile, in the East, established cities grew in population due to industrialization and the job opportunities it created. As industrialization continued in the US, many people left their farms and migrated (moved) to the cities where they could earn higher wages. While cities grew in the West and South, it was northern cities like New York that saw the greatest population growth. As for African Americans, most southern blacks tended to either farm, move west, or migrate to cities within the South. Not until the early 20th century did mass numbers of African Americans migrate to northern cities due to the economic opportunities created by World War I.

IMMIGRATION

Ellis Island

In addition, the second half of the nineteenth century also saw a dramatic increase in **immigration** to the United States. In the East, most of these new arrivals came from Europe, while on the west coast, many immigrated from China. Some immigrants came seeking a better life. Others fled hardships like famine. Many hoped to escape political persecution. By the end of the 1880s, nearly 80% of New Yorkers were foreign born. Industrialization was largely responsible for the flow of immigrants. As industry grew and the need for labor increased, the US became a land of promise, much like it had been for the first colonists nearly 300 years before. To handle the large numbers of people arriving in the country, the federal government opened **Ellis Island** in 1892. A tiny island near the Statue of Liberty in New York, it became a well known reception center for immigrants arriving by ship. As more and more people immigrated to the US, the nation's population became very diverse. Such diversity inspired the phrase, "melting pot." In a melting pot, a person mixes different ingredients together as he or she cooks and prepares an appetizing final product. In the same way, many envisioned the United States as a place where people of all backgrounds could come and assimilate into American society. In reality, however, most immigrants did not want to fully assimilate (become like the US mainstream). They wanted to maintain many of their traditional ways. The nation, particularly the large cities, began to experience **cultural pluralism** (presence of many different cultures within one society).

PROBLEMS AND CONCERNS CAUSED BY IMMIGRATION

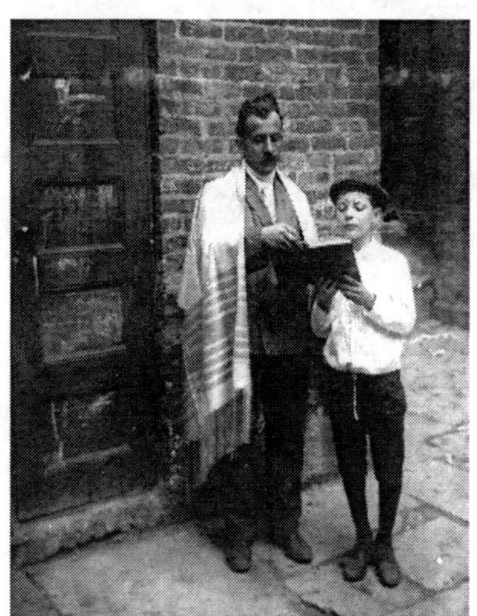
Jewish Immigrants

While immigration had positive effects, such as providing much needed labor for the nation's factories, it also presented problems. Many US citizens looked on immigrants negatively. They felt that immigrants took jobs away from natives (people born in the US), and they often mistrusted foreigners whose cultural ways they could not understand. They also tended to be suspicious of the **ethnic ghettos** within the inner cities. Ghettos were neighborhoods where immigrants from a certain region or country tended to live together due to their common culture, language, and heritage. Many natives saw this as a sign of disloyalty to the United States. **Religious differences** were also a source of tension. Most US citizens were Protestants, while many of the arriving immigrants were Catholics. As a result, an immigrant's religious practices often conflicted with those of native-born citizens. Native citizens also reacted differently depending on where immigrants came from. Before the Civil War, most immigrants tended to come from **Western Europe**. As a result, while there were always some nativists who opposed immigration, most people could at least recognize such immigrants as white Protestants (although there was a great deal of prejudice against the Irish Catholics). Towards the end of the nineteenth century and, however, more and more immigrants arrived from **eastern and southern Europe** (places like Poland, Russia, and Italy). In addition, the number of Jewish immigrants increased. Such immigrants often had to deal with more racism and faced even greater opposition once they arrived due to their ethnic differences. Even among the immigrants themselves, problems existed. As people from different nations and ethnic groups began to live in ghettos that were close together, conflicts arose. As a result, people from one nation or ethnic group developed rivalries with those of another.

Nativism and Restrictions on Immigration

Nativism

As feelings of **nativism** (opposing immigration) grew, anti-immigrant groups began to form. Nativism often made foreign immigrants the victims of violence and discrimination. Eventually, the government reacted to nativist concerns by attempting to pass legislation restricting immigration from certain countries. A number of such efforts failed when they were vetoed by US presidents. Legislation was passed, however, restricting immigration from China. The **Chinese Exclusion Act** of 1882 prohibited Chinese immigrants from legally coming to the US, and was not repealed until 1943.

Living and Working Conditions

Child Labor

While industrialization brought with it a number of innovations and increased job opportunities, it also produced problems within the cities. For poor, unskilled citizens and newly arrived immigrants, urban life could be hard and challenging. Whole families tended to work because wages were low and no one person could earn enough to support a whole household. Men, women, and children worked in mills and factories, usually at least twelve hours/day, six days/week. Women tended to be limited to running simple machines and were given almost no opportunity for advancement. Meanwhile, **child labor** became a common practice. Children — some as young as five years old — had to leave school in order to work. This not only meant that they missed out on a childhood, but without an education, they were inevitably caught in an endless cycle of poverty. Although industrialization did create some opportunities for African Americans in the 1800s, they were extremely limited. Even many labor unions would not accept African American workers among their membership. Most workers feared losing their job, at a time when Social Security and unemployment benefits did not exist.

Sweatshop

Meanwhile, **working conditions** were often difficult. Factories relied on the work of specialized laborers with machines that performed the same task over and over. Work was often monotonous and left employees feeling very little sense of pride. Also, work hours were long, wages were low, and factory conditions were often very dangerous. **Sweatshops** were also hazardous. These were makeshift factories set up by private contractors in small apartments or unused buildings. Since factories often needed more production than they had room to produce, they would hire contractors and pay them by production. Often poorly lit, poorly ventilated, and unsafe, sweatshops relied on poor workers who worked long hours for little pay.

Living conditions were often hard as well. To house the overwhelming numbers of migrants and immigrants, **urban slums** (poor, inner-city neighborhoods) consisting of **tenements** (overcrowded apartments that housed several families of immigrants or poor laborers) arose in the cities. Overcrowded and impoverished, these slums often had open sewers that attracted rats and other disease-spreading pests. The air was usually dark and polluted with soot from coal-fired steam engines and boilers. Meanwhile, the individual tenements were often poorly ventilated and full of fire hazards. Often, they were occupied by more than one family crammed together into a small, sometimes one room, apartment.

Urban Slum

New Urban Lifestyle and Entertainment

As the urban population grew and transformed, urban life transformed with it. Transportation evolved as electric trolleys came into being. Trolleys (soon followed by subways and trains) allowed people to live outside the inner city, while still working and pursuing leisure activities within it. As a result, the nation began to see the development of its first **suburbs**. Increased divisions in economic classes developed as the middle and upper classes moved away and left the inner city to the poorer classes and immigrants.

New means of **leisure and entertainment** began to grow in the cities as well. Among men, saloons became popular places to drink, socialize, forge bonds, and talk politics. Women enjoyed dance halls and cabarets where they could watch musical shows and try the latest dances. For families, there were amusement parks and vaudeville shows (inexpensive variety shows). It was during this time that the movie i and spectator sports (boxing, horse racing, and especially baseball) became popular. In add parks opened, including New York City's Central Park.

Samuel Gompers and the AFL

Samuel Gompers

Out of the challenging conditions facing urban workers, **labor unions** arose. Unions are organizations of workers formed to protect the interests of their members. During this period, a number of notable unions formed. Perhaps the most influential of the era was the **American Federation of Labor (AFL)**, led by **Samuel Gompers**. The AFL focused on such issues as wages, working hours, and working conditions. The AFL used the economic pressures of *strikes* (refusal of employees to work until employers meet certain demands) and *boycotts* (refusal to buy or pay for certain products or services in the hopes of forcing producers to change their policies or actions). The AFL also believed in collective bargaining and mediation. *Collective bargaining* happens when employees negotiate as a united group rather than individuals, thereby increasing their bargaining power. By comparison, *mediation* is when a neutral third party (in some cases, the government) helps negotiate a settlement acceptable to both sides. Unions also called on employers to agree to *arbitration*. Arbitration is a form of mediation in which the mediating third party is granted authority to pronounce a finding that both sides consider legally binding. To increase their ability to negotiate with business owners, the AFL pressed for *closed shop* workplaces in which employers could hire only union members. "Closed shops" forced employers to deal with the union, because they could not look elsewhere for workers.

Employers hated the unions and often took measures against them. They threatened to fire employees who joined unions, or forced them to sign contracts agreeing not to join such organizations. Sometimes they turned to the courts, which often sided with employers and issued injunctions (court orders) declaring strikes illegal. At times, labor disputes erupted in violence. Even the president of the United States sent in troops from time to time to crush strikers' efforts.

Western Migration

Western Farming

In the years leading up to and after the Civil War, more and more settlers moved west, causing a boom in the West's population. Some went for religious reasons. Others sought gold. Still others desired the abundant land and opportunities the region offered. Many settlers moved west intending to be **farmers**. However, they had to adapt to terrain very different from the East's. Since the prairies of the Midwest lacked wood and other traditional building materials, settlers learned to build sod houses. Sod from the thick prairie grass was abundant and proved to be very durable. Meanwhile, technological advances made western farming possible. John Deere's steel plow allowed farmers to plant crops in the Midwestern plains by cutting through the tough prairie sod. Since farmers often had to dig more than 100 feet to reach water, windmills proved crucial because they harnessed the wind's power to pump water to the surface. On the plains, where trees were scarce and there was not enough wood for fences, barbed wire made it possible for farmers to efficiently fence in their land and livestock. Finally, the railroads created a way for farmers to import needed equipment from the East while shipping their own products to different parts of the country. As a result, they could afford to farm western territories without being isolated from the nation's larger markets.

Another industry in the West was **cattle ranching**. Shortly after white settlers arrived in Texas, they learned Mexican cattle ranching techniques. Mexicans taught white settlers how to herd, raise, and drive cattle to market. As a result, white ranchers began imitating not only the Mexicans' ranching techniques, but their dress and culture as well. Cowboy hats and chaps are both examples of Mexican dress that were adopted by western settlers. The growth of the cattle industry contributed to the slaughter of buffalo that otherwise would have competed with cattle for food. It also meant that even more land was taken from Native Americans. "Cowtowns" popped up as settlements to which ranchers would drive their cattle, so that they could be herded onto trains and shipped east to market. Cowboys (those who moved the cattle on long drives to these cowtowns) became legendary figures in western culture.

Western Rancher

Western Miners

The **mining industry** also became important as people of nearly every background headed west to seek gold. Mining camps and towns were established and often had the reputation of being wild and full of vice (gambling, prostitution, drinking, etc.). Eventually, huge corporations moved in with advanced equipment to extract more difficult to reach metals. These corporations came to dominate western mining, causing a great decline in the number of independent miners.

WOMEN, IMMIGRANTS, AND AFRICAN AMERICANS OUT WEST

African American Soldiers

Circumstances on the frontier required a more flexible society and meant that **women** often had the opportunity to take on roles traditionally only open to men. These new freedoms attracted women to the West who otherwise might not have been willing to take on the challenges of the frontier. The West also saw a wave of foreign immigrants. Meanwhile, large numbers of **African Americans** made their way west following the Civil War. Blacks often served as cowhands on western ranches. Although many of the classic movies about the "Old West" fail to depict it, the truth is many cowboys in the 1800s were actually African Americans who moved west after abolition. Many African Americans also served in the West as soldiers in the United States Army.

Impact on Native Americans

Native Americans

As settlers ventured further west, Native Americans continued to feel the impact. For instance, the Plains Indians greatly depended on the buffalo for their livelihood. They used the buffalo for food, clothing, and shelter. As settlers and fur trappers came into the region, they killed great numbers of buffalo for their hides and to make way for herds of cattle. By 1889, only 1,000 buffalo were left. As a result, Plains Indians could no longer continue their way of life. In addition, many Native American tribes were forced to relocate to **reservations** (parcels of land set aside by the federal government for Native Americans), only to be forcibly removed again each time gold was discovered or whites wanted land. Over time, many Native Americans grew bitter and a number of violent wars broke out. Large numbers of Native Americans died from being forced to travel great distances and settle on reservations in lands to which they were not accustomed.

Violent Confrontations

Native American people sometimes chose to resist white settlement rather than accept being moved off their land. Famous battles between whites and Native Americans occurred at Sand Creek, Little Bighorn, and various other sites. The last notable armed conflict between US troops and Native Americans occurred in 1890 at **Wounded Knee** after a Sioux holy man named Wovoka developed a religious ritual called the Ghost Dance. The Sioux believed that this dance would bring back the buffalo, return the Native American tribes to their land, and banish the white man from the earth. Believing that the Sioux leader, Sitting Bull, was using the Ghost Dance to start a Native American uprising, the government sent in the US army. When soldiers tried to arrest Sitting Bull, a gunfight killed 14 people, including Sitting Bull himself. Soldiers then pursued the Sioux to Wounded Knee Creek. Before it was over, more than 150 Native American men, women and children — most of whom were unarmed — lay dead.

Chief Sitting Bull

Practice 5.2 Industrial Growth and Western Expansion

1. Who was John D. Rockefeller and what impact did he have in the United States?

2. What role did railroads play in opening the West and contributing to the rise of big business?

3. Chinese and Irish immigrants are remembered for
   - A. their contributions to the steel industry.
   - B. their contributions to building the nation's railroads.
   - C. their refusal to work for giants of big business.
   - D. working together to found the nation's first trust.

4. Which of the following would be the best way to describe the US government's approach to dealing with Native Americans on the frontier?
   A. Negotiations, in which the aim was to share land peacefully with the tribes that had lived there for generations.
   B. Compensation, in which the US government paid tribal leaders whatever amount of money the two sides agreed the land was worth.
   C. Barter, in which Native Americans surrendered land in exchange for citizenship rights and the guarantee of being given land for families to own and farm.
   D. Conquest, in which the United States used its military to take Native American lands and relocate tribes to areas designated by the US government.

5. What were some of the living and working conditions faced by poor laborers and immigrants to the US in the big cities?

5.3 International Relations and the Progressive Era

Reasons for Expansion

Toward the end of the nineteenth century, a growing number of citizens believed the United States needed to look beyond its borders and acquire more territory; such an attitude is known as **imperialism**. Many business leaders and politicians believed expansion was important because it would provide more markets and greater potential for economic growth. Others backed imperialism because they felt the United States needed to expand to maintain its national security. Some believed it was part of the country's destiny and crucial to maintaining a sense of national pride. With the West conquered, they argued that the country needed to look abroad with a new sense of adventure and purpose. Some leaders harkened back to Manifest Destiny. They saw it as the responsibility and moral obligation of whites in the US to civilize and take democracy to the rest of the world. They believed that darker skinned peoples were naturally inferior to, and in need of leadership from, whites of European descent.

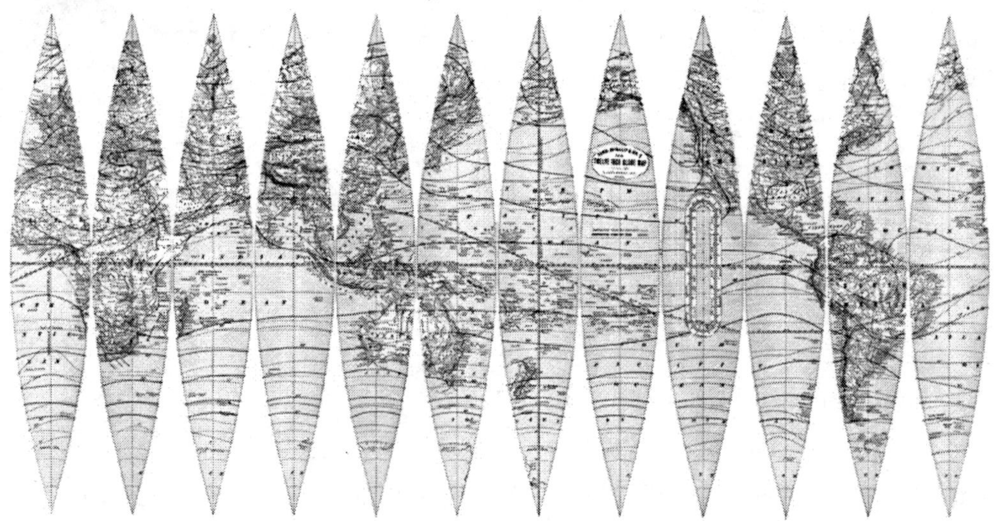

World Map

ISOLATIONISM

Yet, while more and more US citizens were advocating imperialism, others preached **isolationism**. They believed it was not in the best interest of the United States to acquire and exercise control over foreign territories. They felt such acquisitions would inevitably pull the US into foreign conflicts. Others made the case that expansion contradicted the very principles of freedom and self-government on which the United States was founded.

THE PACIFIC

Initially, most expansionists turned their attention towards the **Pacific**. Both political leaders and businessmen in the US wanted to trade with China and other nations in Southeast Asia. To promote access to Southeast Asia, Secretary of State William Seward negotiated the purchase of Alaska from Russia in 1867. Roughly thirty years later, the US annexed Hawaii as well. By acquiring Alaska and Hawaii, the US believed it helped open trade routes across the Pacific while, at the same time, gaining valuable territory.

Alaska and Hawaii

THE CHINESE EXCLUSION ACT

Chinese Exclusion Act

While US politicians and capitalists looked on the markets of Southeast Asia with great excitement, many sought to limit immigration from such countries here at home. In the 1870s, depression hit the west coast of the United States hard. People in places like San Francisco began to resent having to compete with the cheap labor that Chinese immigrants offered. Racism and acts of violence against Chinese immigrants increased. As the need for railway labor lessened, the government felt increased pressure to regulate Asian immigration. In 1882, Congress passed the **Chinese Exclusion Act** which prohibited further immigration from China for ten years. Congress later extended the act and it remained in effect until 1943.

The Spanish-American War

Theodore Roosevelt

In the late 1800s, the island of **Cuba** was still under Spanish rule. In 1895, the Cuban people rebelled, and Spain sent 150,000 troops to restore order. As part of their strategy, the Spanish relocated thousands of Cuban citizens to concentration camps. These camps had miserable conditions and many Cubans died. As pressure mounted for the US to intervene, competing newspapers printed stories about the Spanish abuses against the Cubans. Often exaggerated and untrue, these stories were meant to sell papers rather than accurately report the facts. They also ignited public emotion and calls for war with Spain. One of the many calling for war was Assistant Secretary of the Navy **Theodore Roosevelt**. When war finally came, Roosevelt resigned his position to assume command a of volunteer unit known as the *Rough Riders*.

"A Splendid Little War"

The **Spanish-American War** officially began as a result of what happened on February 15, 1898. A US battleship, the *USS Maine*, exploded while anchored in a Cuban harbor. Immediately, the newspapers blamed Spain and US citizens demanded war. Although it was later determined that the explosion was most likely an accident, Congress adopted a resolution declaring war on Spain in April, 1898. Upon hearing of the declaration of war, US Commodore George Dewey set sail for another Spanish colony — the **Philippines**. Destroying the Spanish fleet there, Dewey quickly seized control of the Philippine Islands. Meanwhile, in Cuba, Roosevelt won praise for leading the Rough Riders in bold charges up Kettle and San Juan Hills. In less than three months, the United States defeated Spain in both Cuba and the Philippines. To people in the US it seemed like a relatively easy victory. John Hay, the future secretary of state and good friend of Theodore Roosevelt, captured what most felt when he referred to the taking of the Philippines as "a splendid little war."

US Commodore George Dewey

Controversy Over Territory

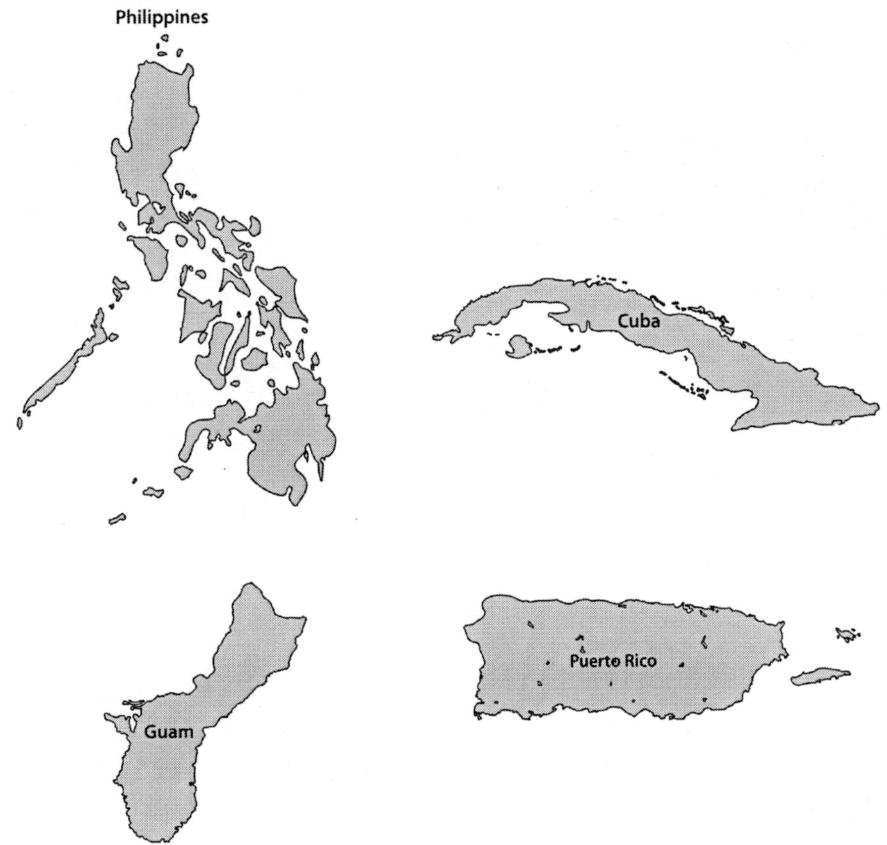

Cuba, Puerto Rico, Guam, and the Philippines

The Spanish-American War officially ended with the signing of the Treaty of Paris. Attached to Congress' 1898 war resolution with Spain was the Teller Amendment, which promised that the United States would allow Cuba to be independent. Meanwhile, Puerto Rico and Guam became US territories. Of all the territories involved in the Spanish-American War, however, it was the **Philippines** that caused the most controversy. People in the US clearly understood reasons for occupying Cuba during the war, but the Philippines were all the way on the other side of the world and seemed to have little to do with events in the Caribbean. Those who opposed expansion argued that annexing the Philippines would undermine democracy and increase the likelihood of future wars in the Pacific. Roosevelt and others, however, saw the Philippines as crucial for protecting US economic interests in Southeast Asia. While debate raged in Washington, Filipinos under the leadership of **Emilio Aguinaldo** launched a resistance movement against US occupation. The Filipinos used guerilla warfare to combat the superior strength of the US. In Guerilla warfare, a weaker army strikes quickly, inflicting damage, then retreats before its stronger enemy can fully retaliate. It is usually intended to frustrate and weaken an enemy's willingness to fight rather than overpower and defeat them in a head-to-head battle. The fighting lasted more than two years and resulted in massacres and atrocities (violent killings and tortures that were unnecessary and/or against innocent civilians) committed by both sides. The US-backed forces finally captured Aguinaldo in 1901 and, in 1902, the Philippines became an unorganized territory of the United States. In 1946, the Philippines officially became an independent nation.

US Involvement in Latin America

The Panama Canal

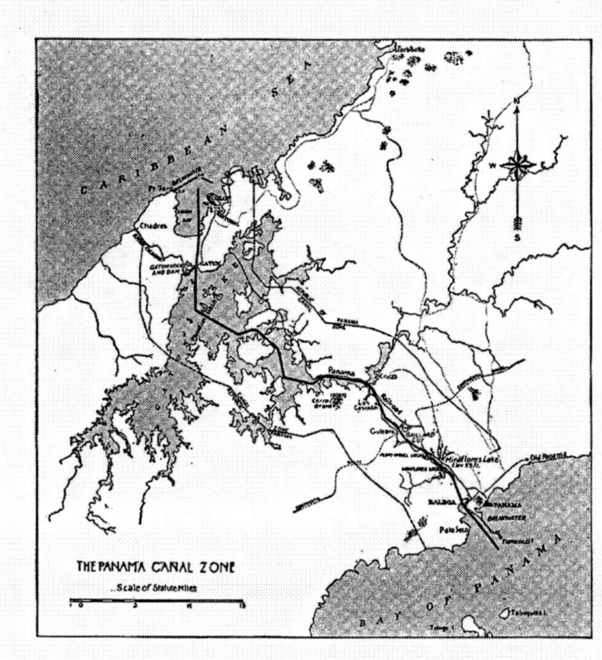

Panama Canal

Following the assassination of President William McKinley in 1901, **Theodore Roosevelt** became the 26th president of the United States. To allow US ships easier movement between the Atlantic and Pacific Oceans, Roosevelt envisioned a canal across the isthmus of Panama. This canal would serve US military and economic interests by allowing ships to travel back and forth between the Pacific and Atlantic oceans without having to go around South America. Unfortunately for the president, the Colombian government which controlled the territory refused to sell or lease the land necessary for the project. Then, in 1903, the Panamanian people revolted against the Colombians. Roosevelt responded by providing US naval support that helped the Panamanians win their independence. In return, the Panamanians allowed the US to lease the land needed for the canal. Construction started in 1905, and, in 1914, workers completed the **Panama Canal**. The US continued to control the canal until President Jimmy Carter signed a treaty in 1977 authorizing the transfer of the canal to the Panamanians. Panama finally took full control of the Panama Canal in December 1999.

The Roosevelt Corollary ("Big Stick" Diplomacy)

Cartoon depicting Big Stick Diplomacy

By the 1900s, the United States was becoming a major player in world affairs. In 1904, President Roosevelt issued **Roosevelt's Corollary**. It was a statement which expanded upon the Monroe Doctrine. Monroe had said that the US would not allow European powers to colonize newly independent nations in the Western Hemisphere, nor would the US interfere with such nations. Roosevelt modified this by saying that the US had the right to intervene in the region *if* a nation had trouble paying its debts. Roosevelt wanted to make sure other imperialist nations did not use debt collection as an excuse to occupy territories in the Caribbean or Latin America. This doctrine came to be known as Roosevelt's *"big stick diplomacy."* The name came from a West African proverb which said, "Speak softly and carry a big stick." It meant that the US did not intend to be a threatening presence in the Western Hemisphere, but neither would it hesitate to forcefully protect its own interests.

The Progressive Era

Upton Sinclair

As the 1800s ended, only a handful of people enjoyed wealth and prosperity, while immigrants and poor laborers continued to live and work under harsh conditions. Meanwhile, the country was riddled with government corruption at all levels. As a result, many citizens and government officials demanded reforms in government, business, and society in general. The turn of the century marked the beginning of the **Progressive Era** and was a time of political, social, and economic change in the United States.

Progressives (those who supported reforms during the Progressive Era) tended to be white, middle class Protestants. They believed that things could be made better through government regulation of society. They called for more regulation of business, improved wages for workers, regulations over work environments, laws governing morality, defined standards for education, and stricter regulation of professions like doctors, teachers, and lawyers. Meanwhile, the progressives raged against the upper class as being exploiters of the poor and slaves to self-indulgence. Many historians look back on the progressives with both praise and criticism. They praise the progressives for their ambition and drive to make society better, and for accomplishing a number of positive reforms. However, they also criticize the progressives for their arrogance. Progressives tended to assume that those of lower economic or social status were helpless without guidance from the middle class and needed the help of "more sophisticated" people to decide for them what was truly best.

The Muckrakers

During the Progressive Era, many writers exposed abuse in government and big business. President Theodore Roosevelt labeled these authors and journalists the **muckrakers** because they uncovered much of the "muck" in US society. Lincoln Steffens exposed political corruption in St. Louis and other cities. **Ida Tarbell** revealed the abuses of the Standard Oil trust. Her writings about Standard Oil threw fuel on an already burning fire, calling for reforms in US business and campaigns against monopolies. Perhaps the most famous muckraker was **Upton Sinclair,** who published a novel called ***The Jungle*** in 1906. The book horrified readers with the truth about the US meat packing industry. Its impact helped lead to the creation of a federal meat inspection program.

Ida Tarbell

THE ROLE OF WOMEN IN THE PROGRESSIVE ERA

Hull House

Women became major players in the progressive movement. **Jane Addams** (nicknamed the "mother of social work") opened *Hull House*, a settlement house, in Chicago. Settlement houses were houses established in poor neighborhoods where social activists would live and offer assistance to immigrants and underprivileged citizens. By 1910, there were more than 400 settlement houses in the United States. Hull House served as a launching pad for investigations into economic, political, and social conditions in the city. It eventually helped fight for and win new child labor laws and other legislation meant to help those in need.

Carrie Nation

During the Progressive Era, momentum grew for the temperance movement. Supporters of the temperance movement believed alcohol was to blame for much of society's ills. They originally only wanted to limit its availability. Ultimately, temperance supporters called for the elimination of alcohol altogether. Many of its leaders were churchgoers and women. One of its most colorful figures was **Carrie Nation**. Already into her mid-fifties by the turn of the century, Nation made a habit of entering saloons and smashing bottles of liquor with a hatchet while her supporters prayed and sang hymns. Although most were not as radical as Nation, the temperance movement continued to gain strength. Ratified in 1919, the **Eighteenth Amendment** prohibited the making, selling, or transporting of any alcoholic beverage in the United States. Commonly referred to as "Prohibition," this amendment later proved to be a failure and was repealed.

More lasting in its impact was the **women's suffrage movement**. Ever since the Seneca Falls Convention of 1848, women had demanded suffrage (the right to vote). By the 1870s, **Susan B. Anthony** was arguably the most recognized leader of this movement. Along with Elizabeth Cady Stanton and others, Anthony helped establish the *National American Woman Suffrage Association (NAWSA)*. Initial attempts to win a constitutional amendment granting women the right to vote failed, although women did win suffrage in a few states. Finally, in 1920, Congress passed the **Nineteenth Amendment** and sent it to the states for ratification. On August 21 of that same year, Tennessee became the last state needed to make the "Anthony Amendment" part of the Constitution. At last, women had the right to vote nationwide.

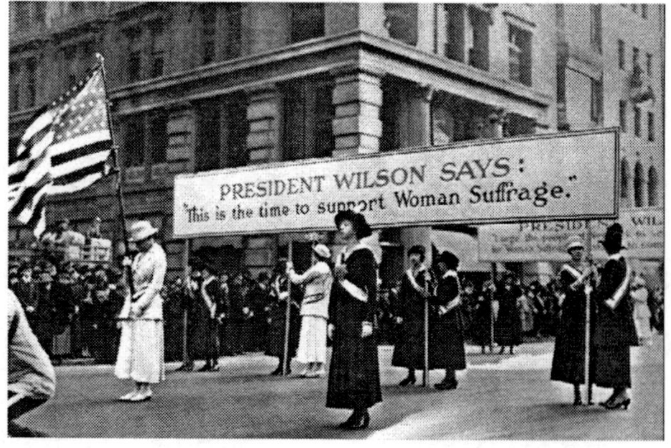

Suffrage March

The Progressive Movement and Race

Homer Plessy

Following Reconstruction, **Jim Crow laws** became common throughout the South. These laws required the **segregation** of blacks and white; Blacks and whites were not allowed to share public spaces. They could not sit in the same dining rooms at restaurants, were not to share railway cars, and were restricted from using the same public facilities. In 1896, the Supreme Court actually upheld such laws as constitutional in ***Plessy v. Ferguson***. The case involved a 30 year old man named Homer Plessy. Plessy, who was one-eighth African American, violated a Louisiana law by sitting in a "whites only" railway car. After being arrested, he sued, claiming the law was unconstitutional. After considering the case, the Supreme Court ruled that segregation was lawful as long as the separate facilities and services were equal. The case set the precedent that segregation was legal so long as separate facilitates held to the standard of "separate but equal." In reality, the facilities for whites were usually far superior to those of blacks.

W.E.B. DuBois

Ironically, many white progressives supported segregation. They believed that African Americans could only develop and advance culturally in their own, segregated society. Since, in reality, conditions in the "black world" were not equal to those in the "white world," many disagreed with the progressives' stance. One such person was **W.E.B. DuBois**. DuBois was the first black Ph.D. from Harvard University and adamantly rejected segregation. He argued that blacks should pursue occupations in the humanities (the arts, social sciences, positions of leadership, etc.) and in white collar (managerial or professional) fields. Unlike some African American leaders, DuBois believed that blacks must be politically, legally, and socially active in order to obtain true equality. DuBois helped to organize a group of black intellectuals known as the *Niagara Movement.* Their goal was to outline an agenda for African American progress in the United States. In 1909, DuBois was instrumental in founding the **National Association for the Advancement of Colored People (NAACP)**. The organization devoted itself to the progress of the African American community. Today, the NAACP continues to be a prominent political voice among the African American community.

Labor Laws and Living Conditions

One area where progressives called for reform was in the **living conditions** of poor, urban laborers and immigrants. One of the key figures in this reform movement was Jacob Riis. Riis, himself an immigrant from Denmark, wrote books like *How the Other Half Lives* that exposed the horrible conditions under which immigrants worked and lived. His writings revealed the cramped space, filthy conditions, and often dangerous hazards that existed in inner-city **tenements** (small, low-income apartments often shared by more than one family). Riis'efforts contributed to New York passing its first laws aimed at improving urban tenements.

Labor laws were another concern. Most workers' wages were low. As a result, men, women, and even children often had to work long hours for little pay. In addition, workdays ran from sunrise to sundown and usually involved dangerous conditions. Many progressives called for shorter workdays, higher wages, and safer work environments for employees.

Minimum Age Laws

Eventually, reformers convinced a number of states to pass *minimum age laws*. These laws set limits on how young employees could be (ages ranged from 12 to 16). Some states also passed laws restricting the hours and occupations of women. Progressives claimed such legislation was necessary to protect the US home and the important role women played as wives and mothers. Legislatures also passed laws restricting work hours and requiring safer working conditions as a result of progressive reforms.

Political Reforms

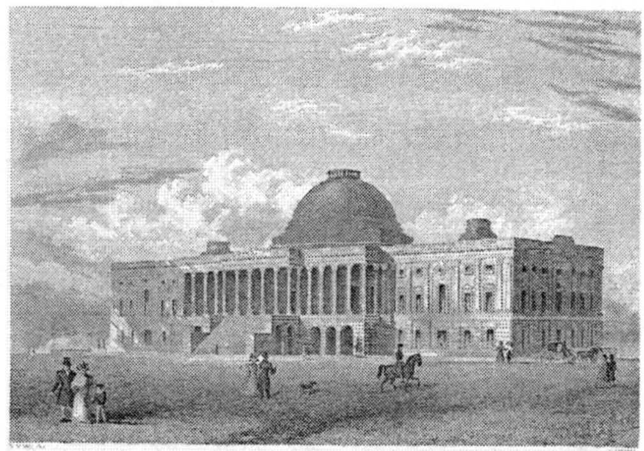

US Capitol Early 1800s

US Capitol 1900

During the late nineteenth century, government became known for political scandal. Corruption existed in city and state governments, as well as at the federal level. Most progressives believed that the solution was to make government officials more accountable to the general public. They believed government officials were corrupt because it was too easy for people to gain political office through favors and corrupt dealings behind closed doors, rather than having to win the support of the people. As a result, several political reforms won popular support during the Progressive Era. Some even prompted changes to the Constitution. For instance, the **Seventeenth Amendment** established that US senators would be elected directly by the people, rather than by state legislatures. Progressives applauded this change because it meant that senate seats would have to be won in open elections rather than awarded as part of a political deal among state legislators.

Other political reforms included the *initiative, recall,* and *referendum*. The **initiative** allowed citizens of a state to force a vote on a certain issue without having to wait for public officials to bring it up. If enough citizens signed a petition, the legislature could be compelled to address a particular concern. The **recall** gave citizens the power to hold special elections to remove corrupt officials from office before their terms were up. Finally, the **referendum** meant that certain proposals would have to be voted on by the general public, rather than passed solely by party bosses or state legislatures.

World War I

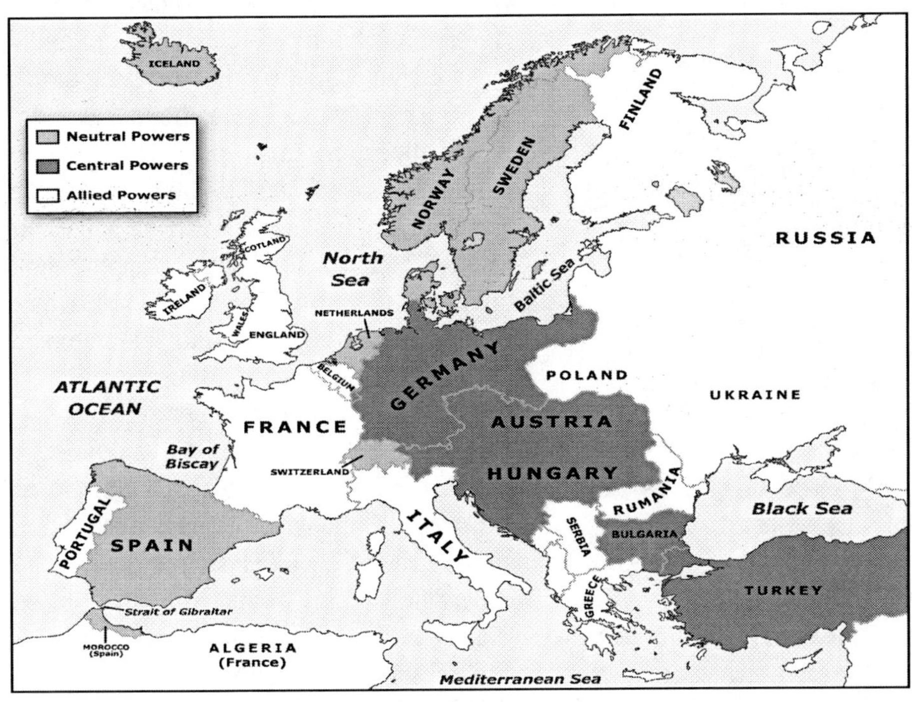

Europe 1914

In 1914, **World War I (WWI)** broke out in Europe. Although it originally began as a conflict between European powers, the war eventually involved the United States and a number of other nations. At first, the United States did not get involved in the war. In fact, in 1914, President **Woodrow Wilson** officially declared the United States neutral (not backing either side). Many in the United States believed in **isolationism** (the philosophy that the United States should stay out of international conflicts) and did not see a war in Europe as being of any concern to the US. Many citizens became peace activists during this period. Others supported a policy of "preparedness", which advocated neutrality while taking steps to prepare for war just in case it became necessary. US policy towards the war became the key issue in the 1916 election. Wilson narrowly won a second term running on the slogan, "He kept us out of war!"

The US Enters the War

Despite Wilson's original desire for neutrality, a number of factors eventually led to US involvement in the war. While many recent immigrants to the US were of German descent and favored the Central Powers (Germany and Austria-Hungary), most public opinion supported the Triple Entente (Great Britain, France, and Russia). This was in large part because US bankers had loaned large amounts of money to Great Britain. In addition, the British had managed to cut the main lines of communication from Germany to the United States. As a result, images of the war that reached the United States predominantly came from Great Britain. As time passed, people in the US came to see Germany as a ruthless aggressor out to destroy democracy and freedom.

Woodrow Wilson

Lusitania Sinking

One of Germany's fiercest weapons in WWI was their dreaded **U-boats**. These were submarines that traveled under water and wreaked havoc in the Atlantic during the war. The Germans warned all nations that they would attack any ships entering or leaving British ports. President Wilson rejected the warning, arguing that no warring party could be allowed to disrupt neutral shipping on the high seas. In reality, however, the US was not entirely neutral. Unknown to passengers, the US had begun shipping military supplies to Great Britain aboard commercial cruise liners. One of these liners, the ***Lusitania***, was torpedoed by a German U-boat in 1915. Twelve hundred people died in the attack, including 128 US citizens. People in the US were furious! A wave of anti-German feeling swept across the country. Not wanting to pull the United States into the war, Germany agreed not to attack anymore US passenger ships. However, in 1917, Germany resumed their attacks on merchant and commercial ships, moving the United States closer to war. The German's policy of attacking all ships was known as **unrestricted submarine warfare**. Although the Germans knew such a policy would encourage the US to enter the war, the fact that Russia had dropped out of the fighting to deal with their own revolution led Germany to believe it could rapidly defeat its remaining enemies before any US troops reached Europe.

WWI Soldiers

It was also in 1917 that the US intercepted the **Zimmerman telegram**. Arthur Zimmerman, the German Foreign Minister, sent a telegram to the German embassy in Mexico. In his telegram, Zimmerman had embassy officials ask Mexico to attack the US if it declared war on Germany. In return, Germany promised to help Mexico win back land the US had acquired as a result of the Mexican-American War. News of this communication did not go over well in the United States. Anti-German sentiment increased even more, and President Wilson broke off diplomatic relations with Germany. Likewise, more sinking of US ships meant that the United States could no longer stay neutral. In March 1917, Wilson made his case for war and proclaimed that the world "must be made safe for democracy." Wilson wanted the US public to see the war as a battle between good and evil; he wanted the people to view it as a fight between democracy and tyranny. His appeals were well received. Congress passed a war resolution soon afterwards. In April 1917, the United States officially entered World War I.

The War Ends

Leaders of the United States, Great Britain, France, and Italy at Versailles

Germany's failure to defeat Great Britain and France before US troops arrived meant that Germany now had to face an additional enemy. Sensing that the war had turned against them, the Germans had no choice but to seek terms of peace. In late 1918, they signed an **armistice** (cease-fire or agreement to stop fighting), ending hostilities. Once the fighting stopped, the leaders of the warring nations met together for a peace conference in Paris. President Wilson went to the conference with no desire to punish Germany, nor did he hope to acquire territory for the United States. Wilson's goal was peace and stability. He put forth a peace proposal known as the **Fourteen Points**. Wilson's plan called for a reduction in weapons and the right of self-determination (power to govern oneself) for ethnic groups like those in Austria-Hungary. Wilson also proposed the founding of the **League of Nations**. The purpose of the League would be to provide a place where countries could peacefully discuss solutions to their differences rather than go to war. A number of nations joined. Ironically, however, the United States was not one of them. Isolationism grew strong again in the US after the war, and the United States Senate would not ratify the **Treaty of Versailles** which ended the war and sanctioned the League of Nations. Opponents feared that commitment to an international organization would lead to binding alliances and drag the nation into another costly war.

In addition, while Wilson wanted peace and stability, many of his European allies wanted retribution. The European countries had suffered longer and lost far more lives than the US (roughly 20 million Europeans died in the war). The Treaty of Versailles made Germany take total responsibility for the war and required the Germans to pay reparations (money to compensate for losses from the war) to the Allies. These conditions ultimately led to economic depression and great bitterness on the part of most Germans. The resentment felt by the German people made it possible for a young, charismatic leader named Adolf Hitler to rise to power and plunge Europe back into war twenty years later. In the meantime, Wilson's plea for the United States to ratify the treaty and join the League of Nations fell on deaf ears. Despite his masterful diplomacy in Paris, Wilson failed to convince his own country to sign the treaty ending World War I.

The Great Migration

There was also an important social impact of the war. The nation's enlarged army needed supplies. The increased demand for products (weapons, supplies, uniforms, equipment, etc.), combined with the reduced number of young men left at home since many fought overseas, meant there were more jobs in northern cities where most of the nation's factories existed. As a result, many African Americans began leaving the South in growing numbers to pursue better economic opportunities and in hopes of escaping southern racism. This mass movement of African Americans from the predominantly rural South to northern cities continued for several decades. It became known as the **Great Migration**.

African American Working During WWI

Practice 5.3 International Relations and the Progressive Era

1. Which of the following would an *isolationist* support?
   A. staying out of WWI
   B. sending US troops to fight in Europe.
   C. the Zimmerman telegram
   D. the League of Nations

2. For what reasons did the US eventually enter World War I?

3. Theodore Roosevelt's attitude about US expansion can best be described as
   A. isolationist.
   B. uninterested.
   C. imperialist.
   D. fearful.

4. What was the Chinese Exclusion Act and why was it passed?

5. Ida Tarbell is best described as a
   A. social worker.
   B. muckraker.
   C. progressive politician.
   D. founding member of the NAACP.

6. Which of the following actions would be illegal under Jim Crow laws?
   A. white citizens joining the NAACP
   B. African Americans receiving Ph.Ds
   C. progressives supporting segregation
   D. blacks and whites riding together on a train

7. What were the progressive changes established by the Seventeenth, Eighteenth, and Nineteenth Amendments?

8. How did progressives feel about the government regulation of society? How did many of them feel about segregation? What were their reasons for these views?

Chapter 5 Review

Key terms, people, and concepts

Presidential Reconstruction
Thirteenth Amendment
black codes
Radical Republicans
Radical Reconstruction
Fourteenth Amendment
Fifteenth Amendment
Johnson's impeachment
sharecropping
tenant farming
Freedmen's Bureau
Ku Klux Klan
Jim Crow Laws
literacy tests
poll taxes
grandfather clauses
railroads
role of Irish and Chinese immigrants
impact of railroads on steel and big business
John D. Rockefeller
Standard Oil
trusts
monopolies
urban growth
immigration
Ellis Island
cultural pluralism
ethnic ghettos
religious differences

immigrants from western Europe
immigrants from eastern and southern Europe
nativism
Chinese Exclusion Act
child labor

women in the West
African Americans in the West
reservations
Wounded Knee
imperialism
isolationism
Pacific
Theodore Roosevelt
Spanish-American War
the Phlippines
Emilio Aquinaldo
Panama Canal
Roosevelt's Corollary
Progressive Era
progressives
muckrakers
Ida Tarbell
Upton Sinclair
The Jungle

Jane Addams
Carrie Nation
Eighteenth Amendment
woman's suffrage movement
Susan B. Anthony
Nineteenth Amendment
segregation
Plessy v. Ferguson
W.E.B. DuBois
National Association for the Advancement of Colored People (NAACP)
urban living conditions
labor laws

Seventeenth Amendment
initiative
recall

urban working conditions
sweatshops
urban slums
tenements
suburbs
urban leisure and entertainment
labor unions
American Federation of Labor (AFL)
Samuel Gompers
western farmers
cattle ranching
mining industry
referendum
World War I
Woodrow Wilson
U-boats
Lusitania
unrestricted submarine warfare
Zimmerman telegram
armistice
Fourteen Points
League of Nations
Treaty of Versailles
Great Migration

Multiple Choice Questions

1. A Radical Republican would have been most opposed to which of the following?
   A. Presidential Reconstruction
   B. the Freedmen's Bureau
   C. the Fifteenth Amendment
   D. impeaching President Johnson

2. A Russian immigrant in 1900 would have been most likely to visit
   A. Hawaii.
   B. the Philippines.
   C. Ellis Island.
   D. Wounded Knee.

3. Which of the following would have been the quickest to defend the rights of poor, immigrant workers?
   A. the NAACP
   B. the AFL
   C. the League of Nations
   D. the Nativist Society

4. Although they often focused on different causes and sometimes disagreed, progressives were united in their belief that
   A. the United States should expand its territory.
   B. segregation based on race is a moral evil.
   C. the US should not enter WWI.
   D. the government should do more to regulate US society.

5. An African American who moved from rural Georgia to New York City in 1919 would have been part of the
   A. Anti-imperialism League.
   B. isolationist movement.
   C. Great Migration.
   D. NAACP.

6. "Segregation is necessary. By separating blacks and whites, society allows the negro to more effectively build and nurture his own customs, culture, and abilities. Why, forcing the races together would most assuredly result in social unrest and, quite possibly, violent upheaval. Surely, the negro would be on the losing end and suffer greatly under such a condition."

The above quote is likely from

A. a progressive.
B. a member of the NAACP.
C. a member of the Ku Klux Klan.
D. W.E.B. DuBois.

7. Why did the US Senate refuse to allow the United States to join the League of Nations?
   A. Many of its members feared it would lead to alliances that would drag the nation into war.
   B. Most senators felt the League did not give enough territory to the US after the war.
   C. The Senate was angry that the League would not approve US plans to invade foreign countries.
   D. Senators did not want to use taxpayer money to pay to join.

8.
- unrestricted submarine warfare
- Zimmerman telegram
- sinking of US ships
- The Lusitania

What would be the best heading for the above list?

A. Reasons Europe Went to War
B. Reasons the US Entered World War I
C. Reasons for the Spanish-American War
D. Reasons Congress Passed the Chinese Exclusion Act

9. "She was nothing short of an angel. If it were not for her founding Hull House and fighting for the rights of the poor and those desperate souls born in foreign lands, God only knows how many would have turned to crime or even perished."

The above quote is talking about

A. Carrie Nation.
B. Jane Addams.
C. Ida Tarbell.
D. W.E.B. DuBois.

10. Who would have benefitted most from the opening of the Panama Canal?
   A. an isolationist wanting the US to stay out of interests in Latin America
   B. a Filipino hoping for independence
   C. Chinese immigrants wanting to enter the US after 1882
   D. a US navy captain needing to sail from Cuba to Southeast Asia.

11. Which of the following would have been unacceptable based on Roosevelt's Corollary?
    A. the United States annexing foreign territories.
    B. foreign nations trading in the Pacific
    C. European nations occupying a South American country to collect debt payments.
    D. the United States making agreements with Latin American nations.

12. Which amendment to the Constitution addressed women's suffrage?
    A. Sixteenth
    B. Seventeenth
    C. Eighteenth
    D. Nineteenth

13. What was *The Jungle*?
    A. a nickname given to the Philippines by US soldiers who fought there
    B. the title of a book by Jacob Riis that described the horrible living conditions of immigrants
    C. the title of a secret telegram sent from Germany to Mexico
    D. a novel by Upton Sinclair that exposed unsanitary conditions in the meat packing industry

14. It was the nation's first trust.
    A. New York's Central Park
    B. J.P. Morgan's purchase of steel
    C. Vanderbilt's railroad
    D. John D. Rockefeller's Standard Oil

15. What was the purpose of the Thirteenth Amendment?
    A. It promised African Americans the right to vote.
    B. It ended slavery in the United States.
    C. It ended Reconstruction.
    D. It made African Americans citizens of the states in which they lived.

16. The first federal relief agency in US history was designed to
    A. help freed slaves.
    B. protect Chinese and Irish immigrants working on the nation's railroads.
    C. open the first African American college.
    D. re-locate Native Americans to reservations.

17. One of the products of immigration during the late nineteenth and early twentieth century was
    A. Reconstruction.
    B. cultural pluralism.
    C. Jim Crow laws.
    D. wars with Native Americans.

18. Who would have been most supportive of a labor union?
    A. a poor immigrant working in a New York sweatshop
    B. a cattle rancher
    C. a Buffalo Soldier
    D. a giant of big business

Chapter 6
United States History: Roaring '20s to the Modern Age

GPS	SSUSH16: The student will identify key developments in the aftermath of WWI. (QCC standard US30)
	SSUSH22: The student will identify dimensions of the Civil Rights Movement, 1945-1970. (QCC standards US37, US43)
	SSUSH24: The student will analyze the impact of social change movements and organizations of the 1960s. (QCC standards US36, US37)

6.1 Prosperity and Depression

The "Red Scare" and Immigration

In 1917, Russia pulled out of World War I due to its own revolution at home. A party known as the Bolsheviks took over and installed a socialist government. In a socialist government, the state owns most of the property, regulates the economy, and runs most of the major industries. Individual freedoms are not nearly as important as the welfare of the state. The Bolsheviks modeled their ideas about government after the teachings of a man named Karl Marx. Marx believed that oppressed workers would eventually rise up and overthrow capitalism, an economic system based on free markets and privately owned industry. He advocated **communism**, a system in which people in society cooperate and own property mutually, thereby making governments unnecessary. According to Marx, socialist governments were meant to provide order while societies made this transition from captitalism to communism. Once they took over Russia, the Bolsheviks installed a government they believed would lead to communism.

Karl Marx

Red Scare

Bolshevik leaders believed that, in order for their vision to become a reality, workers in other countries needed to rise up and establish socialist governments as well. This greatly alarmed people in the United States. Business leaders, government officials, and a growing number of private citizens feared that such a revolution might occur in the US. This led to a period known as the **Red Scare,** in which many people became fearful of anyone who might be a communist or a threat to US freedom. When **anarchists** (those who want to bring down *any* form of government) attempted to assassinate Attorney General A. Mitchell Palmer and Standard Oil icon John D. Rockefeller, many associated the attacks with communism. In response, Palmer authorized the *Palmer Raids*, in which suspected communists and people perceived to be a threat — many of whom were immigrants who had committed no crimes — were arrested and jailed. More than 500 immigrants were deported back to their countries of birth as a result of Palmer's actions.

Immigration Restrictions

Ku Klux Klan in the 1920s

The Red Scare and suspicions about immigrants led to a new rise in **nativism** (opposition to immigration). As a result, citizens pressured the government to place **restrictions on immigration**. Congress passed a temporary limit to the number of immigrants who could come to the US in 1924 and permanent bans beginning in 1929. Racist in nature, many of these laws were designed to allow more immigrants from Western Europe into the country than from Eastern Europe or the Far East. Because few laws addressed immigration from nations in the Western Hemisphere, however, the number of Hispanic Catholic immigrants (both legal and illegal) increased dramatically during this time period and made Latin Americans the fastest growing minority in the United States. Meanwhile, the Ku Klux Klan saw a resurgence due to its willingness to expand its attacks. No longer did it only go after African Americans; the Klan targeted Jews, Catholics, Communists, and foreign immigrants as well. By proclaiming their prejudice and opposition to such groups, the Ku Klux Klan grew to be a national, rather than just a southern, force of hatred.

HENRY FORD AND THE AUTOMOBILE

Ford Assembly Line

The years following WWI saw a number of innovations in business and technology. One key figure of the day was **Henry Ford**. Although he was not the first to invent the automobile, Ford was the first to perfect and successfully market it. In 1907, Ford sold 30,000 of his first, mass-produced car — the *Model T.* What truly set Ford apart was his vision for **mass production**. He decided to produce enough automobiles that he could afford to sell them at greatly reduced prices, thus allowing "ordinary people" to be able to afford his cars. To achieve this goal, Ford relied on the **assembly line**. Assembly lines had existed before, but Ford's was innovative because it had the employees stay in one spot while the assembly line brought the parts to them. Up until that time, parts remained stationary while employees moved from station to station. Ford also saw his workers as consumers. In other words, he wanted those who made his cars to also be able to buy them. For this reason, Ford paid his workers an unheard of $5 per day wage (a good salary back then). From 1907 until 1926, Ford built half the automobiles in the world (16,750,000 cars). The automobile greatly changed the face of US culture by allowing people to become more mobile, live further away from where they worked, and attend activities and events that otherwise would have been inaccessible. His cars, along with the advent of public transportation (electric trolleys, etc.) helped give rise to the new middle class and the US suburb.

CULTURAL INFLUENCES

1920s Fashion

The 1920s was a time of tremendous social and cultural change in the United States. The increased availability of electricity in homes allowed new appliances like refrigerators, sewing machines, vacuum cleaners, and washing machines to greatly reduce the amount of time needed to do traditional chores around the house. As a result, women were not as bound by their traditional roles at home, and more of them began to work and become socially active. New hairstyles and fashions reflected such changes. As technology made work easier and more efficient, both men and women found themselves with more time for leisure activities. Advances in transportation, more free time, and the use of electric power gave birth to a bustling nightlife, in which people ventured into the city after dark to attend shows, have dinner, or take part in evening social events. Simultaneously, a new mass media formed. National magazines allowed news stories and business advertisements to reach people nationwide.

Radio and Movies

1920s Technology

Two of the most impactful developments in media were the **radio** and **movies**. Long before television, radios became the first source of mass communication and entertainment available to people in their own homes. Radio united the nation and molded a national culture like never before, as people across the country enjoyed the same shows and heard the same news reports. It also transformed politics by giving leaders direct access to larger numbers of people.

During this same period, the movie industry boomed in the United States. First to silent pictures, then to movies with sound (called "talkies"), people flocked to be entertained by the big screen. The fashions and lifestyles portrayed in the movies helped define a national culture. People all over the nation wanted to wear the clothes they saw in the movies, drive the cars they saw on screen, and take part in the fads popularized by Hollywood. As a result, movie stars became national icons.

Jazz and the Harlem Renaissance

Jazz Music

The '20s also saw great cultural accomplishments within the African American community. **Jazz** became a popular form of music after World War I, as musical artists from Louisiana and Mississippi brought their talents to the northern cities. Its fast pace rhythm inspired new dances like the "Charleston" and helped create a thriving nightlife. Crossing ethnic boundaries, jazz found a receptive audience among both blacks and young whites. **Louis Armstrong**, a trumpeter and singer from New Orleans, was among the most noted jazz musicians.

An increase in black racial pride and awareness led many black intellectuals to produce works of art portraying the daily lives of working-class African Americans. **Langston Hughes** wrote memorable poetry, short stories, and plays about the black experience that reminded black Americans of their African heritage. Meanwhile, female writer, Zora Neal Hurston, gained fame for her novel *Their Eyes Were Watching God.* Many other black painters, dancers, and musicians also produced enduring works of art. Because much of this cultural movement took place in New York City, it became known as the **Harlem Renaissance**.

Initial Prosperity

Calvin Coolidge

In 1920, Warren Harding followed Woodrow Wilson as president. Under his leadership, the US economy remained relatively strong. Then, after a series of scandals that rocked his administration, Harding died of heart problems in 1923 and was succeeded by his vice president, Calvin Coolidge. The following year, Coolidge was elected to a full term. Coolidge supported big business and believed in laissez-faire economics, the idea that government should not regulate business or try to manipulate the market but rather let the market take its natural course. One of Coolidge's most famous quotes was, "The business of the American people is business." He strongly believed that the government should not interfere with the growth of business and that the natural business cycle would fix any problems in the economy. For most of the 1920s, it appeared Coolidge was right. The stock market did very well as prices reached new highs and continued to climb. People tried to take advantage of the prosperity by buying stock on **speculation** (made high-risk investments in hopes of making large returns on their money). Many investors also engaged in something called **buying on the margin**. Under this practice, investors purchased stocks for only a portion of what they cost. They then borrowed the difference and paid interest on the loan. Many believed that the stock market was doing so well that they could still make money, even while paying such interest.

Technology also helped produce a booming economy in the 1920s. Henry Ford's mechanized assembly line revolutionized the auto industry and was starting to transform other industries as well. **Mechanization** (increased use of machinery for production) meant that products could be produced in far greater numbers and more efficiently. This increase in production meant that manufacturers could afford to charge less money. As a result, more people purchased cars, clothes, appliances, and other goods. **Consumerism** (the practice of people buying and consuming products) became normal and meant that citizens were spending more money than they saved. Money kept pouring into the economy, companies did well, and jobs were plentiful. Economic times were good.

Overproduction

1920s Farmer

Unfortunately, the good times did not last forever. As manufacturers continued to produce goods at a faster rate than ever, they turned out products faster than consumers could buy them. When the market has more of a product than consumers want, it is called **overproduction**. Meanwhile, consumers' reluctance to buy all that has been produced is referred to as **underconsumption**. Overproduction combined with underconsumption leads to falling prices as producers try to convince consumers to pick their goods over a lot of other choices. Eventually, overproduction and the corresponding fall in prices can seriously hurt producers, raise unemployment, and hurt the economy.

One group that understood this better than anyone was farmers. Farmers did not enjoy the same prosperity as the rest of the country during the 1920s. From 1909 through the war years, farmers did well because of high demand for their products. With the war over, however, times changed. New machinery, such as tractors, allowed farmers to produce far more. However, this resulted in overproduction and caused agricultural prices to drop drastically in the 1920s. Although Congress made attempts to pass bills designed to increase farm prices, they were vetoed by Coolidge (remember, Coolidge did not think government should interfere in the economy). As a result, the agricultural industry was unable to recover, and many farms went into foreclosure.

Herbert Hoover

Republican **Herbert Hoover** became president in 1929. Although not as conservative as Coolidge, Hoover also opposed too much government interference in business. Unfortunately for Hoover, he took office at a time when the US economy was about to collapse. On October 29, 1929, a date known as **Black Tuesday**, the stock market crashed! Prices dropped drastically. Many who bought stock on speculation or invested by buying on the margin lost everything. Others were financially ruined as brokers and banks began to call in loans that people had no money to pay. The disaster marked the beginning of the **Great Depression**. The Great Depression lasted for more than a decade and remains the greatest economic crisis in US history.

Causes of the Great Depression

- Overproduction and Underconsumption that led to falling prices.
- Consumerism: citizens began buying and spending more money than they saved.
- Buying risky stocks on Speculation and "Buying on the Margin"
- Stock Market Crash of 1929 ("Black Tuesday")

Great Depression

Hooverville

Following the stock market crash of 1929, the US economy unraveled. People rushed in mass to withdraw money from banks, causing them to close. (Back then, the government did not insure bank accounts. Therefore, if a bank closed and went out of business, anyone who had money in the bank lost all their savings.) People stopped investing in the stock market, causing stock prices to fall even further. Wealthy families suddenly found themselves with nothing. At one point, roughly one out of every four US citizens did not have a job. Countless numbers of people became homeless. Many people had to rely on **soup kitchens** and **breadlines** that provided food for the poor in order to have anything to eat. In larger cities, many of the homeless gathered together to live in homemade shacks. These makeshift villages came to be called **Hoovervilles**, in reference to the president whom much of the nation blamed for its woes. As the United States approached the presidential election of 1932, many citizens felt hopeless and desperate. The nation needed leadership and direction.

FDR Takes Over

In 1932, the nation elected Democrat **Franklin Delano Roosevelt** (FDR) president of the United States by an overwhelming majority. With a broad smile and optimistic demeanor, FDR was a much-needed image of hope for a nation battered by the Great Depression. He became the first president to effectively use radio to his advantage. Speaking directly to the nation in a series of "fireside chats," Roosevelt helped instill confidence and even succeeded in getting many people to redeposit their money in banks. Unlike his predecessors, he was also ready to experiment with government actions to deal with the nation's crisis. Roosevelt believed that the country needed the government to provide **direct relief** (federal help to those hurting from the financial crisis). Many economists and politicians argued that the economy would eventually recover if government left it alone. Roosevelt believed that this policy had already proven to be a failure and was willing to engage in **deficit spending** (government spending of borrowed money) to help get the US economy moving in the right direction. To do this, Roosevelt introduced new legislation and a number of programs known collectively as the **New Deal**. The period from FDR's inauguration in March 1933 through the following June became known as the **first hundred days**. During this time, Roosevelt pushed program after program through Congress in an effort to provide economic relief and recovery.

Franklin Delano Roosevelt

Roosevelt's First New Deal

Roosevelt introduced his New Deal in two parts. The following programs were part of what came to be known as Roosevelt's **First New Deal.**

Civilian Conservation Corps (CCC)	Established in 1933, the CCC provided employment for unmarried men between the ages of 17 and 23. These young men worked in the national parks installing electric lines, building fire towers, and planting new trees in deforested areas. Thanks to the efforts of Eleanor Roosevelt, it eventually provided some programs for women as well.
Agricultural Adjustment Act (AAA)	Passed in 1933, this act approved government loans to farmers and paid farmers not to grow certain crops in order to increase the price of agricultural products.

The Federal Deposit Insurance Corporation (FDIC)	Established in 1933 under the Federal Reserve Act, the FDIC insured bank deposits of up to $100,000 in case of bank failure. This insurance was intended to prevent people from withdrawing their money out of panic.
National Industrial Recovery Act (NIRA)	Passed in 1933, this law sought to bolster industrial prices and prevent US business failures. One part of the NIRA was the **Public Works Administration (PWA)**. The PWA launched a number of public works such as the construction of dams, highways, and bridges. These projects helped provide citizens with desperately needed jobs.
Tennessee Valley Authority (TVA)	Established in 1933, the TVA built hydroelectric dams to create jobs and bring cheap electricity to parts of the South that had previously been without power. The southern Appalachians were historically one of the poorest areas in the nation. With the help of the TVA, this region prospered as never before.

The Second New Deal

After showing cautious restraint through much of 1934, FDR chose to launch a bold new set of programs that came to be called the **Second New Deal**. A few of them are listed below.

National Labor Relations Act (NLRA)	Also known as the **Wagner Act**, Congress passed this law in 1935 and created a board to monitor unfair management practices such as firing workers who joined unions. It protected the right of workers in the **private sector** (non-government employees) to organize unions, engage in collective bargaining, and go on strike. The act demonstrated a strong shift by the federal government towards supporting the interests of workers and made Roosevelt extremely popular among laborers and union leaders.
Social Security Act (SSA)	Passed in 1935, this act established retirement income for all workers once they reach the age of 65. It also provided benefits to certain unemployed workers. Social Security is the only New Deal program still around today. It continues to pay retirement benefits to those over the official age of retirement. One of its architects was Frances Perkins. As Roosevelt's secretary of labor, she was the first woman in history to be appointed to a US president's cabinet.

Revenue Act of 1935	This law raised taxes on those making above \$50,000/year as well as corporate and estate taxes. It won the favor of many on the left and was nicknamed the "soak the rich tax."

Although FDR's New Deal was a revolutionary approach to government, it actually failed to end the Great Depression. On the eve of World War II, much of the nation was still unemployed and the economy was still hurting. It did, however, provide some relief and enabled the nation to stay afloat until the onset of war caused the economy to boom in the 1940s.

Practice 6.1 Prosperity and Depression

1. The term "Red Scare" refers to

   A. US concerns about communism.

   B. citizens' fears concerning the social changes of the 1920s.

   C. specific legislation restricting immigration.

   D. white fears inspired by the Harlem Renaissance.

2. An intellectual movement that occurred in New York City among the African American community and featured the writings of men like Langston Hughes was called the

   A. New Deal.

   B. TVA.

   C. Harlem Renaissance.

   D. Jazz period.

3. Describe Henry Ford's impact on the automobile industry and business practices in general.

4. The greatest economic crisis in US history is known as

   A. overproduction.

   B. The Dust Bowl.

   C. the Great Depression.

   D. Black Tuesday.

5. Describe some of the causes of the Great Depression.

6. Franklin Roosevelt's plan to use government spending to deal with the nation's economic troubles during the 1930s was called the

   A. New Deal.

   B. TVA.

   C. Wagner Plan.

   D. Black Tuesday.

6.2 World War II

International Unrest

Hitler and Mussolini

In the years that followed World War I, a worldwide economic depression devastated Europe. As people blamed government leaders for their hardships, a great deal of political and social unrest began to rise within a number of nations. As a result, totalitarian governments that restricted personal freedoms and prohibited political opposition rose to power. **Benito Mussolini** seized power first in Italy. A few years later, in 1933, a charismatic leader named **Adolf Hitler** emerged as the ruler of Germany. The two soon became allies. Meanwhile, in Southeast Asia, the Empire of **Japan** aggressively conquered parts of China. In 1937, Japan began trying to seize the rest of China as well. By the end of 1938, Japan had captured major cities along the Chinese coast but could not control the inland countryside. In 1939, Hitler's forces invaded Poland, launching World War II in Europe. Less than a year later, he conquered Belgium, the Netherlands, and France as well. In 1940, Germany, Italy, and Japan formed an alliance known as the **Axis Powers**.(See chapter 10, sections 10.2–10.3)

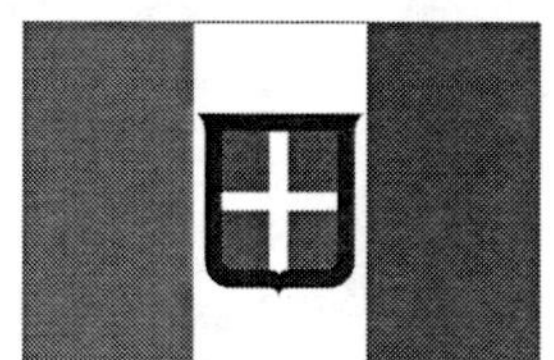
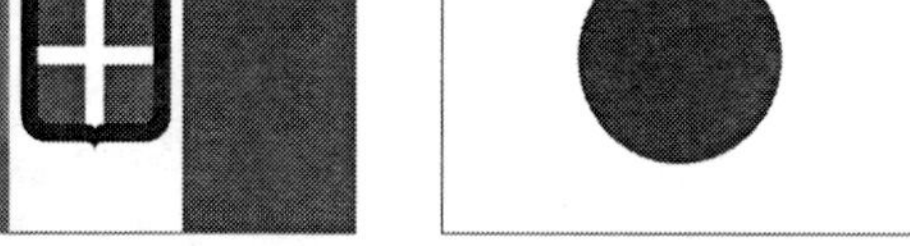
Axis Powers

US Reactions

The United States first tried to stay out of matters in Europe and the Far East. Congress passed the Neutrality Act in 1935 and considered a Constitutional amendment restricting the government's power to declare war. Still, as Japan continued its aggressive behavior and Hitler appeared more and more willing to take what he wanted by force, President Roosevelt grew increasingly concerned. Although he did not yet have enough political support to take a more active stance, FDR kept a suspicious eye on Germany and Japan.

The United States Enters the War

FDR

In 1940, Franklin Delano Roosevelt won a third term as president. Although the majority of US citizens favored neutrality, Roosevelt was already convinced that the United States could not afford to stay out of the war much longer. As Britain struggled in its fight against Germany, Roosevelt proclaimed to the United States public, "If Great Britain goes down, all of us in the Americas would be living at the point of a gun. We must be the great arsenal of democracy." In March 1941, Congress passed the **Lend-Lease Act**. Under this act, the president could send aid to any nation whose defense was considered vital to US national security. If the country had no resources to pay for the aid, the US could send it and defer payment until later. Roosevelt helped win public support for this policy by offering the analogy of a neighbor's house being on fire. "If your neighbor's house is on fire," Roosevelt reasoned, "you don't sell him a hose, you give it to him. Then, you take it back after the fire is out. This helps your neighbor and makes sure that the fire doesn't spread to your own house."

Pearl Harbor

Pearl Harbor Attack

Admiral Yamamoto

While Hitler steamrolled through Europe, the United States also had one eye on Japan. In response to Japan's military actions in the Pacific, the US imposed an **embargo** (refusal to ship certain products to a country) on oil and steel. Japan's leaders then set their sights on the rich natural resources of the Dutch East Indies. Before Japan could go after the territories it wanted, however, it had to deal with one major problem: the US naval Fleet anchored at **Pearl Harbor**, Hawaii. Although he doubted Japan's ability to win a war with the United States, Japanese Admiral Isoroku Yamamoto knew that his country was determined to expand. He developed an all but impossible plan to sail six **aircraft carriers** (huge ships that carry war planes) across the Pacific undetected and launch a surprise attack on Pearl Harbor. Maintaining radio silence the entire way, the Japanese ships reached their destination as planned. US intelligence knew that the Japanese were planning an attack of some kind; they just didn't know where. Believing that the waters of Pearl Harbor were too shallow for planes to drop **torpedoes** (explosive devices that hit the water and then are propelled toward a target), they focused on the Philippines and the threat of **sabotage** (people trying to damage US military equipment, such as planes parked in hangers).

A few minutes before 8 a.m. on **December 7, 1941**, Japanese airplanes began the first wave of bombings on the Pacific fleet at Pearl Harbor. United States military personnel actually detected the incoming planes on radar but ignored them because they thought they were US planes flying in from the mainland. In less than two hours, the Japanese air attack sank or seriously damaged a dozen naval vessels, destroyed almost 200 warplanes, and killed or wounded nearly 3,000 people. The next day, President Roosevelt emotionally described December 7 as "a day which will live in infamy!" Both houses of Congress approved a declaration of war against Japan and later against Germany and Italy as well. Suddenly, the US was plunged into the middle of World War II.

Government Action

War Poster

The government realized that it needed to maintain strong public support for the war in order to successfully defeat the Axis nations. It recognized that a sense of patriotism and high national morale would be crucial. The government paid artists to design patriotic war posters, and movie theaters began playing newsreels depicting the US war effort in a positive light. Ads depicting patriotic themes in magazines and on radio broadcasts also became common.

War meant that the United States' economy had to switch from peacetime to wartime as quickly as possible. To oversee this transformation, President Roosevelt established the **War Production Board (WPB)**. This board re-directed raw materials and resources from the production of civilian consumer goods to the production of materials needed for waging war against Germany and Japan. The economic result of the war was that the US economy boomed and people's standard of living increased. Unemployed men now found themselves employed either as soldiers or in industries producing goods needed for the war effort. Others began migrating to northern cities and out west to fill the jobs needed for wartime production. As a result, the population of states like California, Arizona, Nevada, Texas, and Washington increased rapidly during the war.

Income Taxes and War Bonds

In order for the United States to have the money and resources available to win the war, it called on sacrifices from citizens. The number of people required to pay income taxes greatly increased during the war years. To make sure these taxes were collected, the government introduced the idea of *withholding income tax*. For the first time, the government required employers to withhold taxes from employees' paychecks and give it to the government immediately. Another means of raising money was through the sale of war bonds. By buying bonds, citizens loaned money to the government in return for interest. Thus, **war bond drives** to promote the purchase of such bonds became common as advertisements, posters, even movie stars encouraged people to buy bonds as part of their patriotic duty. Through bonds, the government raised more than 60 million dollars.

War Bond Ad

Citizen Sacrifice

In addition to money, the government also called on people to sacrifice resources. People started growing **victory gardens** of their own so that more food could be sent to feed the soldiers. The government also started a program of **rationing** by which it could control how certain resources were distributed. In 1941, the government began rationing tires. Two years later, certain items were assigned points values. Once a citizen used up all their points, they could no longer obtain these items until they acquired more. In this way, the government forced the public to conserve resources that were needed to support the war effort.

Victory Gardens

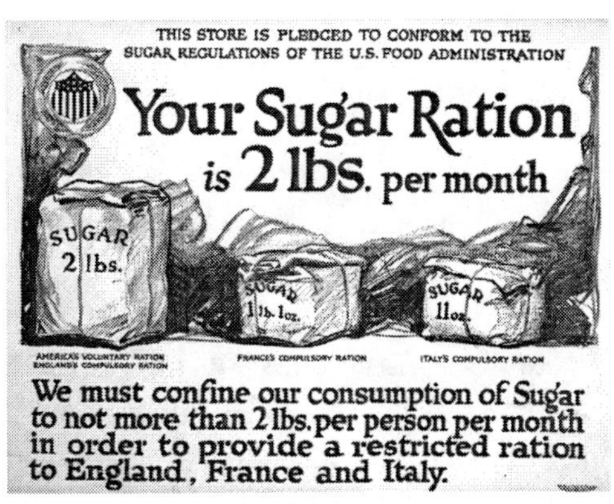

Rationing

"Rosie the Riveter"

Rosie the Riveter

With so many US men going off to fight, women became an important part of the workforce at home. Women of all cultural and racial backgrounds stepped forward to take on jobs traditionally held by men. A popular song of the day was called **"Rosie the Riveter."** It described a woman who worked in the factory as a riveter while her boyfriend served in the marines. *Rosie the Riveter* became the symbol of those women who entered the workforce to fill the gap left vacant by men serving in the war.

Internment of Japanese, German, and Italian Americans

Internment Camp

The Japanese attack on Pearl Harbor fueled suspicion and fear among US citizens. Many suspected that Japanese, German, and Italian Americans would end up supporting the Axis Powers. As a result, thousands of such citizens were forced to relocate to **internment camps**. These camps tended to be located in remote areas and were meant to keep potentially threatening citizens in an isolated location where the government could keep an eye on them.

Although many German and Italian Americans were unjustly interned as well, Japanese Americans suffered the most. At President Roosevelt's order, the US military forced more than 100,000 Japanese Americans from their homes and businesses during the war and placed them in one of the various camps. A great number of these Japanese Americans lost everything as a result. Many of them were US citizens who had lived in the United States for several generations. Others had been born in the US to parents who had immigrated from Japan. In 1944, the US Supreme Court ruled that the government internment of Japanese Americans was lawful and justified due to "...the military urgency of the situation." Eventually, in 1983, the United States government formally recognized the injustice that had been done and authorized payments of $20,000 to each living Japanese American who had suffered under this policy.

THE WAR IN EUROPE

Three days after Pearl Harbor, Germany and Italy declared war on the United States. By this time, Hitler had attacked the Soviet Union and was at war with Stalin as well. The United States, Great Britain, and the Soviet Union now stood together as the **Allied Powers** along with several other nations. After driving the Axis forces out of North Africa and taking parts of Italy, the Allies launched plans for a massive invasion of Western Europe.

Allied Powers

D-DAY

Big Three Meeting

The three leaders — Roosevelt, Churchill, and Stalin — finally met in December 1943. Because the Soviets had lost millions of lives fighting Germany in Eastern Europe while Britain and the US focused on Africa and southern Italy, Stalin desperately wanted the Allies to launch an invasion of France and create a second front against Hitler in Western Europe. After initially being reluctant, the US and Britain finally agreed. They appointed US **General Dwight D. Eisenhower** to serve as the supreme allied commander in charge of planning *Operation Overlord.* The operation involved hundreds of thousands of troops and called for the largest **amphibious invasion** (invasion in which soldiers invade from the sea rather than by crossing borders over land) in military history. The date of the invasion, June 6, 1944, became known as **D-Day**. Hitting the beaches at Normandy, France, the first soldiers ashore received overwhelming gunfire. Despite suffering heavy losses, it took the Allies less than a week to get over 500,000 troops ashore. From their established foothold, these forces were able to advance further into France. On August 25, 1944, the Allies fought their way into Paris, liberating the city from four years of German occupation. After successfully fending off Germany's final major attack at the Battle of the Bulge the following winter, the Allies marched on towards Berlin (Germany's capital).

With Soviet forces bearing down on the capital, Hitler retreated to his **bunker** (underground fortress) in an attempt to somehow salvage victory. Even young boys were armed and placed in the areas around Berlin with orders to defend the city with their lives. Finally, in the spring of 1945, **Berlin fell** before the advancing Soviet army. In the face of certain defeat, Hitler committed suicide on April 30, 1945, rather than be captured. Shortly after, Germany surrendered, ending the war in Europe. Sadly, President Franklin Roosevelt died on April 12 and never saw the day of victory. After many long years of war, people in the Allied countries finally celebrated *V-E Day* (Victory in Europe Day) on May 8, 1945.

War in the Pacific

MacArthur in the Philippines

Within hours of the attack on Pearl Harbor, Japan also attacked the **Philippines**, destroying nearly half of the US airplanes stationed there. A few days later, Japanese forces invaded and eventually took the islands. More than 75,000 US soldiers and Filipinos became prisoners of war as a result. Forced to walk roughly 60 miles to trains waiting to carry them to prisoner of war camps, many of these prisoners died from injuries, sickness, and harsh treatment along the way. The horrid event was labeled the **Bataan Death March**. Those held responsible for it were eventually tried as criminals after the war.

The war in the Pacific had gotten off to a disastrous start for the United States. Not only was one of its most gifted military leaders, General Douglas MacArthur, forced to abandon the Philippines, but the attack at Pearl Harbor badly damaged its Pacific Fleet. Fortunately for the US, the aircraft carriers that the Japanese had hoped to destroy in the attack were not in port on December 7 and were still functioning. This proved to be crucial as the United States tried to turn the tide of the war in the Pacific.

The Battle of Midway and Island Hopping

Battle of Midway

Admiral Yamamoto, considered a military genius for orchestrating the attack on Pearl Harbor, felt that the remainder of the US Pacific Fleet must be destroyed if Japan had any hope of winning the war. He hoped to meet the US Navy in a decisive battle before it could fully recover from Pearl Harbor. The **Battle of Midway** in June 1942 proved to be a turning point in the war. This time, it was the Japanese who failed to detect the location of its enemy's aircraft carriers, and US planes were able to attack the Japanese as they were still attempting to load bombs onto their planes. Midway greatly boosted the morale of the United States' Pacific forces and allowed the US to finally go on offense in its war with Japan.

The United States decided to advance on Japan from two directions. The first path was across the central Pacific under Admiral Chester Nimitz. The second was from the south under General MacArthur and Admiral William Halsey and involved an invasion of the Philippines. MacArthur argued strongly for such an invasion because he had publicly sworn he would return to liberate the islands after being ordered to abandon them at the war's outset.

The United States then began a process of **island hopping**, in which it attacked and conquered one group of islands, then moved on to the next as its forces made their way to Japan. In the South, MacArthur reached the Philippines and, in dramatic fashion, waded ashore before rolling news cameras to proclaim, "People of the Philippines, I have returned." As US troops fought their way inland, the largest naval battle in history raged offshore in the Battle of Leyte Gulf. In desperation, the Japanese turned to the use of *kamikaze pilots* to try and avoid defeat. Kamikazes were pilots who committed suicide by intentionally crashing their planes into US ships in an attempt to sink them. Meanwhile, Nimitz's forces won key battles at Guadalcanal, Iwo Jima, and Okinawa. Each battle was extremely fierce and bloody. Although overpowered, Japanese soldiers often preferred fighting to the death rather than surrendering.

THE ATOMIC BOMB

Atomic Explosion

Harry S. Truman

The capture of Okinawa cleared the way for an invasion of Japan that would end the war. The invasion never happened. Soon after entering the war, the US began work on developing the **atomic bomb**. The top secret endeavor was called the *Manhattan Project.* J. Robert Oppenheimer headed the project and most of the development took place in laboratories at **Los Alamos, New Mexico**. On July 16, 1945, scientists tested the new weapon in the New Mexico desert. The flash was blinding and the explosion so great that it shattered windows 125 miles away. Meanwhile, the new president, **Harry S. Truman**, was at the Potsdam Conference discussing postwar policies with Prime Minister Churchill and Joseph Stalin. Among the conditions of the *Potsdam Declaration*, the allied leaders restated their policy of "unconditional surrender." In other words, the Allies would only accept a surrender in which the Allies dictated the terms of peace without the defeated Japanese insisting on any conditions. When the Japanese refused to surrender unconditionally, but instead insisted that they be given a guarantee that the position of the Emperor would be protected, Truman authorized the use of the bomb.

On August 6, 1945, a specially equipped B29 bomber called the *Enola Gay*, dropped the first atomic bomb on Hiroshima, Japan. The blast leveled the city and killed thousands of civilians and military personnel. Many more died later from radiation released in the blast. Two days later, the Soviet Union declared war on Japan and invaded Manchuria. When Japan delayed in issuing its surrender, the US dropped another bomb on August 9 on the city of Nagasaki. In the face of the massive death and destruction caused by these attacks, and with the Soviet Union now involved in the fighting, Japan finally surrendered to the United States on August 14, 1945. World War II was over. The next day the US celebrated *V-J Day* (Victory over Japan Day). Although the world was shocked by the power of the atomic bomb, Truman defended his decision to use it. He pointed out that by dropping the bomb, an invasion of Japan had been avoided, thereby saving the lives of Allied soldiers.

Practice 6.2 World War II

1. The term "Rosie the Riveter" refers to
   - A. people who raised victory gardens.
   - B. women who worked jobs so men could fight in WWII.
   - C. women who joined the military.
   - D. the head of the War Production Board

2. How did the war affect citizens and the role of women in US society?

3. The US entered the fighting in World War II specifically because of what event?
   - A. Japan's attack on Pearl Harbor
   - B. Germany's invasion of Poland
   - C. Germany and the USSR's non-aggression pact
   - D. the fall of France

4. Who would have been most excited about the US Lend-Lease Act?
   - A. Adolf Hitler
   - B. Isoroku Yamamoto
   - C. Winston Churchill
   - D. Benito Mussolini

5. What was the atomic bomb, why was it used, and what effect did it have on the war?

6.3 The Cold War

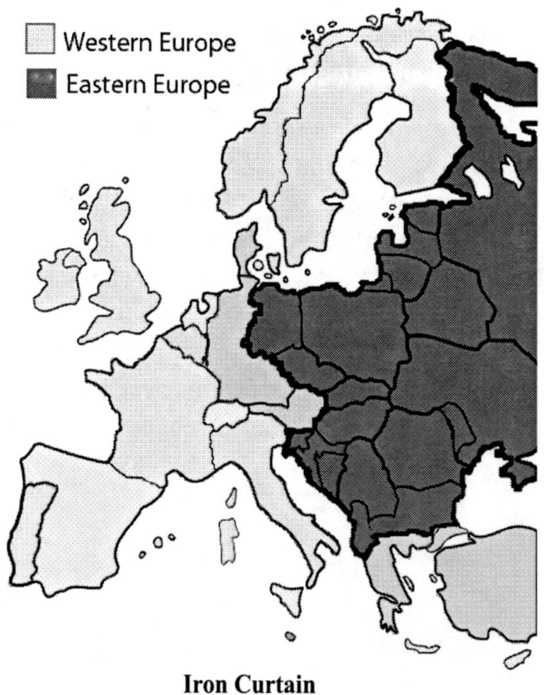

Iron Curtain

Following World War II, tensions were high between the western Allies and the Soviet Union. Neither side trusted the other since the western powers were democracies with capitalist market systems and the Soviet Union was a socialist state led by the Communist Party. After the war, the United States and Great Britain felt strongly that the Allies should not occupy the territories they conquered during WWII. The Soviets, on the other hand, had suffered greater losses in terms of life and property than either of them. They were determined not to be invaded again. Stalin decided that he must maintain control over Eastern Europe in order to keep a buffer between the Soviet Union and western nations. Not only did Stalin make it evident that he had no intention of giving up control of the conquered territories, he also stamped out any opposition to his Communist Party in the nations under his control. The European continent now stood divided between the western democracies and **Soviet satellite nations** (nations answering to and representing the views of the USSR). In a speech given by Winston

Churchill at Westminster College in Missouri, the former prime minister said of Europe, "A shadow has fallen... an *iron curtain* has descended across the continent." As a result of his comments, "iron curtain" became the common term used to refer to the dividing line between Eastern and Western Europe.

US Post-war Policies in Europe

George Marshall

In 1946, a top US diplomat named George Kennan was stationed in the Soviet Union. After observing Soviet behavior and becoming very familiar with the USSR's government, Kennan recommended that the US and its allies focus on a **containment policy**. Kennan believed that Eastern Europe was firmly in Soviet hands and could not be saved. Therefore, the US and the West should focus on *containing* communism to those countries in which it already existed and not let it spread any further. Reaffirming Kennan's philosophy, Truman introduced the **Truman Doctrine**. This doctrine stated that the United States would not hesitate to intervene and aid nations overseas to resist communism. It featured a financial plan to build up Europe, worked out by former army chief of staff and then secretary of state, George Marshall. Labeled the **Marshall Plan**, it provided nations in war-torn Europe with much needed financial support from the United States. This aid served to spark economic revival and prosperity in these countries, alleviating the suffering of many people. Since communist revolutions often started due to economic hardships, the Marshall Plan went a long way towards preventing Soviet advances into Western Europe and became the crowning achievement of the containment policy.

A Divided Germany

When World War II ended, the Allies divided Germany among themselves. Part of the country fell under US control, part fell under British control, and part of the nation fell to the Soviets. Out of the portions allotted to the United States and Britain, France received a portion as well. In addition, the German capital of Berlin, although located within the Soviets' territory, was also divided. The western portions of the city went to the western Allies while the eastern portion went to the Soviets. Great Britain, the United States, and France all saw these divisions as temporary. They envisioned Germany eventually being a unified and independent democracy. Stalin, however, had no intention of giving up the Soviet controlled parts of Berlin or Germany. By 1948, it became obvious that Stalin would not relent. Realizing that a unified Germany would not be possible, the US, Great Britain, and France combined their sectors into one nation, the Federal Republic of Germany (West Germany), and declared West Berlin to be part of this new nation. The USSR responded by establishing the German Democratic Republic (East

France
Russia
Great Britain
United States

Division of Berlin

Germany) under communist rule. Almost immediately, thousands of people wishing to escape communism fled to West Berlin hoping to make their way to freedom. In an effort to stop this, Stalin decided to force the West to surrender its portion of Berlin. He cut off the city, not allowing any needed supplies to reach the people of West Berlin. Wanting to avoid a war, yet deal firmly with Stalin, Truman authorized the *Berlin Airlift*. Over a fifteen-month period, US and British planes delivered needed supplies to West Berlin. The Soviets finally gave up in May of 1949, but the bitterness of the conflict only served to fuel the fires of the **Cold War.** The term "cold war" was first used by presidential advisor, Bernard Baruch, in 1947. It referred to the tension between the United States and the Soviet Union that dominated both nations' foreign policies and which many feared would lead to actual war.

Berlin Airlift

China and Korea

Mao Zedong

In 1949, China fell under communist control after the forces of **Mao Zedong** forced the US-supported Nationalists of Chiang Kai-shek to retreat to Formosa (see chapter 10, section 10.4). Mao's revolution greatly concerned the United States because it feared a communist takeover of Southeast Asia. The US refused to recognize the new government, insisting that Chiang's Nationalists on Formosa still represented the true government of China. It used its veto power to prevent the UN from formally recognizing Mao's government in the newly formed United Nations.

Korean War

Korea was among the countries liberated from the Japanese during World War II. Since both the US and the Soviets played a role in its liberation, the nation was divided along the 38th parallel (line of latitude that runs through Korea). The northern half of the country established a communist government while the southern half put in place a pro-US democracy. In June 1950, the **Korean War** began when North Korean forces crossed the 38th parallel. The United Nations elected to come to South Korea's aid, and President Truman chose General Douglas MacArthur, the man who had liberated the Philippines and oversaw the establishment of a democracy in Japan after WWII, to lead the UN forces. Technically, the conflict was never a declared war, but rather a UN police action.

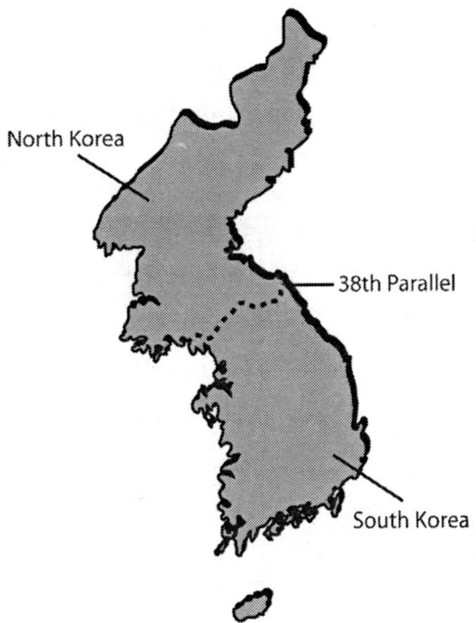

Division of Korea

MacArthur's forces pushed their enemy back across the 38th parallel. Continuing to advance north, the UN forces moved ever closer to the Chinese border. Concerned that US-led forces were so close and wanting to maintain a communist regime in North Korea, the Chinese sent troops across the Yalu River to aid the North Koreans. A stalemate soon developed. To make matters more complicated, Truman fired MacArthur after the general criticized the president's handling of the war. After two more years of fighting, both sides signed a truce in 1953. The agreement left the country divided at almost the same point as when the conflict started.

ATTITUDES AT HOME

Fallout Shelter

Citizens in the United States were very concerned about the Cold War. Unlike before the war, people now lived with the threat of nuclear weapons. The US and USSR were engaged in a *nuclear arms race* in which both sides continually built updated weapons aimed at one another and which provided the possibility of **massive retaliation** (responding to an attack with nuclear weapons). Private citizens began building *fallout shelters,* which they hoped could provide protection if the Soviets launched a nuclear attack. Schools conducted nuclear attack drills and taught students how to "duck and cover" in the event of a missile strike.

In addition to fears of nuclear war, there was also a new wave of fear about communism. During the Great Depression, many US citizens had joined the Communist Party, or at least voiced agreement with certain communist ideals. Most did this because they felt communism offered the economic relief that they needed. When economic times got better and people learned more about Stalin's brutality in the USSR, most no longer had an interest in being Communists. Still, the success of China's communist revolution and North Korea's attempt to invade South Korea convinced many in the US that Communists would stop at nothing short of worldwide domination. The US government inevitably responded to such concerns. In the late 1940s and into the '50s, the government investigated, arrested, and sometimes harassed many people due to their alleged connections to the Communist Party. This period became known as the second **Red Scare**.

GOVERNMENT POLICIES DEALING WITH COMMUNISM

Alger Hiss

Concerned with the threat of communism, President Truman signed legislation creating what became the Department of Defense to preside over military affairs. This act also created the president's National Security Council for the purpose of coordinating national security policies and the Central Intelligence Agency (CIA) to be responsible for spying on the USSR and its allies. Meanwhile, Congress relied on the **House Un-American Activities Committee (HUAC)** to root out Communists in the federal government. The committee became most famous for its investigation of State Department official, Alger Hiss, who was accused of giving the Soviets secret US documents during the 1930s. Hiss denied the charges but was convicted of **perjury** (lying under oath) and sent to prison. HUAC also gained notoriety for its investigations of individuals in the in the movie industry who were suspected of being Communists. The committee called a number of Hollywood actors, producers, and writers to testify in 1947. Believing the committee's actions to be a violation of civil rights, 10 of the accused refused to appear before the HUAC. The "Hollywood Ten" then went to jail for contempt. Some were sentenced to terms as long as a year. Out of fear that they might be targeted next, a number of movie executives denounced the Hollywood Ten and developed a Hollywood blacklist. The list consisted of writers, actors, and directors, that producers refused to work with because of suspected ties to communism. Even today, many in Hollywood remain bitter about the list.

JOSEPH MCCARTHY

McCarthy Hearings

One of the most interesting characters to arise as a result of national concern about communism was Wisconsin Senator, **Joseph McCarthy**. McCarthy was convinced that Communists had infiltrated high levels of government and the US military. He even accused former army chief of staff and secretary of state, George Marshall. At first, Communist aggression in Korea served to help McCarthy and his ideas gain popularity. Eventually, however, McCarthy had to defend his views in a series of televised hearings. By the time the hearings ended in June 1954, most US citizens viewed McCarthy as paranoid at best and downright crazy at worst. *"McCarthyism"* (the ideas and fears of communism voiced by McCarthy and his supporters) began to collapse, and the irrational fear that "Communists are everywhere" ultimately subsided.

THE SPACE RACE

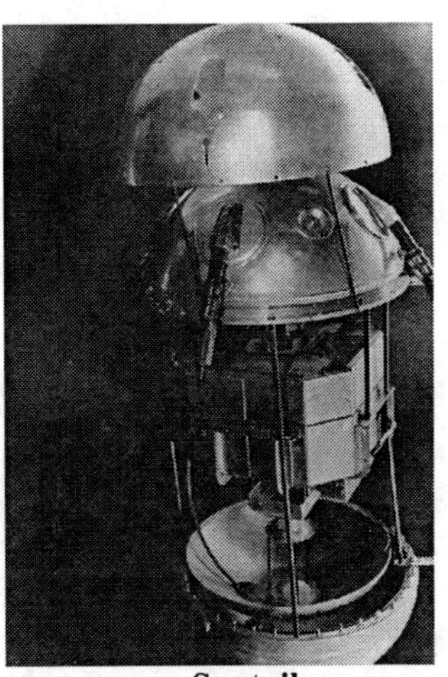
Sputnik

The United States and the USSR distrusted one another even before World War II. The atomic bomb, and later the hydrogen bomb, only intensified the friction between the two nations. Each felt compelled to keep up with the other's nuclear capabilities. In 1957, the Soviets launched **Sputnik,** the first artificial satellite to orbit the earth. Sputnik revealed the superiority of Soviet technology and greatly concerned the US. Realizing that this same technology could be used to launch nuclear missiles, the United States eagerly entered the **space race** (competition with the Soviet Union to gain the upper-hand in space travel and technology). In 1958, Congress passed the *National Defense Education Act*. This law provided aid for education and was geared toward boosting the study of science, math, and foreign languages. It was intended to propel the US in front of the Soviet Union in both the space race and in nuclear technology.

First Moonwalk

In 1961, the Soviet Union once again demonstrated that they were ahead in the space race when they successfully launched the first manned space flight. Yuri Gagarin successfully orbited the earth on board a Soviet spacecraft. Not to be outdone by the Soviets, President Kennedy issued a challenge to the US to put a man on the moon before the end of the decade. Less than a year later, NASA (the National Aeronautics and Space Agency) successfully launched a spacecraft carrying astronaut, John Glenn, into orbit. Seven and a half years later, on July 20, 1969, Neil Armstrong answered President Kennedy's challenge by becoming the first human being to walk on the moon.

Practice 6.3 The Cold War

1. The term "Cold War" refers to
   A. the distrust between the US and USSR that many feared would lead to actual war in the years following WWII.
   B. the war fought in Germany after WWII between Communists and Democrats.
   C. the war fought between North and South Korea.
   D. the war fought between the US and China following the Chinese Revolution.

2. The Truman Doctrine stated that
   A. the US would not tolerate Communists in high levels of US government.
   B. the US would not hesitate to intervene to help foreign nations resist communism.
   C. the US would not cross the 38th parallel during the Korean War.
   D. the US would support Mao's revolution in China.

3. Who was Joseph McCarthy and how did he become famous?

4. What was *Sputnik,* and why did it concern leaders in the United States?

6.4 Social Movements

The Civil Rights Movement

Harry S. Truman

In 1945, **Harry S. Truman** became the nation's thirty-third president following the death of Franklin Roosevelt. Disturbed by reports of violence against southern blacks, Truman quickly became a supporter of civil rights. He also wanted to improve the status of black citizens because of the Cold War. Both the US and the Soviet Union felt it was important to extend their influence around the globe. The United States hoped to keep communism from spreading to Third World countries in Africa, Asia, and Latin America. However, the Soviets made sure that such nations were well aware of racial injustices that occurred in the US. Truman knew that the United States could not allow its prejudice to alienate the rest of the world. He felt strongly that supporting civil rights was a matter of national security as well as social justice.

In 1948, President Truman informed Congress of his intention to support civil rights. He wanted the federal government to take action to ensure voting rights and fair employment practices for minorities. Such views soon caused splits in the Democratic Party. Some Democrats supported Truman and wanted to be even more aggressive about passing civil rights laws. Many southern Democrats, however, were outraged and claimed that the federal government had no right to tell the states what to do. Division over the issue actually led to a number of southern delegates walking out of the Democratic convention and starting a third party that came to be called the "Dixiecrats." The Dixiecrats opposed Democratic positions supporting **integration** (desegregation). They supported segregation and nominated

South Carolina governor, Strom Thurmond, as their presidential candidate. Despite the threat of losing southern support in the upcoming election, Truman stuck to his guns. Shortly after the convention, he signed an executive order **integrating the United States military**. To most experts' surprise, Truman overcame the upheaval in his own party to win the 1948 election. So convinced were most people that Truman would lose to Republican Thomas Dewey, that many newspapers went ahead and printed headlines announcing Truman's defeat. Thanks to Truman's support, the last of the segregated military units were abolished by the end of 1954.

As the nation entered the 1950s, the Civil Rights Movement continued to gain momentum. The NAACP decided that it was time to aggressively go after segregation laws in court. One of the first areas it decided to attack was school segregation. The NAACP sued the Board of Education of Topeka, Kansas, because it would not let a black girl, Linda Brown, attend an all-white school near her home. In ***Brown vs. Board of Education of Topeka* (1954)**, the Supreme Court reversed the *Plessy v. Ferguson* decision and ruled that racial segregation in public schools is unconstitutional. The Court, led by Chief Justice Earl Warren, found that separate facilities were inherently unequal because they did not present minority students with the same opportunities that were offered in white schools. The case also made NAACP attorney, Thurgood Marshall, a well-known figure. Eventually, he became the first African American ever appointed to the Supreme Court.

Thurgood Marshall

WHITE RESPONSE

Despite the Court's decision in *Brown*, many southern leaders were determined to maintain segregation as long as possible. In Little Rock, Arkansas, the governor refused to obey a federal court order to integrate **Little Rock Central High School** in 1957. He called in the Arkansas National Guard to prevent nine black students from entering the school, prompting President Eisenhower to nationalize the Guard and send them home. Eisenhower then mobilized elements of the 101st Airborne to enforce the court's ruling and make sure that the "Little Rock Nine" (the nine African American students) safely gained admittance to the school.

Resistance also occurred at the college level when the governor of Mississippi defied the Supreme Court and attempted to prevent an African American named **James Meredith** from enrolling at the University of Mississippi. The university finally admitted Meredith after President Kennedy sent federal authorities to deal with the situation. Similarly, Alabama's governor, **George Wallace**, tried to prevent the integration of the University of Alabama by physically blocking the entrance in protest. The incident ended when federal authorities again intervened and forced Wallace to comply.

George Wallace at University of Alabama

One city that won national praise for its handling of school desegregation was **Atlanta**, Georgia. Under the leadership of Mayor William Hartsfield, Atlanta managed to avoid much of the violence and turmoil that engulfed other southern cities. Hartsfield owed much of his success to a coalition of black and white business and community leaders that often worked behind the scenes to help the city peacefully deal with race relations. As a result, Atlanta integrated its school system slowly but relatively peacefully during the 1950s. When asked on one occasion how Atlanta managed to avoid much of the racial strife that plagued the rest of the South, Hartsfield responded with his famous quote: "Atlanta is the city too busy to hate."

William Hartsfield

THE MONTGOMERY BUS BOYCOTT

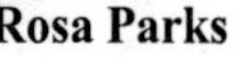
Rosa Parks

Dr. Martin Luther King Jr.

Segregation laws in the city of Montgomery, Alabama, required African American passengers to sit in the rear of public buses. Blacks were also expected to give up their seats to white passengers if the bus was crowded. On December 1, 1955, a bus driver ordered Rosa Parks, an African American woman, to give up her seat to a white passenger. When she refused, the police arrested her and took her to jail.

Rosa Parks' arrest quickly united the black community. NAACP leaders selected a young Baptist minister named **Dr. Martin Luther King, Jr.** to lead them in a boycott of city buses until Montgomery desegregated its public transportation. Almost overnight, the city's 50,000 blacks united in walking to work or carpooling rather than riding buses. The boycott cost the city of Montgomery large amounts of money normally paid by African Americans using public transportation. It lasted over a year until, in November 1956, the Supreme Court ruled that buses in Montgomery must be integrated. The **Montgomery Bus Boycott** was a major victory for African Americans and served to make Martin Luther King, Jr. a national figure. King, an incredibly intelligent man and a gifted public speaker, became the recognized leader of the Civil Rights Movement.

SOUTHERN CHRISTIAN LEADERSHIP CONFERENCE

The Montgomery Bus Boycott also gave birth to the **SCLC (Southern Christian Leadership Conference)**. The group chose Dr. King as its first president and sought to unite leaders from the black community (particularly black ministers) in the cause of civil rights. Early on, the SCLC tended to rely on voter registration and education within the black community as its major method for pursuing civil rights. The SCLC believed that if it could educate average African American citizens and get the right candidates elected to public office, it could successfully bring about the end of segregation and

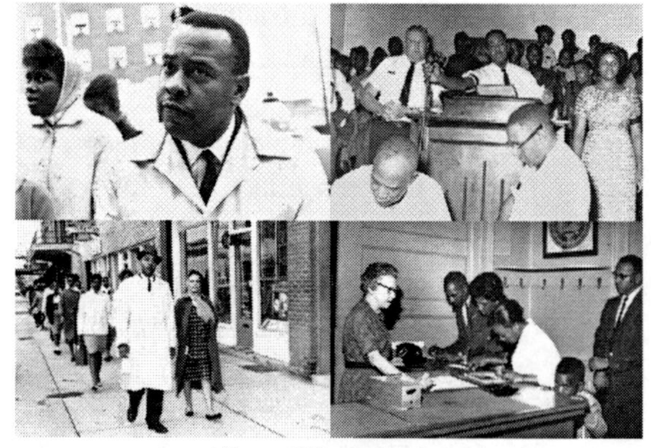
Albany Movement

inequality. However, following their participation in the *Albany Movement* (a student-inspired civil rights movement that occurred in south Georgia during the early '60s), a number of SCLC leaders began to appreciate the value of mass demonstrations and public protests as well.

Dr. Martin Luther King, Jr.

Raised in Atlanta, Martin Luther King, Jr. eventually returned to his home city and made it the center of the Civil Rights Movement. He was an extremely gifted man who believed in non-violent protest. Even if black protestors were beaten, arrested, or killed, King believed that African Americans would win their rights faster by refusing to engage in violence. He was right. As people around the country saw peaceful black marchers and protestors being beaten by white mobs and policeman, the movement gained support.

MLK Jr.

One of King's most famous writings during the Civil Rights Movement was his **"Letter from Birmingham Jail."** King wrote the letter in April 1963 from the jail in Birmingham, Alabama, where he had been arrested following a peaceful civil rights protest. His letter was a response to several white ministers who wrote a statement arguing that the battle for civil rights should be waged in the courts rather than by protests. King's public response eloquently expressed the reasons he disagreed and proclaimed that **civil disobedience** (peaceful refusal to follow unjust laws) was a necessary and acceptable method for achieving equality.

King and others also benefited from international pressure caused by the Cold War. Due to fears that communism might spread, the federal government knew it could not afford to have foreign nations view the US as unjust or a land of racial hatred. Taking advantage of such pressure, King shined in what many feel was his greatest public moment: his "I Have a Dream Speech," delivered before the Lincoln Memorial during the 1963 **March on Washington**. The "march" consisted of 200,000 civil rights activists demanding equality for all citizens.

March on Washington

Civil Rights Legislation

John F. Kennedy

Lyndon B. Johnson

After the March on Washington, President John F. Kennedy proposed new civil rights laws. However, on November 22, 1963, an assassin by the name of Lee Harvey Oswald shot and killed the president in Dallas as he rode in an open car with the first lady and the governor of Texas. The death of the young president left the nation stunned and in mourning. The new president, **Lyndon B. Johnson**, strongly urged the House and Senate to pass the civil rights legislation proposed by Kennedy. Despite fierce opposition from southern members of Congress, Johnson pushed through the **Civil Rights Act of 1964**. The act prohibited segregation in public accommodations (hotels, restaurants, theaters) and discrimination in education and employment. It also gave the president the power to enforce the new law. 1964 was also the year that the states ratified the Twenty-fourth Amendment to the Constitution. This amendment served to protect black voting rights by making the poll tax illegal.

Selma to Montgomery March

Congress passed another key piece of legislation in 1965. That year, protesters in Selma, Alabama, decided to bring national attention to the cause of civil rights by marching 50 miles to the state capital in Montgomery. The march occurred on March 7, 1965. When the 500 marchers reached Selma's city limits, 200 state troopers and sheriff's deputies beat them with clubs and whips, released dogs on them, and showered them with tear gas. Televised scenes of the violence shocked people nationwide and increased support for the Civil Rights Movement. The event became known as "Bloody Sunday" and was called an "American tragedy" by President Johnson. Thousands of whites and blacks descended on Selma to continue the march. Two weeks after "Bloody Sunday," Martin Luther King, Jr. led more than 3,000 marchers out of Selma, including a core of 300 people who walked the entire journey. Four days later, they arrived in Montgomery, where King addressed a rally of nearly 40,000 people in front of the capitol building. Soon after, on August 6, 1965, President Johnson signed the **Voting Rights Act of 1965**. It authorized the president to suspend literacy tests for voter registration and to send federal officials to register voters in the event that county officials failed to do so. This new law led to a huge increase in African American voter registration, as well as an increase in the number of African American candidates elected to public office.

SNCC and CORE versus SCLC

During the Civil Rights Movement, many students joined the SNCC (Students Nonviolence Coordinating Committee). African American college students founded the organization and actively engaged in nonviolent protests and sit-ins to demand their civil rights. At times, students who joined the SNCC criticized the SCLC. Younger African Americans tended to be more radical and wanted to take a more confrontational approach to civil rights. They sought to directly challenge discrimination rather than patiently waiting on court decisions and the political process. Eventually, in the late '60s, some SNCC and CORE members began to reject nonviolent protest as being too slow and ineffective. Instead, they began advocating what they called **Black Power:** a philosophy that held blacks should take great pride in their African heritage and be willing to use violence, if necessary, to attain and protect their civil rights.

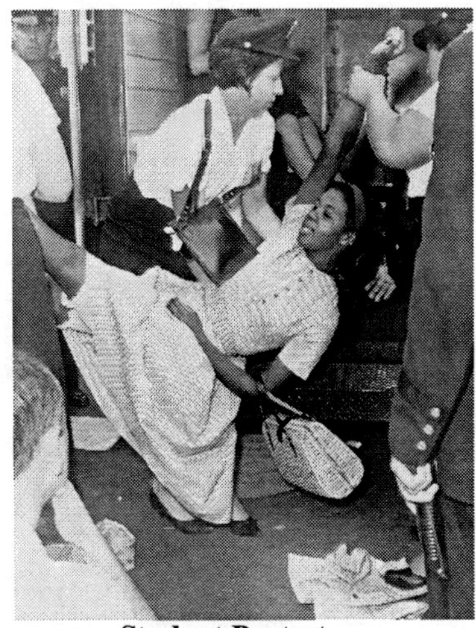

Student Protest

Other Social Movements

The Women's Movement

Women in the 1950s and early '60s were expected to get married, raise a family rather than pursue a career, and adhere to strict societal rules regarding behavior and sexuality. Then, in 1963, Betty Friedan wrote a book called *The Feminine Mystique*. In it, she talked about her own experience in giving up a career to be a homemaker. She suggested that the idea of women being nothing but happy and fulfilled at home was a myth. Her views helped launch the **women's movement** of the 1960s and 70s. This movement, often referred to as "Women's Liberation" or "Women's Lib," rejected traditional gender roles and advocated equality between men and women. Advocates of such positions were labeled "feminists." Friedan also founded the **National Organization for Women (NOW)**, which devoted itself to political activism and feminist causes. Not all women flocked to the women's movement, however. Conservative Phyllis Schlafly campaigned vigorously against it, arguing that many women wanted to remain at home, that there was no more important role than that of a wife and mother, and that "Women's Lib" would destroy family values. Many women in the US joined her in her opposition.

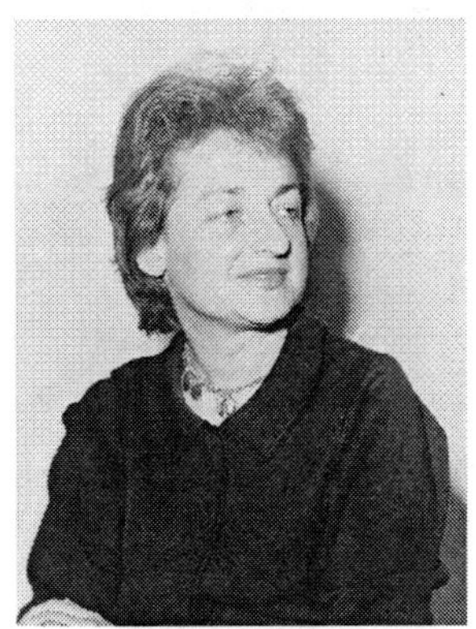

Betty Friedan

The Environmentalist Movement

The 1960s also saw the birth of the modern **environmentalist movement**. Environmentalists are concerned with preserving the earth's resources and species of life. They often focus their efforts on drawing attention to and combating ways in which human beings "negatively affect" the environment. Although calls for government action to protect the environment date all the way back to the late 1800s, the modern environmentalist movement began thanks largely to scientist/writer, **Rachel Carson**. Carson published a book in 1962 entitled ***Silent Spring***, in which she argued that humankind's use of certain chemicals (notably pesticides) was poisoning the environment. Despite protests from several chemical companies, Carson's book won critical acclaim and led to the banning of DDT (a common pesticide). More than that, its message, combined with the activist atmosphere of the '60s to fuel an entire movement. As more and more people flocked to the cause, the United States celebrated its first **Earth Day** in April 1970. Earth Day eventually became an annual event meant to encourage concern for the environment and draw attention to environmental issues. That same year, President Richard Nixon established the **Environmental Protection Agency (EPA)** as a federal agency for the purpose of enforcing laws aimed at maintaining a safe and clean environment.

Rachel Carson

Earth Day

Al Gore

Today, the environmentalist movement continues to gather momentum. Many scientists and citizens agree with Rachel Carson's theory that men and women directly affect the environment based on how they live, what they drive, how they dispose of waste, and so forth. In recent years, former vice president of the United States, **Al Gore**, has been one of the movement's most notable figures. Through his Oscar-winning documentary, *An Inconvenient Truth*, as well as through countless lectures and television appearances, Gore continues to assert that global warming is largely man-made and that it is occurring at a rate that will produce catastrophic consequences. His message is echoed by a number of scientists, political leaders, and activists around the world.

In 2007, he won the Nobel Prize for his tireless efforts. However, there are a number of scientists who dispute such claims. They argue that people like Carson and Gore make the case that global warming and other environmental problems are man-caused without having substantial scientific evidence to back it up. Regardless of who's right, the fact remains that the environmentalist movement continues to march strongly into the twenty-first century.

Practice 6.4 Social Movements

1. What was the significance of Little Rock Central High School in 1957?
   A. It was the first southern school that allowed black students to attend without segregation
   B. The governor called in the Arkansas National Guard to prevent nine black students from entering the school, prompting President Eisenhower to nationalize the Guard and send them home.
   C. The governor of the state attempted to prevent an African American named James Meredith from enrolling in classes.
   D. The principal of the school was determined to maintain segregation and refused to integrate blacks into the classroom.

2. Why was the Southern Christian Leadership Conference established? What was the primary purpose of this group?

3. What philosophy held that blacks should take pride in their African heritage and be willing to use violence, if necessary, to attain and protect their civil rights?
   A. Ku Klux Klan
   B. Black Panthers
   C. Black Power
   D. Red Scare

4. The 1960s saw the birth of a movement that concerned itself with preserving the Earth's resources and species of life. What was this movement called?
   A. the environmentalist movement
   B. the Civil Rights Movement
   C. the Women's Movement
   D. Black Suffrage

5. Describe some events that occurred during the Civil Rights Movement. What impact did these events have on blacks in the United States?

Chapter 6 Review

Key terms, people, and concepts

communism
Red Scare
restrictions on immigration
Henry Ford
mass production
assembly line
radio
movies
Jazz
Louis Armstrong
Langston Hughes
Harlem Renaissance
speculation
buying on the margin
consumerism
overproduction
underconsumption
Herbert Hoover
Black Tuesday
Great Depression
soup kitchens
breadlines
Hoovervilles
Franklin Delano Roosevelt
direct relief
New Deal
first hundred days
First New Deal
Civilian Conservation Corps
Agricultural Adjustment Act
Federal Deposit Insurance Corporation (FDIC)
National Industrial Recovery Act (NIRA)
Second New Deal
National Labor Relations ACT (NLRA)
Social Security Act (SSA)
Revenue Act of 1935
Adolf Hitler
Rosie the Riveter
Internment camps
Allied Powers
General Dwight D. Eisenhower
D-Day
Fall of Berlin
Philippines
Bataan Death March
Battle of Midway
island hopping
atomic bomb
Los Alamos, New Mexico
Harry S. Truman
containment policy
Truman Doctrine
Marshall Plan
Cold War
Mao Zedong
Red Scare
House Un-American Activities Committee (HUAC)
Joseph McCarthy
Sputnik
space race
Harry S. Truman
integrating the United States military
Brown vs. Board of Education of Topeka (1954)
Little Rock Central High School
James Meredith
George Wallace
Dr. Martin Luther King, Jr.
Montgomery Bus Boycott
SCLC (Southern Christian Leadership Conference)
"Letter from Birmingham Jail"
March on Washington
Lyndon B. Johnson
Civil Rights Act of 1964
Voting Rights Act of 1965

Benito Mussolini
Japan
Axis Powers
Lend-Lease Act
Pearl Harbor
War Production Board (WPB)
war bond drives
victory gardens
rationing
Black Power
women's movement
National Organization for Women (NOW)
environmentalist movement
Rachel Carson
Silent Spring
Earth Day
Environmental Protection Agency (EPA)
Korean War

Multiple Choice Questions

1. When too much of a good is on the market it is called
   A. underproduction.
   B. overproduction.
   C. consumerism.
   D. a Red Scare.

2. What was Henry Ford's impact on the automobile industry?
   A. He was the first person to invent the automobile.
   B. He sold automobiles at extremely high prices so only the wealthy could afford them.
   C. He was the first to perfect and successfully market the automobile through mass production.
   D. He sold over 50,000 automobiles in 1907 alone.

Read the list below and answer the following question.

I. Overproduction

II. Consumerism

III. Underproduction

IV. Stock Market Crash of 1929

3. Which of those listed above contributed to the Great Depression?
   A. I, II, III B. I, II, IV C. All of them D. I, IV

4. What was Franklin Roosevelt's plan to deal with the nation's economic troubles in the 1930s called?
   A. TVA
   B. New Deal
   C. Black Tuesday
   D. Wagner Plan

5. What actually ended the Great Depression in the United States?
   A. FDR's New Deal
   B. high tariffs
   C. the US isolationist policy
   D. World War II

6. Which New Deal program is the only one still around today?
   A. Social Security Act
   B. Revenue Act
   C. National Labor Relations Act
   D. Tennessee Valley Authority

7. What is Rachel Carson MOST famous for?
   A. the establishment of Earth Day as a way to encourage environmental concern for the US
   B. the publication of *Silent Spring*, a book that argues humankind's use of certain chemicals are poisoning the environment
   C. the creation of an Oscar-winning documentary, *An Inconvenient Truth*
   D. the establishment of the Environmental Protection Agency

8. The National Labor Relations Act, The Social Security Act, and The Revenue Act of 1935 are all
   A. programs of the First New Deal.
   B. programs designed by Herbert Hoover.
   C. programs of the Second New Deal.
   D. reform movements that contributed to the Civil Rights Act.

9. The US entered World War II in response to
   A. Communism in Eastern Europe.
   B. Pearl Harbor.
   C. D-day.
   D. Hitler's invasion of Poland.

10. Which of the following forced Japan's surrender and launched the nuclear arms race?
    A. US dropping the atomic bomb
    B. the Cold War
    C. D-day
    D. Containment Policy

Chapter 7
World Geography: Africa and Asia

GPS	**SSWG1:** The student will explain the physical aspects of geography. (QCC standards WG2, WG3, WG4, WG11, WG12, WG13, WG14, WG17)
	SSWG2: The student will explain the cultural aspects of geography. (QCC standards WG4, WG11, WG12, WG14, WG33)
	SSWG3: The student will describe the interaction of physical and human systems those have shaped contemporary North Africa/Southwest Asia. (QCC standards WG3, WG4, WG6, WG12, WG14, WG17, WhH3)
	SSWG4: The student will describe the interaction of physical and human systems that have shaped contemporary Sub-Saharan Africa. (QCC standards WG3, WG4, WG11, WG12, WG13, WG14, WG17, WH33, WH34)
	SSWG5: The student will describe the interaction of physical and human systems that have shaped contemporary South Asia, Southeastern Asia, and Eastern Asia. (QCC standards WG3, WG4, WG6, WG11, WG12, WG14, WG17, WH33, WH34)

7.1 The Physical and Human Aspects of Geography

Geography is the study of the earth's surface, land, bodies of water, climate, peoples, industries, natural resources, etc. Why is it important to study geography? It helps us understand how the earth was formed, where energy sources like oil and coal are likely located, what is and is not a danger to the environment, why certain people live in the places that they do, what climate patterns are likely to occur and how they will affect people, and so on. Understanding geography enables human beings to improve their quality of life.

Physical, Human, and Cultural Characteristics

Physical Geography

Physical Geography is the study of how physical characteristics (land, climate, bodies of water, animal life, etc.) define a region or place. A **place** is an area of land that shares common features or is defined by common characteristics. For example, the Gulf Coast is that portion of the United States that borders the Gulf of Mexico. It includes the west coast of Florida, as well as the coasts of Alabama, Mississippi, Louisiana, and Texas. By the same token, the Appalachia region is the portion of the US in North Carolina, South Carolina, Georgia, Kentucky, West Virginia, and Virginia that is part of the Appalachian Mountains. Appalachia is defined by its mountainous surroundings and distinct mountain culture.

Globe

In short, places can be defined in a number of ways. Geographic location and land features, like mountains, vast plains, or proximity to a large body of water, are common means of defining places. However, places might also be defined by the type of wildlife and natural resources that exist there. For instance, parts of the midwest United States are sometimes referred to as the "Wheat Belt" because the soil and climate are ideal for growing large amounts of wheat and grains.

Man-made boundaries are another means of defining places. For instance, the place known as the state of Georgia is not that different from neighboring states in terms of geographic features. However, it is considered a separate place from South Carolina or Alabama because of a human decision.

Physical features are the natural land formations that make up the surface of an area (also called **topography**). The most common features used to describe a place are landforms, bodies of water, climate, soil, natural vegetation, and animal life. A **landform** is one of the features that make up part of the earth's surface such as a plain, mountain, or valley. A **body of water** is a part of the earth's surface covered with water such as a river, lake, or ocean. The **climate** of an area is its average weather conditions over time, including the temperature, humidity, precipitation, sunshine, cloudiness, winds, etc. **Natural vegetation** is the kinds of plants and trees that grow in an area. Finally, **animal life** refers to the types of animals who naturally live in an area.

Human Geography

Multi-ethnic Students

In addition to physical features, human characteristics are also important to geography. **Human characteristics** include language, religion, political systems, economic systems, population, and way of life. **Population settlement patterns** refer to the types of people who live in a place. The population of a region and its culture play a key role in defining a place geographically.

Take the southeastern United States. The region's geography is ideal for raising crops like tobacco, sugar, rice, and cotton. Prior to 1865, the South relied heavily on African slaves to work large agricultural plantations that maintained its economy. Due to the demand for slaves, the African American population in the southern United States grew rapidly. Today, although slavery has thankfully been outlawed for over 140 years, the South continues to have a proportionally large African American population that contributes greatly to defining the region's culture, economy, social norms, etc.

Similarly, due to the southwest United States' proximity to the Mexican border, states like California, Arizona, New Mexico, and Texas have traditionally featured large Hispanic populations. Florida has a large number of immigrants from Cuba and other Caribbean nations. New York has long been defined by its cultural diversity thanks to its role as a key point of entry for immigrants coming to the US from other parts of the world. A distinct Cajun population exists in Louisiana due to its history as a French colony.

Although these are US examples, the pattern is true worldwide. Jewish nationalists settling in Palestine and forming the modern nation of Israel following the Holocaust, Muslims migrating from predominantly Hindu India to settle in predominantly Muslim Pakistan, and French-speaking Canadians dominating the character and culture of Montreal, Canada are all examples of how population settlements play a key role in defining places.

Auto Factory Worker

Human activities also define places. Agriculture is prominent in much of the midwestern United States because the climate makes it ideal for farming. The Northeast and parts of the northern Midwest (i.e., Detroit, Pittsburgh, Cleveland, and Chicago) are known for industries like automobile and steel manufacturing. Silicon Valley, located in the San Francisco area of northern California, and the Research Triangle Park area of North Carolina are all major centers for software and technology. Parts of the western United States are defined by the defense industry. Los Angeles is known for its leading role in the movie industry. New York is the nation's center for business. Meanwhile, southern cities like Atlanta and Charlotte continue to grow in importance as centers of international business and banking.

Farmers

Overseas, growing industry is making China one of the major players in world trade. Japan continues to be a world leader in technology, automobiles, and electronics. India is a growing economy that attracts some of the United States' most promising college graduates. The Middle East has been, and remains, a world leader in the production of oil. Many Latin American nations depend on exports of agricultural products like coffee and sugar. These are all examples of how **agriculture and industry,** as well as human activities, define geographic places.

The Relationship Between Physical and Human Characteristics

Human beings affect their physical environment, and vice versa. As populations grow, human beings use more and more resources and often displace trees, plants, and wildlife as they make room for homes, towns, and infrastructure. The development of new industries often means changes in the landscape and physical features.

Nomads

While development can have positive effects, such as more jobs and a higher standard of living, it can also cause problems as it alters the natural environment. In places like North Africa, for instance, overgrazing of livestock and inefficient farming techniques often result in *desertification* (once fertile, usable land turning into deserts that can no longer support wildlife or agriculture). Desertification results in less farmland, less food, and increased starvation on a continent already familiar with poverty and famine.

The way people live is often determined by climate and the physical features of their environment. In the mountains of West Virginia, for instance, coal mining has long been a way of life for many people because of the abundant resources of coal in the area. In Scandinavian nations, fishing has traditionally been an important industry thanks to their proximity to water. Rural, more secluded, populations in developing nations like Guatemala or Cambodia tend to live by more primitive means than people in urban areas and/or developed nations like the United States. Large cities around the world originally developed along coasts or rivers because such locations could easily be reached by ships for travel and commerce.

Today, understanding the world's physical geography still plays an important role in human behavior. People in the United States try to understand wind and climate patterns to take advantage of windmills and solar energy as alternative sources of fuel. People in North Africa and Southwest Asia need to be very aware of water supplies, as they live in traditionally dry regions. China, with a population of roughly 1.3 billion people, must constantly worry about the availability of land, how to grow and/or import enough food to feed its population, and whether or not its industries and economy are growing at a rate suitable for providing enough jobs. These are just a few examples of how physical and human geographical characteristics are interrelated.

Chinese Population

CULTURAL ASPECTS OF GEOGRAPHY

Woman wearing Kente

Culture is the system of shared beliefs, values, customs, behaviors, etc., that shapes how members of a society live and view their world. These beliefs are transmitted from generation to generation. Some aspects of culture are religion, language, art, music, clothing, and manners. For instance, in West Africa, people wear a cloth called kente. It is made of interwoven cloth strips and is native to the country of Ghana. This cloth reflects the unique culture of West Africa. In parts of the Far East, it is actually considered a compliment to the chef if people eating at a restaurant open the kitchen door and belch after their meal (don't try this at your local diner). In many cultures, senior citizens are revered and ancestors are even worshipped. In others, marriages are arranged by the families of the bride and groom, without the couple having much say. Some cultures depend heavily on religion for their laws and social norms. Others, like the US and much of Western Europe, attempt to keep religion and government separate. Cultures develop over centuries and are impacted by contact with foreign peoples, physical features, and historical events.

IMPACT OF PHYSICAL CHARACTERISTICS ON CULTURE

Physical features affect human culture in a number of ways. People who live on islands, near ocean coasts, or along major rivers, like the Nile in Africa or the Amazon in South America, usually have cultures which rely heavily on these bodies of water. Take, for instance, the island nation of Japan. The Japanese tend to rely on a diet that features large amounts of seafood. Meanwhile, people of Africa's desert and plains regions have traditionally led **nomadic lifestyles**, meaning that they often move from location to location in search of fresh water supplies and areas for their livestock to graze. Religions practiced in these desert regions often depict Paradise as a place of abundant water supplies, because water is so scarce and valued among such people. In South America, many indigenous peoples live in the high and isolated altitudes of the Andes Mountains. Therefore, they depend on the stone and other raw materials of the region to build homes. They also tend to be more self-sufficient. Because their villages are more isolated and harder to reach due to the mountainous terrain, they cannot trade as easily as other societies. Therefore, they must meet most of their own needs locally. By contrast, cultures with easy access to trade, such as cities along rivers, seaport areas, and urban areas within developed countries, tend to feature cultures with greater diversity because they are accessible to different types of people. Physical features impact culture by determining what resources are available, how much contact people have with outside groups and ideas, what types of food are available, and what kind of shelter and clothing will be available.

Meanwhile, climate often determines how people dress, how much they migrate, what kinds of crops they can grow, and how much they must modify their lifestyle based on different seasons of the year. In short, people's natural surroundings play a major role in shaping their culture.

How Cultural Characteristics Define Place

Cultural characteristics are often used to describe a place. For example, religion often describes places. Much of the Middle East is known for its adherence to the religion of Islam (except for Israel, which is officially Jewish). Conversely, India is known for its ties to Hinduism and Buddhism, while China and Japan are also associated with Buddhism, Confucianism, and Taoism. The United States "Bible Belt" is greatly defined by its Protestant, evangelical Christian heritage. Meanwhile, northern cities often feature large Catholic and Jewish populations. Utah was settled as a homeland for Mormons during the 1800s and remains a predominantly Mormon society today.

Jewish Man Praying

Christian Church Service

However, religion is not the only means by which culture comes to define a place. North Africa is viewed as a separate geographic region from the rest of Africa because its climate and ethnic make-up resembles the Middle East rather than the cultures of Central or South Africa. Japan is known as a very fast-paced, high pressure society. Conversely, the Caribbean islands are known for being laid back and having a more relaxed culture. Even within the United States, culture tends to define place. Southern culture is very different from that of northerners. Rural residents of the western United States live very differently than city residents in Chicago or Philadelphia. All of these are examples of how the culture of regions can help define them as distinct places.

Customs and traditions also help to define culture. **Customs and traditions** are ways of doing things passed down from one generation of a people group or society to the next. Particular rituals, ceremonies, beliefs, favored foods, methods of farming, rules for interacting, and methods of tending to home are just a few examples where customs and traditions are evident. Examples of customs and traditions that define culture include wedding rituals, burial ceremonies, traditional celebrations and holidays, methods of showing respect, the manner in which business is conducted, rites of passage from childhood to adulthood, honorable versus dishonorable behavior, and so on.

Practice 7.1 The Physical and Human Aspects of Geography

1. What is *geography* and why is it important to study it?

2. Lakes, mountains, oil reserves, deserts, and open plains are all
   A. aspects of culture.
   B. physical characteristics of geography.
   C. human characteristics of geography.
   D. physical characteristics of culture.

3. What is culture and how is it impacted by physical characteristics?

4. The way a particular society conducts weddings, expects honorable people to carry on business, and who it views as the most important citizens are all examples of
   A. physical geography.
   B. cultural religions.
   C. customs and traditions.
   D. population settlement patterns.

7.2 North Africa and Southwest Asia

Africa and Asia are two of the world's seven continents. A *continent* is a large landmass and usually consists of several countries. Asia is the world's largest continent and Africa is its second largest. On the next page is a map of the world's continents. They are numbered below in order of physical size, with 1 being the largest and 7 the smallest.

1-Asia

2-Africa

3-North America

4- South America

5- Antarctica

6 - Europe

7 - Australia

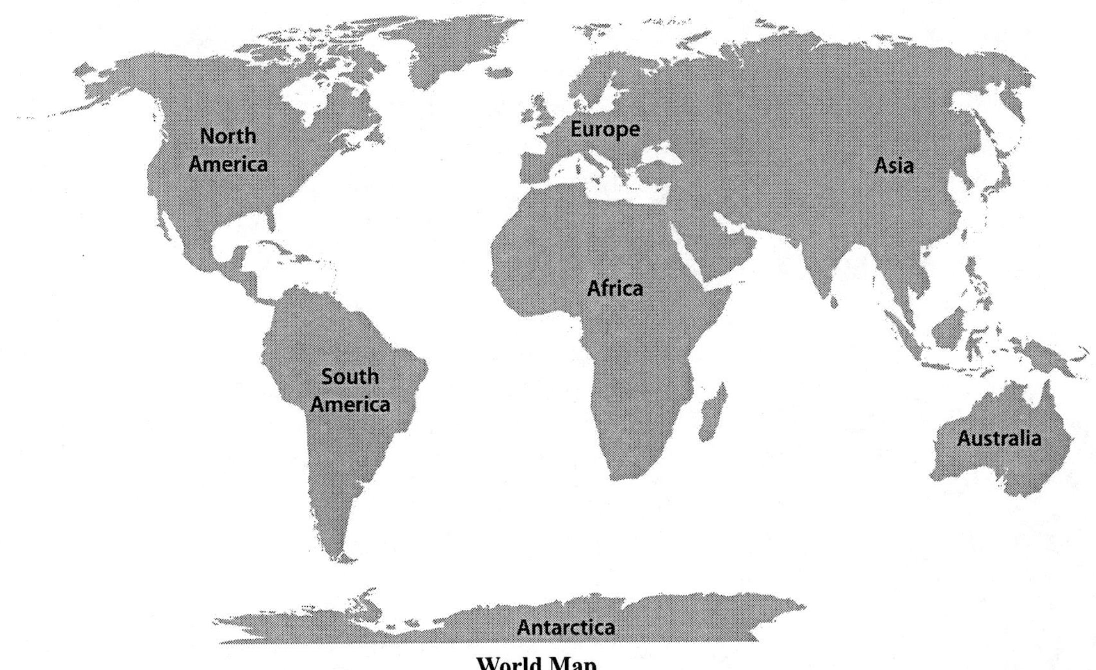

World Map

Although they are located on different continents, **Southwest Asia** and **North Africa** are closely identified by their similarities in climate and culture. Together, they include the tumultuous Middle East and Gulf States. It is a complex area with a fascinating and often violent history. Because of its closeness to the Atlantic Ocean, the Indian Ocean, and the Mediterranean Sea; and because it links three continents (Asia, Africa, and Europe), the area has long been important in terms of commerce and world trade. As a result, nations have often fought wars in the region, trying to secure trade routes and protect themselves from foreign invaders. Even today, violent confrontations frequently occur.

Physical Features

The Landscape

The Sahara Desert

North Africa has a variety of physical features. Mountains are prominent in much of the region. The area is dry with large amounts of territory covered by **deserts** (areas receiving less than 10 inches of rainfall per year). In areas farther north, like Turkey, temperatures are cooler, rain more abundant, and the forests are similar to North America.

The **Sahara** is the world's largest desert (as big as the entire United States) and stretches over most of North Africa. The **Sahel** is a belt of dry grasslands south of the Sahara desert that separates the vast desert from the tropical rainforest of Central Africa. There are three main **mountain ranges** in North Africa and Southwest Asia. They tend to be warm in the summer, but often covered with snow in the winters. When the warm months arrive, their snows melt and produce flooding at lower elevations. The *Atlas* *mountains* run through northern Algeria, Tunisia, and Morocco. They separate the Mediterranean coastal regions from the Sahara Desert. The Atlas Mountains are rich in natural resources such as iron ore, silver, phosphate, coal, marble, and natural gas. The *Taurus Mountains* in southern Turkey are known for beautiful waterfalls, underground rivers, and the largest caves in Asia. Finally, the *Zagros Mountains* in western Iran and eastern Iraq are known for *salt domes*. Salt domes are common where oil deposits are found; therefore, the Zagros Mountains are a rich resource for the oil that is so valuable to the region's economy.

Important Bodies of Water

Ships in the Mediterranean Sea

Because this is a dry region, the bodies of water that exist are very important. The **Persian Gulf** is an extension of the Arabian Sea that provides nations like Iran, Saudi Arabia, Kuwait, and the United Arab Emirates, with access to the sea important for trade and military purposes. Meanwhile, the **Strait of Hormuz** is a narrow waterway connecting the Persian Gulf to the Arabian Sea. It is important because it allows Persian Gulf states to export their abundant oil supplies, as well as receive imported goods from foreign nations. As you might expect, whoever controls it, controls trade in the region. For this reason, nations (even ones outside the Middle East) have often been prepared to go to war to keep the Strait of Hormuz open.

Other important bodies of water include the *Red Sea*, the *Dead Sea* (so-named because its salt content is so high that nothing other than a few microscopic organisms can live in it), the *Black Sea*, and the *Mediterranean Sea*. The **Mediterranean Sea** is the largest body of water in the region. From ancient times, the Mediterranean has provided North Africa, Southwest Asia, and southern Europe with access to travel and trade. In addition, the mild climate of the area also attracted many settlers. As a result, a number of the world's most magnificent cities and civilizations grew along the shores of the Mediterranean (i.e., ancient Greece and Rome).

Nile River

The region also features a number of important rivers. In Southwest Asia, the **Tigris** and **Euphrates** rivers are home to some of the oldest civilizations in the world. They have served as a vital source of water in a dry region. They have also been important routes for water travel and trade. The Tigris begins in Turkey while the Euphrates flows from the northern region of Anatolia south into Syria. Eventually, the two rivers meet in southern Iraq before emptying into the Persian Gulf. In North Africa, the **Nile River** is the longest river in the world (roughly 4,000 miles — that's almost twice the distance between Atlanta and Los Angeles!). The Nile flows north from central Africa, through Egypt, and into the Mediterranean. Areas along the Nile are North Africa's richest farm land. The river provides water and nutrients necessary to grow crops. In the summer, snow in the mountains of Ethiopia (a country in North-Central Africa) melts. The melting snow, along with summer rains, causes the Nile to flood. Once the waters recede, they leave behind fertile soil for farming. Farmers also use the waters of the Nile for *irrigation* (methods used to bring water from a source — in this case the Nile — to areas that otherwise would not have enough water for agriculture).

SINAI AND SUEZ

Two additional important geographic features are the Sinai Peninsula and the Suez Canal. The **Sinai Peninsula** acts as a land bridge between North Africa and Southwest Asia, connecting the two regions. The **Suez Canal** is a man-made waterway connecting the Mediterranean and Red Seas. It is a crucial waterway, allowing ships to sail from one sea to the other without having to go all the way around Africa. For this reason, nations are willing to use military force, if necessary, to make sure that the Suez Canal remains open to trade and travel.

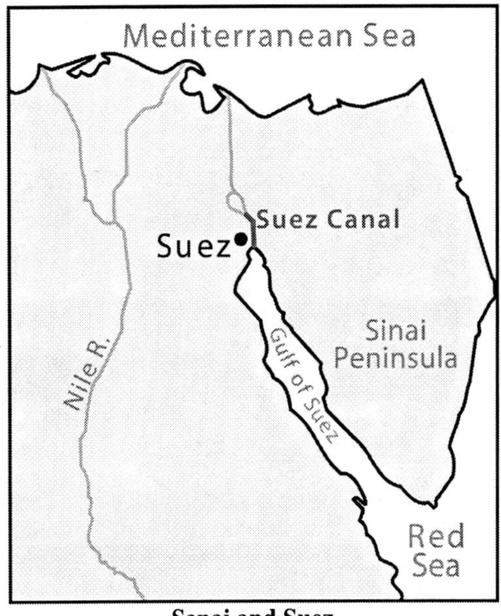

Sanai and Suez

CLIMATE

Desert Oasis

As mentioned earlier, Southwest Asia and North Africa tend to be very dry and are home to large **deserts**. The Libyan Desert, Eastern (Arabic) Desert, and Sahara Desert (mentioned earlier) are the three main deserts of North Africa. Meanwhile, in Southwest Asia, southern Israel is covered by a desert called the Negev, and much of Syria is covered by the Syrian Desert. *Bedouins* inhabit some of these desert regions. Bedouins are people who have lived in the desert regions for generations. They are nomadic, meaning that they move around. They have to move to find areas of fresh water and grazing land for their animals. **Oasis areas** are fertile areas within desert regions that provide water and vegetation. North Africa and Southwest Asia feature a climate in which summers can be extremely hot, with winters remaining fairly mild. Mountainous regions can get quite cold at higher elevations, and areas in the northern portion of Southwest Asia (i.e., Turkey) exhibit a cooler climate similar to areas of northern Europe.

How has climate affected the development of North Africa and Southwest Asia? Due to the harsh conditions of the deserts, major cities and civilizations have tended to grow up around abundant water supplies. Although Egypt is a relatively large country, less than 5% of its area is home to the entire population due to the stretches of uninhabitable desert that cover the rest of the country. In addition, many of these cities became key centers of commerce and trade. As a result, large cultural gaps exist between modernized cities like Cairo and many of the more primitive rural areas. Populations also tend to be smaller in more mountainous regions because of the rugged terrain that make farming difficult and limit travel.

THE IMPACT OF RELIGION

Muslims Praying

Dome of the Rock in Jerusalem

Three major religions impact the culture of North Africa and Southwest Asia: *Judaism*, *Christianity*, and *Islam*. All three began in Southwest Asia. Each of these three religions share a belief in one god (belief in one god is called *monotheism*). **Judaism** looks to the ancient prophet Abraham as its founder. It is the oldest of the three religions and teaches that the Jewish people are God's chosen nation (Israel) and inheritors of His promises. **Christianity** comes out of the Jewish tradition. Its founder is Jesus who claimed to be the Son of God and the fulfillment of God's promise to the Jewish people to send a Messiah (savior). Christians believe that it is the disciples of Jesus who are the true heirs of God's promises to Abraham. Together, they form the *church*, a spiritual nation which they believe has replaced the physical nation of Israel. Finally, **Islam** is the youngest of the three major religions. Whereas Judaism and Christianity both began in Palestine which is part of Israel, the Muslim prophet, Muhammad, founded Islam in what is today Saudi Arabia. Muhammad claimed that an angel dictated to him the words that became the *Qur'an* (Islam's holy book). In 622 AD, Muhammad and his followers had to flee persecution in Mecca and settled in Medina. Muslims view this as the rise of Islam and use this year to mark the beginning of the Muslim calendar. Eventually, Muhammad returned and defeated his enemies in Mecca. From there, the Muslims launched their military campaigns to conquer Arabia and convert its people to Islam. By the time Muhammad died in 632 AD, most of Arabia was Muslim. Eventually, Islam spread across North Africa, reaching southern Spain in Europe. It also moved east into other Asian regions, where it still greatly influences the culture of nations like Pakistan, Afghanistan, India, and Indonesia.

Today, Islam is the most influential religion in the region. With the exception of Israel, which was founded as a Jewish state, Islam is the dominant religion throughout North Africa and Southwest Asia. Unlike the United States where religion and government are kept separate, religion tends to play a major role in Muslim nations, with some countries even relying on the Qur'an to define their laws (i.e., Saudi Arabia).

Because people in the Middle East often define themselves first and foremost by their religion, there is often tension among Jews, Christians, and Muslims. For centuries, the nation of Israel has been at odds with its Arab and Persian neighbors. When modern Israel was established as a formal Jewish state in Palestine in 1948, this tension boiled over. Arabs resented Israel because they believed that Palestine belonged to Arab Palestinians. Since 1948, a number of wars have been fought between Israel and Muslim nations in the Middle East.

Muslim Woman

Today, within Israel's borders, ongoing violence between the Jewish authorities and Palestinians is common. Meanwhile, many nations in the region continue to hate Israel. Some have even sponsored and supported terrorism against Israel and the United States (Israel's ally). Iran has even begun a nuclear program. The US and other nations are concerned that its ultimate purpose might be to launch a nuclear strike or provide terrorists with a nuclear weapon to be used against Israel and/or the United States.

IRAQ

IRAN

Iran-Iraq Border

Tension also exists within Islam. *Sunni Muslims* and *Shi'ite Muslims* disagree over the rightful line of leadership within Islam and tend to see each other as adversaries. Prior to his fall from power in Iraq, Saddam Hussein--a Sunni--was notorious for torturing and executing large numbers of Shi'ite Muslims. In fact, Iraq and neighboring Iran have fought against one another, in large part because Iraq is a majority Sunni nation while Iran is predominantly Shi'ite. Such violence and instability is complicated by the fact that the region is also a key source of the world's oil. For this reason, nations like the United States believe they cannot simply disregard any unrest in North Africa and Southwest Asia.

CONFLICTS OVER CULTURE

Some societies in Southwest Asia and North Africa are more **traditional**. They enforce laws based on the Qur'an more than other nations. In countries like Saudi Arabia, people are required by law to obey the teachings of Islam. For example, according to Islamic law, women in these countries must keep their heads and faces veiled, as well as their bodies entirely covered, while in public. Meanwhile, men must dress and conduct themselves according to the Qur'an as well. Other predominantly Muslim countries (i.e., Turkey) are more **westernized**. People in westernized countries tend to dress and behave similarly to people in the United States and Western Europe. Westernized culture often features the same restaurants, businesses, leisure activities, and trends found in places like the US.

Countries that closely follow Islamic law tend to limit the roles and opportunities afforded women. Meanwhile, in more secular (non-religious) societies, like Egypt, Jordan, and Turkey, women are often well educated, able to dress and act more freely, and may even hold positions of leadership. Conflict often arises between Muslims who prefer westernization and those who follow more traditional ways. Some traditionalists proclaim that westernized Muslims are not true Muslims at all. Radical Islamists who promote **terrorism** (violence against innocent people in the name of a cause) sometimes claim that their actions are a response to westerners who have corrupted Islam and westernized Muslims who have betrayed their own religion.

Practice 7.2 North Africa and Southwest Asia

1. The world's largest desert that covers much of North Africa is called the

   A. Sahel.
   B. Sahara.
   C. Negev.
   D. Maghreb.

2. The Nile is important because it

   A. allows Southwest Asian nations to effectively engage in trade.
   B. provides a land bridge between Africa and Southwest Asia.
   C. provides much needed water to North Africa.
   D. is the holy book of Islam.

3. What are the three major religions that are important to North Africa and Southwest Asia?

4. Describe some of the conflicts that exist between Muslims.

7.3 Sub-Saharan Africa

Physical Features

Sub-Saharan Africa is that portion of the continent below North Africa (below the Sahara Desert). Sub-Saharan Africa consists of *lowlands* and *highlands*. The lowlands lie to the north and west while the highlands are in the south and east. There are many mountain ranges as well. The **East African Mountains** run from Ethiopia in the north through Tanzania in the south. Africans who live in and near these mountains depend on them for farmland, pastures, and water. The higher elevations tend to receive more rainfall and even snow. This precipitation flows down into the lower regions, providing the people and animals with the water and crops needed to survive. The highest mountain is *Mount Kilimanjaro*. In addition to mountains, there are many plateaus and rifts in this region. A *plateau* is a raised area of mostly level land. *Rifts* are cracks in the earth's surface caused by tectonic plates pulling apart. They are recognizable as steep-walled valleys. Most notable is Sub-Saharan Africa's **Great Rift Valley**. It stretches all the way from the Red Sea, south through several countries to Mozambique. Huge lakes in this region include Lake Tanganyika and Lake Victoria. **Lake Victoria** is Africa's largest lake and the second largest freshwater lake in the world. It lies between two rift valleys on the borders of Tanzania, Kenya, and Uganda. These lakes allow for plenty of fishing and fresh water. The **Nile River**, mentioned earlier, also runs through parts of Sub-Saharan Africa. Other key rivers include the Congo and Zambezie. The **Congo River** is almost 3,000 miles long and has served as a major means of travel

Sub-Saharan Africa

and trade within Africa's interior for generations. The **Zambezi River** is known for its awesome waterfalls, including *Victoria Falls*. Victoria Falls is more than a mile across and drops over 350 feet. The roar of Victoria Falls can be heard from miles away.

Paddling Down the Congo River

Victoria Falls

CLIMATE

African Rainforest

Sub-Saharan Africa features four major climates. The *desert climates* are hot with very little rain and few plants and animals. The *semiarid* regions are also high in temperature but have more rainfall (the Sahel is a semiarid region). The *tropical climate* region extends from the semiarid region towards the Equator (line of latitude running east to west around the earth at its center). It has a rainy season of up to six months, with the remaining six months being mostly dry. *Savannas* are flat grasslands with scattered vegetation found within both the semiarid and tropical regions. Savannas cover more than four million square miles of Africa and are home to many of the wild animals most associated with the continent (lions, elephants, giraffes, etc.). Finally, the *equatorial region* which includes the Equator, has high temperatures all year and averages more than four feet of rainfall a year. The region features thick rainforests and abundant wildlife, such as chimpanzees and gorillas.

People and Population Distribution

African Plain

Africa's physical features and climate have a lot to do with its **population distribution**. In other words, they impact where people live and which areas have the highest population. Many of the continent's major cities have grown up along waterways and coastal regions that have traditionally been open to travel and trade. The dry climate and rainforests mean that not all areas are as inhabitable as others. African **urbanization** (the growth and development of cities) is due largely to **modernization** (process of a society leaving primitive methods behind to adopt more modern techniques). More advanced technology, exposure to current trends, better job opportunities, and the ability to live a more modern lifestyle are all factors that attract many Africans to the cities. These cities are often the site of increased industrialization as less developed nations attempt to build infrastructure, improve their economies, and encourage wealthier nations to invest money in their countries.

Of course, urban areas also tend to be overcrowded, more polluted, and have higher rates of crime. Today, many Africans live in urban areas such as Lagos, Nigeria, Johannesburg, South Africa, Cape Town, South Africa, and Nairobi, Kenya. In addition, many Africans still live as small farmers. Therefore, among the rural population, areas accessible to water, rivers, and fertile grazing and farming land have larger populations. Africa's rainforests tend to be populated by people that have adjusted over generations to living and thriving in the jungles, whereas those who live on the African plains adopt a lifestyle centered around vast, open regions. These people are often nomadic, moving according to the seasons and migration patterns of herds they depend on for food. Desert areas, of course, tend to be less populated because of the lack of water.

Johannesburg Nairobi

In the West, people tend to view all of Sub-Saharan Africa as if it were a common culture. However, it is important to understand that Africa is a land full of many different cultures. Its inhabitants descend from thousands of different people groups, each with its own culture, traditions, language, and history. Also, due to European colonization, many societies still reflect Dutch, British, French, and Portugese influences as well. While the majority of Africans south of the Sahara are dark-skinned peoples, there are white-skinned Africans as well. In fact, up until the early 1990s, the nation of South Africa was controlled by its minority white population, while black Africans had almost no rights at all. Islam and Christianity are major religions in the region. However, traditional African religions are still practiced.

Practice 7.3 Sub-Saharan Africa

1. Describe the major physical geographical features of Sub-Saharan Africa.
2. Describe the different climates of Sub-Saharan Africa.

7.4 The Rest of Asia

As mentioned earlier, Asia is the world's largest continent. Because it covers so much territory, its geography varies greatly. We discussed Southwest Asia when we looked at North Africa. Now we will look at the remaining geographic regions that make up Asia: *South Asia*, *Southeast Asia*, and *Eastern Asia*. **South Asia** includes Afghanistan (sometimes Afghanistan is considered part of Southwest Asia), Bangladesh, Bhutan, India, Nepal, Pakistan, the Maldives, and Sri Lanka. **Southeast Asia** includes Brunei, Cambodia, Indonesia, Laos, Malaysia, Myanmar, the Philippines, Singapore, Thailand, and Vietnam. Finally, **Eastern Asia** includes Japan, China, and Korea.

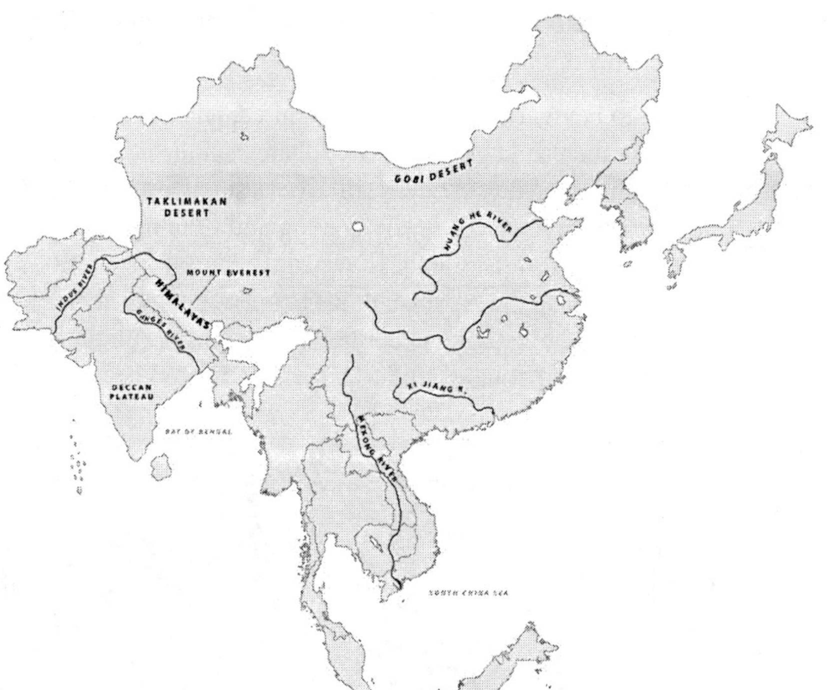

South Asia, Southeast Asia, and Eastern Asia

SOUTH ASIA

PHYSICAL FEATURES

Mt. Everest

South Asia is divided into the *Northern Mountain Rim*, the *Northern Plains*, and the *Deccan Plateau.* Meanwhile, the island nations of Sri Lanka and the Maldives are part of South Asia as well. India is the largest country in South Asia and is second in the world only to China in population. The **Northern Mountain Rim** has several mountain ranges, including the Hindu Kush and the Himalayas. The **Himalayas** are the tallest mountains on earth. They stretch across northern India and Nepal for roughly 1,500 miles. At certain points, the Himalayas are 200 miles wide. World-famous *Mount Everest* is located in the Himalayas and is the tallest mountain on earth (although geologists believe there are even taller mountains located under the surface of the ocean). Mount Everest is more than five miles high, more than 20 times higher than New York City's highest skyscraper. Lying between Hindu Kush and the Himilayas is the Karakoram Range. Farming is difficult in the mountainous terrain of northern South Asia. Therefore, very few people live there. In addition, the various mountain ranges have often acted as a natural barrier between South Asia and northern parts of the continent. For this reason, parts of South Asia are sometimes referred to as a *subcontinent* (part of a continent that is set off from the rest by some physical feature).

The **Northern Plains** can be found between southern India and the Himalayas. The **Indus and Ganges Rivers** run through these plains. The Indus runs southwest through Pakistan and empties into the Arabian Sea. The Ganges runs southeast through Bangladesh and empties into the Bay of Bengal. Large *deltas* (rich soil deposits at the mouth of a river) exist where these rivers empty into the ocean. Areas along these major rivers tend to be fertile for farming. In addition, flooding during the rainy season causes the rivers to deposit nutrients in the soil, making the land even more useful for agriculture. Many people live in these fertile areas. In fact, more than 130 million people live in the small country of Bangladesh. Much of the remaining Indus River Valley, however, is dry desert. As a result, few people live in these areas.

The **Deccan Plateau** covers a large portion of southern India. It features rich mineral deposits, large forest areas, and is home to many herds of elephants. The Eastern and Western Ghats (mountain ranges) border the region to the east and west, with a coastal plain running between the mountains and the oceans on both coasts. The coastal plain features rich, fertile soil and lots of water. While the soil between the mountain ranges is not as fertile, people still manage to farm there despite the drier, hotter climate. Because of the challenges the region presents, fewer people live here than in the more fertile Northern Plains.

Effects of the 2005 Tsunami in Sri Lanka

Sri Lanka and The Maldives are beautiful islands off the South Asian coast. Many of them are covered in mountains. Sri Lanka is located 23 miles from the tip of India. The Maldives are more than 1,200 flat coral islands that stretch roughly 400 miles south of the Asian mainland. Only about 300 of these islands are inhabited by humans. Like much of southern Asia, because of their location, Sri Lanka and the Maldives are very vulnerable to natural disasters like *typhoons* (harsh storms that form over the ocean; in the Western Hemisphere they are called "hurricanes"), earthquakes, and *tsunamis* (giant waves that strike land with devastating effects; often they are the result of earthquakes that occur beneath the ocean).

Climate

Monsoon

South Asia has three main seasons: cool, rainy, and hot. Higher elevations and mountainous regions, of course, experience cooler temperatures than lower elevations and areas further south. In fact, in South Asia's northernmost territories and the Himalayas, temperatures can be brutally cold. Larger countries, like India, experience a wide climate range. Northern India experiences cooler temperatures during certain parts of the year in places like the Northern Plains. Meanwhile, southern India tends to be more tropical and remain hot year-round. The summer months usually feature the arrival of *monsoon season*. Monsoons are seasonal storms that blow in from the Indian Ocean and bring heavy rains. The heaviest rains fall from June to October, with the months that follow being cooler and dry. They are important because farmers use them to time their crops. Most years, the monsoons are predictable. However, sometimes they come early or bring more rain than anticipated, destroying or preventing the planting of crops. Other years these storms may arrive late or not come at all, causing crops to fail for lack of water. Agricultural failure means less food and increased starvation in a region already burdened by extreme poverty.

SOUTHEAST ASIA

PHYSICAL FEATURES

The two major regions of Southeast Asia are the mainland and the many islands. **The mainland** is the Malay and Indochinese peninsulas. The countries in this region are Cambodia, Laos, Myanmar (Burma), Thailand, Vietnam, and part of Malaysia. This region produces a lot of rice and is highly populated due to the **Mekong River** (Southeast Asia's longest river). This river drains more than 300,000 square miles, starting in the Plateau of Tibet and ending in the South China Sea. The region also depends on other rivers, such as the *Chao Phraya River* flowing through Thailand. Parts of the mainland, such as northern Myanmar, are mountainous. With the exception of Laos, which is **land-locked** (surrounded by land), every country in mainland Southeast Asia has a coastline giving it access to the Indian Ocean. Most people in Southeastern Asia are still rural farmers, although the region does feature major cities like Bangkok, Thailand, Ho Chi Minh City, Vietnam, and Phnom Penh, Cambodia. Vietnam boasts the region's largest population.

Indonesia

The islands of Southeast Asia include Singapore, Borneo, the Philippines, and Indonesia. Indonesia and the Philippines are both *archipelagos* (groups of islands). Indonesia is made up of more than 17,000 islands (roughly 10,000 of which are not inhabited) and is the largest country in the region. It has the fourth largest population in the world and is home to the world's largest Muslim population (this might surprise you since we tend to associate Islam with the Middle East). Indonesia has a tropical climate with large amounts of rainfall. Although fertile soil in Indonesia is very limited, many Indonesians still farm. By comparison, the Philippines consists of over 7,000 islands, over 6,000 of which are uninhabited. It, too, has a tropical climate with limited fertile areas. Like Indonesia, much of the population depends on agriculture for a living.

CLIMATE

Southeast Asia generally has two seasons: rainy and dry. From mid-spring to late summer, Southeast Asia experiences its hot, rainy, monsoon season. The remaining months tend to be cooler and dry. Since most people in this region are rural farmers, predictable monsoons are just as important in Southeast Asia as they are for South Asia. The rainy seasons and the fertile river deltas that exist in the area make the climate ideal for raising crops like rice, sugarcane, beans, peanuts, sweet potatoes, bananas, and coffee. Although the higher elevations of the mountains in north Myanmar can get cold, South Asia experiences an overall warm, tropical climate.

Eastern Asia

Physical Features

Tibetan Monk

The major countries of Eastern Asia are China, Japan, and Korea. **China** is the largest of the three countries. Much of the country is covered by mountains that are part of the **Himalayas**. The Himalayas separate China from Nepal in the west. Eastern China features a lot of rivers and plains. High plateaus define the southwest, including the **Plateau of Tibet** which is the highest plateau in the world. Vast, dry **deserts** cover the northwest portion of the country. Most notable are the *Taklimakan* and *Gobi* deserts. The Taklimakan stretches roughly 600 miles and is one of the world's largest sandy deserts. During summer months, violent dust storms featuring hurricane strength winds commonly occur in the Taklimakan, raising desert sands thousands of feet into the air. The Gobi rests in central northern China. It is extremely dry (in fact, its name means "waterless place"). It also features extreme temperatures. During the summer, the desert can reach 113° F. In the winter, it may dip as low as 40° below zero. China's **major rivers** are the *Huang He*, *Chang Jiang*, and *Xi Jiang*. The Chang Jiang is China's longest river, running almost 3,500 miles across the country. Meanwhile, the Huang He is nicknamed the "Yellow River" because of the color of the silt that covers the plains along the river. It often overflows, producing dangerous floods. Due to the death and destruction sometimes caused by these floods, the Chinese nicknamed the river "China's Sorrow."

Hong Kong

Tokyo

Japan is a country of islands that stretches for 1,500 miles. The four main islands are *Hokkaido*, *Honshu*, *Shikoku*, and *Kyushu*. Honshu is the largest island and home to Japan's capital and most famous city, Tokyo. Mountains cover over 80% of Japan's land. However, instead of forming ranges, these mountains are separated by lowlands. Some are volcanoes. The largest stretch of lowlands is the Kanto Plain, where Tokyo is located. The tallest mountain in Japan is Mount Fuji, an active volcano. Because Japan sits above two tectonic plates, it is more susceptible to volcanic eruptions and earthquakes than many other parts of the world. It is part of an area nicknamed the "Ring of Fire" for its high volcanic activity. Most of the world's volcanoes and earthquakes are in this region.

North Korea

South Korea

Korea sits on a peninsula bordering northwest China. It is west of Japan across the Sea of Japan. Because of its location, Korea has often been the object of Japanese military invasions. Even today, many Koreans resent and mistrust the Japanese. Since the end of World War II, the peninsula has been divided into two countries: North and South Korea. The primary difference between these two nations is that North Korea is communist and South Korea is a capitalist democracy. As a result, North Korea struggles much more economically than South Korea. North Korea is very mountainous with numerous valleys, while South Korea is a mix of rugged mountain ranges, coastal plains, and river valleys. Major rivers include the Yalu and the Tumen in North Korea, and the Han, Kum, and Naktong in South Korea.

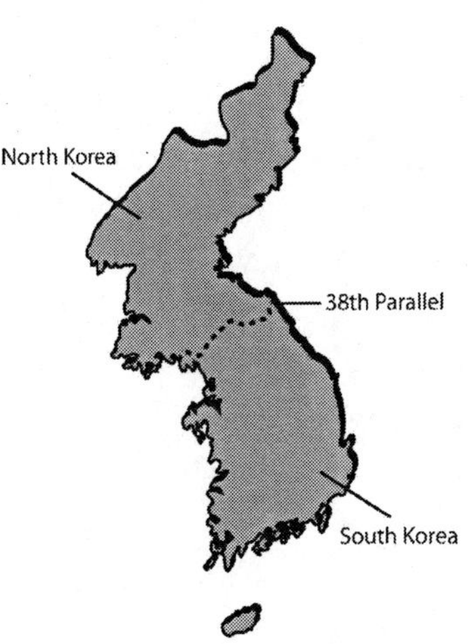

North and South Korea

CLIMATE

The climate of Eastern Asia varies greatly. Parts of **China** have subtropical climates, while northern and moutainous areas can experience great amounts of snowfall and freezing temperatures during the winter. China's major rivers help provide fertile land for the country's millions of rural farmers. Certain areas are covered by large deserts that are extremely dry and face extreme temperatures. Such harsh conditions make these regions basically uninhabitable. By comparison, much of **Japan** is covered in forests and mountains. Monsoons play a major role in the Japanese climate. They cause cold rains and snow in the higher elevations and along the western coast during the winter, and warm rains to the south and east during the summer. From summer through early fall, typhoons are also frequent. Cold winters and cool summers persist in the north, while warmer climates are present in the central highlands and the south. Warm, wet, tropical climates are common to many of Japan's islands. Finally, **Korea** features a temperate climate with hot, humid summers and winters that are cold and dry. From June through September, the region experiences most of its yearly rainfall, thanks to the seasonal monsoons.

Mt. Fuji

Population and Culture

Climate and topography affect where people live in a given region and the type of culture that develops. The Himalayas, other mountain ranges, and often bodies of water (i.e. the Sea of Japan) act as natural barriers that have contributed over centuries to the development of diverse cultures in various areas. Few people live in the Himilayas because of the rough terrain, high altitude, and harsh conditions. Deserts are scarcely populated as well. People live in urban areas that have developed along coasts and rivers providing access to travel, trade, and contact with other cultures. Like most regions, much of southern and eastern Asia's population lives in cities. Cities provide modern technology, jobs, transportation, more advanced medical care, and schools.

However, in other southern and eastern Asian countries, the majority of citizens still live in the countryside. These people reside in areas that traditionally receive enough water and are good for farming and raising livestock.

Kim Jong Il

The quality of life in different nations varies greatly. Japan, as a major capitalist and industrialized nation, is one of the wealthiest nations on earth, and its citizens tend to enjoy a fairly high standard of living. Meanwhile, China is a vast nation with the world's largest population (well over 1 billion people). Its cities are packed. Its rural population tends to be very poor. Because of its population, China fights each year to provide enough food and jobs for its ever-growing population. Thanks to implementing aspects of capitalism into its communist society, however, China is developing at a faster pace in recent years. In India, parts of the country are extremely poor while some urban areas are developed and even feature growing centers of international business. South Korea, like Japan, benefits from its post-World War II history as a capitalist nation and features a prosperous economy. North Korea's citizens, on the other hand, live in extreme poverty under a totalitarian socialist regime. These are just a few examples of how the make-up and distribution of the region's population vary widely from country to country.

Practice 7.4 The Rest of Asia

1. The Himalayas are part of the
   - A. Deccan Plateau.
   - B. islands of Southeast Asia.
   - C. largest Muslim nation in the world.
   - D. Northern Mountain Rim.

2. China, Japan, and Korea are
   - A. the three major countries of Eastern Asia.
   - B. the three major countries of South Asia.
   - C. island nations in Eastern Asia.
   - D. nations outside the "Ring of Fire."

3. Describe two distinctive things about Indonesia.

CHAPTER 7 REVIEW

Key terms, people, and concepts

geography
physical geography
place
physical features
topography
landform
body of water
climate
natural vegetation
animal life
human characteristics of geography
population settlement patterns
human activities
agriculture and industry's effects on geography
culture
customs and traditions
Southwest Asia and North Africa
deserts
Sahara
Sahel
North African and Southwest Asian mountain ranges
Persian Gulf
Strait of Hormuz
Mediterranean Sea
Tigris and Euphrates Rivers
Nile River
Suez Canal
Sinai Peninsula
deserts
Judaism
Christianity
Islam
traditional Muslim societies
westernized Muslim societies
Sub-Saharan Africa
East African Mountains
Great Rift Valley
Lake Victoria
Congo and Zambezi rivers
climate regions of Sub-Sahara Africa
population distribution
urbanization
modernization
South Asia
Southeast Asia
Eastern Asia
Northern Mountain Rim
Himalayas
Northern Plains
Indus and Ganges Rivers
Deccan Plateau
Sri Lanka
The Maldives
climate of South Asia
mainland Southeast Asia
Mekong River
islands of Southeast Asia
climate of Southeast Asia
China
Plateau of Tibet
China's deserts
China's major rivers
Japan
Korea
climate of Eastern Asia

Multiple Choice Questions

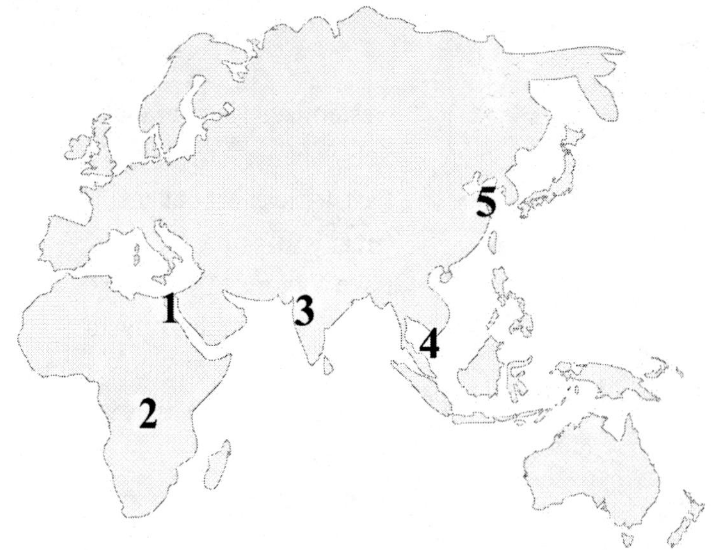

1. In which numbered region of the map would one find the country of China?
   A. 1 B. 2 C. 4 D. 5

2. In which numbered region of the map would one find the country with the world's largest Muslim population?
   A. 1 B. 3 C. 4 D. 5

3. Which region covers portions of two continents?
   A. 1
   B. 3
   C. 5
   D. None cover territory on more than one continent.

4. In which region would one find the world's longest river?
   A. 1 C. 1 and 2
   B. 2 D. 1, 2, and 3

5. Which of the labeled regions is the birthplace of Islam?
   A. 5 B. 3 C. 2 D. 1

6. The study of how land, climate, and bodies of water define a region/place is referred to as
   A. topography. C. physical geography.
   B. climatology. D. geology.

7. Which of the following is an example of how human activity helps to define a region?
   A. rainy seasons. C. religious rituals
   B. the Mediterranean Sea D. race

8. North Africa and Southwest Asia share which of the following in common?
   A. They both have rainy seasons with more than 50 inches of rain per year.
   B. They both have been greatly impacted by Islam.
   C. They both depend heavily on the Tigris River.
   D. They both contain portions of the Himalayas.

9. The Nile, Tigris, Euphrates, Strait of Hormuz, Congo, and Zambezi are all
   A. important bodies of water in Asia.
   B. important bodies of water in Africa.
   C. rivers in North Africa and Southwest Asia.
   D. important bodies of water west of South Asia.

10. The relationship between Muslims and Israel can best be described as
    A. hostile.
    B. trusting.
    C. united.
    D. indifferent.

11. Urbanization and modernization means that larger populations tend to live in
    A. cities.
    B. rural areas.
    C. mountainous regions.
    D. deserts.

12. African societies that live in the equatorial region are most likely adapted to living in
    A. savannas.
    B. rainforests.
    C. the Sahel.
    D. semiarid areas.

Chapter 8
World Geography: Europe, the Americas, and Oceania

GPS	SSWG6: The student will describe the interaction of physical and human systems that have shaped contemporary Europe. (QCC standards WG2, WG4, WG6, WG11, WG12, WG13, WG14, WG17, WH33, WH34)
	SSWG7: The student will describe the interaction of physical and human systems that have shaped contemporary Latin America. (QCC standards WG2, WG4, WG6, WG11, WG12, WG13, WG14, WG17, WH33, WH34)
	SSWG8: The student will describe the interaction of physical and human systems that have shaped contemporary Canada and the United States. (QCC standards WG2, WG4, WG6, WG12, WG13, WG14, WG17, WH33, WH34)
	SSWG9: The student will describe the interaction of physical and human systems that have shaped contemporary Oceania, including Australia, New Zealand, and Antarctica. (QCC standards WG12, WG17)

8.1 EUROPE

PHYSICAL FEATURES

The continent of **Europe** is surrounded by several major bodies of water. The Arctic Ocean lies to the north, the Atlantic Ocean to the west, and the Mediterranean Sea hugs the southern coast of Europe. Asia sits to the east. The **Ural Mountains** serve as a natural barrier dividing Europe (the world's second smallest continent) from Asia (the world's largest). The continent features a number of **peninsulas** (land surrounded on three sides by water). The *Iberian Peninsula* is made up of Spain and Portugal and forms the westernmost

Ural Mountains

territory of Europe. The *Scandinavian Peninsula* consists of Norway and Sweden and is located in northern Europe. Scandinavia features magnificent *fjords* (long, narrow inlets surrounded by steep cliffs on both sides) full of breath-taking beauty. Finally, the country of Italy and part of Greece form peninsulas as well.

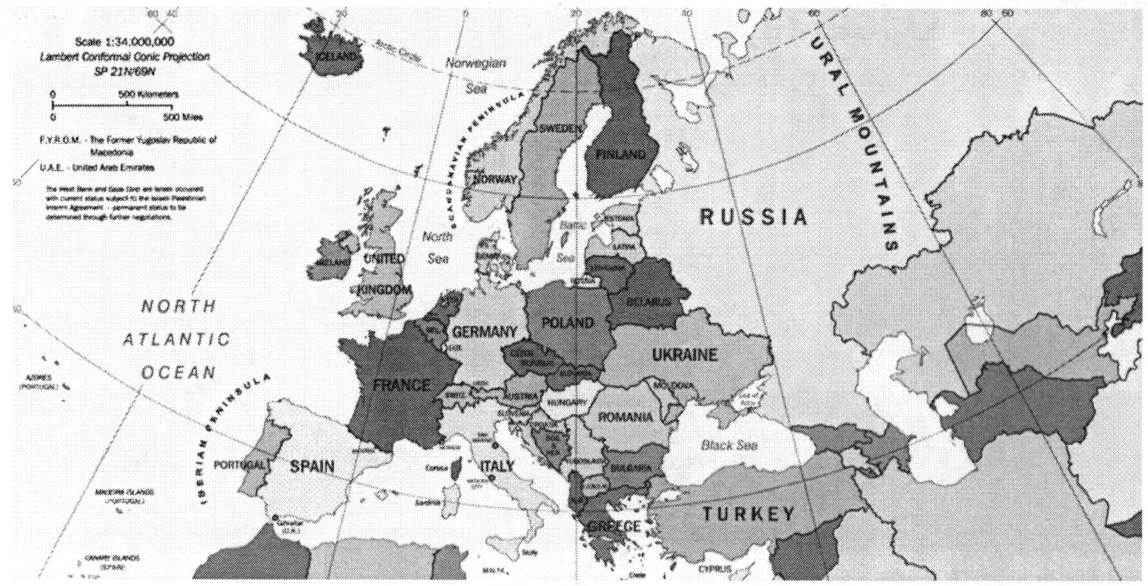

Map of Europe

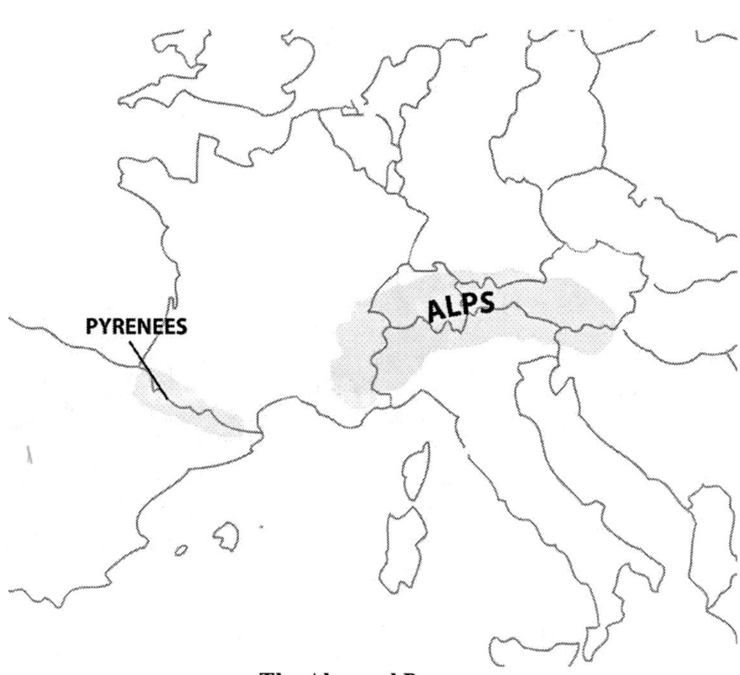

The Alps and Pyrenees

Much of Europe is mountainous. Major mountain ranges include the Ural Mountains, the **Alps**, and the **Pyrenees**. The Alps stretch from Austria westward into France. The Pyrenees separate the Iberian Peninsula from the rest of the continent. Because the ranges serve as barriers, different cultures and nations formed despite the continent's small size. Europe also consists of *lowlands* and *plains*. A *plain* is a large, flat, open area of land. The **Great European Plain** stretches from France to the Urals and features some of the richest farmland in the world. Unlike the mountains, people could travel and engage in trade more easily in the Great European Plain. As a result, many of Europe's major cities, like Paris, Berlin, and Moscow, developed in this region.

Europe also features important waterways. The Mediterranean Sea and Atlantic Ocean have long provided a means of travel, trade, and livelihood. In fact, thanks to Europe's location along the Atlantic Ocean, many of the continent's countries (i.e., Great Britain, France, Spain, Portugal, and the Netherlands) eventually established colonies in both hemispheres and came to dominate the world economically and militarily from the sixteenth to the early twentieth century. **Major rivers** in Europe include the *Rhine, Danube*, and *Volga*. Before trains and air travel, rivers allowed Europeans to travel, interact, and trade. Many of Europe's most influential cities grew up along rivers and bodies of water.

European Rivers

CLIMATE

The Alps and Pyrenees mountains impact Europe's weather. They act as a natural barrier between the regions around the Mediterranean and Iberian Peninsula and regions farther north. Winters in higher elevations and north of these mountain ranges tend to get very cold due to winds blowing southward from the Arctic Ocean. Because the mountains shield southern Europe from these winds, the Mediterranean and Iberian coast enjoy milder, warm temperatures most of the year. The Mediterranean climate tends to be dry, while northern Europe has greater amounts of precipitation that produces green forests and vast stretches of fertile farmland. Farther north, in places like Scandinavia and Russia, it is not uncommon to experience winter temperatures well below 0° F. The Siberian **tundra** region has wide-open spaces covered with ice and snow by the year-round freezing temperatures. Because of its harsh conditions, few people live in the tundra.

Skiing in the Alps

POPULATION, ECONOMIC DEVELOPMENT, AND WORLD INFLUENCE

Middle Ages Church

Europe's geography has greatly impacted its ability to develop and influence the rest of the world. In ancient times, the Roman Empire conquered much of Europe, uniting the continent for a time. Although the Empire eventually fell and the continent broke into separate regions, the roads developed by the Romans allowed different areas to experience a common culture and share common languages. They also provided a means by which Christianity could make its way across the continent. During a period known as the Dark Ages, in which much of Europe's government and structure collapsed, Christianity played a vital role in maintaining a civilized society in the absence of any overriding government. Since Europe's **mountain ranges** served as a natural barrier, many nations developed on the small continent. The Pyrenees separate the people of Spain and Portugal from France and the Germanic peoples. Many Slavic peoples stand divided from other Europeans by the Ural Mountains. Meanwhile, water also serves as a barrier. The UK sits on islands just off the coast of mainland Europe. Since overland travel was often difficult on the mountainous continent, Europeans depended on its many rivers for travel and trade. As a result, cities like Paris, Vienna, Warsaw, London, and Geneva grew up along European waterways. Because Europe is bordered on three sides by water, Europeans also learned master of the sea. Nations like England, France, Spain, the Netherlands, and Portugal built some of the world's most efficient ships for trade and military conquest. Many of the continent's most influential cities grew up along the coast because of the trade and travel that took place by ship (i.e., Naples, Lisbon, and Venice). Combined with a desire to expand their territories, Europeans' ability to navigate the oceans eventually led to the colonization of parts of Africa, Asia, and the Americas. Colonization meant the spread of European philosophies, schools of thought, ideas about social order, and Christianity. Even today, Europe's cultural, social, religious, and economic influences are felt in many parts of the world.

As Europe took advantage of its natural trade routes, its economic markets expanded. Expansion created more opportunity for wealth. New markets and products created a demand for better and more efficient ways to produce and distribute goods. As a result, Europe was the birthplace of the **industrial revolution** in the 1700s. People began to develop new machines and innovative technology that made mass production of goods possible. Thanks to its colonies and industrialization, many parts of Europe became very wealthy. After World War II, western nations remained open to relatively free markets which allowed them to grow their economies and thrive. Today, **Western Europe** (nations that remained free of communist rule after World War II) continues to prosper and be an important center of international business. By comparison, **Eastern Europe** (nations that fell under the rule of the USSR and its communist government after World War II) has suffered economically. Because the governments of these nations heavily regulated the economy, limited private ownership of property, and prevented free market competition, people in these nations did not experience the same prosperity as those in the West. Since the fall of communism in Eastern Europe in the late 1980s and early '90s, many of these nations have struggled to develop and put in place free market economies.

London

Paris

Moscow

Today, Europe remains **ethnically diverse**. People of various ethnic backgrounds live on the continent. In larger cities, people of different ethnic groups often live close to one another. In more rural places, they often live within their own regions and/or villages. While diversity is embraced by many people, it sometimes leads to conflict. Over the centuries, certain ethnic groups have developed a history of being at odds with one another. Resentments and mistrust between certain ethnic groups have existed for generations. As a result, peace is often hard to maintain in certain parts of Europe. For instance, when the former Soviet Union collapsed in the early 1990s, a number of East European territories formerly under the control of the Soviet government suddenly found themselves free. While freedom is generally a good thing, it also meant that the rival ethnic groups within these nations were once again free to resume old wars and act on age-old hatreds.

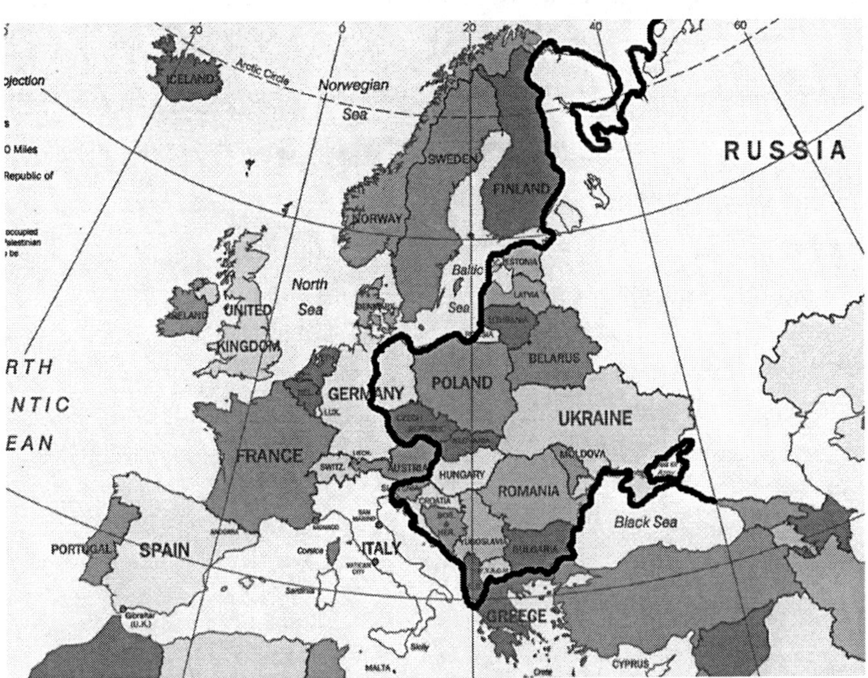

Eastern and Western Europe

European Urban Area

Many Europeans live in large, **urban areas**. Cities like London, Paris, Moscow, Rome, Madrid, and Berlin, are among the oldest and most beautiful cities in the world. In Western Europe, most of these cities tend to resemble the big cities of the United States. They are modern, culturally similar, centers of international commerce, etc. Meanwhile, in Eastern Europe, large cities are often less developed, further behind, and face more economic difficulties, due to the effects of communism. As one might expect, areas with milder temperatures, fertile soil for farming, and access to urban areas tend to be more populated than extremely cold, more isolated, and/or mountainous regions.

THE EUROPEAN UNION

European Union Leaders

The **European Union (EU)** is a group of European nations that have joined ranks to encourage economic and political progress. These nations hope that by working together on the continent, they will experience greater economic benefit and prevent future military conflicts. Most EU nations are in Western Europe, but more eastern nations are joining over time. The EU even has its own currency, the *euro*. Traditionally, each country has had its own currency. The euro is innovative because it allows Europeans to use the same currency in member nations. EU nations have also eliminated tariffs (taxes on foreign goods) on products from fellow EU countries and are continually implementing measures which encourage European nations to become more environmentally responsible.

Practice 8.1 Europe

1. Southern Europe is best described as
   A. extremely cold.
   B. similar to Africa's equatorial region.
   C. full of fjords.
   D. mild and dry.

2. The Pyrenees, Alps, and Urals are
   A. important rivers in Europe.
   B. major mountain ranges in Europe.
   C. key peninsulas in Europe.
   D. native Iberian people groups.

3. How have mountain ranges, rivers, and oceans impacted Europeans?

8.2 Latin America

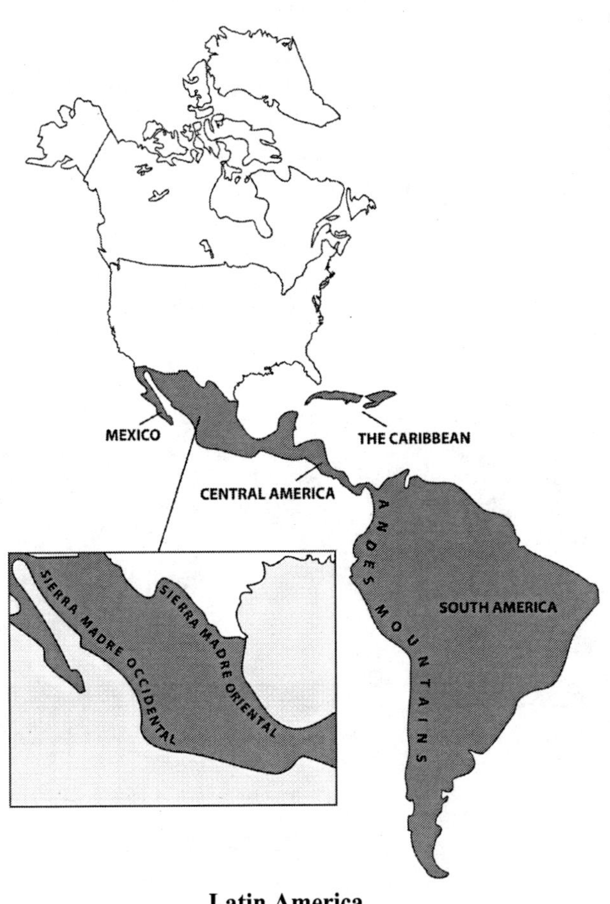

Latin America

Together, Mexico, Central America, South America, and the Caribbean compose **Latin America**. The region gets its name from the mainly Spanish and Portuguese colonists who share a common Latin derived language and culture.

Physical Features

Mountainous regions occupy much of Latin America. Mexico is the northernmost Latin American country. Its two major mountain ranges are the **Sierra Madre Occidental** and the **Sierra Madre Oriental**. In between sits **Mexico's Central Plateau** (sometimes called the "Mexican Plateau"). Mountain regions covered in rainforests stretch south through **Central America** which rests to the south of Mexico. Although the countries in this region are part of North America, the region is called Central America because it sits on a narrow strip of land connecting North and South America. Seven countries make up Central America: Guatemala, Honduras, El Salvador, Nicaragua, Costa Rica, Panama, and Belize. Most of the region is hilly or mountainous and is covered with rainforests. Along the west coast of South America run the **Andes Mountains.** The Andes is the longest series of mountain ranges in the world, stretching more

The Andes

than 4,500 miles. Mountains are found on the Caribbean Islands. Many of these islands are actually the peaks of ancient volcanoes, the base of which sit below the ocean. **Volcanoes** are openings in the earth's surface (usually a mountain) through which lava (hot, molten rock), volcanic ash, and gases escape. When enough pressure builds up beneath the surface of the earth to push lava, ash, etc., through the opening, volcanic eruptions occur. Major eruptions can cause massive death and destruction. Volcanoes are located throughout many of Latin America's mountainous regions. In fact, more than forty volcanoes line hundreds of miles along the west coast of Central America, forming the most active group of volcanoes in the Americas. Because much of the region is located above tectonic plates (pieces of the earth that move), Latin America is also prone to **earthquakes**. When these tectonic plates move, they often cause violent shaking. Small earthquakes may only cause light tremors that are barely detected. However, large quakes can destroy buildings and even entire cities, causing injuries, destruction, and death.

A number of major plains also cover Latin America. Mexico and Central America are marked by narrow coastal plains, while parts of South America are covered by large inland plains, including the *pampas* of Argentina and the *llanos* of Columbia. South America is also home to the **Amazon Basin,** the largest lowland area on the continent. It rests at the basin of the **Amazon River**, which is the longest river in the Western Hemisphere and home to the feared *piranha* (aggressive, flesh eating fish with razor-sharp teeth) and the world's largest snake, the *anaconda*. It runs through the heart of the **Amazon Rainforest**. The Amazon Rainforest covers portions of nine countries and represents more than one half of the world's remaining rainforests.

Piranha

Anaconda

Other major rivers and waterways in Latin America include the *Rio Grande* (this river separates the United States from Mexico along the Texas border), the *Gulf of Mexico*, the *Caribbean Sea*, and the many tributaries that feed the Amazon River in South America. One man-made waterway that is important to the region is the **Panama Canal**. The canal was built across the isthmus (thin stretch of land) of Panama by the United States in the early 1900s. In 1999, the Panamanians assumed control of the canal. The Panama Canal allows ships to travel between the Atlantic and Pacific oceans without having to travel around South America.

Rainforest

DEFORESTATION

Amazon Tribe

Deforestation is the destruction of rainforests. Over the last two decades, the rate of deforestation has greatly increased. As rainforests disappear, wildlife is forced to retreat further into the interior until certain species become endangered or extinct (no longer exist). Deforestation also affects the human inhabitants of the rainforest. The Amazon is home to native peoples whose existence and way of life has long depended on the rainforest. Finally, there are concerns about the environmental effects. Because the Amazon Rainforest is so immense, its vegetation puts out large amounts of oxygen and clears the air of vast amounts of carbon dioxide. Some argue that, by destroying large portions of the rainforest to make way for development, people are altering air quality and damaging the environment. Deforestation is a side-effect of an ever-growing population and attempts by South American nations to further industrial and economic development.

CLIMATE

Atacama Desert

Because the Equator runs through northern South America, much of Latin America has a *tropical climate.* Large portions of the region are hot most of the year and subject to dry and rainy seasons. Although temperatures are cooler at higher elevations, even in the mountains, the tropical climate keeps the area fairly warm. As one moves further south or north of the equator, temperatures become cooler and rainfall is less. As a result, parts of northern Mexico and southern Argentina are similar in climate, featuring dryer areas and deserts. The mountains in these regions are much colder than those closer to the Equator. Along Chile's coast lies the **Atacama Desert**, one of the driest places on earth. Due to the warm waters of the Caribbean Sea, it is not uncommon for **hurricanes** (storms forming over the ocean with winds greater than 75mph) to sweep across the Caribbean Islands during summer and autumn months. Often these storms head north, crashing into the southeastern United States.

El Nino

One key aspect of Latin America's climate that impacts other parts of the world is **El Ñino**. The name is a Spanish reference to the Christ child because the phenomenon usually occurs around Christmas every few years. El Ñino features warmer than usual ocean currents which form in the Pacific off the coast of northern South America. These currents warm the normally cool air. As a result, El Ñino tends to change normal weather patterns, causing different parts of the globe to be dryer or experience more rainfall than normal. Since farmers depend on predictable rain patterns to plant and harvest their crops, El Ñino can have drastic effects. In less developed nations, it has contributed to vast famines and starvation.

Hurricane

People and Population Distribution

The cultures of Latin America feature a combination of Native American and European influences. Latin America is also home to a diverse ethnic population. Native American peoples, blacks of African descent, and people of European ancestry all occupy the region. Much of the population consists of people who are a mix of these various people groups. Because Spain and Portugal colonized much of the region, Spanish or Portuguese is often the official language. However, since France and Great Britain colonized parts of the Caribbean, modified French and English dialects are spoken there as well. Many people mix the European languages with local dialects. Some still speak local, native languages, especially in rural, less developed areas.

Today, many Latin Americans live in **urban areas**. Mexico's capital, **Mexico City**, is one of the most populated cities in the world. Although it offers great opportunities for jobs, education, business, and culture, it also presents problems. Because it is surrounded by mountains, pollution produced by the vast population is often trapped and lingers in the air. Overcrowding, unemployment, and crime are ongoing challenges as well. Mexico City's location also exposes it to earthquakes which may cause extensive damage and injure or kill thousands of people. Rio de Janeiro and Sao Paulo in Brazil; Buenos Aires, Argentina;. and Santiago, Chile are other large Latin American cities. Many of the region's most populated areas rest in the fertile areas of the plains or along the coasts or waterways. Rivers and waterways allow for easier travel, while coastal regions have long been accessible to trade and international contact. In South America, coastal regions are areas of high population because these areas are easier to inhabit than the thick rainforest regions of the continent's interior or the rugged terrain of the Andes Mountains.

Practice 8.2 Latin America

1. *Deforestation* refers to
   A. the amount of forests in Central America.
   B. the number of people living in Latin American rainforests.
   C. the destruction of rainforests to make way for development.
   D. the largest rainforest on earth.

2. What is El Niño and what impact can it have on the world?

3. Describe some of Latin America's key physical features.

8.3 The United States and Canada

Map of North America

The **United States** and **Canada** are part of the continent known as **North America,** the third largest continent after Asia and Africa. Mexico, the Caribbean Islands, the nations of Central America, and Greenland (the world's largest island, located in the north Atlantic Ocean) are also part of North America. Canada is the largest country on the continent and the second largest in the world. While Mexico, the Caribbean, and Central America are part of Latin America the United States and Canada were influenced more by Great Britain and France. To the east of North America is the Atlantic Ocean, to the west is the Pacific, to the north the Arctic Ocean, and to the south lies South America.

PHYSICAL FEATURES OF CANADA AND THE US

The Great Plains

Mountain ranges are common to both the United States and Canada. Along the Pacific coasts of both nations run stretches of rugged peaks. Further inland, the **Rocky Mountains** stretch over 3,000 miles from the southwestern United States to Alaska. Finally, through much of the eastern United States and into southern Canada run the **Appalachian Mountains**. Although not as high as the Rockies, the Appalachians are much older and feature beautiful scenic areas, such as the New River Gorge in West Virginia. Between the Rockies and the Appalachian mountains sit the **Great Plains**. This area covers central portions of both countries and features wide open spaces. Although a number of major cities now occupy the Great Plains, it has long been known as a major region for agriculture and cattle ranching.

Mississippi River

In addition to the oceans that surround the continent, there are a number of other important bodies of water. The **Mississippi River system** is the largest in North America. It includes the two longest rivers in the United States, the Mississippi and the Missouri. The **Mackenzie River** is the longest in Canada. It runs north into the Arctic Ocean and, because of the freezing temperatures and ice, is only navigable five months a year. Other major bodies of water include the **Great Lakes**, the *Gulf of Mexico*, *Chesapeake Bay*, *Gulf of California*, *Hudson Bay*, *St. Lawrence River*, *Gulf of Alaska*, and *Bering Sea* that separates North America from eastern Asia. All of these bodies of water, as well as many other rivers and waterways, have long provided people with a means of travel and trade. As a result, many great cities, such as New Orleans and Memphis along the Mississippi

River; Kansas City along the Missouri River; Toronto, Detroit, Chicago, and Milwaukee along the shores of the Great Lakes; Montreal along the St. Lawrence River; New York, Boston, and San Francisco along the US coast; and Vancouver on the western edge of Canada have grown up along these locations.

Canada and the Mackenzie River

The Great Lakes

Climate of Canada and the US

The Tundra

Georgia Drought

Since North America is so big, it has a variety of climate regions. To the far north of Canada and Alaska lies the frozen **tundra**. As one travels south, the tundra gives way to thick, evergreen forests. Still, because of the great distance from the equator, temperatures remain extremely cold during the winter time and fairly cool to cold during the warmer months with very brief summers. Along the Pacific coast of Canada and the northern US, people experience a mild, wet climate, with chilly winters and comfortable summers. Warmer temperatures are common in southern California. The high Pacific mountains that line the coastal regions block the moist air from reaching the areas just to the east. As a result, deserts are common in places like Nevada, Utah, and Arizona. The Great Plains experience hot summer months and cold, snow-filled winters. The northeastern United States and eastern Canada also experience cold, snowy winters and mild to hot summers, while much of the southeast United States has chilly winters with little to no snow and extremely hot and humid summers. The southeast also experiences high counts of pollen during spring and autumn months, often causing discomfort for people with allergies. In places like Georgia, **droughts,** or periods without rain, can be a problem. In 2007, Georgia was hit with one of the worst droughts in its history. As a result, a number of wild fires burned in southern Georgia and north Florida unchecked for several months and laws the state governments passed laws restricting water usage to cities like Atlanta did not run out. Finally, southern Florida around Miami and the Florida Keys (series of small islands off Florida's mainland) enjoy the mildest temperatures in the US. These areas are the only region in the US or Canada that enjoy a tropical climate.

Population Distribution and Regional Growth

New York City

Today, most US citizens and Canadians live in urban areas. Many of these cities grew up along major rivers and along ocean coasts because of the access to travel and opportunities for trade and commerce such bodies of water provided. For this reason, such areas and regions surrounding the Great Lakes tend to boast higher populations and more urban areas than places in extremely mountainous regions or in the middle of the Great Plains. The US' largest urban area is *New York City.* New York's population boomed in the second half of the 1800s as it became the main point of entrance for people immigrating from Europe. Similarly, San Francisco grew rapidly on the west coast due to the easy access it provides to the Pacific ocean. Meanwhile, Montreal along the St. Lawrence River, Toronto on the shores of Lake Ontario, and Vancouver on the Pacific coast, are among Canada's largest and most important cities.

Although the northeast United States has traditionally been home to more people than any other part of the US, in recent decades, the southern United States has experienced a boom in population. The region that stretches from the Carolinas across the nation to southern California is called the *Sun Belt.* Because of the availability of land, affordable cost of living, economic opportunities, and mild climate, this region has attracted more residents and businesses in recent years. Meanwhile, increasing numbers of immigrants from Mexico have served to rapidly increase the Hispanic population in these areas. As a result, cities like Atlanta, Charlotte, San Antonio, Phoenix, and others are among some of the fastest growing and developing cities in the country.

Montreal

Practice 8.3 The United States and Canada

1. The largest river system in North America is the

   A. Missouri. B. Mississippi. C. Mackenzie. D. Appalachian.

2. Canada is

   A. the largest country in terms of land area in the world.
   B. the largest country in terms of population in the world.
   C. the largest country in terms of land area in North America.
   D. the second largest country in terms of land area in North America.

3. Describe why major urban areas in North America tended to grow up around bodies of water.

4. What is the Sun Belt and why is its population growing?

8.4 OCEANIA

Oceania includes *Australia, New Zealand, Antarctica,* and more than 20,000 islands stretching across the Pacific Ocean. Australia and Antarctica are often considered separate from the rest of Oceania because of their size and the fact they are both continents. **Australia,** the smallest continent on earth, is also a country. Meanwhile, **Antarctica,** at the South Pole, is uninhabitable because it is buried in ice. Antarctica's ice holds roughly 70% of the world's fresh water and, in some places, reaches a thickness of two miles.

Oceania

PHYSICAL FEATURES

Great Barrier Reef

Kangaroo

Australia consists mostly of flat lands, relatively unpopulated deserts, and wilderness—commonly known as the outback. The vast majority of Australia's population and its major cities, such as Sydney, Melbourne, and Perth, are located along the coast. Along the continent's eastern edge runs the **Great Dividing Range**, which is a series of mountains and hilly regions. Along the northeastern coast lies the **Great Barrier Reef**. Home to a multitude of underwater wildlife, it is the world's largest coral reef and stretches over an area nearly 133,000 square miles. So vast is the Great Barrier Reef that it can actually be seen from outer space. Just across the *Tasman Sea* lies the nation of **New Zealand**. It consists of two main islands and a number of smaller ones. New Zealand features sandy beaches along the coasts, rolling green hillsides, various plateaus, and mountainous regions with peaks covered in snow. As for the rest of Oceania's islands, some were formed by volcanoes, while others are coral islands surrounded by reefs.

CLIMATE

Although the coast of Australia does receive rainfall, its high mountains prevent much of the moisture from ever reaching the dry interior. Since New Zealand is much smaller (all of the country is within 90 miles of the ocean) its climate is mild throughout, with plenty of rainfall. The many islands have mostly tropical climates with wet and dry seasons, and temperatures that tend to remain hot year-round. Finally, Antarctica is a frozen climate.

Penguin

Practice 8.4 Oceania

1. What two parts of Oceania are sometimes considered separate from this region because they are continents?

   A. Australia and New Zealand
   B. the outback and Great Barrier Reef
   C. Antarctica and Tasman
   D. Antarctica and Australia

2. Where would one find the driest climate?

   A. New Zealand's interior
   B. Oceania's islands
   C. Australia's outback
   D. Antarctica

3. Where do we find the majority of Australia's population? Describe why.

CHAPTER 8 REVIEW

Key terms, people, and concepts

Europe
Ural Mountains
Europe's peninsulas
Alps
Pyrenees
Great European Plain
major rivers of Europe
Europe's climate
tundra
impact of Europe's mountain ranges on population distribution
industrial revolution
economic difference between Western and Eastern Europe
ethnic diversity in Europe
Europe's urban areas
European Union (EU)
Latin America
Sierra Madre Occidental and Oriental
Central Plateau
Central America
Andes Mountains
volcanoes
earthquakes
Amazon Basin
Amazon River
Amazon Rainforest
Panama Canal
deforestation
climate of Latin America
Atacama Desert
hurricanes
El Nino
urban areas in Latin America
Mexico City
United States
Canada
Rocky Mountains
Great Plains
Mississippi River system
Mackenzie River
Great Lakes
droughts
areas of high/growing population in US and Canada
Oceania
Australia
Antarctica
Great Dividing Range
Great Barrier Reef
New Zealand
climate of Oceania

Multiple Choice Questions

1. Which of the following develops along rivers and ocean coasts on nearly every continent?
   A. tundra B. deserts C. urban growth D. rainforests

2. The Andes, Pyrenees, Alps, and Urals are all
   A. important bodies of water that have opened regions up to increased trade and travel.
   B. mountainous regions made up mostly of volcanoes.
   C. parts of Europe featuring high altitudes, cold temperatures, and lots of precipitation.
   D. important mountain regions that serve as natural geographic barriers and affect climate.

3. One could expect to find tundra covering parts of
   A. the United States and Canada. C. North America and Russia.
   B. the Andes and the Urals. D. New Zealand and Antarctica.

4. Look at the map below. Which of the labeled areas most likely depicts a major city in Europe?

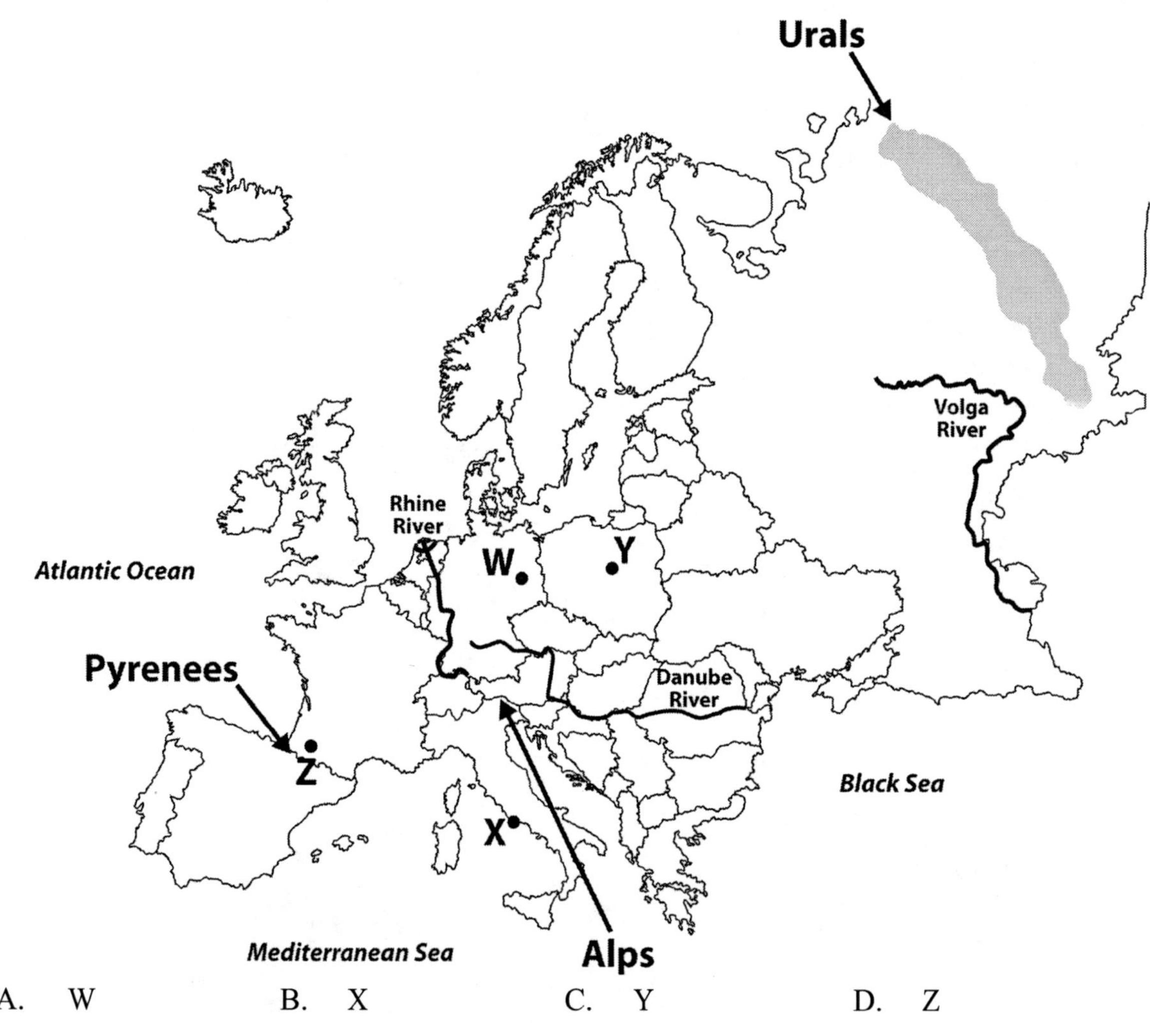

   A. W B. X C. Y D. Z

5. Using the map below, where would one expect to find the most fertile farmland?

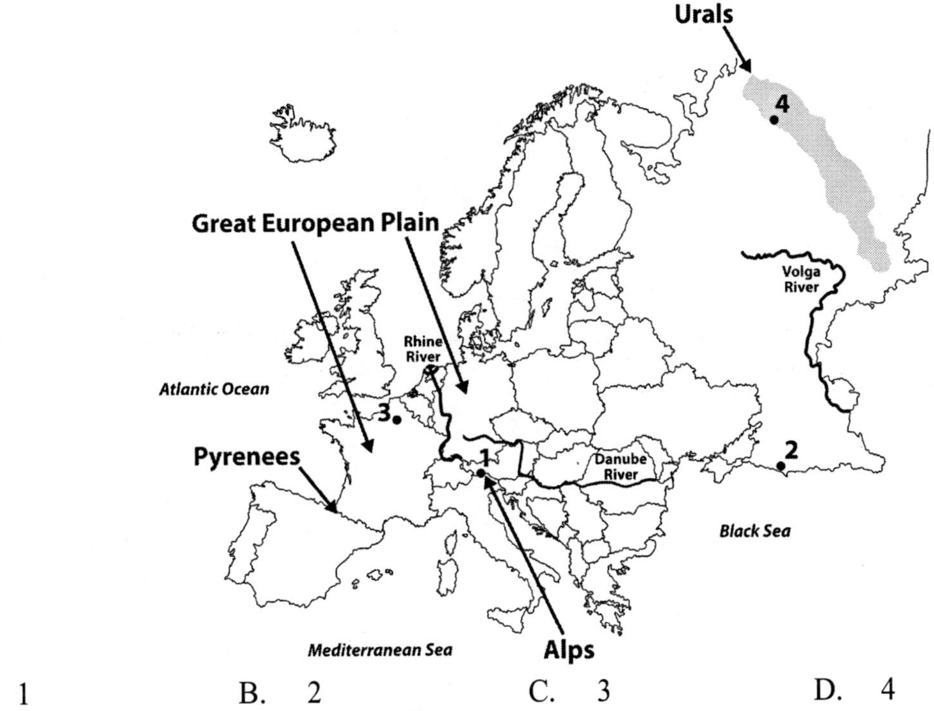

A. 1 B. 2 C. 3 D. 4

6. Australia's major cities are found
   A. in the outback.
   B. along its coast.
   C. more than 200 miles inland.
   D. in New Zealand.

7. The industrial revolution and the establishment of the European Union are both
   A. factors contributing to deforestation.
   B. reasons why Eastern Europe is more developed than Western Europe.
   C. important events in Europe's economic history.
   D. organizations devoted to Europe's economic development.

8. Tropical climates are typically found in
   A. Europe.
   B. Central America.
   C. Australia.
   D. the Great Lakes region

Chapter 9
World History: From the Renaissance through Napoleon

GPS	SSWH9: The student will analyze change and continuity in the Renaissance and Reformation. (QCC standard WH10)
	SSWH10: The student will analyze the impact of the age of discovery and expansion into the Americas, Africa, and Asia. (QCC standard WH11)
	SSWH13: The student will examine the intellectual, political, social, and economic factors that changed the world view of Europeans. (QCC standards WH10, WH12, WH13)
	SSWH14: The student will analyze the Age of Revolutions and Rebellions. (QCC standards WH13, WH14)

9.1 Renaissance and Reformation

The Renaissance

From around 1350 AD to the mid 1500s, Europe experienced the **Renaissance**. The term means "rebirth." It was an era in which artists, architects, philosophers, political thinkers, scientists, and even theologians believed in reviving the classical ideas of ancient Greece and Rome. The Renaissance was a "rebirth" of culture, thought, and civilization after a period of disorder in Europe known as the Dark Ages. Europeans came in contact with many of these ancient ideas thanks to Muslim philosophers and scientists who had already been influenced by them for centuries.

The City of Florence

The Renaissance began in Italy and soon spread to other parts of Europe. Before the Renaissance, people tended to see themselves as members of a community or social order. Individual worth was not highly valued. The Renaissance put more emphasis on the worth and potential of individuals. Several Italian city-states became important centers of the Renaissance. Milan's government grew rich off of its innovative tax system. Venice took advantage of its location along the coast of the Adriatic sea to become a wealthy center of international trade. Among all the city-states, none rose to more prominence than **Florence**. After winning a series of wars, Florence came to dominate much of northern Italy and became the cultural center of Italy and the Italian Renaissance.

Florence, Italy

Machiavelli

Niccolo Machiavelli

The Renaissance featured new ideas in political thought. Among political theorists of the day, **Niccolo Machiavelli** was one of the most influential. Before the Renaissance, most European writers emphasized the importance of monarchs ruling according to Chrisian ethics and principles. Machiavelli rejected this reasoning. In his classic work, *The Prince*, he wrote that a ruler should make decisions based on human nature and what is best for the state. When possible, a ruler should seek to behave ethically. However, they should not be bound by such principles in matters of government. According to Machiavelli, a leader should, "...not deviate from what is good, if that is possible, but he should know how to do evil, if that is necessary." Machiavelli's theory that rulers should act according to the needs of the state rather than religious principles of morality greatly influenced leaders.

The "Renaissance Man"

The Renaissance introduced the idea that human beings are limitless in what they can accomplish. Therefore, people can achieve great things in several areas (the arts, politics, philosophy, science, etc.) rather than being limited to just one. People labeled men who showed such gifted diversity the **Renaissance man.** Two men who exemplified such an image were Leonardo da Vinci and Michelangelo. **Leonardo da Vinci** was a renowned painter, sculptor, inventor, scientist, architect, engineer, and mathematician. Among his most famous works are the paintings the *Mona Lisa* and *The Last Supper.* Long before they were ever invented, da Vinci drew diagrams for a helicopter and a calculator and envisioned harnessing solar power. By comparison, **Michelangelo** was also a gifted painter, sculptor, and builder. He is most remembered for his *David*, a fourteen foot statue sculpted out of a single piece of marble, and his vast painting covering the ceiling of the Sistine Chapel in Rome.

Leonardo da Vinci

Mona Lisa

Michelangelo

David

HUMANISM

Petrarch

Humanism arose out of the Renaissance as well. This movement placed great value on the study of ancient literary works. Humanists focused on grammar, poetry, philosophy, history, ethics, and rhetoric (public speaking and debate). Today, we often refer to such subjects as *the humanities*. Several became major in the humanist movement. **Petrarch** is often remembered as "the father of humanism" and played a key role in uncovering forgotten Latin manuscripts. During the Middle Ages, Christian monks collected and copied many ancient manuscripts and stored them away in hidden libraries. Petrarch led an effort to find these libraries and recover such works. He also emphasized the use of Latin as the "purely classical" language and is credited with perfecting the sonnet (popular form of poetry). Petrarch's efforts ultimately contributed to the more modern Italian language.

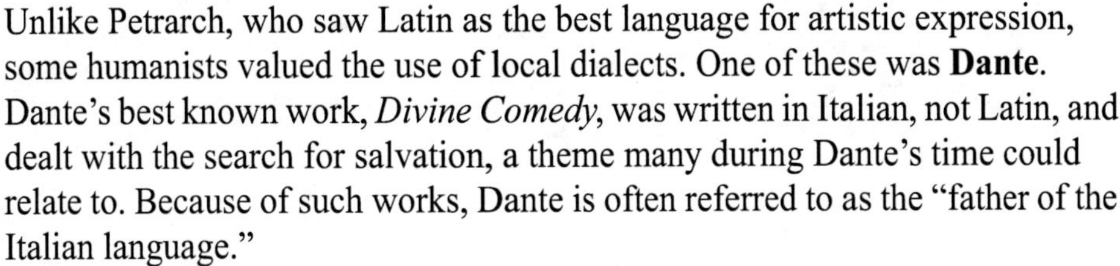

Unlike Petrarch, who saw Latin as the best language for artistic expression, some humanists valued the use of local dialects. One of these was **Dante**. Dante's best known work, *Divine Comedy*, was written in Italian, not Latin, and dealt with the search for salvation, a theme many during Dante's time could relate to. Because of such works, Dante is often referred to as the "father of the Italian language."

Dante

ERASMUS

Humanism also affected religious thought. Among Christian scholars, **Erasmus** became known as the "Prince of Humanists." He was a towering figure in a movement aimed at reforming the church and ending corruption. Much of this corruption flowed from the wealth and political power of popes, bishops, and the nobility. Humanism meant re-examining what the church was doing in light of ancient Christian writings. Erasmus and many others concluded that many of the church's practices were wrong and needed to change. In particular, he taught that obedience to the Bible and sincere devotion to God were more important than religious rituals. Erasmus did not want to break from the Catholic Church, he simply wanted to reform it. Leaders of the Reformation later adopted many of his ideas.

Erasmus

THE REFORMATION

LUTHER AND THE PROTESTANT REFORMATION

Martin Luther

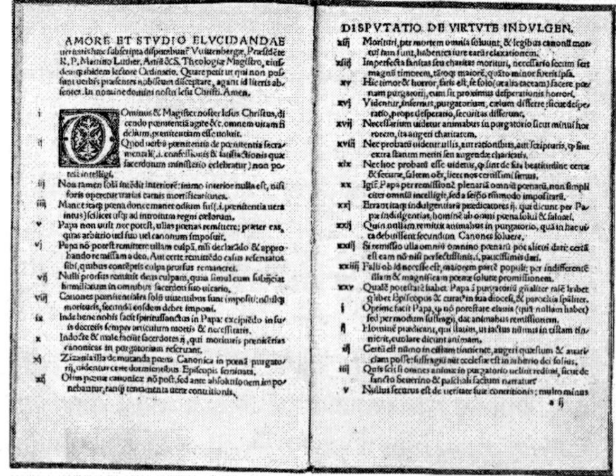
AMORE ET STVDIO ELVCIDANDAE

DISPVTATIO DE VIRTVTE INDVLGEN.

Ninety-five Theses

Up until the early sixteenth century, the Roman Catholic Church was the only recognized Christian church in Europe. Due to circumstances that occurred during the Middle Ages, it also possessed tremendous political power. Often, emperors and kings relied heavily on their alliances with the pope and paid taxes to Rome. Then, in 1517, a German monk named **Martin Luther** took action that shook the church and changed Christianity forever. Luther believed that the Bible taught people are saved only by the grace of God and not religious works. One of the practices that upset Luther the most was the Catholic practice of selling *indulgences*. Indulgences allowed people to pay money in exchange for forgiveness, either for themselves or for loved ones who had died and were in purgatory. Purgatory is a place many Catholics believe people who have died without living a good enough life must be purified before they can go to heaven. Pope Leo X authorized the sale of indulgences in order to allow a political official, Albert of Brandenburg, to raise enough money to pay for the completion of St. Peter's Basilica in Rome. On October 31, 1517, Martin Luther nailed what came to be known as his *Ninety-five Theses* to the door of the castle church in Wittenberg, Germany. He voiced his protest against indulgences and various other Catholic teachings he found contrary to the Bible. Although his original goal was to see Catholic leaders change their ways rather than start a new church, his actions ultimately led to the **Protestant Reformation**. It was called "Protestant" because, in 1529, a number of German princes *protested* efforts by the Catholic emperor to impose Catholicism on all the territories of Germany. Although much of southern Germany remained Catholic, northern Germany looked to Luther as the founder of a new church that rejected many Catholic teachings and did not answer to the pope. In reality, many of these princes protected and supported Luther more for political than religious reasons. Because the emperor needed their support, he granted them the right to establish whatever church they wanted in their respective territories (Protestant or Catholic). Individuals, however, were expected to hold to whichever faith their local princes chose.

Pope Leo X

John Calvin

While Luther challenged the Catholic church in Germany, a reformation movement took hold in Switzerland as well. Originally, Ulrich Zwingli led this movement. However, when Zwingli was killed in a battle against Catholic forces, leadership of the cause fell to **John Calvin**. Calvin wrote *Institutes of the Christian Religion* in which he put forth many arguments that came to define Protestant thought. One of his most famous and controversial doctrines was that of *predestination*, the belief that God has already decided who is saved and who is lost, and humans can do nothing to change it. Eventually, Calvin became the recognized ruler of Geneva and made it a city ruled by Protestant ideas. Calvinism eventually became the foundation of the Presbyterian Church.

John Calvin

The English Reformation

Unlike Luther and Calvin's reformation movements, the **English Reformation** was sparked by political and personal concerns rather than religious. The English king, **Henry VIII**, wanted to divorce his wife, Catherine, because she had "failed" to produce a male heir. However, the pope refused to sanction such a divorce because Catherine was the aunt of the Holy Roman emperor, Charles V. During the 1500s, kings often used marriage as a way of forming political alliances. The pope opposed the divorce because he feared it would cause political instability. Enraged, King Henry established the Church of England in 1534, proclaiming it

Henry VIII

free from the influence of the pope and making the king the, "...only supreme head on earth of the Church of England." One of the new church's first acts was to grant the king his divorce. Outside of leadership, the Church of England kept many of the same beliefs and ceremonies of the Catholic Church.

The Counter Reformation

Ignatius Loyola

The Protestant Reformation prompted a response from the Catholic Church known as the **Counter Reformation**. The Counter Reformation was an attempt to reform the Catholic Church while rejecting the Protestant Reformation. One key group that emerged during this period was the **Jesuits**. A Spaniard named Ignatius Loyola founded the order following a religious revelation. Loyola believed that Christians should totally submit to the will of the Church because it is Christ's body on earth. This meant total obedience to the pope as the "Vicar of Christ" (Christ's earthly representative). In 1540, the pope officially recognized the Jesuits, who swore a vow of allegiance to the pope and became enforcers of his policies. Jesuits used their education to counter arguments against Catholicism. In an effort to turn back the tide of the Protestant Reformation, the Jesuits became great missionaries, taking Catholicism to many parts of the world.

Council of Trent

Another important part of the Counter Reformation (sometimes called the "Catholic Reformation") was the **Council of Trent**. The council met over a period of eighteen years. During three major sessions it attempted to strengthen the church and encourage Protestants to return to the Catholic fold. In the end, however, it only hardened the lines between Catholics and Protestants. It upheld traditional Catholic teachings regarding salvation, the seven sacraments (Protestants recognize only two: baptism and the communion), celibacy of clergy (idea that clergy are not to marry and are to abstain from sexual relations), purgatory, and even the selling of indulgences when done "properly." The Council of Trent provided the Catholic Church with a clearly stated doctrine and unified the church as never before. With the pope's power reaffirmed, the Catholic Church met the Protestants head-on, both in Europe and across the globe.

Gutenberg's Printing Press

Johannes Gutenberg's printing press had a profound impact on the Renaissance and Reformation. The printing press mass produced written works so that they could be distributed more widely. Without the printing press, the Protestant Reformation may have failed. Not until some of Luther's followers began printing his Ninety-five Theses and several of his other works did his ideas ignite a mass following in Germany. The printing press also allowed the Bible to be printed and distributed in common languages. Gutenberg's invention played a major role in both the religious and political transformation of Europe.

Johannes Gutenberg

Printing Press

Practice 9.1 Renaissance and Reformation

1. He greatly impacted political thought by asserting that leaders should rule according to the needs of the state rather than simply relying on what is considered ethical or moral.
   - A. Martin Luther
   - B. Erasmus
   - C. Machiavelli
   - D. Leonardo da Vinci

2. Martin Luther and John Calvin were both regarded as key leaders of the
   - A. Renaissance.
   - B. Protestant Reformation.
   - C. Counter Reformation.
   - D. Humanist movement.

3. What was the Protestant Reformation and what inspired it?

4. Describe the Counter Reformation. Who were the Jesuits and what was the importance of the Council of Trent?

5. Describe the impact of Gutenberg's printing press.

9.2 Discovery and Expansion

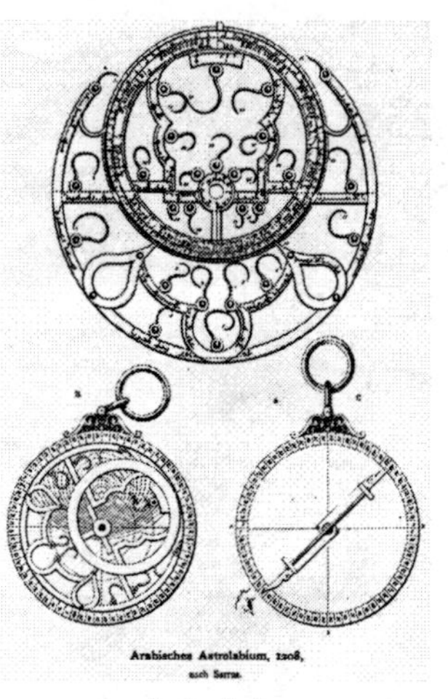

Astrolabe

From the late fifteenth to the nineteenth centuries, many European nations embarked on an era of discovery and expansion that took their culture, political ideas, and religion to other parts of the world. Their ventures led to European colonies in Asia, Africa, and the Americas. European nations established dominance over much of the globe economically and militarily, forever impacting foreign cultures.

A number of factors led to European exploration and expansion. National leaders had grown in power and wealth and could afford to finance voyages. In addition, new technology made available the ships and means of navigation necessary to successfully travel across vast oceans. The **astrolabe**, for instance, allowed navigators to determine their position on the high seas using the location of the sun and stars. Finally, there were motivations that convinced monarchs to pay for such expeditions. One was economic. Countries like Spain and Portugal hoped to discover territories and trade routes that would make them rich. There were also religious motivations. Expansion was seen as a way to spread Christianity. For many of the explorers who embarked on these journeys, there was the promise of personal wealth and glory. They would be hailed at home as national heroes. **God, gold, and glory** served as major motivations for European expansion.

Key European Explorers

The Portuguese

Africa and Portugal

The Portuguese were the first to impact the age of exploration. They began venturing into **Africa** in search of new territories and riches. Before long, Portuguese ships were returning to Europe with resources and black Africans, many of whom were sold into slavery. Eventually, the Portuguese acquired land from local African rulers and built forts. From these locations they welcomed and loaded European ships with goods and slaves returning to Portugal. As Portugal established colonies in the Americas, these forts served as gathering points where African slaves could be bought and held until they could be loaded on ships and transported across the Atlantic.

Portugal also wanted to find a sea route to **Asia** around the southern tip of Africa. Since the Middle Ages, Europeans had been aware of Asia's rich markets and the raw materials it offered. They hoped to find quicker trade routes and establish their presence in coastal areas that could serve as commercial ports. In 1498, Portuguese explorer, **Vasco da Gama**, successfully rounded Africa and made his way to India. The profit he made from this voyage encouraged other Portuguese sailors to follow him. Thanks to their skills as seamen and military technology, the Portuguese defeated Arab, Turkish, and Indian navies to establish their dominance over the Indian Ocean and its trade routes.

Vasco da Gama

Spanish Explorations

Christopher Columbus

While da Gama opened the way east, **Christopher Columbus** ventured west across the Atlantic. Financed by Spain, the Italian adventurer set sail believing that he, too, would eventually reach Asia. In October 1492, Columbus reached the Americas, exploring the coast of Cuba and landing in Hispaniola (modern-day Haiti). Columbus, however, had no idea that he had "discovered" a new world. He thought he'd reached Asia. Overall, he made four voyages to the region, reaching several Caribbean Islands and part of Central America. Although he was wrong in his assumption that he had reached Asia, Columbus made rulers in Europe aware of a previously "unclaimed" territory (Europeans considered these lands open to colonization even though many native peoples already lived there). Eventually, other navigators realized that Columbus had discovered an entirely new continent and launched their own voyages. On one of these voyages, a man named Amerigo Vespucci wrote letters describing the new lands. The popularity of these descriptions led people in Europe to label the new territory **America.**

Ferdinand Magellan believed there must be a water route through the Americas. If located, he could use it to sail on to the Far East. Finally, after sailing down the entire coast of South America, Magellan found his open waterway in 1520 (today known as the Strait of Magellan). Unfortunately, however, he greatly underestimated the size of the Pacific Ocean that awaited him on the other side and many of his men grew ill or died of starvation before finally reaching the Philippines (they named the islands the "Philippines" after King Philip of Spain). Natives of the islands killed Magellan, but a remnant of his crew returned to Spain, making his expedition the first to officially sail around the world.

Ferdinand Magellan **Magellan's Route**

Samuel de Champlain

France's most successful early North American colony was established at *Quebec* in 1608 by the French explorer **Samuel de Champlain**. The colony rested on high ground along the shores of the St. Lawrence River, thereby giving the French an excellent settlement for carrying out their fur trade and establishing more colonies along the river. It also provided them with a good military position for protecting their interests from any European rivals who might try to navigate the St. Lawrence.

Samuel de Champlain

The Columbian Exchange

Columbus Discovery

When Columbus "discovered" America in 1492, he established contact between two worlds. The **Columbian Exchange** refers to the exchange that arose between the Western and Eastern hemispheres. It included the exchange of raw materials, people (both willing travelers and slaves), ideas, religion, products, and even diseases. The Columbian Exchange drastically affected society on both sides of the Atlantic. It introduced new foods, vegetation, and forms of livestock to both Europe and the Americas. It also transformed the cultures as new commodities, like sugar, tobacco, cotton, and rice, transformed European culture and Europeans imposed new ideas on Native American societies. The Columbian Exchange had detrimental effects on native peoples who were subjected to conquest, slavery, and the devastation of diseases brought by their European invaders.

Practice 9.2 Discovery and Expansion

1. He believed that India could be reached sailing west and, in the end, discovered what would be known as the Americas.

   A. Vasco da Gama
   B. Christopher Columbus
   C. Ferdinand Magellan
   D. Samuel de Champlain

2. Which country was the first to successfully embark on long range voyages during the age of exploration?

   A. Portugal B. Spain C. France D. England

3. What was the Columbian Exchange and what effect did it have on Native Americans?

4. What was the astrolabe and how did it impact exploration?

9.3 Enlightenment and Revolution

Scientific Discoveries

Prior to the Renaissance, most Europeans believed that the Earth sat at the center of the universe, with the sun and other heavenly bodies rotating around it. In 1543, however, an astronomer and mathematician named **Copernicus** published a work entitled *On the Revolutions of the Heavenly Spheres*. He argued that it was actually the sun that sat at the center of the universe. He also asserted that the Earth, along with other planets, rotated around the sun and that the moon rotated around the Earth. His findings are largely credited as marking the beginning of modern understanding about the universe.

Copernicus

Another brilliant mathematician and astronomer, **Johannes Kepler**, expanded on Copernicus' work. Kepler more accurately documented the paths of the planets' rotations. He showed that they actually rotated following an elliptical course (egg-shaped) with the sun sitting towards the end of the ellipse rather than at the center of a circular rotation. **Galileo** was the first known scientist to regularly observe the universe using a telescope. Through his observations, Galileo gained knowledge regarding the surface of the moon as well as the planets. His work confirmed many of Copernicus' theories and made the Catholic Church very upset. The Church felt that Copernicus' conception of the universe contradicted the Bible and considered Galileo a heretic (someone who teaches false ideas about God). Galileo eventually recanted many of his findings under pressure from the Church. Eventually, an Englishman named **Isaac Newton** tied together the work of Copernicus, Kepler, and Galileo and explained how gravity is responsible for planetary motion.

Galileo

Isaac Newton

THE ENLIGHTENMENT

John Locke

Jean-Jacques Rousseau

The late sixteen and seventeen hundreds witnessed **the Enlightenment**, a period which produced new ideas about government. Newton had discovered natural laws governing the universe, many believed there were natural laws governing politics, economics, and other aspects of society as well. Two key figures of this time were Englishman John Locke and Jean-Jacques Rousseau of France. **John Locke** held that knowledge and worldview comes from one's environment and experiences. He praised reason above simple faith. According to Locke, people could be changed by altering their surroundings. He also challenged the old view that monarchs possess a God-given right to rule. Locke believed that people were born with natural rights that included life, liberty, and property. He also advocated *social contract theory.* For the good of society, people give up certain freedoms and empower governments to maintain order. Locke taught that citizens have the right to replace any government that fails to serve the public good. Years later, **Rousseau** published a work actually entitled *The Social Contract*, in which he argued that the general will of the people acted as a "social contract" which all (citizens and government) should be forced to abide by. His ideas later influenced socialism, nationalism, and the French Revolution.

Revolutions in England and North America

New political ideas led many to believe in the basic rights of human beings. Eventually, such thinking contributed to key revolutions that impacted the western world and forever altered the course of history.

The English Revolution and "Glorious Revolution"

Parliament

During the 1600s, conflict arose between the king of England and the British Parliament. At the heart of the controversy was the question of power. Who really ruled England? King James I believed that God, Himself, gave kings their thrones and therefore it was he, as king, who should have ultimate say over the affairs of England. Parliament, however, disagreed. Parliament is Great Britain's legislative body. It originally began during the Middle Ages as a body of noblemen who counseled the king. It eventually developed into an official body of government consisting of two houses: the House of Lords, which consisted of noblemen; and the House of Commons, elected by the people and consisting of representatives from among those classes below the nobility.

Charles I

Oliver Cromwell

Revolution erupted during the reign of James' successor, Charles I. Charles tried to resist limitations placed on his power by Parliament and sought to impose Catholicism on the Church of England. This greatly offended members of the House of Commons because many of them were **Puritans.** The Puritans saw Charles' actions, not only as a dangerous abuse of power, but as an offense to God as well. In 1642, a Puritan leader named **Oliver Cromwell** led an army in open rebellion against the king. The **English Revolution** resulted in the overthrow and execution of Charles I, with Cromwell assuming leadership and expelling members of Parliament who opposed his actions. A short time later, he dissolved Parliament, assumed the title "Lord Protector of England," and established a military dictatorship until his death in 1658.

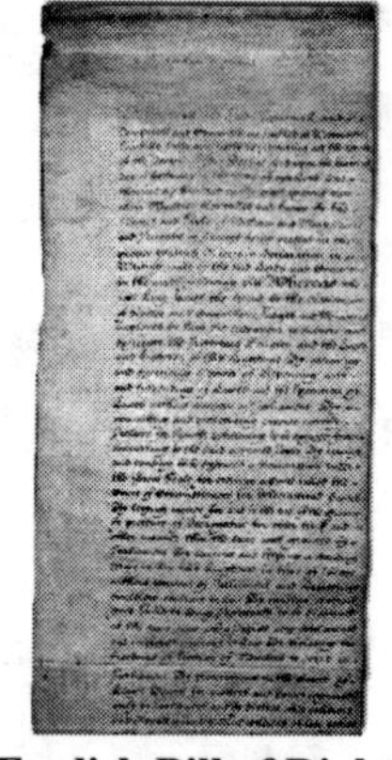
English Bill of Rights

Following the death of Cromwell, England re-established the monarchy under Charles' son, Charles II. Under the new monarchy, Parliament had to approve all taxes and the king recognized that he needed its consent to carry out many of his decisions. Following Charles II, his brother, James II, became king of England. James was a Catholic and viewed as a threat by members of the Anglican Church (another name for the Church of England). Since James had no male heir and both his daughters were Protestants, many trusted that after he died one of them would become queen. However, when James' second wife, also a Catholic, gave birth to a son, Protestant leaders invited James' son-in-law, a Dutchman named **William of Orange**, to invade England and assume the throne. With the support of the Church of England, William and his wife, Mary, raised an army and landed in England in 1688. James and his family fled to France, surrendering the throne without a fight. The **Glorious Revolution** resulted in William and Mary assuming leadership of England. In exchange for Parliament's support, they agreed to give even more power to the legislature and accepted an **English Bill of Rights**. This Bill of Rights increased the powers of Parliament while limiting the powers of the king. It also granted freedom of worship to Puritans while continuing to limit the rights of Catholics. Together, the English and Glorious revolutions ripped apart old beliefs about the divine rights of kings, firmly established Parliament as the ultimate power within the British government, and laid the foundation of England's limited monarchy (monarchy in which the king/queen is limited by laws rather than given unlimited authority).

The American Revolution

American Revolution

Less than a century later, another revolution occurred that forever changed the world and established new principles of government. Thirteen of Great Britain's North American colonies declared independence in 1776 and launched what came to be known as the **American Revolution** (review chapter 3, section 3.2). The revolution was based on many of the ideas of the Enlightenment, such as the notion of *natural rights* and the idea that a *social contract* exists between governments and citizens. In the Declaration of Independence, the Founding Fathers of the United States asserted that such natural rights existed and that the British government had violated its social contract. Just as Parliament had accused the king of assuming too much power to justify the English Revolution, the colonies now claimed that Parliament had assumed too much power by taxing them without representation. Against all odds, the American Revolution succeeded, establishing the United States' independence and a new representative government that would serve as a model for future democracies.

The French Revolution

Many historians regard the **French Revolution** as the most important social, political, and economic event in modern history. It marked the end of Europe's old order of a world dominated by rich aristocrats and the beginning of a new order valuing equality, representative government, individual rights, and nationalism. The revolution occurred over the course of a decade and came in a number of stages.

Causes of the French Revolution

Prior to 1789, French society was divided between three *estates*. The First Estate was the clergy (Catholic bishops, priests, etc.). The Second Estate was the nobility (rich, land-owning aristocrats), which occupied many of the nation's positions of leadership and influence. The Third Estate consisted of the more common classes and made up the majority of the population. The Third Estate included peasants, farmers, shopkeepers, and the **bourgeoisie** (middle class) consisting of bankers, merchants, lawyers, etc. Many members of the bourgeoisie supported the political ideas of the Enlightenment and, along with many of the nobility, wanted to reform the French monarchy. In the late 1780s, economic hardship, food shortages, discontent over the nation's tax system and land policies, and the near financial collapse of the government forced King Louis XVI to call an assembly of France's legislative body in 1789 (it had not met for over 150 years). Although each estate was represented, members from the Third Estate quickly seized control, called themselves the National Assembly, and drew up a new constitution. When the king threatened to use force to put down the new assembly, an angry mob stormed a prison and armory known as **the Bastille**. The mob cut off the head of the garrison leader defending the fortress and marched it through the streets of Paris. Soon, peasant uprisings filled the French countryside. Revolution had come!

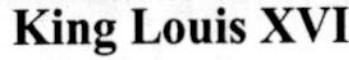

King Louis XVI

Three Estates

Bastille

The Limited Monarchy

The National Assembly's Constitution of 1791 replaced the old order of French government with a limited monarchy. Meanwhile, other European nations grew alarmed. Foreign kings feared that the revolutionary spirit alive in France might spread to their countries as well. Soon, France found itself at war with many of its European neighbors. Early military defeats and continued economic hardships led to another change in government. A radical mob stormed the royal palace, took the king captive, and forced the assembly to suspend the French monarchy. The new National Convention took charge, abolished the monarchy, and executed the king of France. Many Frenchmen felt that such actions were too drastic and refused to support the National Convention. At the same time, other European nations were appalled by the king's execution and prepared to invade France. Desperate, the National Convention empowered a group called the *Committee of Public Safety* to deal with the crisis.

The Terror

Maximilien Robespierre

A party of radicals known as the **Jacobins** soon controlled the Committee of Public Safety. Under the leadership of **Maximilien Robespierre**, they quickly raised an army of well over one million Frenchmen that pushed back France's foreign enemies. France's ability to enlist so many citizens demonstrated that a new era had arrived. Previously, wars were seen as battles between rulers. Now, for the first time, they were perceived as a fight for one's nation. In this way, the French Revolution greatly contributed to the rise of **nationalism** (pride in one's country).

Robespierre and his followers then set their sites on enemies inside France. They launched a period known as **the Terror**. The state executed thousands of French citizens on the *guillotine* (contraption that cut off people's heads). Eventually, the Terror ended when a rival group seized control of the National Convention and executed Robespierre in July, 1794.

The Directory

In 1795, a new constitution passed power to five directors, known as the **Directory**. Unfortunately, the period of the Directory was riddled with corruption and political rivalries between royalists who wanted to return the monarchy and radicals still enraged by ongoing economic problems. More and more, the Directory looked to the army to maintain its position of power. Finally, in 1799, one of the army's most popular generals took advantage of the political situation to seize power and eventually declare himself emperor of France.

The Haitian Revolution

Toussaint L'Ouverture

Revolution in France soon spread to some of its colonies. In 1791, black slaves in Saint-Dominique rebelled against their white masters after learning of the revolution in Europe. A gifted and educated slave named **Toussaint L'Ouverture** quickly became their leader. Toussaint, who continually claimed to be a Frenchman acting in the spirit of the revolution, proclaimed himself ruler and freed all the slaves. When French troops arrived in 1802, Toussaint was deceived and taken prisoner. He died soon after in a French dungeon. His followers, however, did not give up the fight. They successfully turned back the French and established the new nation of **Haiti**.

Revolutions in Latin America

During the early 1800s, many **creoles** (people of European descent who were born and lived in Latin American colonies) began to feel a great deal of discontent towards Spain and Portugal. They resented what they saw as unfair economic policies. Inspired by the United States' success, a number of successful **Latin American revolutions** occurred during the first quarter of the nineteenth century. By 1810, **Jose de San Martin** led forces that expelled the Spanish from Argentina. Believing that all of South America must be free of Spain's rule, he then crossed the Andes Mountains to surprise the Spanish and defeat them at the Battle of Chacabuco in 1817. Meanwhile, another great leader, **Simon Bolivar**, liberated Venezuela, Colombia (then called New Granada), and Ecuador. The two eventually joined forces to finish driving the Spanish out of South America. Mexico declared independence in 1821. By 1823, Central America was also free and eventually divided into five republics. Meanwhile, in 1822, Brazil declared independence from Portugal. Concerned that European nations might act to reinstate their authority, US President James Monroe issued his *Monroe Doctrine* guaranteeing the independence of the new Latin American nations (review chapter 3, section 3.3). However, Monroe's bold words alone were not enough to deter European action. Fortunately for Latin Americans, Great Britain wanted them free so that they could engage in trade with England. More than any promise by a US president (at the time, the US was not very powerful), it was Britain's navy that shielded the new nations from the threat of European invasion.

Jose de San Martin

Simon Bolivar

NAPOLEON BONAPARTE

Napoleon Bonaparte

In 1799, **Napoleon Bonaparte** rose to power in France. In 1804, he had himself crowned Napoleon I, Emperor of France. Napoleon made peace with the Catholic Church (previously viewed as an enemy of the revolution) and solidified his support among many landowners. Napoleon also provided France with its first set of national laws since the revolution: the *Napoleonic Codes*. These laws guaranteed equality under the law and upheld many principles of the revolution. Napoleon is most remembered, however, for his military campaigns. He defeated Austria, Prussia, and Russia by 1807, making him master over much of Europe. Under Napoleon, France's borders extended from the Rhine River to northern Italy. Meanwhile, he exercised authority over various dependent states (Spain, Italy, the Netherlands, Switzerland, and parts of Germany). He also forced nations he defeated to join him in his wars with Great Britain. As Napoleon acquired more territory and influence, ideas and principles of the French Revolution, such as equality, nationalism, and religious toleration, spread to other countries.

THE FALL OF NAPOLEON

Napoleon's Russian Retreat

Napoleon eventually fell for several reasons. For one, he could never defeat the British. Because England is on an island, Napoleon's impressive army could not march across its borders as it had other nations. Secondly, as the French empire spread, so did nationalism. Citizens of other nations now began to develop the same sense of pride in their country. As a result, they grew ever more bitter against Napoleon, viewing him as a foreign oppressor. Finally, despite his military brilliance, Napoleon made some key mistakes. Most notably was his decision to invade Russia in 1812. Although he knew an invasion was risky, he felt he had little choice given Russia's unwillingness to remain unified with Napoleon in his efforts against the British. Rather than engage Napoleon in a head-to-head battle, the Russians continually retreated, drawing Napoleon further and further into their territory. Along the way, they burned their own towns and destroyed crops to deny the French any supplies or food. The Russians even burned Moscow. Napoleon's forces, tired and starving, then retreated in winter temperatures well below freezing. Many died along the way. Other European armies rose up and attacked the staggering French army, conquering Paris in March 1814 and exiling Napoleon to the island of Elba. The European powers then supported France in re-establishing its monarchy under King Louis XVIII, believing they had heard the last of the French emperor. Napoleon escaped, however, and returned to France. French authorities quickly dispatched troops to arrest and, if necessary, kill the former emperor. When Napoleon found himself halted by a regiment of soldiers, he dismounted from his horse, took several steps towards them, held open his coat and called out, "If you would shoot your emperor, then do so now!" Rather than firing, the inspired troops fell in behind their hero. Thus began Napoleon's **One Hundred Days** from March to June 1815, in which he made one last attempt to re-establish his empire. It appeared that he might be successful until the **Battle of Waterloo** in Belgium.

At Waterloo, he met a combined European force under the command of the British Duke of Wellington. Wellington lured Napoleon onto a battle field with which the British were more familiar and defeated the French army, ending Napoleon's campaign.

Battle of Waterloo

Practice 9.3 Enlightenment and Revolution

1. John Locke and Jean-Jacques Rousseau were both key figures of the
   A. age of exploration.
   B. French Revolution.
   C. Enlightenment.
   D. Haitian Revolution.

2. Johannes Kepler, Copernicus, Galileo, and Newton each contributed greatly to
   A. better understandings of the universe.
   B. the discovery of new territories.
   C. advances in new technology that allowed for wider exploration.
   D. political theories that led to major revolutions.

3. How would someone who believed that power should not rest in the hands of a single monarch have felt about the effects of the English and Glorious Revolutions?
   A. discouraged B. fearful C. indifferent D. encouraged

4. In what ways did the French Revolution introduce a new social and political order to France?

5. Describe the impact of Napoleon Bonaparte on France and Europe. What led to his downfall and what was "the Hundred Days"?

CHAPTER 9 REVIEW

Key terms, people, and concepts

the Renaissance
Florence
Machiavelli
"Renaissance Man"
Leonardo da Vinci
Michelangelo
humanism
Petrarch
Dante
Erasmus
Martin Luther
Protestant Reformation
John Calvin
English Reformation
Henry VIII
Counter Reformation
Jesuits
Council of Trent
Gutenberg's printing press
astrolabe
"God, gold, and glory"
Africa
Asia
Vasco da Gama
Christopher Columbus
America
Ferdinand Megellan
Samuel de Champlain
Columbian Exchange
Copernicus
Johannes Kepler
Galileo
Isaac Newton
the Enlightenment
John Locke
Rousseau
Puritans
Oliver Cromwell
the English Revolution
William of Orange
Glorious Revolution
English Bill of Rights
American Revolution
French Revolution
bourgeoisie
the Bastille
Jacobins
Robespierre
nationalism
the Terror
Directory
Haitian Revolution
Toussaint L'Ouverture
Latin American Revolutions
Jose de San Martin
Simon Bolivar
Napoleon Bonaparte
One Hundred Days
Battle of Waterloo

Multiple Choice Questions

1. A nationalist would most passionately support
   A. the king over Parliament.
   B. ideas that challenged their nation's old form of government.
   C. exploration for the sake of religion.
   D. going to war in the name of defending their country.

2. The Renaissance was a time in which
   A. the Church was reaffirmed as the highest authority.
   B. new discoveries were discouraged.
   C. modern ideas were praised above the ideas of ancient societies.
   D. people sought to apply the ideas of classic Greek and Rome to the world in which they lived.

> "A ruler answers first of all to God. He is obligated to obey the Word of God, regardless of the consequences. It is by the Hand of God that he rules; it is before Holy God he will stand in judgment. No despot can claim that his position alleviates him of his moral responsibility."

3. How would Machiavelli have felt about the above quote?
   A. He would have opposed it.
   B. He would have agreed.
   C. He would have had no real opinion.
   D. He would have agreed, but cautioned that rulers must also answer to the pope.

4. Humanism was a/an
   A. political movement that rejected the idea of morality as a guiding principal for rulers.
   B. intellectual movement that placed importance on the study of ancient literary works.
   C. new religion that formed due to the Reformation.
   D. answer to the Reformation put forth by the Jesuits.

5. Martin Luther and Calvin sought to reform the church and became key leaders of the
   A. Renaissance.
   B. Humanist movement.
   C. Protestant Reformation.
   D. Counter Reformation.

6. Look at the map below and answer the following question.

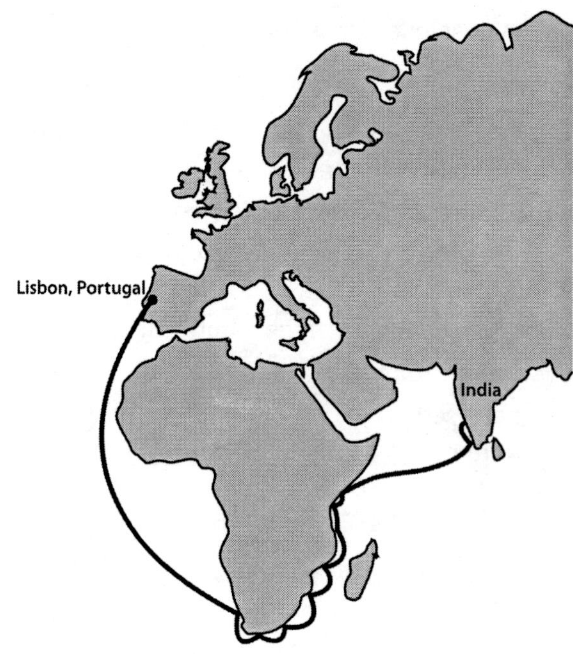

The route depicted in the map above was first traveled by

A. Christopher Columbus.
B. Vasco da Gama.
C. Magellan.
D. Erasmus.

7. Beginning in the late fifteenth century, Native Americans were exposed to European religion and culture. Many of them were also conquered and forced to work as slaves or were taken back to Europe. Some died of European diseases. At the same time, American crops and resources became popular in Europe and transformed the way Europeans lived. Many European settlers also learned native languages, married native wives, and adopted aspects of native cultures. Together, these are examples of the

A. Columbian Exchange.
B. Atlantic trade.
C. Counter Reformation.
D. Enlightenment.

8. A shopkeeper in a remote town of Europe reads a copy of the New Testament and some of John Calvin's writings during the late 1500s. He is inspired by what he reads and, for the first time, begins to question the established church. This shopkeeper has been greatly impacted by the work of

A. Galileo. B. John Locke. C. Gutenberg. D. Isaac Newton.

9. Oliver Cromwell, Simon Bolivar, and Toussaint L'Ouverture each

A. introduced new political ideas during the Enlightenment.
B. provided scientific discoveries that increased knowledge about the universe.
C. explored portions of the Americas during the age of discovery.
D. led revolutions that greatly changed the face of government in the western world.

10. Upon hearing that the Bastille had been stormed, King Louis XVI exclaimed, "It is a revolt!" One of his subordinates quickly answered, "No Sire, it is a revolution." To which revolution was the subordinate referring?
    A. the English Revolution
    B. the Glorious Revolution
    C. the French Revolution
    D. the American Revolution

11. What country was born out of the only successful slave revolt in the Western Hemisphere?
    A. Mexico
    B. Haiti
    C. Argentina
    D. Brazil

Read the following excerpt from a letter and answer the following question.

> "My love, I fear I shall not see you again. The cold is unbearable. We are reduced to eating the snow; fantasizing that it is a piece of meat or bread. Some even cut away flesh from their dead comrades and cook it over what fire they can muster to stay alive. When there is nothing to burn, what they eat is raw. May God save us! May God forgive us for some of what we have done! May God let me forget some of what we have seen! Once the most feared force in all of Europe, we are reduced to a band of poor beggars. Is this the army of an empire? I think not."

12. The above letter was probably written by
    A. a member of Cromwell's army during the English Revolution.
    B. someone fighting with Simon Bolivar.
    C. a soldier in Washington's army at Valley Forge.
    D. a soldier in Napoleon's army retreating from Russia.

Chapter 10
World History: World War I to Modern Day

GPS	SSWH16: The student will demonstrate an understanding of long-term causes of World War I and its global impact. (QCC standards WH19, WH21, WH22)
	SSWH17: The student will be able to identify the major political and economic factors that shaped world societies between World War I and World War II. (QCC standards WH19, WH21, WH22)
	SSWH18: The student will demonstrate an understanding of the global political, economic, and social impact of World War II. (QCC standards WH21, WH22, WH25)
	SSWH19: The student will demonstrate an understanding of global social, economic, and political impact of the Cold War and decolonization from 1945 to 1989. (QCC standards WH22, WH25, WH26)
	SSWH20: The student will examine change and continuity in the world since the 1960s. (QCC standard WH26)
	SSWH21: The student will analyze globalization in the contemporary world. (QCC standards WE30, WH26, WH27)

10.1 World War I

The Roots of War

In 1914, **World War I (WWI)** broke out in Europe. Because of its size and the incredible amount of death and destruction it produced, it came to be called "The Great War." The war had a number of causes. The **nationalism** (loyalty to one's country) born in France and spread by Napoleon was growing ever stronger across Europe. Countries wanted to expand their influence and pursue their own interests. In **the Balkans**, various ethnic groups launched successful revolutions against the Ottoman Empire and won their

Soldiers Fighting in WWI

independence. Other Balkan territories were annexed by Austria-Hungary. Serbs within Bosnia wanted to establish their own independence. Poles under Russian rule and the Irish under the British Empire also desired their freedom. Conflicts arose within many existing nation-states.

The Balkans

Many nations adopted a policy of **militarism**. They chose to look out for their own interests by building up their military forces to intimidate other countries. This approach led to large armies and an arms race in which countries continually tried to produce more advanced weapons. By 1914, the Russian army boasted over a million soldiers, while Germany and France each had roughly 900,000. Countries also formed alliances. **Alliances** are agreements between nations to help each other in the event of war. If one country in an alliance is attacked, then the other countries in the alliance agree to come to that nation's defense. This policy meant that an attack against one nation could drag several countries into war, creating a domino effect. By 1914, almost no nation in Europe could become involved in a war without the whole continent being pulled in with it.

The War Begins

Francis Ferdinand

The spark that ignited World War I occurred on June 28, 1914, when a Serbian nationalist assassinated Archduke Francis Ferdinand, the heir to the throne of Austria-Hungary. Austria-Hungary accused Serbia of being involved in the assassination and threatened war. Russia, which was allied with Serbia, vowed to intervene if Austria-Hungary attacked. This brought Germany into the mix because of its alliance with Austria-Hungary. Within two months, the dominos had fallen. Due to the existing alliances, Europe was soon divided and at war. Great Britain, France, and Russia formed an alliance called the Triple Entente. Meanwhile, Germany and Austria-Hungary lined up against them as the Central Powers.

The War Front

The war featured new technology and advanced weapons. Machine guns allowed soldiers to fire more rounds of ammunition faster and with more deadly results than ever before. Both sides learned to use poisonous gases to kill enemy soldiers, and sometimes their own when the winds changed unexpectedly. Eventually, tanks and airplanes became important weapons. As a result of all the new weaponry, leaders on both sides had great difficulty adjusting their tactics. The war was soon a stalemate, with neither side gaining an advantage.

Trench Soldiers

Kaiser of Germany

Life along the **front** (area where opposing armies meet in battle) was difficult. Soldiers died by the thousands, as neither side could defeat the other. Eventually, millions of civilians would die as well. Unable to advance, armies on both sides found themselves mired in **trench warfare**. Trenches were long ditches in which soldiers would take cover while they fired on the enemy. In between the two sides rested a "no man's land." Soldiers considered it a no man's land because it was open, exposed to enemy fire, and *no man* could hope to survive there. Since they could not advance without suffering heavy losses, both sides lived for long periods in dirty, rat-infested trenches.

The End and Aftermath of World War I

Big 4 at Versailles

Treaty of Versailles

In 1917, the United States entered the war on the side of the Triple Entente (review chapter 5, section 5.3). By September of the following year, Germany realized defeat was inevitable and sought terms for peace. The warring parties finally signed an armistice (agreement to stop fighting), but not until after the deaths of roughly 20 million Europeans. The Allies ignored President Wilson's pleas not to seek revenge and drafted a treaty designed to punish Germany. The **Treaty of Versailles** forced Germany to accept blame for the war and to pay **reparations** to cover the cost of its destruction. In addition, the face of Europe changed drastically. With the defeat of Germany and

Austria, the **Hapsburg Dynasty**, which had ruled much of Europe since the tenth century, fell from power and faded into history. Finally, the postwar treaties dismantled the **Ottoman Empire**. Over the centuries, the Ottoman Turks had built a vast empire in Eastern Europe, parts of Asia, and portions of North Africa. However, by the twentieth century, their power had weakened, and their empire was already in decline. The final blow came after the Ottoman Empire chose to ally itself with Germany in WWI.

Once the war ended, the Allies redrew national borders in ways meant to promote their own interests and to ensure their future security. A number of new countries emerged. Many of them contained ethnic groups that rivaled one another. In addition, the Allies promised independence to a number of Arab nations, and then went back on their word. Lebanon and Syria fell to France, while Britain took control of Iraq and Palestine (modern-day Israel). Such arrangements were called *mandates* and became known as the **mandate system**. The mandate system was seen as a betrayal by many in these Arab nations and served to instill bitterness against the West in many parts of the Middle East. Political and economic instability during the postwar years, combined with the resentment felt by the German people towards the Treaty of Versailles, eventually led Europe back into war within just a few years.

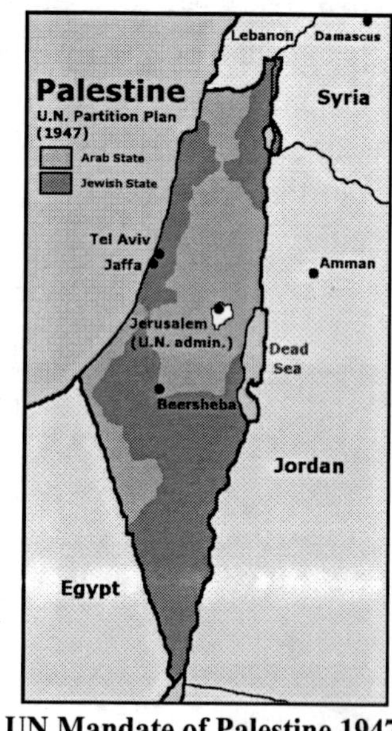

UN Mandate of Palestine 1947

THE LEAGUE OF NATIONS

Following World War I, President Wilson proposed the **League of Nations**. The League's purpose was to provide a place where countries could peacefully discuss solutions to their differences rather than go to war. A number of nations joined the League. Ironically, the United States was not one of them. (Review chapter 5, section 5.3.) Eventually, without any means to enforce its decisions, the League of Nations proved powerless to stop the onset of a second world war.

Practice 10.1 World War I

1. The mandate system caused bitterness on the part of many nations because
   A. it blamed Germany for the war.
   B. it ended the Hapsburg Dynasty.
   C. it ended the Ottoman Empire.
   D. it went back on promises to grant many Arabs their independence.

2. Which of the following nations was most supportive of the Treaty of Versailles?
   A. France
   B. United States
   C. Germany
   D. Ottoman Empire

3. What is *nationalism* and how did it contribute to the beginning of World War I?

4. How do you think requiring Germany to pay war reparations may have contributed to unrest in Europe?

10.2 The Rise of Communism, Fascism, and Totalitarianism in Europe and Asia

Russia Between the Wars

The Russian Revolution

Czar Nicholas II

Russian Revolution 1917

Russia entered WWI under the leadership of **Czar Nicholas II**. However, the country lagged behind much of the rest of Europe. Its technology was not as advanced, and it lacked modern industrialization. Despite Nicholas' willingness to fight, Russia was not prepared for war. The nation was poor. Many peasants were starving. The fighting only sapped more money and food away from Russia's citizens to support the war effort. Millions of Russians, both soldiers and civilians, suffered and died. As the war and misery dragged on, the czar became more unpopular. People of all classes began calling for change in the Russian government. The **Russian Revolution** finally erupted in 1917. Among the lower working classes, strikes broke out. When Czar Nicholas II ordered troops to put down the uprisings, many of his soldiers switched sides and joined the rebellious crowds. On March 12, Czar Nicholas II surrendered power to a new government.

Lenin

Meanwhile, a Russian revolutionary named **Lenin** watched from exile. Lenin had long opposed the czarist regime and fled to Switzerland after being arrested for his revolutionary views and imprisoned in Siberia. He was a *Marxist* and became the leader of a socialist party known as the **Bolsheviks**. (Review chapter 6, section 6.1 regarding the views of Karl Marx.) With the support of Germany, Lenin returned to Russia and led the Bolsheviks in their quest for power. Promising to redistribute land and food to the poor, put power in the hands of the people, and pull Russia out of WWI, Lenin's party soon seized control of the Russian government. A three-year civil war then followed between the Bolsheviks and other Russian factions that opposed their communist ideas. A number of allied countries (Great Britain, France, Japan, and the United States) also sent troops to Russia to support the anti-Communist forces and to encourage Russia to re-enter the war. However, because of a well trained military force and a ruthless secret police force that arrested and killed citizens opposed to their regime, the Bolsheviks eventually won the civil war. By

1921, Russia was firmly in Communist hands. Its new leaders never forgot, however, the way Western nations sided with the anti-Communists, and a wall of mistrust between the West and Communist East remained firmly in place for decades to come.

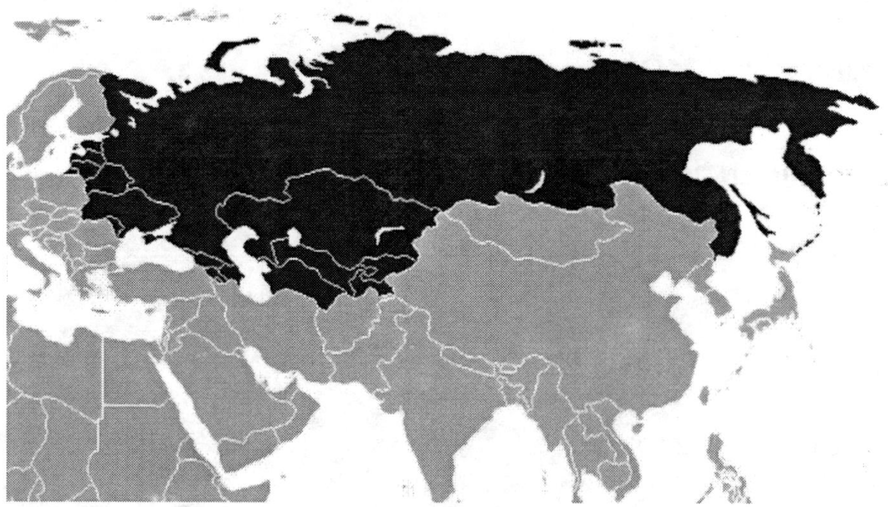

Russia 1917

JOSEPH STALIN

Joseph Stalin

Leon Trotsky

Following a famine that killed millions in Russia and the collapse of the nation's industry, Lenin had no choice but to modify some of his communist views. He allowed a limited amount of private ownership, while still maintaining state control over large industries and banks. In 1922, he and his Communist Party established a new state: The Union of Soviet Socialist Republics (USSR) or **Soviet Union**. Thanks to improved agricultural conditions and new policies that revived the economy, Lenin successfully saw the USSR through its first year. However, in 1924, Lenin died. An intense struggle for power followed. One faction, led by Leon Trotsky, wanted to turn back Lenin's economic changes, allowing the state to seize all property and launch a massive program of industrialization. These "Trotskyites" also believed that the Soviet Union should do all in its power to encourage communist revolutions in other nations. Unless communism spread internationally, they believed the USSR would not survive. Others, however, disagreed. They favored keeping Lenin's new policies in place and felt that the Soviet Union should focus on strengthening its government at home rather than worrying about foreign revolutions.

Soviet Propaganda Poster

Eventually, one of these leaders, **Joseph Stalin**, emerged as the nation's dictator. Stalin joined the Bolsheviks in 1903 and eventually won Lenin's favor after leading a bank robbery to get money for the party's cause. As general secretary of the party under Lenin, Stalin was responsible for appointing people to important party posts. He used his position to appoint people who later helped him seize and maintain his power. Once in control, he launched a plan for economic and military development known as his **Five Year Plan**. Stalin's "Five Year Plan" sought to increase industrialization in the Soviet Union. It established new, industrial cities and focused on the production of capital goods (goods used to make other goods, such as machines). His plan also transformed agriculture. Instead of independent farms owned by peasants, Stalin *collectivized* agriculture. Rather than own private land, people worked state-owned land together. Many peasants resented this move and responded by hoarding crops and killing livestock. Such protests contributed to a famine that killed millions of Soviets during the early 1930s. While Stalin's policies did successfully increase industrial production, they did little to care for the new industrial workforce these changes produced. Many Soviet workers lived in poverty as they worked long hours to produce what the government demanded. Since communism offered no promise of more money or promotions for hard work, Stalin's government appealed to national loyalty and used the fear of punishment as motivations for Soviet workers.

Stalin was as ruthless as he was ambitious. To establish his power, he began a **purge**, in which he systematically eliminated those he perceived to be a threat. He had Bolshevik leaders and a number of military officers tried and convicted of crimes. Many were executed. Others were shipped to prison camps in Siberia, never to be heard from again. Trotsky fled to Mexico, only to be murdered with a pickax in 1940. Before his regime finally ended in 1953, Stalin murdered millions of his own people.

Effects of the Revolution

The Russian Revolution marked one of the most influential turning points in world history. It affected social structure, economics, international relations, culture, and Russia's development as a nation. The czar's fall marked both the end of the **Romanov Dynasty** and the transfer of power in Russia from aristocrats to leaders from the lower classes. The revolution also ushered Russia into the industrial age. Many people moved out of the country and into the cities, transforming Russia from an agricultural society dominated by rural peasants, to an urban society dependent on industrial workers. The importance of education also reached new heights as the Communist USSR sought to catch up to the West.

Czar Nicholas II and His Family

The Bolsheviks did not forget how Western nations had sided with their enemies, and they were determined to become as self-sufficient as possible. Although the USSR would side with a number of these nations during World War II, its different beliefs about government and economics ultimately laid the groundwork for a new kind of war that would last for decades and spread across the entire globe.

Totalitarian versus Authoritarian Governments

Benito Mussolini

Stalin's government in the USSR was one of several **totalitarian states** that arose following World War I. A totalitarian state is different from an **authoritarian state**. Under either system, democracy does not exist. Rather, the government is led by an authoritative figure or party. In an authoritative state, the government usually is only interested in political power. It simply seeks to maintain control over government policies and expects its people to accept its authority as they conduct their independent, daily lives. Often, they are led by conservative forces who simply want to protect the nation's traditional way of life and resist radical changes. Under a totalitarian government, however, the government seeks to control, not only politics, but the economy, culture, and social life of the people as well. The people are expected to actively participate in national goals, such as conquering foreign territories, building a strong military, or establishing a fascist or socialist state. Such governments often use terror and fear to force members of society to go along with their plans. They also use large amounts of *propaganda* (biased information, often untrue, to win the loyalty of the people) through state-controlled advertising and education. Following WWI, a number of authoritative and totalitarian states arose in Europe and parts of Asia.

Fascism and Mussolini

Italy

Fascism is a nationalistic movement that is both anti-democratic and anti-communist. Fascism uses propaganda, rallies, beatings, and intimidation to gain power and popular support. Fascist leaders are charismatic, promising better times and national glory while blaming outside groups for the country's problems. The first fascist government emerged in Italy in 1922 under **Benito Mussolini**. After being kicked out of the Socialist Party for supporting Italy's entrance into WWI, Mussolini started the Fascist Party. Taking advantage of Italy's ineffective postwar government, Mussolini's Fascists used violence to put down a number of industrial strikes and deal with social unrest. Such moves won support from middle-class industrialists and large landowners. Meanwhile, the Fascists support for Catholicism, condemnation of communism, and appeals to Italian nationalism, only increased their popularity. Finally, Italy's king, Emmanuel III, had no choice but to name Mussolini prime minister. Within a few years, Mussolini was known as *Il Duce* ("the Leader") and had firmly established himself as dictator of Italy.

Although he attempted to control every aspect of Italian society and envisioned himself as the restorer of Italy's ancient Roman Empire, Mussolini never effectively established the totalitarian regime that Stalin did in the Soviet Union or that Adolf Hitler eventually would in Germany.

Italian Black Shirts Under Mussolini

ADOLF HITLER

Adolf Hitler

In 1921, an obscure Austrian named **Adolf Hitler** took control of a right-wing political party in Germany and re-named it the National Socialist German Worker's Party, better known as **the Nazis**. Hitler's nationalist speeches, promises to return Germany's honor following its defeat in WWI, and his natural skills as a leader and speaker contributed to his rapid rise to power. In 1933, Hitler became chancellor of Germany and methodically seized more power. He claimed the title "Fuhrer" (guide of Germany) and established his own totalitarian, fascist state. Hitler labeled his new government the "Third Reich," and he envisioned it as an empire that would last a thousand years. Winning the loyalty of conservatives, anti-communists, and many of the nation's churches, Hitler set Germany on a course that eventually led to war and its own destruction.

NAZI IDEOLOGY AND THE HOLOCAUST

Hitler Speaking

The Nazis ascended to power with several aims in mind. One, Hitler believed strongly in German nationalism. Like many Germans, he considered the country's defeat in WWI and the Treaty of Versailles a national humiliation. He took advantage of the nation's discontent and the economic depression of the 1920s to win the hearts and minds of many Germans. He set about rebuilding Germany's military, enlarging its territory by marching troops into the Rhineland, annexing Austria, and claiming parts of the Sudetenland. In an effort to try and avoid war, Great Britain and France signed a treaty with Hitler in which they agreed to Germany's capture of the Sudetenland in exchange for its promise not to invade any more territories. (Such a policy is called "appeasement" because it assumes that by giving aggressors what they want, they will be satisfied and stop their aggressive behavior. History has proven that appeasement rarely works.) One member of the British Parliament who opposed this approach was Winston Churchill. Churchill voiced his opposition stating, "Britain and France had to choose between war and dishonor. They chose dishonor. They will have war."

Russia
Germany
Germany and Russia

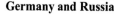

WONDER HOW LONG THE HONEYMOON WILL LAST?
Hitler and Stalin Meeting

Ultimately, what the Nazis sought was ***lebensraum*** (living space) for their new "empire." They believed that the Aryan race (people of white, West European descent) was biologically superior to all other races. Therefore, Aryan Germans had a right to claim the territory of inferior races. In this case, Hitler viewed the Slavic peoples of Russia and Eastern Europe as inferior, and he wanted the Soviet Union for his own. In 1939, he signed a non-aggression pact with Joseph Stalin, in which the two vowed not to attack each other. Hitler never intended to stick to the agreement, however, and used it only to keep the USSR from attacking him from the east while Germany battled France in Western Europe. Meanwhile, Stalin was not fooled. He knew Hitler would attack, but he signed the pact to give him time to build up his military before the German invasion came.

German Concentration Camp

Stemming from the Nazis racism was a ruthless **anti-Semitism** (hatred of Jewish people). Anti-Semitism had long existed throughout Western Europe. However, beginning in the late nineteenth century, it became more intense. Ironically, among European nations, Germany initially protected the rights of its German residents more than most countries. As a result, a large Jewish population existed in cities like Berlin. When the depression of the 1920s hit, many of these Jewish citizens occupied important positions in business and education within German society. Hitler raged against, not only these individuals, but also the entire Jewish community as anti-German and a major source of the nation's woes. Combined with the fact that Jewish Germans had also played a role in the leadership that agreed to the Treaty of Versailles, anti-Semitism grew prior to 1933 and helped propel Hitler to power.

Once in control, Hitler continued to paint the Jews as a national enemy. Gradually, over the course of less than a decade, he and his Nazi Party passed law after law that reduced the rights of Jewish people in Germany. Finally, as Germany began its invasion of the Soviet Union, Hitler authorized his **"Final Solution."** It called for the total elimination of the Jewish people. Whether or not Hitler intended from the very beginning to exterminate the Jews remains an issue of debate. Regardless, Hitler's regime murdered more than six million Jews before his death in 1945. Some were killed right away. Others were shipped to concentration camps and gassed to death upon arrival. Still others were forced to live under horrible conditions in these camps as slave labor before eventually being executed. The Jews were not the only ones to suffer such unspeakable horrors. Other "undesirables," such as Gypsies, Slavs, the mentally and physically disabled, homosexuals, Jehovah's Witnesses, political enemies of the state and Christians opposed to the Nazis, also met terrible fates. Still, no group suffered in such great numbers as the Jews. This horrible episode came to be known as **the Holocaust**, and will forever remain one of the darkest times in human history.

Jewish Man Being Executed

HIROHITO AND JAPAN

Unlike Mussolini and Hitler, **Emperor Hirohito** of Japan was not a fascist ruler. He reigned from December 25, 1926, until his death in 1989. Ruling for longer than any other emperor, he oversaw many significant changes in Japan. Although emperor, he did not exercise absolute control over the government. Political rivalries resulted in the military seizing power. An army general named **Hideki Tojo** ultimately assumed the role of Japan's premier and led the nation through World War II.

Emperor Hirohito

Practice 10.2 The Rise of Communism, Fascism, and Totalitarianism in Europe and Asia

1. Who was the totalitarian dictator who rose to power in Germany and aggressively seized foreign territory, setting the stage for another world war?

   A. Benito Mussolini
   B. Adolf Hitler
   C. Hideki Tojo
   D. Joseph Stalin

2. Which nation became the world's first communist state?

   A. Germany B. Italy C. Russia D. France

3. He was the general secretary of the Communist Party in 1922 and eventually established a totalitarian regime over the USSR.
   A. Adolf Hitler
   B. Vladimir Lenin
   C. Benito Mussolini
   D. Joseph Stalin

4. What were some important outcomes of the Russian Revolution?

5. What is the difference between a *totalitarian* and an *authoritarian* government?

10.3 World War II

Aggression Leading to War

In addition to Hitler's invasion of the Rhineland, Austria, and the Sudetenland, Japan began aggressively expanding its territory during the 1920s and '30s. As a tiny series of islands, Japan did not have access to many natural resources despite being a fairly modernized country. To get the resources it needed, Japan's leaders decided to conquer territory in the South Pacific. When Japan invaded the Chinese province of Manchuria in 1931, the League of Nations demanded that it leave China. Japan responded by leaving the League of Nations instead. In 1937, Japan began trying to seize the rest of China as well. By the end of 1938, Japan had captured major cities along the Chinese coast but could not control the inland countryside. In 1940, Germany, Italy, and Japan formed an anti-communist alliance known as the **Axis Powers**.

Parts of China Conquered by Japan

War in Europe

Polish Invasion and the Fall of France

Nazis Invading Poland

On September 1, 1939, Hitler launched **World War II** in Europe when he invaded western Poland. Most of Poland fell to the Nazis in less than a month. Great Britain and France responded by declaring war on Germany because of a promise they had made to defend Poland. Once again, Europe found itself at war. Hitler really wanted the Soviet Union; however, he first needed Poland because it stood between Germany and Russia. Hitler also felt that, before attacking the Soviets, Germany must first defeat France to the west. Otherwise, the French might come to the Soviet's aid, leaving Germany caught in between two enemies.

Hitler in Paris

After a lull in the fighting over the winter of 1939, Germany conquered Denmark and Norway in April 1940, and then quickly overwhelmed Belgium, the Netherlands, and France less than a month later. As a symbol of redemption for Germany's defeat in WWI (and in an attempt to humiliate the French), Hitler insisted that France sign their surrender in the very train car where Germany had been forced to sign the armistice ending World War I. With France now defeated, Hitler hoped to establish peace with Great Britain and turn his attention east. However, once it became evident that Great Britain would not make peace with an aggressor like Germany, Hitler decided that the British must also be defeated. With the US still neutral and the Soviet Union not yet involved in the fighting, Britain's new prime minister, Winston Churchill, found himself standing alone against German domination of Europe.

Battle of Britain and US Entrance Into the War

Hitler knew that he had to destroy Britain's mighty Royal Air Force before he could cross the English Channel and launch an invasion of England. In the **Battle of Britain** that raged from July – October 1940, thousands of German planes bombed British airfields and cities. During the almost nightly air raids, residents of London slept in subways for cover and woke up to find more and more of their city reduced to smoke and rubble. Churchill, however, proved to be a great leader who inspired the British people with a strong sense of nationalism and hope. Thanks to the heroism of their Royal Air Force, the British were able to fight off the German assault and resist long enough to force Hitler to give up his plans of invading Great Britain.

Battle of Britain

Pearl Harbor

For more than a year after the invasion of Poland, the United States remained officially neutral. Then, on December 7, 1941, Japanese planes bombed the US Pacific Fleet anchored at **Pearl Harbor** in Hawaii (review chapter 6, section 6.2). The US responded by declaring war on Japan and, because of the Axis alliance, soon found itself at war with Germany and Italy as well. The United States, Great Britain, Soviet Union, and several other countries fought together as the **Allies** against the Axis countries.

Tehran, Yalta, and Potsdam

Tehran Conference

By the summer of 1941, Hitler's invasion of the Soviet Union was underway. The Nazis quickly advanced deep into Russia. They nearly took the Soviet capital of Moscow and the city of Stalingrad before Russia's Red Army and the fierce Russian winter turned back the German march. Because of the death and destruction the war inflicted on his country, Stalin pleaded with the other Allied powers to launch an invasion of Western Europe right away. US President Franklin Roosevelt and British Prime Minister Winston Churchill, however, chose a different strategy. They decided to drive the Nazis out of North Africa first, then invade Italy. Once the Allies drove the Axis forces from Africa and took most of Italy, Roosevelt and Churchill finally met with Stalin at the **Tehran Conference** in 1943. They agreed to an invasion of Europe that came to be known as **D-day** (review chapter 6, section 6.2). Involving troops from numerous Allied countries, the invasion worked and trapped Hitler's army between western Allied forces and the advancing Soviet army. In less than three months, Paris was free and victory seemed inevitable.

Anticipating Germany's defeat, the "Big Three" (Roosevelt, Churchill, and Stalin) met in February 1945 at the city of Yalta and conducted the **Yalta Conference**. Stalin restated his promise to declare war on Japan after the defeat of Germany. He also agreed to allow free elections to establish democratic governments in Eastern European countries freed from German occupation. In return, Roosevelt and Churchill agreed that the USSR would retain land in Poland (the US and Britain considered this only temporary) and would have special rights to certain islands and Chinese lands presently under Japanese control. Furthermore, because of the tremendous losses inflicted on the USSR by the war, the Soviet Union would receive half of the war reparations from Germany. The resolutions of the conference were stated in the *Yalta Declaration* and included a provision to divide Germany into four zones after the war. These zones would be administered by the United States, Britain, France, and the USSR. In addition, the leaders scheduled a conference in San Francisco for the following April to establish the United Nations as a permanent peace-keeping organization.

Hitler committed suicide in April, 1945, and Mussolini was killed by his own people. The war in Europe ended by early May. All that remained was Japan. The new US president, Harry S. Truman (Roosevelt died before the war ended) met with Stalin and Churchill in Potsdam for the **Potsdam Conference**. At Potsdam, the Allies reaffirmed their policy of *unconditional surrender* (review chapter 6, section 6.2). While at Potsdam, President Truman also learned that tests on the atomic bomb were a success. Less than a month later, US atomic bombs leveled the Japanese cities of Hiroshima and Nagasaki. Unable to answer such a powerful weapon and soundly beaten by the Allied forces, Japan surrendered. By the fall of 1945, the war was officially over.

Potsdam Conference

Tehran, Yalta, and Potsdam were significant for a number of reasons. Despite Stalin's bitterness towards the West for waiting so long, Tehran finally paved the way for the invasion Stalin wanted and proved vital to ending the war. Yalta laid out significant policies that resulted in the division of Europe between free-democratic Western Europe and communist, Soviet-led, Eastern Europe. The dividing line between the two came to be known as the **iron curtain**. Potsdam was crucial because it reasserted "unconditional surrender." This led to the decision by President Truman to drop the atomic bomb. Not only did this devastate Japan and force its unconditional surrender, it also launched a **nuclear arms race** between the United States and the USSR that lasted through the 1980s.

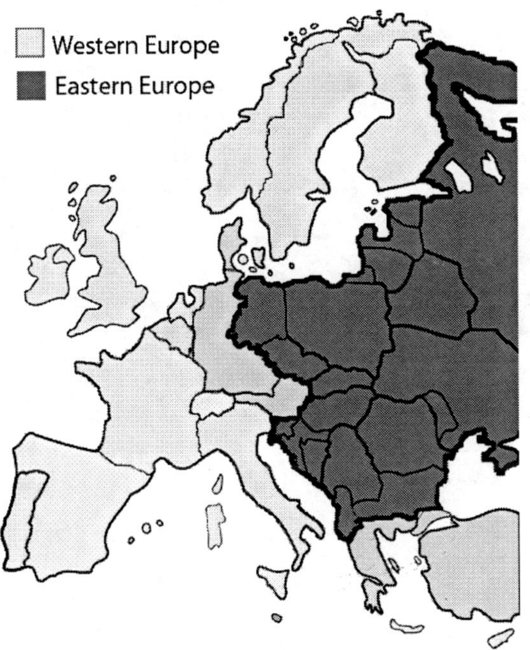

Iron Curtain

Practice 10.3 World War II

1. Germany began World War II in Europe when it invaded

   A. the Soviet Union.

   B. Poland.

   C. France.

   D. Great Britain.

2. Who were the leaders who met at Tehran, Yalta, and Potsdam? What was the significance of each of these meetings?

10.4 The Post-World War II Era

Postwar Europe and Japan

Douglas MacArthur

The end of World War II marked the beginning of the **Cold War**. The term described the great tension between the United States and the Soviet Union that many feared might lead to nuclear war. The Cold War divided most nations of the world into two opposing camps: those that supported the USSR and those that supported the United States. Fearing that the Soviets would attempt to spread communism across all of Europe, President Harry Truman authorized the **Marshall Plan** to boost Western Europe's economy and help rebuild countries devestated by the war. By providing such countries with money to rebuild and meet the needs of their people, the US hoped to remove any incentive people might have to support communist revolutions. The Marshall Plan was a key part of the United States' containment policy, through which it hoped to limit communism to those parts of Europe where it already existed (review chapter 6, section 6.3).

Tokyo

Meanwhile, the US general who had re-taken the Philippines and contributed greatly to the Allied victory in the Pacific, oversaw **postwar Japan**. MacArthur set about establishing a new government. Japan drafted a new constitution based on democratic ideals and decreased its military, maintaining only enough forces for national defense. The constitution allowed for the emperor but did away with the notion that he was a "god." It also guaranteed certain human rights and extended women the right to vote. Eventually, Japan became independent again in 1951. However, it maintained a close alliance with the US and continues to allow US military troops to be stationed in Japan to this day. As a result of its adoption of democratic and capitalist ideas, Japan's economic growth occurred rapidly. Today it is one of the most modern, industrialized, and wealthiest nations on the face of the earth.

The United Nations

The United Nations

After WWII, the international community established the **United Nations** as an organization where representatives of different countries could meet and seek peaceful solutions to their problems. The intent of the UN was to prevent future wars like the ones that had devastated Europe and Asia during the first half of the twentieth century. Unlike the failed League of Nations, the UN enjoyed the support of the US government and power to enforce its policies, either through economic sanctions or military actions. The United Nations resides in New York City and is led by a Security Council. The Security

Council consists of five permanent members: The United States, Great Britain, France, Russia (originally the Soviet Union), and China. It also includes seats for temporary members who sit for two-year terms. Before the UN can approve any military action, it must have the consent of all five permanent members to the Security Council.

The Nuclear Arms Race

H-Bomb

The United States produced the first atomic bomb in 1945. Soon after, the Soviet Union followed with its own. To maintain its nuclear superiority, the United States developed a **hydrogen bomb**, or "H-bomb," a thousand times more powerful than the first atomic bombs. Once again, the USSR followed suit. By 1964, France, Britain, and China all had nuclear weapons. Others soon followed. Meanwhile, scientists developed nuclear missiles that could travel from one side of the globe to the other within minutes. The nuclear arms race continued throughout the Cold War, with both sides creating ever more powerful weapons. The US and USSR eventually developed enough weapons to destroy the entire earth several times over. Finally, in the late '80s and early '90s, the Cold War ended. The Soviet economy could not afford to continue spending billions of dollars on weapons. The USSR had no choice but to make policy changes that ultimately brought the communist regime to an end. The Soviet Union dissolved with many of its territories becoming independent nations. Meanwhile, the US found itself carrying a huge debt caused largely by the massive military spending necessary to continue the arms race. Unfortunately, though the Cold War is over, its legacy of nuclear weapons remains.

Independence Movements, New Nationalism, and Ethnic Conflicts

Indian Independence

Mohandas Gandhi

The twentieth century featured a period of **decolonization**, in which a number of European colonies sought freedom and independence. One of the most notable movements occurred in **India**. For decades, Indians lived under the rule of the British Empire. Top positions of leadership went to white Europeans. Darker skinned Indians suffered discrimination and unjust treatment in their own homeland. Eventually, under the leadership of **Mohandas Gandhi**, an Indian independence movement began that led to the nation's independence. Gandhi was a Hindu who believed in the use of non-violent protest and stressed the importance of unity among Hindu and Muslim Indians (the two largest religions in India). Gandhi preached peaceful resistance to unjust laws. At his direction, Indians peacefully resisted the British government, enduring beatings and even death at the hands of colonial authorities. Such passive resistance won the support of outsiders and even many British citizens. These pressures finally resulted in India's independence in 1947. Sadly, the religious unity Gandhi longed for was always fragile. Unable to sustain religious peace, Indian leaders agreed to the establishment of **Pakistan** as an independent Muslim state.

Gandhi's methods proved effective and inspired future leaders who sought social justice, such as Dr. Martin Luther King, Jr. A Hindu radical assassinated Gandhi in 1948, believing he had made too many concessions to Muslim Pakistan.

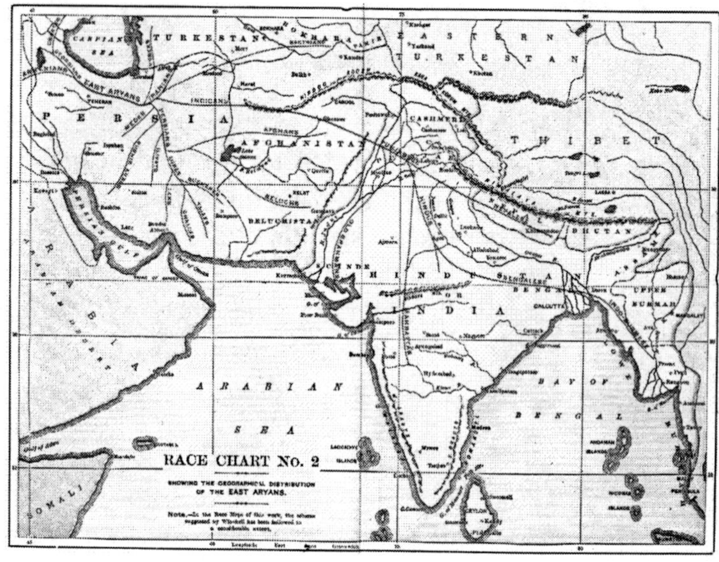

India

China's Communist Revolution

Mao Zedong

Prior to World War II, Communist rebels waged a civil war against Nationalist ruler, Chiang Kai-shek, in China. When Japan attacked, however, the two sides stopped fighting one another to resist the Japanese. After the war, hostilities between the Nationalists and the Communists started up again. After a US attempt to mediate the conflict failed, the United States reasoned that it could not allow a communist takeover of such a key country. Therefore, it decided to send financial aid to Chiang Kai-shek. The Soviets responded by sending support to the Communist forces of **Mao Zedong**. By 1949, Mao's Communists won control of the mainland, forcing Chiang and his supporters to flee to the island of Formosa, known today as Taiwan.

The Founding of Israel

After the Holocaust, **Zionism** (Jewish nationalism) increased. Hundreds of thousands of Jewish refugees wanted to enter Palestine and establish a Jewish homeland. On May 14, 1948, with the support of the newly formed United Nations, the new state of **Israel** was officially proclaimed as an independent Jewish state. President Truman showed the United States' support for the new nation by immediately recognizing it. Arab nations, however, greatly resented the decision to give part of Palestine to the Jews. They claimed that the entire territory rightfully belonged to Arabs. A series of wars between Arab states and Israel soon followed. To this day, conflict continues between Israel and the surrounding Arab states that refuse to recognize its right to exist. Meanwhile, within Israel's borders, violence and bloodshed between Israelis and Palestinians remains common. The decision to officially recognize Israel as a Jewish nation also had an impact on the Cold War. The US and Israel grew to be staunch allies, while the Soviets supported many of its Arab enemies.

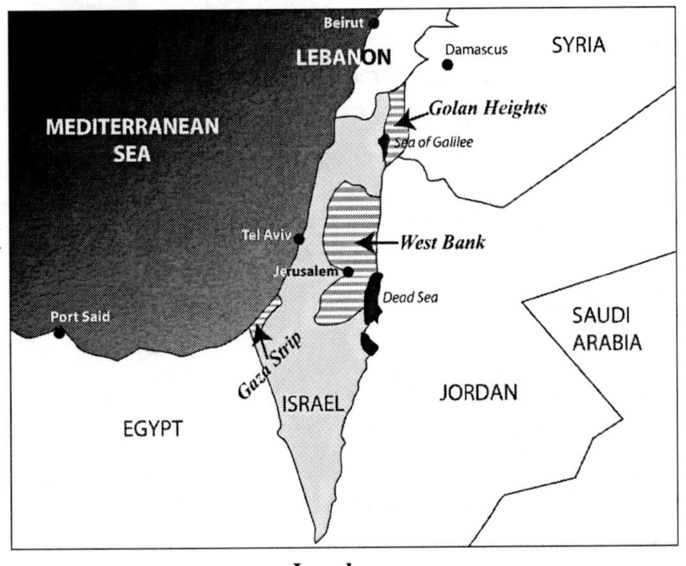

Israel

Former Prime Minister of Israel, Golda Meir

LATIN AMERICA

Many postwar nationalist movements occurred in poorer nations, historically colonized by western powers. Often, they leaned towards socialism. Although they did not want the Soviet Union telling them what to do, nationalists identified with the Russian Revolution and depended on Soviet support.

Fidel Castro

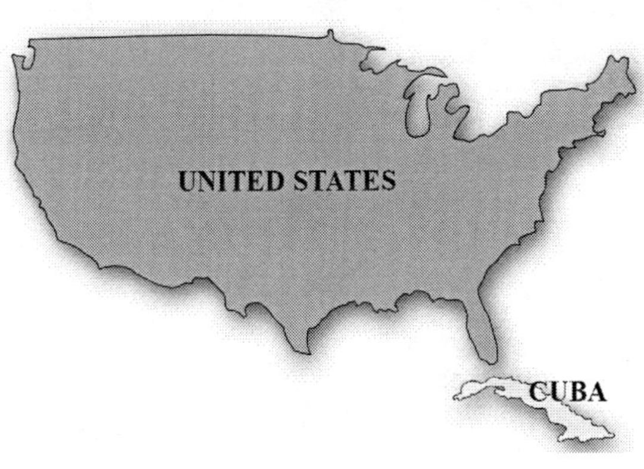

Cuba

During the twentieth century, the US became the largest investor in Latin America. US businesses owned much of the land and industry. To protect these businesses, the United States government backed leaders who supported US policies. Latin American nationalists viewed these leaders as oppressors and the United States as an imperialist power. In Cuba, Fidel Castro's communists overthrew the nation's pro-US regime in 1959. Later, in 1970, the people of Chile elected the socialist leader, Salvador Allende, president. In the late '70s and early '80s, a Marxist party called the *Sandinistas* seized control of Nicaragua. Even the United States' immediate neighbor, Mexico, experienced **Latin American nationalism**. An indigenous revolutionary group called the *Zapatistas* declared war on the Mexican government in 1994. Originating from Chiapas, one of the poorest regions of the country, the Zapatistas first attempted a violent overthrow. Overmatched by the Mexican army, however, they quickly changed their strategy. Today, the Zapatistas attempt to educate people at home and abroad through lectures, the Internet, and various forms of mass media, hoping to win support.

Hugo Chavez

Worried by Castro's victory in Cuba, the United States quickly decided that no other Latin American nations could fall to communism. As a result, nationalist movements like the ones mentioned above invited US opposition and led to political instability. In Chile, the US supported the ruthless, anti-communist dictator Augusto Pinochet. After overthrowing and executing Allende, Pinochet led Chile until 1989. In Nicaragua, the United States supported an anti-Sandinista force known as the Contras. Eventually, the Nicaraguan people voted the Sandanistas out of power.

Today, Venezuela and Bolivia both boast governments opposed to the US. Venezuelan president, Hugo Chavez, took office in 2002 and has repeatedly denounced the United States, winning him a nationalist following. In 2005, Bolivians elected leftist leader Juan Evo Morales Ayma, as president. A member of Bolivia's indigenous population, Morales won support championing the cause of the poorer classes and standing up to the United States.

SOUTHEAST ASIA

Ho Chi Minh

Southeast Asian nationalism grew as western powers promised a number of countries the right to self-determination once WWII ended. The US granted independence to the Philippines, and Great Britain gave up control of Burma. Despite reluctance from the Netherlands, Indonesia gained independence in 1949. In Vietnam, a communist leader named Ho Chi Minh seized control of the country's northern territory and began a movement that eventually defeated both France and the United States. As Southeast Asia entered the '60s and '70s, a number of nations experienced unrest. Indonesia's President Sukarno suspended democracy and tried to implement communist policies. Meanwhile, military dictatorships took control of Burma and Thailand. Today, a number of these nations have reinstated representative governments.

The most notable nationalist movement occurred in Vietnam. From 1946 until 1975, Vietnamese nationalists fought to drive western powers from their country. After forcing the French to withdraw, communists used guerilla warfare to outlast US forces sent to prevent the fall of South Vietnam to communism. Following the withdrawal of US troops, the communists overran the southern capital of Saigon in 1975, placing the entire country under their rule.

AFRICA

European powers had no choice but to recognize postwar **African nationalism** and give up their colonial possessions. Most African nations gained independence during the 1950s and '60s. Only Portugal clung to its colonial territories. A series of bloody wars finally convinced the Portuguese to grant independence to Mozambique and Angola in the 1970s.

Nelson Mandela

South Africa

Of all the African nationalist movements, South Africa's was, perhaps, the most unusual. For years, the white Afrikaans (descendants of Dutch colonists) ruled South Africa despite being a racial minority. Over time, they implemented oppressive policies against the nation's black, majority population. Most infamous was an official policy of racial segregation known as *apartheid.* Opposition to apartheid sparked a nationalist movement. One of the movement's key leaders was Nelson Mandela. The government arrested Mandela in 1962 and imprisoned him for twenty-seven years. Eventually, a progressive leader named F.W. de Klerk became president and released Mandela. In 1994, South Africa held its first elections in which its black population was allowed to fully participate. Mandela won the election and served as president until 1999.

THE MIDDLE EAST

The founding of Israel fueled **Arab nationalism**. Arab states saw the move as a betrayal of the Palestinian people and resented western nations that supported it. A key figure to emerge during this time was Gamal Abdul Nasser. Nasser became the leader of Egypt in 1954 and won the admiration of the Arab world for his willingness to stand up to the West. Nasser advocated Arab states working together to improve their economies and to oppose Israel. Under his leadership, Egypt also played a key role in establishing the PLO (Palestinian Liberation Organization) to act on behalf of the Palestinian people.

Abdul Nasser

Ethnic Conflicts

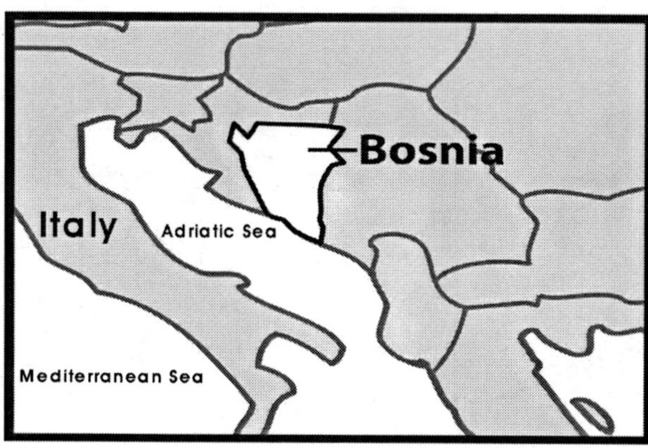

Map of Bosnia

While nationalist movements have resulted in independence for many countries, they have also opened the door for more **ethnic conflicts**. Under colonial and Soviet rule, ethnic violence was suppressed by powerful governments. Without such authority in place, ethnic rivalries resurfaced. In Africa, bloody wars between opposing tribes are common. Kurds, Persians, Arabs, and Jews consistently battle one another for land in the Middle East.

Some of the most notorious ethnic violence has occurred in Eastern Europe. With the fall of communist governments, ethnic nationalist groups have fought one another for territory. In Croatia and Bosnia-Herzegovina, ethnic conflicts among Serbs, Bosnians, and Croats have been some of the bloodiest in history. After conquering much of Bosnia during the 1990s, Serbians began a process of *ethnic cleansing*. Sparking memories of the Holocaust, Serbians murdered or forcibly removed more than a million Bosnians. After the international community initially did little, the United States eventually helped negotiate a truce and led a NATO military force to help maintain peace in the region. (NATO stands for North American Treaty Organization and is an alliance between the United States and various Western European nations.)

Terrorism

Terrorism is the use of violence against innocent people in the name of a cause. Usually, victims of terrorism are civilians, including women and children. Terrorism has been a tactic of nationalist groups for centuries. Today, terrorism is commonly associated with the Middle East. The largest and most active terrorist group is **Al-Qaeda**. Led by **Osama bin Laden**, Al-Qaeda believes in an extreme interpretation of Islam. Its members are Muslim radicals devoted to using terrorist actions against Israel, the United States, and other western nations. In 1998, Al-Qaeda attacked a US ship as it sat anchored in Yemen. Two years later, it bombed US embassies in Africa. On **September, 11, 2001**, Al-Qaeda

Osama bin Laden September 11, 2001

terrorists hijacked four US airliners. They purposely crashed two of them into the World Trade Center in New York City, destroying both towers. Terrorists flew the third plane into the Pentagon, which is the center of US military operations. The fourth airliner crashed in Pennsylvania after passengers on board revolted. Most believe the hijackers intended to strike the White House or the US Capitol. Thousands of innocent people died. The nation and most of the world were shocked. As the country mourned, President George W. Bush began coordinating international support for a response to the attacks. In October 2001, the United States led an invasion of Afghanistan to bring down the government that sheltered bin Laden. The invasion, part of Operation Enduring Freedom, marked the beginning of a **war on terror** aimed at finding and defeating terrorists before they kill, rather than waiting to respond to their attacks.

Operation Enduring Freedom in Afghanistan

The September 11 attacks greatly changed the world. Travel by air, train, and ship now require much tighter security measures than they used to. New laws allow government officials to hold suspected terrorists for longer periods of time without formal charges and permit closer monitoring of private phone calls and emails. The Department of Homeland Security was created as part of the US government to protect the nation from future attacks. In addition, illegal immigration has, once again, become a topic of intense debate. Most US citizens feel that more must be done to secure the borders against illegal immigrants because they fear terrorists might slip into the country to carry out more deadly attacks. In the twenty-first century, terrorism is a serious problem that impacts the entire world.

GLOBALIZATION

Globalization

Technology allows faster travel and communication than ever before. Computers and the Internet allow citizens and business leaders to correspond across continents within seconds. Satellites and television mean that people living in Georgia can see what happened in Pakistan minutes before. Militaries possess weapons that allow them to attack from thousands of miles away. What happens in one region of the world affects people in other regions. The world is connected through trade, business, and political alliances, creating an international community. Such worldwide interdependence is called **globalization**.

A number of organizations exist due to globalization. The **United Nations** allows political representatives to negotiate peacefully, provides humanitarian aid to nations in need, and occasionally backs international military forces to maintain stability in the world. The **World Trade Organization** monitors countries and makes sure they stick to international trade agreements. **OPEC** (Organization of Petroleum Exporting Countries) consists of several oil producing nations and controls the cost and supply of oil. These are just a few of the organizations resulting from increased globalization.

Practice 10.4 The Post-World War II Era

1. The United Nations was formed for the purpose of

   A. monitoring international trade agreements.
   B. controlling the export of oil.
   C. battling terrorism.
   D. preventing wars.

2. Who was the leader who used non-violence to win independence for his country in 1947?

   A. Mao Zedong
   B. Mohandas Gandhi
   C. Osama bin Laden
   D. Gamal Abdul Nasser

3. How did nationalism affect the continent of Africa after WWII?

4. How did most Arabs respond to the founding of Israel? What are relations between Israel and Arab states like today?

5. Why have nationalist movements often been anti-US?

CHAPTER 10 REVIEW

Key people, terms, and concepts

nationalism
the Balkans
militarism
alliances
front
trench warfare
Treaty of Versailles
reparations
Hapsburg Dynasty
Ottoman Empire
mandate system
League of Nations
Czar Nicholas II
Russian Revolution
Lenin
Bolsheviks
Soviet Union
Joseph Stalin
Five Year Plan
Stalin's Purge
Romanov Dynasty
totalitarian state
authoritarian state
fascism
Benito Mussolini
Adolf Hitler
the Nazis
lebensraum
anti-Semitism
Hitler's Final Solution
the Holocaust
Emperor Hirohito
Hideki Tojo
Axis Powers
World War II
Battle of Britain
Pearl Harbor
Allies
Tehran Conference
D-day
Yalta Conference
Potsdam Conference
iron curtain
nuclear arms race
Cold War
Marshall Plan
postwar Japan
United Nations
hydrogen bomb
decolonization
Mohandas Gandhi
India
Pakistan
Mao Zedong
China's communist revolution
Zionism
Israel
Latin American nationalism
Southeast Asian nationalism
African nationalism
Arab nationalism
ethnic conflicts
terrorism
Al-Qaeda
Osama bin Laden
September 11, 2001
War on Terror
globalization
World Trade Organization
OPEC

Multiple Choice Questions

Look at the map below and answer the following question.

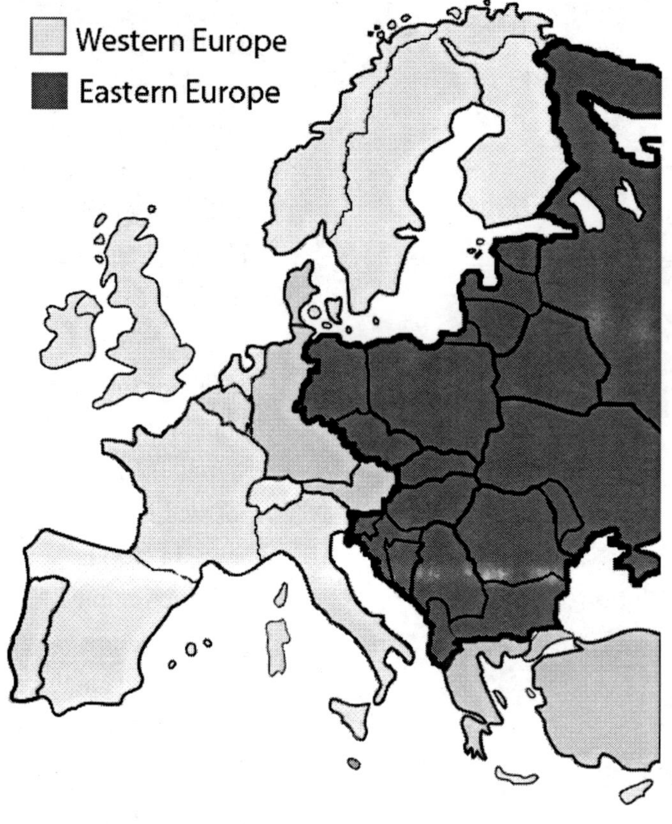

1. The thick, dark line in the center of the map depicts
   A. the iron curtain.
   B. ethnic conflict.
   C. Arab nationalism.
   D. lebensraum.

2. Nationalism, militarism, and alliances all contributed to
   A. ethnic conflicts after WWII.
   B. India's independence movement.
   C. the fall of communism.
   D. the start of WWI.

3. Karl Marx inspired
   A. the founding of the United Nations.
   B. Zionism.
   C. the Bolshevik Party.
   D. terrorism.

Look at the map below and answer the following question

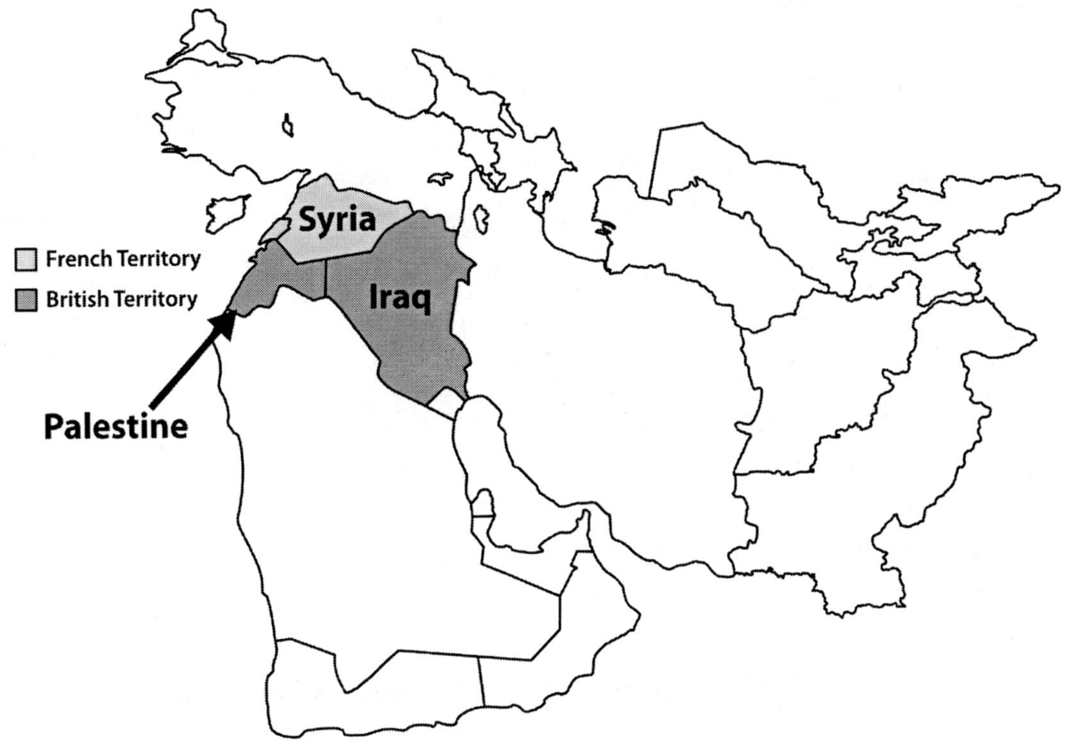

4. The map depicts
   A. the Cold War.
   B. Arab nationalism.
   C. the mandate system.
   D. the World Trade Organization.

5. Which of the following leaders would have disagreed with totalitarianism?
   A. Joseph Stalin
   B. Mohandas Gandhi
   C. Adolf Hitler
   D. Benito Mussolini

6. Many Jews became Zionists because of
   A. the Holocaust.
   B. Arab nationalism.
   C. African nationalism.
   D. communism.

7. Roosevelt and Churchill finally agreed to an Allied invasion of Europe when they met with Stalin in
   A. Yalta. B. Potsdam. C. Tehran. D. Bosnia.

8. In addition to ending the war with Japan, the atomic bomb started the
   A. Cold War.
   B. nuclear arms race.
   C. nationalist movement in Southeast Asia.
   D. Chinese revolution.

9. If representatives of two nations wanted to settle their differences peacefully following World War II, they could turn to the
   A. League of Nations.
   B. PLO.
   C. United Nations.
   D. Zapatistas.

10. Increased security at airports, laws allowing greater government intervention into the lives of citizens, greater concern about illegal immigration, and wars in the Middle East are all side-effects of
   A. nationalism.
   B. communism.
   C. the mandate system.
   D. terrorism.

11. What do Ho Chi Minh, Mao Zedong, and Mohandas Gandhi all have in common?
   A. They were all devout communists.
   B. They were all supporters of Zionism.
   C. They all rebelled against the mandate system.
   D. They all led independence movements in Asia.

Read the quote below and answer the following question.

> "The international community must intervene. Not since Hitler's Final Solution has the world seen such evil. We must not let such horrors go unchecked again. Have we learned nothing? Must we wait until millions have died as they did under the Nazis?"
>
> – official addressing the UN during the early '90s.

12. The official quoted above is most likely talking about
   A. the Holocaust.
   B. apartheid.
   C. ethnic violence in Eastern Europe.
   D. the Israeli-Arab conflict.

Georgia HSGT Practice Test 1

The purpose of this practice test is to measure your progress in United States Social Studies. This test is based on the GPS-based Georgia HSGT in Social Studies and adheres to the sample question format provided by the Georgia Department of Education.

General Directions:

1. Read all directions carefully.

2. Read each question or sample. Then choose the best answer.

3. Choose only one answer for each question. If you change an answer, be sure to erase your original answer completely.

1 The president can be charged with wrongdoing (impeached) if he/she is suspected of treason, bribery, or other crimes while in office. What does this process involve? SSCG14

A The president stands trial in the Senate. If two-thirds of the senate finds him/her guilty, then he/she is removed from office.

B The president stands trial in front of the Supreme Court. The Chief Justice makes the final decision.

C All leaders of the three branches of government vote. If two out of three find him/her guilty, then he/she is removed from office.

D The president goes on trial, and the people of the US vote for or against his innocence.

2 When British Prime Minister Winston Churchill heard that Pearl Harbor had been bombed, he is reported to have said, "We've won the war!" His reaction to Japan's attack on the United States is evidence that SSUSH19

A Great Britain desperately needed the US to join them as an ally in the fighting.

B Churchill did not trust the US and was relieved that it would be distracted fighting the Japanese for a while.

C Japan and Great Britain were allies.

D Churchill resented the US for not helping Great Britain and was glad that they had suffered.

Read the description below and answer the following question

> "He had brought few supplies, even by the standards of the short campaign he had planned for, since he expected his army to be able to live off of the land they were in, as was his usual practice. The desperate Russians, however, adopted a "scorched-earth" policy: whenever they retreated, they burned the places they left behind. His army had trouble finding supplies, and it grew progressively weaker the farther it marched."

3 What is this description referring to? SSWH14

A Napoleon's invasion of Russia

B Jose de San Martin's Russian defeat

C Simon Bolivar's liberation of Russia and Spain

D Napoleon's march across Belgium

4 What protects citizens from double jeopardy, self-incrimination, and prevents the government from taking citizen's private property for public use without cooperation? SSCG6

A equal protection

B due process

C public interest

D individual liberties

Use the map below to answer the following questions.

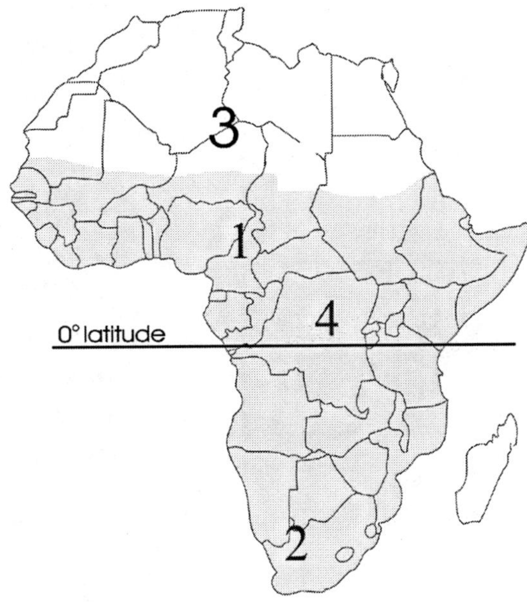

5 Which climate extends from the semi-arid region toward the equator? SSWG4

A 3 **B** 2 **C** 4 **D** 1

6 Which climate is numbered 4 on the map? SSWG4

A equatorial **B** semi-arid **C** desert **D** tropical

7 He preached non-violent, civil disobedience as the most effective method for blacks to obtain civil rights, became a national figure after the Montgomery Bus Boycott, led the March on Washington, and was eventually assassinated in Memphis, Tennessee. Who was he? SSUSH22

A Dr. Martin Luther King, Jr.

B Robert Kennedy

C Jackie Robinson

D A. Philip Randolph

8 What was one of the greatest impacts of the cotton gin during the Industrial Revolution? SSUSH7

A It allowed people to harvest cotton much faster making it the basis of the South's economy during the 1800s.

B It allowed the North to become more industrialized and prosperous.

C It ended the South's dependence on agriculture and freed the slaves.

D It improved Henry Ford's assembly line with faster seat production.

Read the quote below and answer the following question.

> "Congress shall make no law respecting an establishment of religion, or prohibiting the free exercise thereof, or abridging the freedom of speech, or of the press; or the right of the people peaceably to assemble, and to petition the government for a redress of grievances."

9 This quote is in reference to which amendment? SSCG6

A Fourth

B Ninth

C First

D Sixth

10 Which one of the following was a product of the Harlem Renaissance? SSUSH16

A the writings of Machiavelli

B the speeches of Frederick Douglass

C the writings of Langston Hughes

D the works of Michelangelo

11 The city of Florence was most influential during SSWH9

A the Reformation.

B World War II.

C the French Revolution.

D the Renaissance.

12 Which philosophy recognizes an implied agreement that entitles citizens their freedom and natural rights but also empowers government to maintain order? SSCG2

A Declaration of Independence

B Social Contract theory

C natural rights

D the letters of enlightenment

13 What is the major difference in climate between North and South Europe? SSWG6

A It is much colder along the coasts of the South than the plains of the North.

B The South consists of high winds that increase temperatures.

C Southern Europe has greater amounts of precipitation that produces green forests and fertile farmland

D The South is dryer and more mild than the wet fertile, and sometimes cold, North.

14 What was the main reason Charles the II of England wanted New Amsterdam? SSUSH16

A to establish complete dominance of all new territories in America

B to give the Duke of York his own colony

C because it was successful in trading and ideally located as a key port

D because the English did not want the Dutch to have control of any region

Look at the chart below and answer the following two questions.

Andrew Johnson's Presidential Reconstruction Plan	Radical Reconstruction Plan
Southerners who swore loyalty to the Union were pardoned.	Southern states would be put under military rule.
Former Confederate states could hold constitutional conventions to set up state governments.	African Americans were allowed to vote.
States had to cancel secession and ratify the Thirteenth Amendment.	Southerners who had supported the Confederacy would temporarily lose their right to vote.
After the Thirteenth Amendment was ratified, southern states could then hold elections and be part of the Union.	Southern states had to guarantee equal rights to African Americans.
Permitted southern states to enact black codes.	Southern states had to ratify the Fourteenth Amendment.

15 Which of the following is true about Johnson's Reconstruction Plan? SSUSH10

A Southern states created laws that limited the rights of freed blacks so much that they basically kept them living like slaves.

B No southerners were forgiven of any crimes against the US.

C All southerners were allowed to vote regardless of race or gender.

D Previous Confederate states were allowed to hold conventions but could not set up independent state governments.

16 Which of the following fails to describe the Radical Reconstruction Plan? SSUSH10

A required southern states to give citizenship to African Americans

B did not allow confederate leaders to vote

C designed to punish the South

D called for the president to make final decisions concerning Reconstruction

Read the list below and answer the following question.

- The Ottoman Empire
- The Hapsburg Dynasty
- The Romanov Dynasty

17 Which of the following is the best heading for the list above? SSWH16

A Empires Established by the Mandate System

B Communist Dictatorships

C Totalitarian Regimes in Europe During World War II

D Powers That Fell Due to World War I.

18 Colonists responded negatively to such measures as the Stamp Act, the Proclamation of 1763, and various other British laws after the French and Indian War because SSUSH3

A they had declared their independence and saw them as attempts by a foreign power to seize control of North America.

B they favored the French over the British method of taxation.

C they felt that these laws did not do enough to raise government revenue to support the colonies and Great Britain.

D they felt that they were having taxes and regulations imposed on them without being granted a voice in government.

19 Why did the British believe they would have greater success fighting the Americans in the South than they did in New England and the middle colonies? SSUSH4

A Most of Britain's soldiers were stationed in the South when the war began.

B The southern colonies had never agreed to the Declaration of Independence.

C General Washington was only concerned with gaining independence for the northern colonies.

D There were more colonists in the South who remained loyal to the king.

20 What was a MAJOR cause of ethnic conflicts after World War II? SSWH20

A The destruction and economic decline created instability, leading to the creation of new identities around the world.

B The destruction seen by Hitler made all nations fearful of control by other countries.

C People no longer wanted to govern themselves because of the burden of responsibility this involved.

D Wartime occupation caused many blacks to never want their independence.

21 The principle that authority to govern should be divided between different branches in order to respect and uphold the natural rights of citizens is known as SSCG3

A Separation of Powers.

B the Tenth Amendment.

C popular sovereignty.

D the Bill of Rights.

Look at the map below and answer the following question.

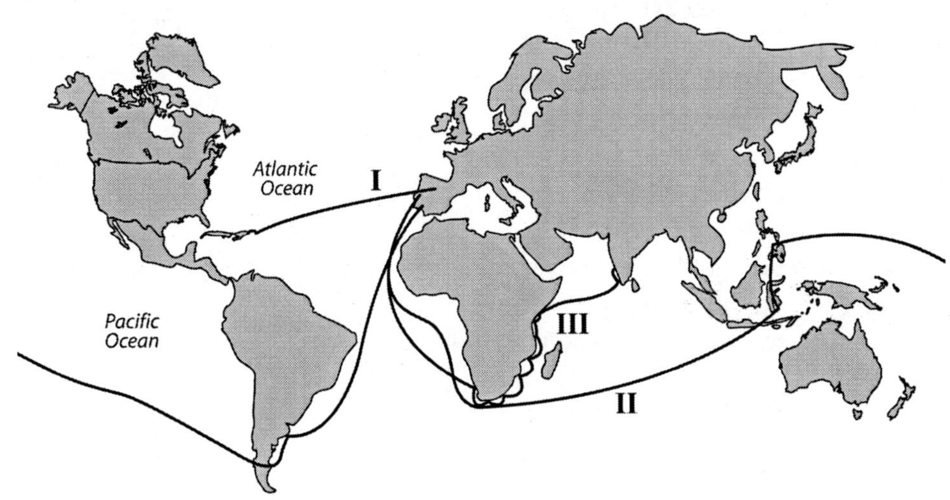

22 Route II depicts the voyage of SSWH9

A Christopher Columbus.

B Magellan.

C Vasco da Gama.

D Amerigo Vespucci.

23. What were the "Fourteen Points"? SSUSH15

A Woodrow Wilson's proposals for peace following World War I

B Great Britain and France's demands for peace from Germany

C conditions imposed upon Germany at the end of the war

D reasons officially presented to President Wilson by the US Senate explaining why that body had refused to approve US membership in the League of Nations

24 Deserts, Arabic culture, Islam, terrorism, and conflicts between Israelis and Palestinians are associated with SSWG3

A Southeast Asia and Eastern Asia.

B Africa and Southern Europe.

C North Africa and Southwest Asia.

D North Africa and Southern Europe.

Read the quote below and answer the following questions .

> "Provided that, as an express and fundamental condition to the acquisition of any territory from the Republic of Mexico by the United States, by virtue of any treaty which may be negotiated between them, and to the use by the Executive of the moneys herein appropriated, neither slavery nor involuntary servitude shall ever exist in any part of said territory, except for crime, whereof the party shall first be duly convicted."

25 Where is this quote from? SSUSH8

A Missouri Compromise

B Dred Scott Case

C Wilmot Proviso

D Compromise of 1850

26 He challenged the selling of indulgences and other Catholic practices which he felt contradicted the Bible. Eventually, his teachings led to a new church in Germany and a religious movement known as the Protestant Reformation. Who was he? SSWH9

A John Calvin

B Martin Luther

C King Henry VIII

D Ignatius Loyola

27 Elizabeth Cady Stanton is most famous for SSUSH1

A supporting abolition.

B calling for education reform.

C advocating women's suffrage.

D opposing Jacksonian democracy.

28 Which of the following correctly lists the world's continents in order of size, from largest to smallest? SSWG1

A Asia, Africa, South America, Australia, North America, Antarctica, Europe

B Asia, Africa, Antarctica, South America, Australia, North America, Europe

C Asia, Africa, North America, South America, Antarctica, Europe, Australia

D Europe, Africa, Asia, North America, South America, Antarctica, Australia

29 A resident of Savannah in 1864 would have been MOST terrified by news of SSUSH9

A Sherman's march to the sea.

B Sherman's attack on Atlanta.

C Jackson's unexpected death.

D Lee's defeat at Gettysburg.

30 How did the Fifteenth and Nineteenth amendments change voting in the US? SSCG8

A They encouraged free speech and individual rights.

B They allowed poor people to vote.

C They extended voting rights to blacks and women.

D They established the use of primary and recall elections.

Use the map listed below to answer the following questions.

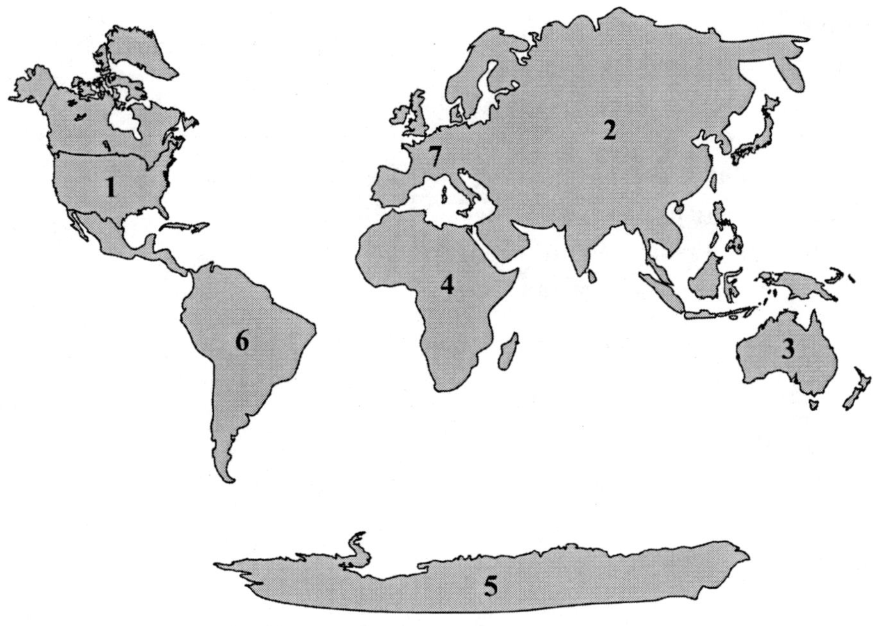

31 Which continent is the largest? SSWG3

A 4

B 2

C 1

D 7

32 Rather than attempting to force the Soviet Union to give up the portions of Eastern Europe it had inhabited during WWII, the US elected to concentrate its efforts on preventing the expansion of communism into Western Europe and other parts of the world. This policy was known as SSUSH20

A containment.

B detente.

C the Marshall Plan.

D the Great Society.

33 Which of the following statements is true regarding the Enlightenment? SSWH13

A It led to the mixing of European and Native American cultures during the age of exploration.

B It gave birth to political ideas that eventually impacted the United States.

C Florence was its cultural and political center.

D It ended when William of Orange invaded England.

Read the quote below and answer the following question.

> **"It must be built! Now that the US is responsible for territories on both sides of the Americas, our ships must be able to travel quickly from ocean to ocean. By aiding the rebels against the Colombians, our nation betters its chances of acquiring the land needed for this necessary construction."**
>
> **Public official, 1906**

34 The above quote is referring to SSUSH14

A the Erie Canal.

B the Panama Canal.

C the Roosevelt Corollary.

D the transcontinental railroad.

35 The United States Constitution does not grant the federal government the power to determine curriculum for public schools. Under the Tenth Amendment, this power is SSCG5

A unconstitutional.

B reserved for the states.

C implied under the supremacy clause.

D a violation of civil liberties.

36 An area that shares common geographical features, like the Amazon rainforest, is best described as a/an SSWG1

A place.

B tundra.

C natural barrier.

D arid region.

37 The NAACP was founded in 1909 to SSUSH13

A improve the lives of laborers.

B reveal corrupt politicians in big cities.

C promote the interests of African Americans.

D protect segregationist policies in the South.

38 Chinese immigrants played a major role in the SSUSH11

A opening of Ellis Island.

B construction of western railroads.

C rapid growth of northern cities.

D organized labor movement.

39 The Five Year Plan was SSWH17

A Napoleon's plan to conquer Europe.

B Stalin's plan to industrialize the Soviet Union.

C Hitler's plan to exterminate the Jewish people.

D the United States' plan to establish democracy throughout Latin America.

40 In order for US society to function efficiently, citizens must fulfill SSCG7

A individual liberties.

B civic responsibilities.

C military obligations.

D family chores.

Look at the map below and answer the following question.

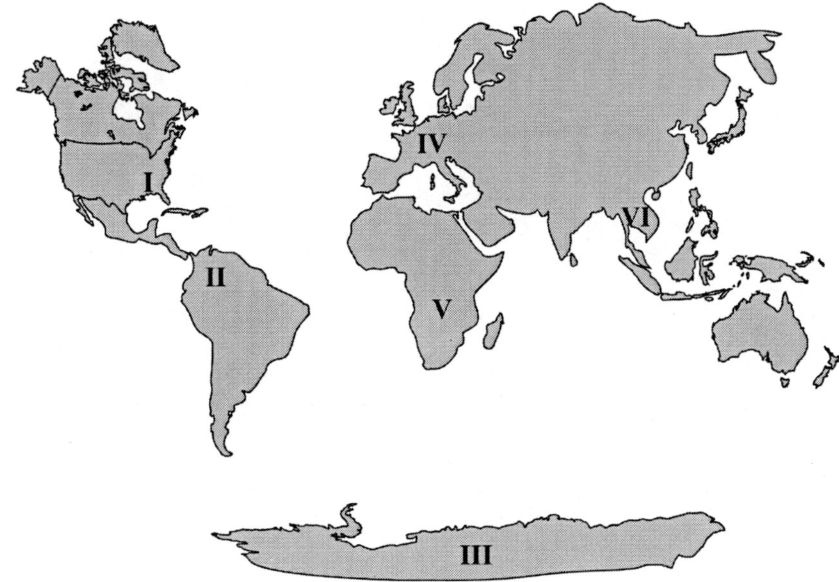

41 Which of the regions on the globe would be MOST LIKELY to suffer from a drought? SSWG8

A I

B II

C III and IV

D IV and V

42 Why did the federal government open Ellis Island? SSUSH12

A to protect New York

B to deal with the number of immigrants coming into the United States

C to act as a central processing center for immigrants arriving by ships

D to encourage immigrants to come to New York

43 The federal bureaucracy consists of SSCG15

A Congress, the president, and the federal courts.

B federal departments of the executive branch.

C Congressional committees.

D Federal and state agencies.

SESSION II

DO NOT BEGIN UNTIL INSTRUCTED TO DO SO

44 Janet serves her state in the federal legislative branch of government. She will serve 2 years before having to run for re-election and is one of fifteen representatives from her state. She hopes that, in time, she might become speaker and lead the entire house in which she serves. Janet serves in the SSCG9

A US Senate.

B state house.

C US House of Representatives.

D General Assembly.

45 Which of the following lists events of World War II in the correct chronological order? SSUSH19

A Pearl Harbor, Germany's invasion of France, V-E Day, D-day

B Germany invades the USSR, D-day, Pearl Harbor, the atomic bomb

C the USSR conquers Berlin, the atomic bomb, D-day, President Roosevelt dies

D Lend-Lease, Pearl Harbor, D-day, the atomic bomb

46 The divisions of Germany and Korea were both effects of the SSWH18

A Treaty of Versailles.

B Japanese surrender in World War II.

C Surrender of Germany in World War II.

D Cold War.

47 What three major countries comprise Eastern Asia? SSWG5

A Afghanistan, India, and China

B Japan, China, and Korea

C Thailand, Vietnam, and China

D China, Cambodia, and Nepal

Read the list below and answer the following question.

- fought against the British
- made Andrew Jackson a national hero
- led to the end of the Federalist Party
- resulted in a new sense of national identity

48 What is the list above referring to? SSUSH6

A the French and Indian War

B the American Revolution

C the War of 1812

D World War I

49 Who of the following was not a communist? SSWH19

A Karl Marx

B Lenin

C Mao Zedong

D Mohandas Gandhi

50 The idea of a strong central government was supported at the Constitutional Convention by SSCG3

A the Anti-federalists.

B Thomas Jefferson.

C the Federalists.

D popular sovereignty.

Look at the illustration below and answer the following question.

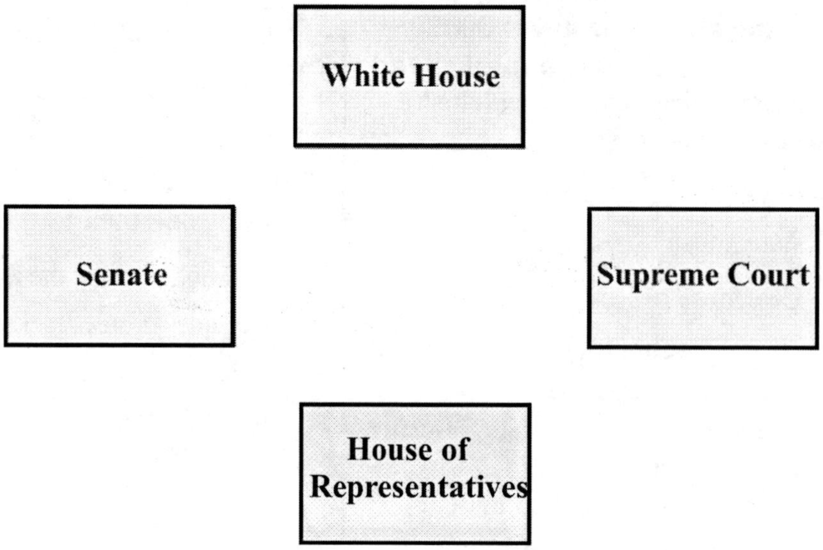

	White House	
Senate		Supreme Court
	House of Representatives	

51 The picture above is meant to illustrate the process by which a presidential nominee takes his/her place on the Supreme Court. The arrows to illustrate the correct process should be drawn SSCG4

A from the White House, to the Senate, to the Supreme Court

B from the White House, to the House of Representatives, to the Senate, to the Supreme Court

C from the White House, to the Senate, to the House of Representatives, to the Supreme Court

D from the White House, to the Senate, to the people, to the Supreme Court

52 In which of the following states was slavery legal in 1860? SSUSH9

A Ohio

B New York

C Georgia

D New Hampshire

53 The Red Scare led to SSUSH16

A violent conflicts on Native American reservations.

B the end of the Cold War.

C ratification of the Thirteenth Amendment.

D increased restrictions on immigration.

Examine the table below and answer the following question.

Casualties by Country for WWI		
	Population	Deaths due to WWI
France	39,600,000	1,697,800
Italy	35,600,000	1,240,010
Great Britain	45,400,000	994,138
Germany	64,900,000	2,462,897
United States	92,000,000	117,465

54 The table above offers evidence why SSUSH15

- **A** Germany refused to sign the Treaty of Versailles.
- **B** Germany's enemies wanted retribution after WWI.
- **C** the United States opposed the League of Nations.
- **D** the Cold War began after WWII.

55 Various tribes still live in the Amazon. Which of the following problems most directly affects these people? SSWG7

- **A** urban pollution
- **B** deforestation
- **C** drought
- **D** terrorism

56 What caused the French and Indian War of 1754? SSUSH3

- **A** the signing of the Treaty of Paris
- **B** tension between French and British colonials
- **C** tension between Native Americans and Spanish explorers
- **D** France's decision to help the British colonists

57 The belief that countries must grow wealthier and maintain their national security by consistently exporting more than they import is SSUSH1

- **A** trade.
- **B** trans-Atlantic trade.
- **C** mercantilism.
- **D** middle passage.

58 Which of the following Asian countries most closely resembles the United States' form of government? SSUWG1

- **A** Japan
- **B** China
- **C** North Korea
- **D** Afghanistan

Read the list below and answer the following question.

1. commander-in-chief of the armed forces
2. leader of his/her party
3. foreign policy leader
4. power to impeach
5. head of state

59 Which of the above powers/responsibilities belong to the president of the United States? SSCG12

A 1 and 5

B 1 and 4

C 1,2,3,5

D 1,2,5

60 Sputnik concerned leaders in the United States because SSUSH21

A it was an agreement between the USSR and Cuba that placed nuclear missiles within ninety miles of the United States.

B it was a Soviet satellite that signaled the US was far behind the Soviets in the space race.

C it was a submarine that US ships were defenseless against.

D it was a bomb ten times more powerful than the atomic bomb dropped on Japan.

61 Mountainous regions tend to be SSWG2

A hotter.

B more populated.

C colder and less populated.

D accessible to trade and travel.

Read the quote below and answer the following question.

"It is best when a sovereign rules morally. However, no ruler should feel bound by the laws of morality—not where the state is concerned. His duty is to the state, and thus, what is good for the state, for the time *is* ethical."

62 The statement above is consistent with the beliefs of SSWH9

A Erasmus.

B Machiavelli.

C John Calvin.

D Martin Luther.

63 The Columbian Exchange contributed to SSWH10

A the invention of the printing press.

B the rise of Florence as an influential city.

C the spread of Christianity to the Americas.

D trade between Europe and China.

Use the map below to answer question number 64.

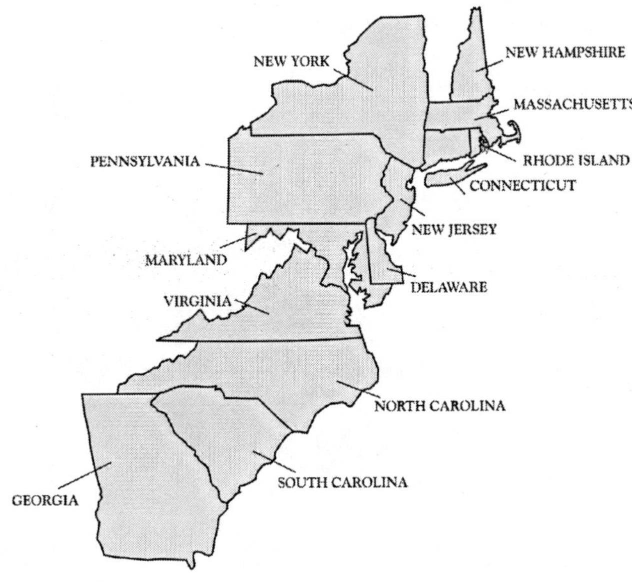

64 Which of the following states would have MOST LIKELY been supportive of the Virginia Plan? SSUSH5

A Delaware

B Rhode Island

C New Hampshire

D New York

65 A poor family living in the Appalachian mountains of north Georgia in 1934 would have benefitted most from the SSUSH18

A Great Migration.

B Tennessee Valley Authority.

C Wagner Act.

D. Truman Doctrine.

66 The Great Depression occurred, in part, because farmers and other producers were filling the market place with more products than consumers could buy. This caused a drastic fall in prices that eventually drove many out of business and hurt the stock market. Such a phenomenon is called SSUSH17

A underconsumption.

B overproduction.

C a stock market crash.

D consumerism.

Look at the map below and answer the following question.

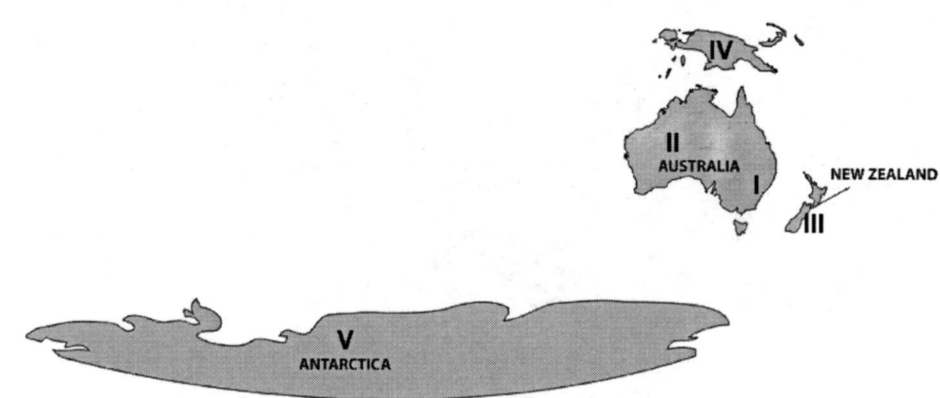

67 Where would one find a frozen climate, uninhabitable by human beings? SSWG9

A II

B III

C IV

D V

68 Bills passed by Congress then go to SSCG10

A the president for approval or veto.

B the House of Representatives for a vote.

C the Supreme Court to determine constitutionality.

D the states for ratification.

69 Which of the following MOST LIKELY resembles the role of the US Senate during the impeachment process? SSCG14

A fans at a sporting event

B spectators at a political debate

C jury at a trial

D citizens at a town meeting

Look at the chart below and answer the following questions.

Louis and Clark Expedition	led to the rapid migration of settlers to the Pacific Northwest
War of 1812	X
Louisiana Purchase	turning point for the US as it began to pursue prosperity within its own borders
Monroe Doctrine	the US declared no tolerance for European Intervention

70 What goes where the X is? SSUSH6

A allowed Native Americans to have their land back

B gave more control of the United States to Britain

C helped the US produce a stronger sense of national identity

D Great Britain defeated the US at Fort McHenry

71 Congress passes a new federal law making it illegal to call public officials "boneheads." The president gladly signs it. However, the Supreme Court nullifies the law by ruling that it violates citizens' First Amendment right to free speech. What power has the Court exercised? SSCG16

A the power to impeach

B judicial appointment

C judicial review

D constitutional amendment

72 In an effort to bring down the government of Fidel Castro, the United States adopted a policy of refusing to trade with Cuba. More than 40 years later, this policy remains in effect. Which of the following is an attempt to punish another country by refusing to trade with it? SSCG20

A a tariff

B a negative trade balance

C an embargo

D a trade treaty

Read the quote below and answer the following question.

> **"He totally transformed the economies of two regions, but in entirely different ways. How could one man have taken one region of the nation down a path of increased reliance on factory workers, while at the same time making the South a region totally dependent on slaves."**
>
> **US Economist in the mid-1800s**

73 Who is the above quote MOST LIKELY referring to? SSUSH7

A Benjamin Franklin

B Thomas Edison

C Eli Whitney

D W.E.B. DuBois

74 Speaking in front of the Lincoln Memorial, Martin Luther King, Jr. gave his famous "I have a Dream" speech. Which of the following statements is true regarding this speech? SSUSH22

A It occurred at the March on Washington and greatly influenced Kennedy to push for civil rights legislation.

B It occurred at the March on Washington just months after the Kennedy assassination and re-focused the nation on civil rights.

C It occurred in Montgomery, Alabama and was King's final speech before his assassination.

D It occurred in Selma, Alabama and led to Governor George Wallace apologizing for many of his segregationist views.

75 Where was the meeting between Roosevelt, Churchill, and Stalin held, in which the Allies agreed to the division of Germany and parts of Europe after the war, although the US and Great Britain viewed these divisions as only temporary? SSWH18

A Yalta

B Tehran

C Potsdam

D Berlin

76 In which of the following areas would one expect to find the greatest population? SSWG1

A Great European Plain

B Australian Outback

C Siberia

D Amazon Rainforest

77 The War of 1812 SSUSH4

A closed the West to any further expansion.

B improved US manufacturing and farming.

C hindered US manufacturing and farming.

D reduced US nationalism.

78 Popular sovereignty is based on the belief that SSCG3

A the people should have the deciding voice in government.

B leaders are not to be trusted.

C monarchs have a divine right to rule.

D fascism is better than totalitarianism.

Use the chart below to answer the following question.

1776	
January	*Common Sense*
February	Battle of Moore's Creek Bridge
March	British Evacuate Boston
April	
May	
June	
July	?
August	British Conquer New York City
September	
October	
November	
December	Washington Crosses the Delaware

79 Which of the following should appear where you see the question mark? SSUSH4

A the Declaration of Independence

B the Great Compromise

C Battle of Saratoga

D France formally supports America's war for independence.

80 Castro's revolution in Cuba, the Sandanista's in Nicaragua, and the rise of Evo Morales in Bolivia are all examples of political movements inspired by SSUSH20

A Latin American nationalism.

B radical Islam.

C the United States.

D terrorism.

Read the quote below and answer the following question.

> "Each of us places his person and authority under the supreme direction of the general will, and the group receives each individual as an indivisible part of the whole."

81 Who is this quote most likely from? SSWH14

A Rousseau

B Galileo

C Kepler

D Newton

82 The Declaration of Independence was based largely on the ideas of SSCG2

A the Renaissance.

B the French Revolution.

C the Enlightenment.

D Karl Marx

83 Which of the following would most concern OPEC? SSWH21

A The United States passes stricter immigration laws.

B A corporation in Canada successfully markets vehicles that do not require gasoline.

C Riots erupt in Haiti.

D Egypt and Russia sign a treaty.

Look at the cartoon below and answer the following question.

84 According to the above cartoon, political candidates often SSSCG8

A depend heavily on campaign contributions.

B are part of the mass media.

C tend to oppose freedom of the press.

D avoid saying things that might offend voters.

85 Upton Sinclair, Ida Tarbell, and Jane Addams can all be described as SSUSH13

A muckrakers.

B nativists.

C progressive.

D imperialists.

86 Flat grasslands which are home to most of the wild animals one associates with Sub-Saharan Africa are called SSWG4

A equatorial regions.

B tropical zones.

C tundras.

D savannas.

Use the quotation below to answer the following question.

> "Gentlemen, I believe that this compromise presents the best possible solution to this dilemma. Since those in the North feel strongly that slaves are not citizens and therefore should not be counted in the population, while our Southern representatives feel just as adamantly that they should be, I see no other solution."

87 The above quote is referring to which of the following? SSUSH5

A the Three-fifths Compromise

B the Connecticut Plan

C the Slave Trade Compromise

D the Virginia Plan

88 President Thomas Jefferson negotiated the Louisiana Purchase despite the fact that the Constitution does not specifically grant the president power to acquire new territory. Given the fact that Jefferson held to a strict interpretation of the Constitution, his decision to acquire Louisiana is seen by many historians as SSUSH6

A consistent with the views Jefferson originally held concerning the Constitution.

B inconsistent with Jefferson's past views.

C supportive of arguments Jefferson made when he was secretary of state under President Washington.

D dishonest considering he did not notify Congress of his decision.

89 Where was the meeting between Truman, Churchill, and Stalin held, in which the Allies reaffirmed their policy of unconditional surrender and at which Truman learned the atomic bomb had been successfully tested? SSWH9

A Yalta

B Potsdam

C Tehran

D Washington, DC

90 African American students in the early 1960s who wanted to be part of a movement that actively resisted segregation would have been most drawn to the SSUSH24

A NAACP

B SCLC

C NATO

D SNCC

Georgia HSGT Practice Test 2

The purpose of this practice test is to measure your progress in US social studies. This test is based on the GPS-based Georgia HSGT in Social Studies and adheres to the sample question format provided by the Georgia Department of Education.

General Directions:

1. Read all directions carefully.
2. Read each question or sample. Then choose the best answer.
3. Choose only one answer for each question. If you change an answer, be sure to erase your original answer completely.

Use the following table to answer question 1.

Historical Figure	Influence on the Colonial Period
Nathanial Bacon	led an army of discontented Virginia farmers
Chief Powhatan	leader of a tribal confederation in Virginia
King Philip	X
King Charles II	took New Amsterdam from the Dutch

1 **Which of the following should appear where you see the X?** SSUSH1

A a leader who united Native Americans in New England in an unsuccessful attempt to drive out English settlers

B a British King who took control of Virginia and enslaved many Native Americans

C first leader of New England

D a leader who successfully united Native Americans by gaining firm control over New England

2 **The Constitution involves checks and balances. It also allows each branch to check the powers of the other two. What is the purpose of this system?** SSUCG4

A to strengthen federalism

B to keep any one branch from becoming too authoritative

C to allow judicial review

D to give absolute power to the president

3 **He preached that a ruler should make decisions based on human nature and what is best for the state rather than religion or ethics.** SSWH9

A Leonardo Da Vinci

B Michaelangelo

C Machiavelli

D Petrach

Read the list below and answer the following question.

1. Raw materials
2. Religion
3. Ideas
4. Disease
5. People
6. Animals

4 The Columbian Exchange drastically affected society by establishing contact between two worlds. Which from the list above were things shared between the West and East as a result of the Exchange? SSWH10

A 1 – 6

B 1,2,3,5,6

C 1 – 4

D 1,2,5

5 Bob notices Nick's accent and asks him what country he is from. Ten minutes after responding to Bob's questions, Nick is also asked by Melissa what continent he grew up on. Nick responds to Melissa's question with the exact same answer he gave Bob. Nick must be from SSWG9

A Europe.

B Australia.

C America.

D North Africa.

6. Which of the following tended to be true of the immigrants who came to the US from other countries during the late 19th and early 20th centuries? SSSH16

A They tended to be wealthy and had the money to book passage to the United States.

B They were usually dispersed once they arrived in the US, so as to better assimilate into US society and not be easily recognized as foreigners.

C They tended to live together in ghettos, where they shared the same language and cultural background.

D They refused to join unions because they tended to favor business owners over immigrant workers.

7 Omar lives in Southwest Asia and holds to a strict form of Islam. He believes strongly in the Qur'an and believes that all aspects of European and US culture should be rejected. Meanwhile, Ahmed, who lives in the same country and also considers himself a devout Muslim, dresses in suits and ties and listens to the rock music. Omar and Ahmed are an example of SSWG3

A racial conflict.

B the difference between terrorism and Zionism.

C tension between traditional and westernized culture.

D the Arab-Israeli conflict.

Go On

Look at the map below and answer the following question.

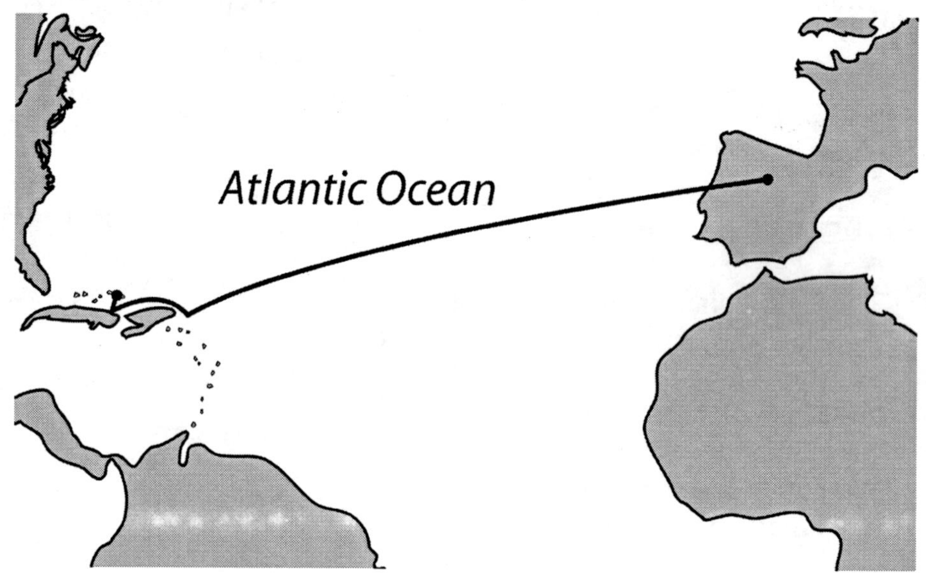

8 What famous explorers route is depicted in the map above? SSWH10

A Christopher Columbus

B Vasco da Gama

C Magellan

D Samuel de Champlain

9 What did Frederick Douglass and William Lloyd Garrison have in common? SSUSH8

A They were both leaders of the abolitionist movement.

B They were both determined to expand slavery.

C They were each early black leaders in the United States.

D They both participated in John Brown's raid.

10 A defense attorney argues in court that the case against his client should be thrown out because the police violated his defendant's right to due process. The attorney is claiming that the government violated SSCG6

A Article I of the Constitution.

B the Fifth Amendment of the Bill of Rights.

C his client's right to a jury trial.

D the doctrine of nullification.

Read the statement below and answer the following question.

> "These settlements were often formed in unpleasant neighborhoods or desolate areas and consisted of dozens or hundreds of shacks and tents that were temporary residences of those left unemployed or homeless by the Depression."

11 What is this quote referring to? SSUSH17

A Civilian Conservation Corps

B National Industrial Recovery Act

C Hoovervilles

D internment camps

12 The Great European Plain is known for SSWG6

A being the westernmost territory of Europe.

B some of the richest farmland in the world.

C acting as a natural barrier that divides Europe from Asia.

D magnificent fjords that are full of breathtaking beauty

13 Which of the following is a principle dividing authority among different branches of governments in order to respect and uphold the natural rights of citizens? SSCG3

A Separation of Powers

B the Tenth Amendment

C popular sovereignty

D the Bill of Rights

14 The English Revolution and the Glorious Revolution had what effect? SSWH14

A They increased the powers of Parliament and decreased the powers of the king.

B They increased the powers of the king and decreased the power of Parliament.

C They ended the monarchy and established a republic.

D They allowed Napoleon to escape from exile and launch his One Hundred Days.

15 What was the purpose of the Civil Rights Act of 1964? SSUSH22

A It prohibited segregation in public accommodations and discrimination in education and employment.

B It authorized the president to suspend literacy tests for voter registration and to send federal officials to register voters in the event that county officials failed to do so.

C It provided assistance and benefits to civilians who were unemployed.

D It was an attempt to punish the southern members of Congress who opposed civil rights.

16 Which of the following is considered a civic responsibility? SSCG7

A going to church

B waking up on time

C voting in elections

D studying hard in school

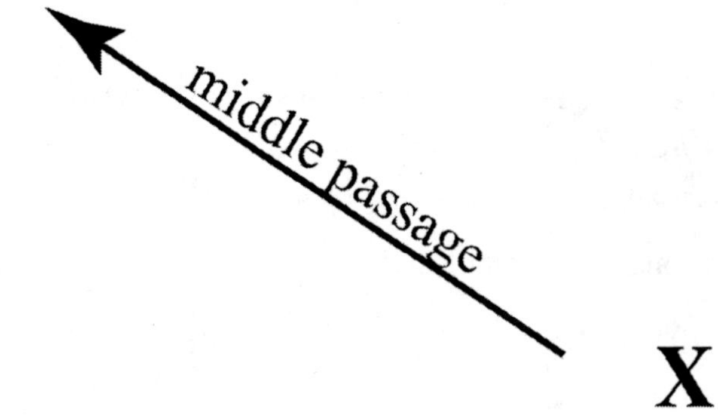

17 Which of the following should replace the X in the diagram above? SSUSH2

A France **B** Africa **C** Spain **D** Britain

18 Nikira is a member of a remote African society. She has been pledged by her father to marry a young man from her village named Obaruku. When the day of their wedding arrives, Nikira and Obaruku pour cups of water over each other, engage in a special ceremonial dance, and each offer a bowl of berries to their gods, asking them to bless their marriage. Nikira and Obaruku's actions are an example of SSWG2

A authoritative rules.

B nomadic lifestyles.

C customs and traditions.

D cultural diversity.

19. What role did children often play in the US urban labor force at the beginning of the 20th century? SSUSH12

A They worked long hours for low pay.

B They rarely worked because they were in school.

C They worked limited hours because of strict child labor laws.

D They were rarely hired because, unlike adults, employers had to pay them a minimum wage.

Read the quote below and answer the following question.

> "He is a heretic! His teachings are but the ravings of a demon. Satan, himself, has sent him here to deceive and draw the faithful away from the church. He supports Copernicus' lies that the earth is not the center of all. If the earth is not the center of the universe, then who is to stop others from saying that man is not the center of God's creation. And, if it is claimed that man be not the center of creation, then is it not God, Himself, who made us in his image, who is being attacked?"
>
> Catholic bishop
> 1614

20 The above quote is most likely talking about SSWH13

A Isaac Newton.

B John Locke.

C da Vinci.

D Galileo.

21 The United States wanted to win the space race because it SSUSH21

A wanted to start a colony on the moon to deal with the earth's overpopulation.

B wanted to start a colony on the moon that US citizens could relocate to in the event of a nuclear war.

C feared that the USSR would use its space technology to develop nuclear weapons capable of destroying the US.

D hoped to fulfill Kennedy's dream of developing a satellite shield capable of destroying Soviet missiles.

22 Which of the following is not evident in the Constitution? SSCG5

A the supremacy clause

B enumerated powers

C separation of powers

D implied powers

Read the quote below and answer the following question.

> "The new sovereign also enacted several wise and wholesome laws for his colony, which have remained invariably the same to this day. The chief is, to ill-treat no person on account of religion, and to consider as brethren all those who believe in one God."

23 Which colony does this quote MOST LIKELY describe? SSUSH1

A Virginia

B Massachusetts

C Haiti

D Pennsylvania

24 What was the name of the top secret endeavor which involved building the atomic bomb? SSUSH19

A the Los Alamos project

B the Truman Doctrine

C the Manhattan Project

D Nagasaki

Use the map to answer the following question.

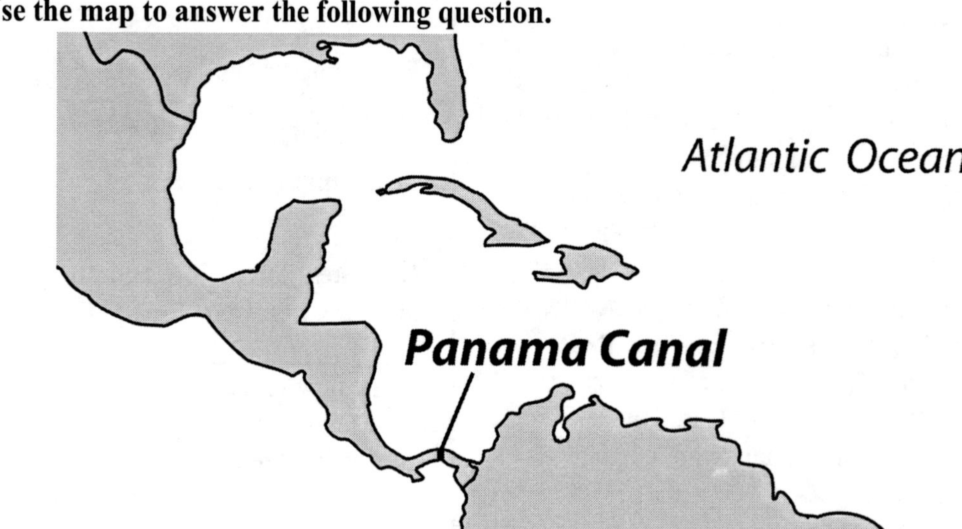

25 Why did President Theodore Roosevelt want a canal built across the isthmus of Panama? SSUSH14

A to serve the US military and economic interests by allowing ships to travel back and forth between US territories in the Pacific and Atlantic without having to go around South America

B to establish a better relationship with the Columbian government who controlled the territory between the Pacific and Atlantic Oceans

C to assist the Panamanian people who had revolted against the Columbian government

D to capture the Philippines

26 Which is a power granted solely to the Senate? SSCG9

A impeach public officials

B confirm or reject presidential appointments

C borrow money and regulate foreign trade

D propose taxes and raise revenue

27 Canvassing, propaganda, public funding, and political endorsements are part of SSCG8

A the electoral college.

B campaigns.

C party coalitions.

D recall elections.

Look at the map below and answer the following question.

28 What nationalist leader led a revolutionary movement that eventually drove western powers from the country above and established a communist government throughout the entire nation in the by the mid-1970s? SSWH20

A Fidel Castro

B Ho Chi Minh

C Mao Zedong

D Gamal Abdul Nasser

29 In which of the following areas would one expect to find the greatest population? SSWG1

A middle of the Sahara

B along the Nile

C the tundra

D Himalayas

30 At the end of World War I, President Wilson introduced a peace proposal known as the SSUSH15

A League of Nations.

B Treaty of Versaille.

C Fourteen Points.

D Zimmerman Telegram.

Read the quote below and answer the following question.

> "We do further declare it to be Our Royal Will and Pleasure, for the present as aforesaid, to reserve under our Sovereignty, Protection, and Dominion, for the use of Indians, all the Lands and Territories not included within the Limits of Our new Governments, or within the Limits of the Territory granted, as also all the Lands and Territories lying to the Westward of the Sources of the River."

31 This quote is MOST LIKELY from SSUSH3

- **A** Treaty of Paris.
- **B** Proclamation of 1763.
- **C** *Common Sense.*
- **D** Intolerable Acts.

32 Why did the North want to capture Atlanta during the Civil War? SSUSH9

- **A** It interfered with trade on the Mississippi River.
- **B** The war would be over if it was captured.
- **C** It was a major railroad hub and its capture would disrupt southern industry.
- **D** It would end Georgia's support of slavery.

Read the excerpt below and answer the following question.

> Dear Mary,
>
> Death is my constant companion. Many of my fellow men have died. We are surrounded by vicious rats who live off the remains of deceased soldiers. Lice, fever, and infections of the feet are also quite common. Please pray for me.

33 Who is this letter most likely written by? SSWH16

- **A** an Ottoman Turk fighting over his Empire in Asia
- **B** a soldier fighting during the Russian Revolution
- **C** a soldier in trench warfare during World War I
- **D** Germans rebelling against Hitler in violent battles

34 During President Bill Clinton's second term in office, he was accused of lying to a grand jury during a criminal investigation. The House of Representatives voted to charge the president, and the case was tried before the US Senate. When less than two-thirds of the Senate voted against the president, he was allowed to remain in office. This was an example of SSCG14

- **A** a recall election.
- **B** impeachment.
- **C** judicial review.
- **D** Federalism.

Look at the illustration below and answer the following question.

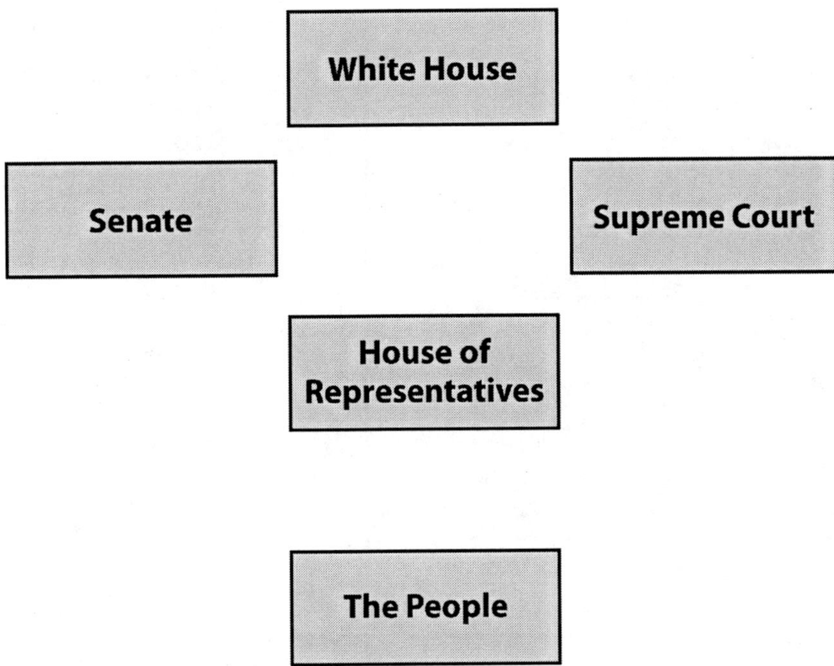

35 The picture above is meant to illustrate the legislative process. If a tax bill originates in the House of Representatives, then to which block should the first arrow be drawn? SSCG10

A from the House of Representatives to the White House

B from the House of Representatives to the Senate

C from the House of Representatives to the Supreme Court

D from the House of Representatives to the people

36 By roughly doubling the size of the United States, it opened the way to western expansion and meant that the US did not have to depend as heavily on imports from other nations. What was it? SSUSH6

A the Gadsden Purchase

B the Northwest Ordinance of 1785

C the Louisiana Purchase

D the Missouri Compromise

37 If one were hiking and heard the roar of Victoria Falls over twenty miles away, then one would be in SSWG4

A Europe.

B Sub-Saharan Africa.

C North Africa.

D Japan.

Look at the picture below and answer the following question.

38 The picture above MOST LIKELY depicts SSWH14

A Maximilien Robespierre.

B Napoleon Bonaparte.

C Toussaint L'Ouverture.

D Mohandas Gandhi.

39 After World War II, Zionists called for the establishment of a Jewish homeland. The UN agreed and established the independent state of Israel in 1948. Support among the international community for a Jewish state increased greatly due to the SSWH19

A mandate system.

B establishment of Pakistan as a Jewish state.

C Holocaust.

D fall of communism.

40 "Jacksonian Democracy" can BEST be described as SSUSH7

A government that favors an elite few.

B representative government in which property owners are the only ones that vote.

C a system of government in which even poorer white men have a voice.

D democracy based on equality, regardless of social standing, gender, or race.

Read the list below and answer the following question.

1. commander-in-chief of the armed forces
2. chief agenda setter
3. foreign policy leader
4. power to impeach
5. chief of state

41 The President of the United States has many different roles. Which roles listed above is he/she responsible for? SSCG12

A 1 and 5

B 1 and 4

C 1,2,3,5

D 1,2,5

SESSION II

DO NOT TURN PAGE UNTIL INSTRUCTED TO DO SO

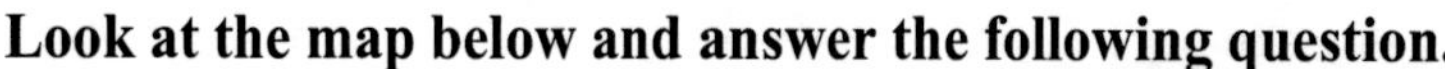

Look at the map below and answer the following question.

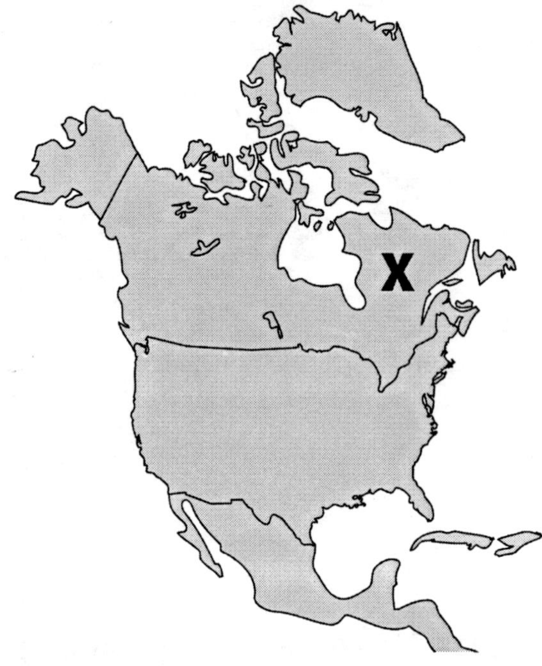

42 Which European explorer was responsible for establishing a settlement at the location labeled X in the map above? SSWH10

A Christopher Columbus

B Marquis de Canada

C Samuel de Champlain

D Amerigo Vespucci

43 Compared to the Republicans in Congress, President Andrew Johnson's approach to Reconstruction can BEST be described as SSUSH10

A lenient.

B harsh.

C about the same.

D far more complicated.

44 Which of the following public officials is part of the judicial branch of government? SSCG16

1. attorney general
2. secretary of state
3. chief justice
4. secretary of the judiciary

A 1 **C** 1 and 4

B 3 **D** 1 and 3

45 Today, airports have tighter security, the government can monitor phone calls and emails with less restraint, prisoners are occasionally held for long periods without being formally charged and tried, and US troops occupy Iraq and Afghanistan. Each is a direct result of SSWH20

A imperialism.

B socialism

C nationalism.

D terrorism.

46 Mao Zedong concerned leaders in the United States because he was SSUSH20

A a militaristic leader who led Japan down an aggressive path.

B the communist leader of North Vietnam who was intent on conquering the South.

C a communist leader who allowed the USSR to place missiles ninety miles off the coast of Florida.

D a communist revolutionary who ultimately took over China.

47 Someone living along the shores of the Great Lakes would live in either SSWG8

A Asia or Europe.

B North America or South America.

C Canada or the United States.

D Mexico or the United States.

48 The Three-fifths Compromise SSUSH5

A established a legislative branch comprised of two houses.

B made George Washington president in exchange for maintaining slavery in the South.

C. allowed southerners to count slaves in the population in exchange for immediately ending the slave trade.

D allowed slaves to be partially counted as part of the US population.

Read the list below and answer the following question

- active volcanoes
- Amazon Basin
- Andes Mountains
- Mexico City
- deserts
- Isthmus of Panama

49 One would find the places on this list in SSWG7

A Mexico.

B Panama.

C South America.

D Latin America.

50 The completion of the transcontinental railroad would not have been possible without the help of thousands of SSUSH11

A African American slaves.

B Native Americans.

C Irish and Chinese immigrants.

D wealthy businessmen.

Use the timeline below to do exercise number 51.

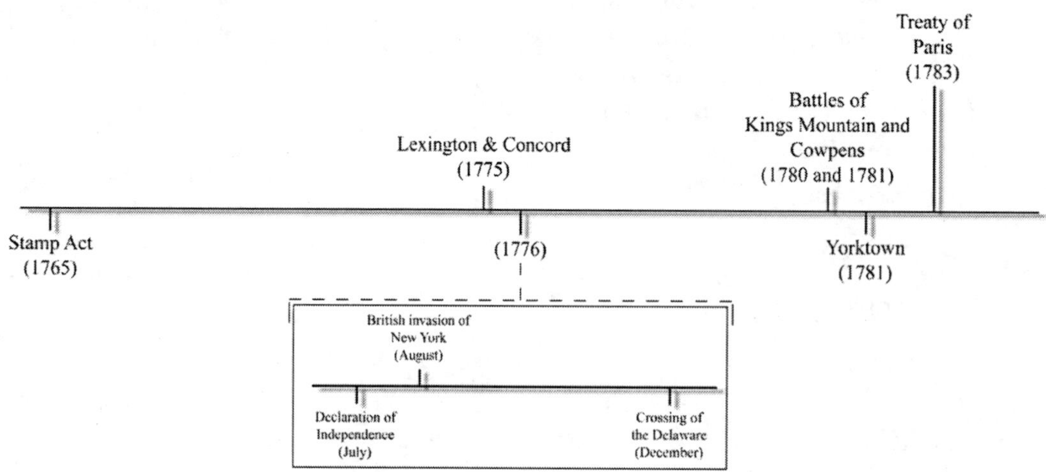

51 The Continental Army's winter at Valley Forge should fall in between SSUSH4

A adoption of the Declaration of Independence; Washington's crossing of the Delaware.

B Yorktown; signing of the Treaty of Paris.

C fighting at Lexington and Concord; British invasion of New York.

D Washington's crossing of the Delaware; Cowpens and Kings Mountain.

52 Anti-Semitism, a belief in Aryan superiority to other races, and a determination to eliminate those deemed undesirable and a burden to the state all led to SSWH18

A the Five Year Plan.

B conflict between Serbs and Bosnians.

C the decision to drop the atomic bomb.

D the Holocaust.

53 What type of foreign aid consists of giving money, supplies, and manpower to help relieve those suffering from poverty or war in other countries? SSCG20

A humanitarian aid

B treaties

C economic aid

D military aid

54 What occurred in response to Upton Sinclair's novel, *The Jungle*? SSUSH13

A It horrified readers to learn about the abuses of the Standard Oil Company.

B Hundreds of factories went on strike and refused to work unless they received higher wages.

C Its impact helped lead to the creation of a federal meat inspection program.

D It enlightened readers as it uncovered the excellent working conditions of factories.

55 Which of the following is true regarding the Social Security Act of 1935? SSUSH18

A It is the only New Deal program still around today.

B It established retirement income for all workers once they reach the age of 55.

C It created projects to help provide citizens with desperately needed jobs.

D It created a board to monitor unfair management practices such as firing workers who joined unions.

56 Which mountain in Asia is the tallest on Earth? SSWG5

A Hindu Kush

B The Himalayas

C Mount Kilamanjaro

D Taklimakan

Read the quote below and answer the following question.

> "I made efforts to swallow tears and to protect the species of the Japanese nation."

57 Who is this quote MOST LIKELY spoken by? SSWH17

A Mussolini

B Mao Zedong

C Hirohito

D Ho Chi Minh

58 Which of the following is true regarding the president's cabinet? SSCG15

A It is established by Article II of the Constitution.

B It consists of several committees appointed by Congress.

C It oversees different areas of government and advises the president.

D Its members are elected at the same time as the president and vice president.

59 Which of the following inventions most impacted Europe by allowing new ideas to spread more quickly and educate the masses as never before? SSWH9

A the cotton gin

B the printing press

C the astrolabe

D the telescope

Go On

60. Which statement is true regarding the Treaty of Versailles? SSUSH15

A It was Germany's official surrender and divided the country in half between the democracies of the West and the Soviet Union.

B It was a treaty that ended World War I and basically returned conditions to what they were before the war.

C It ended WWI and imposed harsh conditions on Germany.

D It was never signed because Adolf Hitler came to power and plunged the world right back into war.

61 Someone inspired by Rachel Carson's book, *Silent Spring*, would MOST LIKELY become an active member in the SSUSH24

A anti-war movement.

B civil rights movement.

C environmentalist movement.

D women's movement.

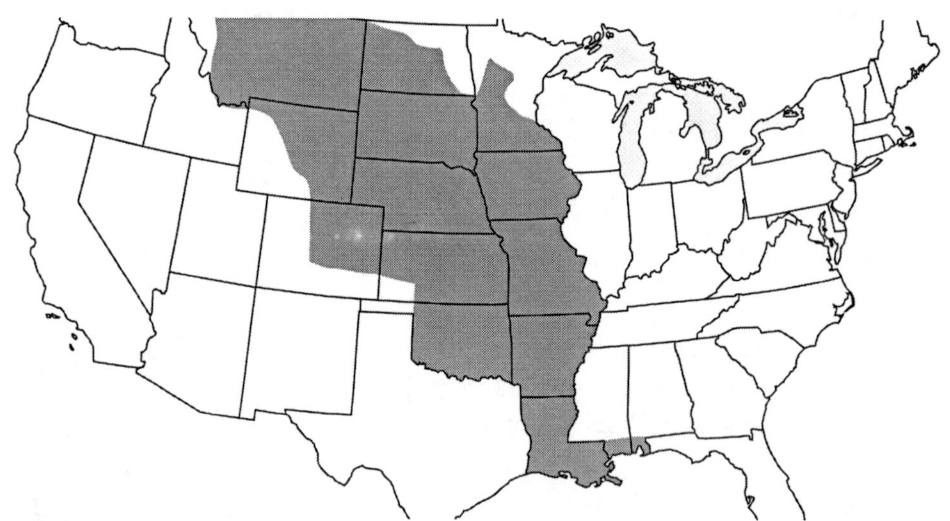

62 Which of the following is associated with the area highlighted on the map above? SSUSH6

A the Louisiana Purchase

B the Northwest Ordinance

C the Erie Canal

D the Compromise of 1850

Read the list below and answer the following question.

1. television
2. satellites
3. H-bomb
4. astrolabe
5. Internet

63 From the list above, what helped strengthen the growth of world communication after World War II? SSWH21

A 1–5

B 1,2,5

C 2,5

D 1,5

64 Many social reform movements occurred in the 1800s. Which movement wanted to moderate the use of alcohol? SSUSH7

A Abolitionist Movement

B Temperance Movement

C Women's Suffrage

D Awareness Movement

65 Which two regions are often identified together because of their similarities in climate and culture? SSWG3

A South America and Europe

B Europe and Antarctica

C Australia and Asia

D North Africa and Southwest Asia

66 Following Hiroshima and Nagasaki, the USSR also developed an atomic bomb. The US then developed a hydrogen bomb. The USSR soon developed a hydrogen bomb as well and launched Sputnik. Soon, both the US and USSR were developing nuclear missiles capable of striking each other in minutes and destroying the entire planet. This describes SSWH19

A the space race.

B nationalism.

C the nuclear arms race.

D diplomacy.

Read the quote and answer the following question:

> "…We hold these truths to be self-evident, that all men are created equal, that they are endowed by their Creator with certain unalienable Rights, that among these are Life, Liberty, and the pursuit of Happiness. That to secure these rights, Governments are instituted among Men, deriving their just powers from the consent of the governed…"

67 The statement above is consistent with SSCG2

A totalitarianism.

B authoritarianism.

C the Renaissance man.

D social contract theory.

Go On

68 **From which point would Stalin's army have been advancing on Germany?** SSUSH19

A A

B B

C C

D D

69 **What freed the slaves in the Confederate States, while maintaining slavery in the few slave states that had remained loyal to the Union?** SSUSH9

A The Abolitionist Movement

B The Second Battle of Bull Run

C The Emancipation Proclamation

D The Battle of Chancellorsville

70 **Marissa is the editor of a political magazine. In her latest addition, she prints an editorial critical of state leaders. Her right to print such an article is protected by the** SSCG6

A Supremacy Clause.

B Sixth Amendment.

C Declaration of Independence.

D First Amendment

71 What would a supporter of popular sovereignty have MOST LIKELY felt about the Dred Scott case and the Kansas-Nebraska Act? SSUSH9

A He/she would have been supportive of both because the Court's decision meant that states could reject slavery if enough people voted against it, while the Kansas-Nebraska Act maintained balance by admitting one state as free and the other as a slave state.

B He/she would have opposed the Dred Scott decision because it meant that a person could not be deprived of property (a slave) even if a state's citizens voted against slavery; however he/she would have supported the Kansas-Nebraska Act because it instituted popular sovereignty.

C He/she would have opposed both because together the two abolished slavery without ever allowing citizens the right to vote on the issue.

D He/she would have supported the Dred Scott decision because it allowed citizens to decide for themselves whether or not their state would have slaves, but he/she would have opposed the Kansas-Nebraska Act because it showed favoritism toward free states.

72 Geography tends to affect which of the following? SSWG1

A population settlement patterns

B totalitarian governments

C diplomacy

D the legislative process

73 Which of the following MOST contributed to a suspicion of immigrants and a mistrust of those with different political beliefs in the years following WWI? SSUSH16

A the opening of Ellis Island

B the Red Scare

C the Cuban Missile Crisis

D the Soviet invasion of Germany

74 The three main branches of government are SSCG4

A House of Representatives, Senate, and Executive.

B Electoral College, legislative, and president.

C president, vice president, and Executive.

D Legislative, Executive, and Judicial.

75 Someone who supported John C. Calhoun and backed the state of South Carolina during the Nullification Crisis MOST LIKELY supported SSUSH8

A a strong central government.

B state's rights.

C the Union during the Civil War.

D Abraham Lincoln in the election of 1860.

76 In the United States, a conservative is MOST LIKELY a member of which political party? SSCG8

A Democratic

B Republican

C Communist

D Socialist

Go On

77 What does the following list describe? SSUSH1

- Bacon's Rebellion
- House of Burgesses
- Development of Slavery
- Tobacco Cultivation

A development of the trans-Atlantic trade

B development of Virginia

C loss of the Massachusetts charter

D the French and Indian War

78 What revolution introduced a new social and political order to Europe, gave birth to nationalism, and is considered by many historians to be the most important social, political, and economic event in modern history? SSWH14

A the Russian Revolution

B the English Revolution

C the French Revolution

D the American Revolution

79 What determines how many elected officials a state has in the House of Representatives? SSCG9

A the Electoral College

B population

C the geographical size of the state

D how long a state has been part of the Union

80 The Progressive Era was a period from approximately 1900 to about 1918 which was marked by a drive for social and economic reform. What two amendments listed below would be considered to have resulted from the Progressive Movement? SSUSH13

A 16th — allowing a federal income tax, and the 17th — providing for the direct election of senators

B 21st — repealing Prohibition, and the 24th — eliminating poll tax

C 10th — limiting the power of the federal government, and the 12th — modifying presidential elections

D 21st— repealing Prohibition, and the 22nd — creating presidential term limitations

81 Which of the following correctly list the world's continents in order of size from largest to smallest? SSWG1

A Asia, Africa, South America, Australia, North America, Antarctica, Europe

B Europe, Africa, Asia, North America, South America, Antarctica, Australia

C Asia, Africa, Antarctica, South America, Australia, North America, Europe

D Asia, Africa, North America, South America, Antarctica, Europe, Australia

> "We oppose abortion, but our pro-life agenda does not include punitive action against women who have an abortion. We salute those who provide alternatives to abortion and offer adoption services."

82 The above quote was MOST LIKELY made by a member of which major party? SSCG8

A Republican

B Liberal

C Democratic

D Independent

83 How might one describe the way in which the 13th, 14th, and 15th Amendments to the US Constitution are related? SSUSH10

A They are all a part of the Bill of Rights.

B They all dealt with Prohibition or its repeal.

C They created direct election for the president, Senate, and state legislators.

D They were passed to give full rights of citizenship to former slaves

84 Many Puritans believed that it is already predetermined by God who is saved and who is lost. Such a doctrine is called *predestination* and is attributed to SSWH9

A Martin Luther.

B Ignatius Loyola.

C Galileo.

D John Calvin.

85 The Great Rift Valley is one of the most notable features of SSWG4

A North America.

B Europe.

C Southeast Asia.

D Sub-Saharan Africa.

86 The search for gold, religious faith, and the desire for land were all SSUSH7

A major causes of the Civil War.

B reasons for conflict with Spain.

C reasons why settlers moved west.

D causes of the Nullification Crisis.

87 Lenin was most influenced by SSWH17

A Karl Marx.

B Napoleon.

C Machiavelli.

D Martin Luther.

88 According to the Supremacy Clause SSCG5

A the US Constitution takes precedence over any state laws.

B any power not granted to the national government is reserved for the states.

C the president is the supreme head of state.

D Congress makes the final decision regarding foreign policy and aid

Go On

89 Which of the following MOST accurately depicts the process for creating a law? SSCG10

A The president first signs a bill, and then presents it to Congress. Congress then sends it to a committee in each house. If the committee approves the bill, it then goes to a subcommittee. If the subcommittee votes in favor of the bill, both houses of Congress then vote on it. If both houses vote in favor of the bill, it becomes law.

B If one house of Congress votes in favor of a bill, it then goes to a committee within that same house. If the committee recommends the bill, it then goes to the other house of Congress for a vote. If that house also votes in favor of the bill, it then presents the bill to one of its own committees. If that committee recommends the bill, the bill then goes to the president who will either sign or veto the bill.

C Once a senator or representative introduces a bill, it goes to a committee. If the committee decides to send it to the house of Congress of which the committee is a part, the entire body then votes on the bill. If it passes by a majority vote, it then goes to the other house. Once a bill passes both houses, it goes to the president, who will either sign or veto it.

D All bills must originate in the House of Representatives. Once this occurs, they go to the House Rules Committee, which then assigns them to subcommittees. Once a subcommittee recommends a bill, it then goes to the whole House for a vote. Once the House passes it, it then goes to the Senate. If the Senate passes it as well, the bill then goes to the president, who will either veto or sign it.

90 What was Abraham Lincoln's official position on slavery when he was elected president in 1860? SSUSH9

A He planned to end slavery throughout the United States.

B He wanted to prevent slavery from expanding to new territories.

C He favored slavery because it was not outlawed by the Constitution.

D He took no official position because he was afraid he would lose support.

Numerics

49ers 104
54-40, or fight 103

A

abolitionist 110
abolitionist movement 107
Adams, John 90
  Federalist party 90
  president 91
Addams, Jane 140, 141
Afghanistan 50, 277
African American
  abolitionist movement 110
  Buffalo Soldier 132
  in the War 114
  indentured servant 73
  labor 129
  limited rights 122
  migration 127
  Niagra Movement 141
  Radical Reconstruction 122
  Reconstruction 123
  schools 175
  segregation 141
  slavery 80
  West 132
  white resistance 124
African-American
  transition to freedom 123
Agricultural Adjustment Act 157
agriculture 94
Aguinaldo, Emilio 137
Alaska, purchase 135
Alexander Hamilton 31
Alien Act 91
alliance 256
Allied Powers 165
Allies 168
Amendment
  10 56
  12 36
  14 57
  17 33
  2 55
  22 36
  24 178
  25 38
  3 55
  4 56
  5 56, 57
  6 56
  7 56
  8 56
  9 56
  Eighteenth 140
  Fifteenth 123, 124
  Fifth 112
  Fourteenth 123
  Nineteenth 140
  Seventeenth 142
  Thirteenth 122, 123
American Anti-Slavery Society 110
amusement park 130
Andrew Jackson 93
Antietam 114
anti-federalists 31
Appeal to the Colored Citizens of the World 110
Appomattox Courthouse 116
Appomattox Courthouse, 121
arbitration 131
armistice 145
Armstrong, Louis 154
Armstrong, Neil 173
Article
  II 36
  III 39, 40
Article I 33
Article II 37
Articles of Confederation 27
assembly line 153, 155
Atlanta
  burning 116
Atlanta campaign 116
Atlantic slave trade 79
atomic bomb 167
Australian ballot 142
Axis forces 165
Axis nations 162
Axis Powers 160, 266

B

Bacon's Rebellion 73
barbed wire 132
Bataan Death March 166
battle
  Britain 267
  Bulge 165
  Kettle and San Juan Hills 136
  Midway 166
Battle of Bull Run 117
Battle of Horseshoe Bend 93
Battle of New Orleans 93
Battle of the Bulge 165
Bennett Place 116
Berlin Airlift 170
Bessemer process 126
big stick diplomacy 138
bill 34
Bill of Rights 30, 55, 57
black codes 122
Black Tuesday 156
Bleeding Kansas 111
Bloody Sunday 178
Bolsheviks 151
Booth, John Wilkes 121
Boston Tea Party 83
boycott 83, 131
breadline 156
Britian, Battle of 267
Brooks, Preston 111
Brown vs. Board of Education of Topeka 175
Brown, John 110
Bull Run, Battle of 117
Burr, Aaron
  duel with Hamilton 92
Bush, George HW 62
Bush, George W. 65
buying on the margin 155

C

cabaret 130
Calhoun, John C. 109
campaign 65
candidates 61
canvassing 66
cattle ranching 132
caucus 64
Central Powers 256
Chancellorsville 115
checks and balances 29
Chiang Kai-shek 272
child labor 129
Chinese Exclusion Act 129, 135
Churchill, Winston 264, 267, 268
CIA 172
Civil Rights Act of 1964 178
Civil War 113
  key battles 114, 115, 116
  northern advantages 117
Civilian Conservation Corps 157
Clark, William 93
Clinton, Bill 62
closed shop 131
cloture 44
coalitions 64
Coercive Acts 83
Cold War 170, 177
collective bargaining 131
Committees of Correspondence 83

D

E

F

G

N

O

P